AF257904

Divine Commander Par Excellence

Military Management in the Battles of the Prophet (s)

Muhammad Dhāhir Watr

Translated from Persian by

Abu Zahrā Muhammadi

Name of the book: Military Management in the Battles of the Prophet (s)
Original Arabic title: *al-Idārat al-Askariyya fi Hurub al-Rasul Muhammad (s)*
Author: Muhammad Dhāhir Watr
Project Supervisor: Abu Yahya al-Hussaini
Persian Translation: Asghar Qaidān
English Translation: Abu Zahrā Muhammadi
ISBN: 978-1-7330284-2-4
Year: 2019

There has certainly been for you in the Messenger of Allah an excellent pattern (role model) for anyone whose hope is in Allah and the Last Day and [who] remembers Allah often.
[Holy Qur'an, 33:21]

Contents

SECTION III

Translator's Introduction

Orientalists have, from the very beginning, propagated that Islām is a violent religion that was spread by the sword. This myth is even promulgated today albeit in a different form and context. At present, the 'violence' of Islām is portrayed by small fanatic groups who kill innocent civilians. Ironically, these extremist groups like the Daesh, Tālibān and their like, kill more Muslims than people following any other creed.

Yet since 9/11, the world has been bombarded with repeated messages against this 'violent religion'. As if those who are making these accusations are themselves any less violent. The USA is the only country in the world to use the A-bomb and kill a large civilian population without any remorse or apology. They are the ones who violently invade and ravage lands belonging to others and yet have the audacity to call Islām what they have called it. This is the highest form of hypocrisy.

Human beings are dynamic creatures with the ability to be peaceful and loving in one instance while being hostile and aggressive the next. The same person may be smiling one minute and fuming with rage just moments later. Islām recognizes these intrinsic features in human beings and trains one to mould them and harness them properly, when to be angry and when to be happy, when to be kind and when to be fierce.

Islām does not condone the idea of humiliation and subjugation by other human beings. For this reason we find that, after years of persecution at the hands of the Quraysh, the divine ordinance for battle was received by the Holy Prophet (s). Initially, some of the weaker Muslims showed hesitation at the idea of picking up weapons and fighting for their rights. Some lacked the courage while others were content being in the camp of the oppressed. However, the Prophet (s) recited to them the Holy verses wherein the believers were called to arms to protect their rights and property, and the Muslims complied.

The beauty of the battles that followed was the humanity that was displayed by the Prophet (s) and his followers. Usually, when one goes to war, they tend to lose their ability of distinguishing right from wrong and many atrocities are committed by soldiers because of this. The adrenaline rush caused by life threatening situations clouds their judgment and they end up killing innocents and doing all sort of beastly things. The latest example of this is what the USA did (and continues to do) in 'Iraq, Afghanistan and Guantanamo.

The Prophet (s) warned his soldiers not to fight in such a manner that they end up neglecting the basic principles that make a human being human. They were not to kill innocent women, children, old people and the handicapped. They were not permitted to cut down trees or fill up wells. They were to offer the enemy an opportunity to surrender and not pursue those who fled from battle. These were just some of the numerous injunctions that the Holy Prophet (s) laid down for the Muslims at a time when the norm among the Arabs was to treat the enemy ruthlessly and without any mercy whatsoever.

The Holy Prophet (s), or the 'supreme commander' as the author of this work refers to him time and again, had no interest in building a large empire. Rather, he readily made those who were willing to live peacefully, his allies. The sword was only raised against open enemies who were out to destroy Islām and the Muslims.

Further, many of the defeated prisoners of war became Muslims when they saw how the Prophet (s) treated them. Contrary to their expectation of harsh and brutal treatment, they were treated with kindness and mercy. Just this was enough to make many of them Muslims. This was how Islām really spread, not at the tip of the blade as wrongly hypothesized by Western Orientalists.

Translating this work posed a number of challenges. First, the enormous amount of transliteration. In Arabic, different dialects pronounce words differently. We have tried as much as possible to conform with the standard Arabic transliteration but this has not been a priority and at times one Arabic name may have been transliterated in two or three similar ways. Care has been taken, however, that this should in no way cause any confusion about who or what is being referred to and it should only be deemed a handicap of the English language, nothing more.

Second, one will notice that this work, which was originally a dissertation for the author's PhD, has a string of footnotes as long as the eye can see! These footnotes only serve to provide a basis for his statements and refer the reader to where he or she can turn if more information or detail is required.

Third, I have taken the liberty of adding my own notes wherever I thought a clarification was required. As the translator of this work, probably the hardest thing for me was to contend with some conclusions that are made by the author. Unfortunately, the esteemed author has not endeavored to carry out any scrutiny of the sources he has referred to and has taken these reports at face value. As a student of history, the importance of carefully analyzing reports and looking for possible loopholes and inconsistencies is well known to me.

II

However, since my task was to translate this otherwise important work, I only added very brief notes in areas where I disagreed with the author. Readers who are interested can of course delve deeper and conduct their own research in those areas.

Finally, I would like to extend my thanks and gratitude to Dr. Abu Fizza Heydari for meticulously going through my final draft, editing and proofreading it. And of course thanks is due to the publishers Heritage International Inc. for undertaking the task of getting this work translated and published. All praise, in the end, belongs only to the Almighty.

Abu Zahrā Muhammadi

Author's Introduction

All praise belongs to the Lord of the Worlds. The Most Beneficent, the most Merciful. Master of the Day of Reckoning. Thee alone do we worship and Thee alone do we seek help from. Guide us to the straight path; the path of those whom Thou hast blessed, not those with whom Thou art angry, nor those who have strayed.

O Allah send Thy blessings on Muhammad and the progeny of Muhammad just as Thou have sent Thy blessings on Ibrahim and the progeny of Ibrahim in the worlds, indeed Thou art the Owner of Praise, the Owner of Glory. And bless Muhammad and the progeny of Muhammad just as Thou have blessed Ibrahim and the progeny of Ibrahim in the worlds, indeed Thou art the Owner of Praise, the Owner of Glory.

This research and study under the heading: 'Military Management in the Battles of the Prophet of Allah, Muhammad (s)' was presented as a doctorate thesis in the field of history at the Université Saint-Joseph, Lebanon, and is now before the respected readers. We have tried to spare no effort in this work with the hope that we would be successful in arriving at the truth [about the Prophet (s) as an exemplary military commander].

The present work has been arranged as follows:
1. Preface: Here the genesis of the techniques and strategies of battle in Islām and its most salient characteristics have been mentioned.
2. Introduction: I begin by explaining my methodology of choice in this study based on what I have discussed in the different sections and precede this by mentioning the narrators and important figures who have written about the history of the Prophet (s) and those who wrote war chronicles.
3. Section One: In this section, the characteristics of the Arab military before Islām have been discussed.
4. Section Two: Here 'military command' and that which pertains to it is, including the qualities of a commander, have been discussed.
5. Section Three: Here the different types of 'army command centers and headquarters' in the Muslim army have been explained.
6. Section Four: In this section the branches of 'security and intelligence' and related issues are mentioned.
7. Section Five: Details about the 'base of operations' along with its arrangement and plans have been outlined.

8. Section Six: Here 'relief support units', 'munitions', 'medical services', 'management of booty' and, in the end, 'role of women' in the Muslim army have been explained.

9. Conclusion: Finally, the issue of 'growth and development of the Muslim army and the causes and factors that led to their victory in battle' is discussed; after which I have listed the most important sources and references that have been used in this study.

Muhammad Dhāhir Watr
5 Dhu al-Qa'adah 1405 AH

[1] *The Glorious Qur'an (Q1:1-7)*

SECTION I

Preface

The establishment of 'the art of Islāmic warfare' emerged after the migration of the Holy Prophet (s) to Madina with the implementation of the first Sariya mission.[1] During this period, battles took place continuously and the Muslim army had hardly recovered from one conflict when it was faced with another battle. Wars[2] were also fought in a similar sequence. The foundation that the [continuous] battles and wars of the Prophet (s) formed[3] was like a spring that never stopped gushing in strengthening the structures of military management, which were responsible for designing the strategies of war.

The supreme commander of these battles, due to his perfect genius and insight, made this form of management perdurable and complimented it with determination, dynamism and practicality. To such an extent that many of the documenters of war chronicles, in their books of 'Expeditions and Wars'[4] have made efforts to outline and survey this and present it as the principles, laws and regulations that can be referred to [and implemented] in future events by those who read [and study] about these battles in the books of expeditions and history. Indeed, because of the [consecutive] battles and wars that took place between Islām and the enemies and adversaries of this faith and its teachings, there was a need for a strong army that would be led by a skilled and capable leader who was well versed in military management and universally accepted and supported, so that he could implement Jihād as one of the most important ordinances and commandments of Islām.[5] And in addition to these principles, he would give importance to the humanitarian aspect of warfare[6] and the understanding of the human condition while calling for, and sparing no efforts in trying to achieve, global reform.[7]

With regards to war and its military aspects, by having clear goals that he would strive to attain and with strong foresight that results from a dynamic intellect, and also by being quick to act and carry out surprise attacks[8] and implementing new strategies, he (s) became an excellent commander. With observation we find that this form of [military] management was superior in terms of 'the sublime ethics of war' meaning bravery, boldness, fearlessness and lack of lassitude in difficult situations. Aside from this, with greater intelligence and contemplation, and with insight and illumination, he sought to evaluate the important issues and take advantage of the resources and means at his disposal without negligence or indolence, presenting plans of action, and relying on dynamic organization and diverse leadership.[9]

As in the present age 'ideology' was similarly accepted as a sublime spiritual fountainhead which armies are supposed to take benefit from,[10] any commander who would read about their ideology [in the future, even] after centuries would take inspiration from it and follow it.

Acquiring techniques of warfare depends upon various external factors, conditions and available resources that are beyond time, place[11] or numbers, and are tools that the commander has at his disposal. Verily, the most important factor that distinguishes this form of military management from other types of military management that came later is the 'ethics and moral attributes' of the military command, which developed from war. It is an undisputed fact that the Prophet (s) had all the qualities of a political, social and universal leader in himself, and that he sought help from the Almighty with complete faith.[12] He had the attributes of faith, valor, steadfastness and insight in matters of principles and military sciences,[13] and he inherited these lofty traits from his forefathers.[14]

Similarly, in his social interaction with friends and foes,[15] he was magnanimous and would always keep his word and fulfill his vows and promises.[16] He would spend time in contemplation and then form his opinion with regards to planning and strategizing [for battle][17] and would employ exemplary organization skills.
As for the relationship between the commander and the army, he (s) was distinguished for his sacrificing and ever-friendly[18] disposition. Obedience [to him] was strengthened by full cognizance and acceptance of his prophethood by the people under him; therefore this was an impetus for them to believe in his orders out of conviction [that he was commanded by the Almighty].[19]

The Prophet was always aware of the problems being faced by his troops. He would be sympathetic towards them and would always, both in times of war and peace,[20] be with them and act as a good role model for them so that they could emulate him in all matters and follow him.[21] He would never proceed with his forces without seeking counsel first, as is observed in the battles of Badr, Uhud etc.[22] His relationship with the troops was always based on the principles of humanity, compassion, compromise, sympathy, reform, magnanimity,[23] aiding the oppressed, assisting in the doing of good, actively opposing tyranny and transgression, and equality among the people.[24] And this would include all the people despite their differences.[25] In order to achieve this objective, he had to bring the community together at the same level under one common rubric and imbibe love and compassion for each other in their hearts.[26] He needed to establish a link of brotherhood between them and counter their lassitude and uncertainty. Because of this, those who had gathered around him[27] were all pleased with him and had come to accept this matter.

All the goals that he worked towards and strived to attain, and the preparations that he made so that the brutal battles may be won internally and externally, are truly astounding for the people who read about them, and all the people who have learnt about this type of leadership are left with no option but to admit its greatness. The American Michael Hart says: 'My choice of Muhammad to lead the list of the world's most influential persons may surprise some readers and may be questioned by others, but he was the only man in history who was supremely successful on both the religious and secular level.'[28]

The Englishman Montgomery Watt says: 'His readiness to undergo persecutions for his beliefs, the high moral character of the men who believed in him and looked up to him as leader, and the greatness of his ultimate achievement - all argue his fundamental integrity. To suppose Muhammad an impostor raises more problems than it solves. Moreover, none of the great figures of history is so poorly appreciated in the West as Muhammad.'[29]

As for the reason behind my choosing this subject, it is because of the military and historic significance[30] that it has. It clarifies aspects of ingenuity, management and administration that have been largely ignored by researchers or have only been mentioned by them in passing. This is because they only try to concentrate their efforts in approaching the subject of military expeditions[31] in a specific manner, not in the way the great documenters of expeditions and battles[32] have presented them. In this regard, this present research can be taken as an example for the personal and social interactions between all the nations and peoples of the world.[33] We will present certain parts of this in summary.

NOTES AND REFERENCES

[1] The Sariya missions were military missions in which the Holy Prophet (s) would send contingents under the command of his companions, to find out about the enemy, carry out raids and assaults, assassinate the enemy chiefs etc. In the age of Jāhiliyya, Sariya referred to a group that was sent at night (under the cover of darkness and secrecy). (Tr.)

[2] Wars, unlike Sariya missions, were fought in the open, with a large army, after having been declared against the enemy openly. The Holy Prophet (s) participated in many of the wars, but never took part in any Sariya missions. Wāqidi narrates that among the wars in which the Holy Prophet was not present were: the Battle of Abnā', Waddān and Muta.

[3] Wāqidi, al-Maghāzi 1:8-10; Ibn Hishām, al-Seerah al-Nabawiyyah 4:256; Ibn Sa'd, al-Tabaqāt al-Kubrā 2:1

[4] See: Ibn Is'hāq, Zuhri, Wāqidi, Ibn Hazm, Kalā'i, Ibn Sayyid al-Nās, and from the contemporary scholars see: 'Ammād Talās, Liwā' Sheet Khattāb, Faraj and others

[5] Bukhāri, *Sahih* (Bāb al-Maghāzi, hadith no. 53); Tirmidhi, *Sahih* (Bāb Fadhā'il al-Jihād, hadith no. 22); the Glorious Qur'an (Q8:65)

[6] Bukhāri (al-Jihād, hadith no. 102); Muslim (Bāb al-Imārah, hadith no. 117)

[7] The Holy Qur'ān 2:211; Ibn Hanbal, al-Musnad 5:437

[8] Wāqidi 2:496, 3:903; Ibn Hishām 3:213; Ibn Sa'd 2:53, 77, 3:2, 90; Montgomery Watt, Muhammad fi al-Madina, translated into Arabic by Sha'bān Barakāt

[9] Ibn Hishām 3:50, 4:42; Ibn Sa'd 1:147, 2:24; Muslim 3:1386; Abu Dāwud, *Sunan* (al-Jihād hadith no. 89); Tabari, *Tārikh al-Tabari* 2:355; see also: Watt, *Muhammad fi al-Madina*: 130, 511; Cobuld, *al-Bahth 'an Allāh*, translated into Arabic by 'Umar Abu al-Nasr: 121

[10] Q8:65; Zuhri, *al-Maghāzi al-Nabawiyya*: 86; Wāqidi 1:182; Bukhāri (al-Jihād hadith no. 110); Ibn Mājah, *Sunan* (al-Jihād hadith no. 1); Nasā'i, *Sunan* (al-Jihād hadith no. 18)

[11] Wāqidi 1:335; Bukhāri (al-Maghāzi 29); Abu Dāwud (al-Jihād 156); al-Kalā'i 1:105

[12] Bukhāri (al-Janā'iz 80, al-Maghāzi 18); Tirmidhi (al-Da'awāt 82)

[13] Bukhāri (al-Jihād 82); Tirmidhi (al-Shamā'il 1); Tabari 2:326; Kalā'i 1:101

[14] Ibn Bakār, Jamharah Nasab Quraysh 1:362; Ibn 'Abd Rabbih, al-Iqd al-Fareed 3:321

[15] Ibn Hanbal 1:406; Ibn Hishām 4:55; Tabari, Tafseer al-Tabari 14:131

[16] Bukhāri (al-Jizyah, al-Adab, al-Eimān, al-Sayd, al-Maghāzi); Ibn Mājah (al-Sadaqāt, al-Janā'iz, al-Jihād)

[17] Ibn Sa'd 1:147; Tabari 2:355; Suhayli, al-Rawdh al-Anf 2:252; Kalā'i 1:88

[18] Wāqidi 1:275; Ibn Sa'd 2:29; Tabari: 520; Ibn Atheer, al-Kāmil fi al-Tārikh 2:158

[19] Q8:65; Bukhāri (al-Jihād 110); Nasā'i (al-Jihād 18)

[20] Q6:54; Q9:128; Bukhāri and Nasā'i (*Ibid.*)

[21] Q33:33

[22] Before the start of the Battle of Uhud, the Holy Prophet (s) went on the pulpit in the Masjid and said: Last night I saw a dream in which I was surrounded by shields and protected while the sword, Dhul Fiqar, had been broken from one side and I saw a cow being slaughtered. The companions asked the Prophet (s) to interpret this dream so he said: As for the shields that were surrounded, it is the city of Madina, and as for the broken sword, it means that I will lose someone from my family (in the battle), and as for the cow being slaughtered, it means that some of my companions will be killed. Having

4

said this, the Prophet (s) recommended that they remain in Madina and defend themselves against the attackers, however, some of the youth who were eager for battle insisted that they should leave the city and meet the enemy outside saying: If we don't go out to meet them in battle, the enemies will take this to mean that we are afraid of them. The Prophet (s) gave in to their insistence and prepared the army. Later, these same youth came to the Prophet (s) and said: We do not wish to force you to do something that you do not wish to do O Prophet of Allāh, and we will obey your command whatever it may be. But by this time it was too late and the Prophet (s) said: It is not appropriate for those who have put on their armor and prepared for battle to remove their armor now. In this instance we see how the Prophet (s) acted against his own wishes and accepted the view of the majority (See: Wāqidi 1:212-215) (Tr.)

[23] Q6:33; Q7:206, 168; Q8:1; Q15:88; Bukhāri (al-Hanbalā' 50, 54, al-Jizya, al-Adab, al-Eimān, al-Sayd, al-Maghāzi); Muslim (al-Fadhā'il 65); Ibn Mājah (al-Zuhd 33); Abu Dāwud (al-Jihād 44, 54)

[24] Q16:90; Q42:15; Wāqidi 1:182, 194; Bukhāri (al-Madhālim 5, 6); Muslim (al-Amārah, al-Birr, al-Jihād, al-Fadhā'il 63); Nasā'i (Ishrat al-Nisā' 1)

[25] Q6:19; Abu Dāwud (al-Sunan 10)

[26] Ibn Sa'd 2:1; Suhayli 2:252; Tabari 2:421, 499, 3:389

[27] Q33:71; Wāqidi 1:21; Bukhāri (al-Ahkām 4)

[28] Michael H. Hart, *The 100: a ranking of the most influential persons in history*, New York: Hart Publishing Company, Inc., 1978, p. 33.

[29] W. Montgomery Watt, *Mohammad at Mecca*, Oxford, 1953, p. 52

[30] Ibn Sa'd 2:770; Ibn 'Asākir, *Tārikh Madinat Dimishq* 15:397; Ibn Sayyid al-Nās, *'Uyun al-Athar fi Funun al-Maghāzi wal-Siyar* 1:7; Mārglyuth, *Dirāsāt 'an al-Muwarrikheen al-'Arab*, translated into Arabic by Husayn Nassār: 108

[31] Ibn Hishām 2:264, 4:170

[32] Wāqidi 1:177; Ibn Hishām 3:245; Ibn Sa'd; Tabari 2:583

[33] Bukhāri (al-Jihād 102); al-Dārimi, *Sunan* (Bāb al-Siyar 8)

PART ONE: THE MILITARY AND ITS HISTORICAL SIGNIFICANCE

From the time he entered Madina, the Prophet (s) started raising an army in order to counter the threats of the enemy. He organized numerous secret fact-finding military missions,[1] sending them to different parts of the Arabian Peninsula.[2] By sending these secret missions and appointing commanders for each of them, the Holy Prophet (s) was able to fight both the internal and external[3] (i.e. outside the Arabian Peninsula) enemies. The result of these wars was the foundation of faith and conviction in humane warfare that became fundamental for the Muslims and others. Numerous scholars like Ibn Shihāb al-Zuhri, Wāqidi, Ibn Hishām and others have written about this. It is certain that this belief originated from faith in God and it was evident that it bestowed a special energy to the fighters that made them fearless and as a result, their struggles and bravery became unmatched and not even the slightest inkling of fear remained in them.

As for the factors and motivations of this ideology, they were manifested in the most beautiful form in faith in a specific goal that consisted of the establishment of justice and the struggle towards universal peace and security, and also in countering oppression and exploitation, treachery, greed, evil habits and imprudent patrimony of authority and power that was practiced by the Arabs in the age of Jāhiliyya. I have studied this ideology and its basis after the advent of Islām. During the reigns of the Umayyad and Abbasid Caliphates and after that, many wars took place and in all of them lessons were taken from the past. They would refer to this very period (i.e. the time of the Prophet) and seek to take lessons from it. That which transpired later, after the battles in the early days of Islām, was all a continuation of that which took place during the time of the Prophet (s) in its basis, motivations and factors except that it transpired under a different set of circumstances.[4] Thus we find this ideology being adopted after the companions of the Prophet (s) such as Abu ‘Ubayda Ibn Jarrāh,[5] Sa’d bin Abi Waqqās[6] and Khālid Ibn Walid[7] had become accustomed to it, having implemented it with precision and understanding in the battlefields alongside the Holy Prophet (s), and after him in Qādisiyya and Yarmuk, and later during the time of the Caliphs.[8] Therefore, they and others gained guidance through this ideology and fundamental principle that was observed in the first battles, and these principles were like a keepsake that was brought from the biggest wars and battlefields of victory. However, with the passing of time, their successors began to forget these principles and became lax and negligent in preserving them, and for this reason they had to face losses in battles.

This is a plain indication and a stro[9]ng proof for the necessity of studying and analyzing the art and method of warfare at that time. So even now, after so much time has passed, the importance of studying these wars and battles has not waned. It continues to seek an in-depth reading and a profound understanding in order to deduce and discover matters concerning warfare that are lesson-giving, because it is this aspect that does not expire. The ideas and effects related to the 'principles of war' have not perished or reduced in value over the period of time.

NOTES AND REFERENCES

[1] The number of Sariya missions that the Prophet (s) sent has been recorded as being anywhere between 35, 38, 48 and 66 (Tr.)

[2] Q28:57; Bukhāri (al-Manāqib, al-Maghāzi); Abu Dāwud (al-Jihād)

[3] The Prophet (s) had created an institution that was known as the Intelligence and Security Branch through which information about the enemies both within and without the Arabian Peninsula was gathered. (Tr.)

[4] Of course this may be true for a specific period of time, during the reign of the first Caliphs, but when the Umayyads and Abbasids took over, the situation was quite the opposite. Their motives for war was mostly material and in order to gain control and occupy fruitful and thriving lands for their own benefit. Unfortunately, the respected author has neglected this fact. (Tr.)

[5] To find out more about him refer to: Ibn 'Abd al-Barr, *al-Isti'āb fi Ma'rifat al-Ashāb* 4:170; Ibn Atheer, *Usd al-Ghāba fi Ma'rifat al-Sahāba* 5:249

[6] Ibn 'Abd al-Barr 2:606; Ibn Atheer 2:291

[7] Ibn 'Abd al-Barr 2:427; Ibn Atheer 2:101

[8] The respected author has followed a wrong track with regards to Khālid bin Walid. Contrary to what he mentions, Khālid bin Walid was in no way a man of strong faith and moral principles. Before becoming one of the commanders of the Muslim army, he was a commander of the disbelievers who had strong inclinations to the practices of Jāhiliyya. It was because of the continuous victories of Islām over the disbelievers that he joined the Muslims. It was for his own personal benefit that he accepted the faith. This can be clearly witnessed by his actions after becoming a 'Muslim'. His various infringements caused the Prophet (s) much displeasure, so much so that he (s)

even reproached him. (See: Muhammad al-'Aqqād, *'Abqariyyatu 'Umar*: 172-174). After the death of the Prophet (s) Khālid bin Walid was responsible for killing numerous innocent Muslims. The incident of his killing Mālik bin Nuwayra, despite his professing Islām, just in order to marry his wife, is well documented. So is his attack on the Bani Yarbu' who were standing for prayer and had borne testimony to Islām. (See: Ya'qubi, *Tārikh* 2:110; Ibn Katheer, *al-Bidāya wal-Nihāya* 6:311; Kalā'i al-Balansi, *Tārikh al-Radda*: 2; Ibn Atheer, *al-Kāmil* 2:359; Dhahabi, *Tārikh al-Islām* 1:253). It is very unfortunate that despite all this some Muslims insist on referring to this man as the 'Sword of Allāh'! (Tr.)

PART TWO: NOVEL WARFARE

The Prophet (s) gave real meaning to the term 'military management' and aside from being a science, he gave it originality; something that the Arabs before him were unfamiliar and unacquainted with.[1] The wars of the Muslims would take place in a manner which was unlike the wars based on vengeance and barbarism. These wars were not for personal pleasure or blind hatred in useless matters, nor were they chaotic, unplanned and disorganized onslaughts.

When the Prophet (s) was appointed to Prophethood, he made a lot of efforts regarding this matter. The most important issue that he would concentrate on in war was the constant readiness for it. Many of the missions and expeditions that took place were in actuality a kind of preparation and military exercise that the troops needed. The advantage in the end, when these missions and expeditions returned home, was the invention of new arts and strategies of warfare which played an important role in the organization of the ranks of the army in the Battle of Badr,[2] in commanding these ranks, procuring arms and the necessary equipment, and the distribution of tasks among the troops.

Aside from this, the most important instrument that he (s) used was the sending out of spies in order to gather information about the enemy during the preparatory stages of war, and through this he was able to secretly gain knowledge about the numbers of the enemy and their accoutrements. For example, he sent Hudhayfa in the Battle of the Confederates (Ahzāb), telling him: 'Go and gather information about this group and during this mission do not make contact with anyone until you return back to me.'[3]

The Holy Prophet (s) used 'psychological warfare' as one of the most important strategies of war and in this way he was able to put fear and awe in the hearts of the enemy so that they may be forced to flee or surrender without the need for combat. This is just what he did in the Conquest of Makkah. He ordered that the army should light ten thousand fires, so that by this he could put fear and anxiety in the hearts of the enemy.[4]

Similarly, the Prophet (s) initiated pre-emptive war[5] in order to avert possible threats from the enemy that he was unable to counter. In this way, before the enemy could gather all its forces for war, he would take quick action. For this type of war, he put in place rules and regulations and encapsulated them with perfect precision and profound understanding. He then placed them alongside 'speed, agility and stealth'. In this method, by conducting 'surprise attacks' on the enemy, they would end up being stunned and straggled and became, from the start of the invasion, crippled and rendered helpless in their very own land, and this action would bring with it many other advantages and benefits.[6]

In the same way, the Prophet (s) would conduct 'lightening-strikes' which was a form of war wherein it would not take a significant amount of time and would be 'swift, short, unexpected and stealthy'. It would also require a smaller force with fewer accoutrements. This type of operation would be carried out in the face of an enemy that was larger in number and in many instances,[7] with [other] new strategies, it gave an upper hand to the Muslims, especially in the battles of Badr, Khandaq and Hunayn.

The Prophet (s) also employed the 'war of uprising'[8] and through it, he would raise the inhabitants of a town, including their men, women and children, to stand up and fight against the invading armies that were intent on destroying them. This type of action was clearly seen in the Battle of the Confederates. In this instance, he made all the people participate jointly to dig a ditch in the battlefield, and this was considered a novel tactic that was previously unknown.[9] This method then became an example for those who took part in later wars.

He (s) similarly used the strategy of 'laying siege' and completely surrounding the enemy so that in this way, they would be cut off from the outside world and could not send for reinforcements and support. Of course he was careful to ensure that they were out of the range of enemy arrows and would set camp in a place where he and the forces would be safe from the reach and view of the enemy, continuing this until those who were besieged were forced to come out and surrender.[10]

The Holy Prophet (s) made use of the 'war of impediments' which was previously unknown to the Arabs and with which they were unfamiliar.[11] When the Prophet (s) was informed that the enemy had gathered at night in order to carry out a dangerous attack against him, he sought counsel from his troops. The advisers agreed with the proposal made by Salmān al-Fārsi that a ditch be dug (around the city of Madina).[12] Thus by digging a ditch, the basis of a unique and new form of war, meaning the 'war of impediments' was created, which was in line with the idea of defense and using of the appropriate weapon in the given situation.

The result of this tactic was that it made the enemy perplexed and baffled. They did not know how to react to what they saw. Being unable to pass over or go through the ditch, they turned back hopeless. This later became known as the 'Battle of the Ditch' because of this great feat.

When the Holy Prophet (s) foresaw rebellion, siege and one on one combat from the side of the defenders of the city, he would turn to the 'war of the city and streets'[13] which consisted of precise and particular measures. The Conquest of Makkah is indeed one example of this type of warfare.[14] In this case, the army of Islām entered the city of Makkah in order to conquer it, after having strengthened its siege in the four corners of the city. Troops were placed in each corner according to the importance of that part of the city, and specific accoutrements were used and commanders appointed. The effect of this was that the people in Makkah became terrified as they looked at the great numbers of soldiers in the Muslim army. When this strong army entered Makkah, no blood was spilt.[15] This was something the likes of which has never been witnessed, nor has anything like it been recorded or reported in the past.[16]

The Prophet (s) had some strategies that he would always use against the enemies in all the battles. Some of these strategies were: 'creating a possibility for easy movement', 'sending secret information gathering missions', 'carrying out surprise attacks on the enemy' along with 'movement with stealth and furtiveness'[17], 'use of traps and artifices'[18], 'taking advantage of the most suitable time and place and appointing the most appropriate commanders for each mission'[19]. And in all these issues he displayed no lassitude nor did he fall short from implementing them perfectly.

In order to promote the needed balance, create hope and increase the morale of the army,[20] he would try to study the facets of the tactics and strategies used either before, during or after the battle.[21] Every factor that contributed in giving the Muslims an upper hand over the enemy in battlefield[22] was considered carefully and studied by him, because victory is a goal that every commander strives for in the wars he fights.

At this point it is necessary mention the issue of attacking those who were fleeing and running away from the battlefield – about which many have erred. The Prophet (s) never used to attack those who were fleeing from the battlefield after having lost the battle, just in order to fulfill his desires or act upon his inclinations. However, some have said that the Muslim army would pursue the defeated enemy, especially as in the case of the battle of Hunayn. It must be said that the Prophet (s) would avail the opportunity to the defeated enemy to flee if they so wished; because throwing a spear towards the back of the enemy was something that would lower the respect of the commander in the eyes of the soldiers and would cause him to be despised. In the battles of Dhāt al-Suwayq, Dhāt al-Ruqā' and al-Ghābah, he did not attack those who were fleeing; and also in the battle of Hunayn, he only pursued those enemies who were not surrendering or fleeing,[23] but were instead trying to move to a better position in order to regroup and launch further attacks on the Muslims, because at this stage the battle had not ended and it only came to an end when the forces of the Hawāzin were defeated and Ṭā'if came under siege.[24] [25] Similarly, in other missions that resulted in war, the fleeing enemy was never attacked.[26]

NOTES AND REFERENCES

[1] The Arabs in the age of Jāhiliyya had no specific organization in their wars and never used to comply with any principles and rules of warfare. Obeying the commander, moving in an orderly fashion, being organized, following a plan etc. were not given importance by them. For this reason, even when they had large numbers and many resources, they would often lose their battles. (Tr.)

[2] Bukhāri (al-Maghāzi 31, 38); Muslim (al-Jihād 42). Today it is necessary to have the armed forces ready and on alert at all times. This is achieved by giving them continuous training. The Holy Prophet (s) would also train his army, but not through unreal war games (as is done today), rather he would send them for real missions. This would keep them ready and enable them to practice new tactics of war and would also strike fear into the hearts of the enemy (Tr.)

[3] In the Battle of Ahzāb, the Holy Prophet (s) sent Hudhayfa ibn al-Yamān to spy on the enemy and find out what they were doing. When Hudhayfa set forth, the Prophet (s) prayed for his success. Hudhayfa went into the enemy camp and sat beside them without anyone realizing that he had been sent to spy on them. Then he returned to the Prophet (s) and informed him of what he had heard. (For more details on this, refer to: Wāqidi, *al-Maghāzi* 2:490) (Tr.)

[4] Wāqidi 2:670; Ibn Hishām 3:344. During the Conquest of Makkah, the Holy Prophet (s) commanded all the soldiers, who numbered about ten thousand and were camped a few kilometers outside Makkah, to light torches and when the Makkans saw ten thousand lights in the night, they lost all hope of resistance and in this way the Muslims were able to enter Makkah without spilling any blood as the Qurasysh simply surrendered without putting up any resistance (See: Wāqidi 2:814; Ibn Hishām 3:402) (Tr.)

[5] Wāqidi 1:182, 194; Ibn Hishām 3:46; Ibn Sa'd 2:21, 35, 44

[6] It has always been the case that gaining an advantage over the enemy in all aspects is considered one of the primary tactics and this is as true today as it was in the past. Countries gather large arsenals and buy or manufacture weapons in order to ensure that they are prepared to face any enemy that would dare to attack them. The Holy Prophet (s) also took this very seriously and because of this, he was able to gain numerous victories over his enemies. (Tr.)

[7] See: al-Harb al-Khātifah in Ibn Hishām 2:248, 3:69; Ibn Sa'd 2:7, 2:53 onwards; Wāqidi 1:11; Ibn Sayyid al-Nās 2:79

[8] Zuhri: 86; Ibn Hishām 3:181; Bukhāri (al-Jihād: 38)

[9] The Holy Prophet (s) commanded the digging of a trench around the city of Madina in the Battle of Ahzāb in accordance with the suggestion made by Salmān al-Fārsi. Because this task was very difficult and required a lot of time to complete, the Holy Prophet (s) instructed all the forces and even the youth to assist. They would not stop digging until the task was completed and even the Prophet (s) did his share of the work. In this way, the task was completed quickly and in time. (See: Wāqidi 2:445-460) (Tr.)

[10] The Prophet (s) used this strategy in the Battle of Khaybar, Bani Quraydha and Bani Nadhir, and he besieged the Jewish forces in their fortresses. This made things difficult for them and they eventually came out and surrendered. (Tr.)

[11] For more details see: Asghar Qā'idān, *Tārikh wa Athāre Islāmiye Makkeye Mukarrame wa Madineye Munawware*: 72

[12] When Salmān gave the suggestion that the Muslims should dig a trench in the Battle of Ahzāb, the Muslims became so happy with the idea that each group claimed Salmān to be part of them. But the Prophet said: Salmān is from us – the Ahl al-Bayt, and this Salmān became known as Salmān al-Muhammadi. See: Wāqidi 2:455-460; Tabari 2:574; Ibn Sayyid al-Nās 2:61 (Tr.)

[13] Wāqidi 2:792, 803; Ibn Hishām 4:44; Ibn Sa'd 2:98; Tabari 3:56

[14] War of the city and streets is one of the most important types of warfare that has been fought both in the past and present and has played a decisive role in the outcome of many battles. The same is true for the Conquest of Makkah. This can be seen in the

books of history. (For example, see Bakri Shāfi'i, *al-Durar al-Mukallalah fi Fath Makkah al-Mukarramah al-Musharrafah al-Mubajjalah*, and also Wāqidi's *al-Maghāzi* and Ibn Hisham's *Seerah*) (Tr.)

[15] Wāqidi 2:825; Ibn Hishām 4:44; Tabari 3:54

[16] After the polytheists had broken the Treaty of Hudaybiyya, the Prophet (s) gave the order to mobilize all the forces so that he could uproot the very existence of polytheism and disbelief from the Arabian Peninsula. With ten thousand strong, the Prophet (s) marched towards Makkah. When Abu Sufyān saw the Muslim army up close and knew that there was no hope of defeating them, he sought the intercession of the Prophet's uncle 'Abbās ibn 'Abd al-Muttalib and professed Islām. In turn, the Prophet (s) granted amnesty to all those who sought refuge in Abu Sufyān's house. After taking over the city, the Prophet decided to free all the disbelievers, and spared their lives. The way this conquest was carried out was unprecedented. An entire city was taken without the use of any force and without shedding a single drop of blood. (For more details, see: Ibn Hishām 3:400; Wāqidi 2:780; Ibn Sayyid al-Nās 2:223-244; Ya'qubi 2:58 onwards; Ibn Sa'd 2:135) (Tr.)

[17] Wāqidi 1:195, 2:496; Ibn Hishām 3:50; Ibn Sa'd 2:23; Tabari 2:181 & 9:3

[18] Shaybāni, *Sharh Siyar al-Kabir* 1:119; Ibn Sayyid al-Nās 2:64

[19] Wāqidi 1:404; Ibn Hishām 3:302; Ibn Atheer, *Usd al-Ghābah* 4:2, 330; Ibn Hajar, *al-Isāba fi Tamyeez al-Sahāba* 1:29, 3:194, 4:11, 176

[20] Q4:84; Bukhāri (al-Maghāzi 17); Muslim (al-Amārah 117)

[21] Wāqidi 2:245 onwards; Ibn Hishām 2:267, 4:37, 39

[22] Zuhri: 63, 71; Wāqidi 1:9 & 2:534; Ibn Hishām 4:161, 2:241, 3:107; Tabari 2:448

[23] Wāqidi 2:658 onwards; Suhayli 4:65; Ibn Sayyid al-Nās 2:201

[24] Wāqidi 3:927; Ibn Sa'd 2:114; Ibn Sayyid al-Nās 2:201 onwards

[25] The Battle of Hunayn took place in 8 A.H. after the Conquest of Makkah. When the enemy ambushed the Muslims, many of those who had just become Muslims after the Conquest of Makkah fled and then, with the exception of ten individuals, everyone left the side of the Holy Prophet and took to their heels. When the ten brave individuals put up a strong resistance, the army eventually returned and regrouped.

Eventually the Muslims defeated the Hawāzin army and six thousand of them were captured. A group fled to Tā'if and another group went to Autās where they set up defenses. The Prophet (s) sent Abu 'Aāmir Ash'ari to follow them and he was able to capture nine more of them from Autās. In the end, the Muslims were victorious. (For more details, see: Ibn Sa'd 2:147; Ibn Hishām 2:72; Nuwayri, Nihāyat al-Urub fi Funun al-Adab 2:295-297). Here, it was only because the enemy intended to regroup and launch further attacks on the Muslims that the order to pursue them was given. (Tr.)

26 Zuhri: 151. Such an incident never transpired in any of the battles and the Prophet (s) never ordered that the fleeing enemy should be pursued. (Tr.)

PART THREE: MANAGEMENT OF SUPPLIES AND MUNITIONS

With the advancement of different facets of daily life and its changes, it can be observed that the issue of 'munitions and support' was very serious and had an important impact on the outcome of the war; because if the needs of an army are not met, the forces are faced with inconvenience, loss and dispersion, and the enemy is also likely to take the first opportunity and overpower them. In this way, its paramount importance in terms of the management of war and the tactical and strategic planning, become evident.

It is necessary that different aspects of this matter and its hardships and difficulties be discussed, because people in the past have not recounted the conditions of the management of warfare for us in a way that can be relied upon or trusted.[1]

If one wanted to learn about the strength of the military infrastructure of the Muslim army at the time of the Holy Prophet (s), he would find that the first thing that the Prophet gave importance was the abundance of locally available resources[2] that would be utilized, whether it be in the form of foods – the most important of which were dates – or other resources that the soldiers and troops would take as provisions for the war.[3] The Muslim army never gave importance to the idea of storing or hoarding foodstuffs and for this reason, in many of the battles, the soldiers would suffer from hunger due to lack of sufficient food, and this forced the commanders to distribute the little available resources among the soldiers in an equitable manner,[4] and in situations where soldiers had nothing, they were forced to eat the meat of horses, wild donkeys etc.[5] With respect to drinks like water, which was not always enough or accessible due to the lack of wells, the situation was very difficult[6] and the same procedure of equal distribution was applied.[7]

As for the modes of transport that mostly consisted of camels and other animals, the soldiers would use them for traversing long distances and transferring booty that was gained from the battles. Actually, this booty was considered an important source for the acquisition of weapons and military provisions, in addition to the sale of horses and other equipment which constituted another source.[8]

On the other hand, the Noble Prophet (s) gave importance to the disabled and the handicapped,[9] because they would always remain with the army until the necessary resources for tending to their needs became available. For this type of forces, there was no special arrangement in the Muslim army (as is the case today). Their role and important responsibilities included: Keeping watch and constant surveillance, providing partial reinforcements, tending to the injured, removing the bodies of those who were killed from the battlefield and burying them, patrolling and serving during the night, taking care of those who were in shock, gathering and settling,[10] selecting suitable places where there were no plagues or infectious diseases – in which the commander would himself assist them – and in the end, the injured would be taken [by them] to a tent in Madina that was erected for them next to the Masjid of the Prophet (s).[11]

Despite all the difficulties [they faced], and the lack of provisions and reinforcements, the army of Islām would overpower the enemy that was better equipped in all these respects. The reason for this was that the Prophet (s) would use various forms of warfare according to what he deemed appropriate given the circumstances, based on his experience and brilliance.[12]

NOTES AND REFERENCES

[1] From the past up till today, the issue of supplies and provisions has been of paramount importance in war, and it can be said with some confidence that in every war where the matter of provisions and supplies was adequately addressed, victory was attained. And this issue has also played a key role in the loss of many a battle. This issue would always be taken very seriously by the Holy Prophet (s) in all of his battles. (Tr.)

[2] The author gives more details about this in the fifth section. (Tr.)

[3] Bukhāri (al-Maghāzi 17); Muslim (al-Amāra 143)

[4] Bukhāri (al-Maghāzi 65); Abu Dāwud (al-Ati'mah 46); Ibn Sayyid al-Nās 2:158

[5] Ibn Hanbal 6:346; Bukhāri (al-Maghāzi 35); Kalā'i 1:132

[6] Wāqidi 2:578; Ibn Hazm: 251; Ibn Katheer, al-Bidāya wan-Nihāya 5:9

[7] The fact that the Prophet (s) never used to store food and grain can be derived from the Qur'ānic injunctions against hoarding and maybe also from the economic situation in Madina at the time. In any case, the Prophet (s) would mostly get his own food supplies from his own lands and from the enemies and would give less burden to the soldiers by nor requiring them to carry and transport it, so that their movement would not be slowed down. (Tr.)

[8] Wāqidi 1:378; Bukhāri (al-Jihād 80); Muslim (al-Jihād 49)

[9] Dārimi (Muqaddima 2); Abu Dāwud (al-Jihād 107); Kalā'i 1:130

[10] Wāqidi 2:644; Bukhāri (al-Madina 12); Abu Dāwud (al-Tibb 24)

[11] These missions in the Muslim army were carried under the Department of Supplies and Provisions.

[12] Wāqidi 1:26, 396; Ibn Hishām 3:181, 346; Tabari 2:513, 3:10

PART FOUR: THE SUBJECT FOR DISCUSSION

In this study, the important events in the battles of the Prophet (s) have been discussed with the view of outlining the profundity of thought and consideration that was employed. In order to make things easy for the readers and students, we shall discussed the details of the subject at hand in such a manner and at such length that they would find no need to refer to numerous other available sources on the subject. This discussion regarding all the different aspects and the conclusions drawn will be presented separately. For example, the matter of *istitlā'*[1] (gathering information and intelligence) which includes the modes, types and importance of intelligence gathering in battles and military missions and also the ways and methods that are used for this. In this discussion, all the tactics that are employed in information gathering, the role of every individual and group including [that of] the commander of the army and its leaders, their responsibilities and the conditions that need to be met by them and also how the information should be gotten from the enemy, the means that must be used, how to send this information to the commander of the army and how the information is used by the commander, are all explained.

In these discussions, we give another example of the organization of the soldiers and their formations in different situations.[2] They would sometimes be arranged into one, two or three groups. The 'arrow makers' would be in the first or second group along with the archers, and the infantry would be behind the cavalry. The commander and the central watcher would be positioned in the center of the formation.

Taking this into consideration, the subject being discussed comprises of both detailed and general topics about effects and consequences, and explanation of the important points and goals.[3] Actually, we find that this subject includes a variety of topics, some of which are examined closely and thereby linked to others. All these topics are important for arriving at a clear and conclusive understanding of the subject.

NOTES AND REFERENCES

[1] Wāqidi 1:9; Ibn Sa'd 2:2; Suhayli 3:27; Kalā'i 1:139; Ibn Sayyid al-Nās 2:108

[2] Ibn Hishām 2:287; Ibn Hanbal 5:420; Abu Dāwud (al-Jihād 107)

[3] In the third chapter of this book, the issue of parading the army and organizing it has been explained in detail.

PART FIVE: STRIVING FOR HUMANITY

The Prophet of Allah (s) was truly a mercy for the entire human race.[1] He never excluded anyone because of color or ethnicity. All people were considered servants of God by him.[2] For this reason, he (s) would invite and call people towards the following:

1. Growth and advancement of humanity as a whole.[3] He would say: *All of you are from Adam, and Adam was from clay.*[4]
2. Agreeing to a peace treaty before war.[5]
3. Forgiveness and pardon before punishment.[6]
4. Leniency and clemency before retribution.

Therefore, we find that all the battles he fought were always for the good of humanity, so he would not seek to punish anyone before they had done anything wrong, as [opposed to what] we see in our present day.

The Prophet of Allah (s) would prevent the killing of the aged, women, children, prisoners and those who did not participate in the war and did not help the enemy.[7] He would prohibit this fervently. He also forbade torture and the disfiguring of dead bodies.[8] He instructed the Muslims to be good, kind and compassionate to the people and to be affable and friendly with them.[9]

He gave a perfect example of mercy in the Conquest of Makkah where, despite victory over the enemy, he treated them with the utmost kindness and compassion. If he wanted, he could have just as easily taken revenge on all of them, but instead he forgave them saying: *Go, you are all freed.*[10] In the battle of Dhat al-Ruqā', 'Amr bin Hārith was captured trying to assassinate the Prophet,[11] however the Prophet pardoned him and set him free.[12]

The Prophet (s) would treat the captives and prisoners of war with mercy and kindness. He would do favors to many of them (and set them free).[13] At the same time, he told the soldiers to treat them well.[14] For example, in one of the battles, he personally untied the hands of one of the prisoners whom he heard wailing.[15]
He propagated the idea of World Peace and instituted the word 'peace' as a greeting among all the children of Adam.[16] He showed this in the Treaty of Hudaybiyya when he sent Uthmān bin 'Affān to negotiate with the Quraysh, and he accepted a number of representatives and groups that were selected to carry out this task. According to this treaty, he accepted the conditions put forward by the oppressive enemy for the cessation of war.[17] During the conquest (of Makkah), he deposed the commander whom he had given the order to take the

city[18] because of the slogans that he was chanting which gave a totally different impression about the goals of the conquest.[19]

He paid special attention in choosing pious and righteous representatives to take the message to the rulers and kings of the world, because these representatives would have to convey the message using logic and wisdom in order to successfully invite them to accept Islām.[20]

In the present age, there is no need that is greater than what the Prophet (s) was striving for. A strong need is felt for sincere action that is free from vain desire and hostility and for leadership that is truthful and righteous, which can lead the people towards humanity and a moral ethic of warfare that is far from mere bloodshed and slaughter.

These issues encompass a vast plethora of discussions that a humble person such as myself feels incapable of doing justice to. However, I shall spare no effort in trying my utmost to work on it. I do not claim that this research is complete and final, but I pursued this subject because I found it delectable and interesting, and I realized that the fruits of this research would be very beneficial.

I would truly like to express my gratitude to Dr. Ibrahim Baydhun of the University of Lebanon for his help and guidance in the arrangement and layout of this work and his attention to detail regarded the material presented in it. I will never forget his mentoring and the explanations and elucidations that he shared with me and assisted me with, to such an extent that he would at times leave his entire library – which is filled with many valuable works – at my disposal and I was able to gain access to many original sources and handwritten manuscripts.
I take this opportunity to thank the administrator and staff of the Dhahiriyyah Damascus Library who facilitated the access to important texts and manuscripts that I needed. I also would like to thank all those who participated in this work with me and even those who found out about my research proposal and went through it. I thank them all.

Was-salaam
Muhammad Dhāhir Watr

NOTES AND REFERENCES

[1] Q21:107; Muslim (Bāb al-Birr wal-Jannah)

[2] Muslim (Bāb al-ʿItq 16)

[3] Bukhāri (al-Jihād 102); Muslim (al-Amāra 117)

26

[4] Tirmidhi (al-Manāqib)

[5] Q2:208; Q8:61; Ibn Hanbal 2:246; Bukhāri (al-Adab 91)

[6] Bukhāri (al-Anbiyā 50, 54); Tabari 3:49

[7] Shaybāni, *Sharh al-Siyar al-Kubrā* 1:42; Abu Dāwud (al-Jihād 82)

[8] Bukhāri (al-Madhālim 30, al-Dhabā'ih 25, al-Maghāzi 36); Abu Dāwud (al-Jihād 110, al-Amārah 33)

[9] Bukhāri (al-Adhān 17,18); Muslim (al-Nadhr 8); Abu Dāwud (al-Eimān 21)

[10] The Holy Prophet (s) conquered Makkah and purified this holy sanctuary of the impure idols. Many of those who had persecuted him over the years gathered around him in the hope of seeking his mercy and forgiveness. The Prophet (s) let them go saying 'Antum al-Tulaqā' – *I have set you free.* (Tr.)

[11] Suhayli 3:253; Kalā'i 1:112; Qurtubi, al-Jāmi' al-Ahkām al-Qur'ān 3:217; Ibn Qayyim, *Zād al-Ma'ād fi Hudā Khayril 'Ibād* 2:275

[12] 'Amr ibn Hārith was from the tribe of Bani Mahārib. He approached the Prophet (s) with the intention of killing him. When the Prophet (s) was resting, he took his sword and threatened him with it saying: Don't you fear me now that I have your sword and am about to kill you? He (s) replied: No, I am not afraid of you because I know that Allāh is there to protect me. When 'Amr heard this he could not move forward and dropped the sword and ran away. (Ibn Hishām 2:205) (Tr.)

[13] Bukhāri (al-Ahkām 35); Muslim (al-Jihād 58); Abu Dāwud (al-Jihād 120); Bayhaqi, *Sunan al-Kubrā* 6:319

[14] Ibn Hishām 2:199; Tabari 2:46

[15] This person was 'Abbās ibn 'Abd al-Muttalib, who was taken as a prisoner in the Battle of Badr, whereas he had been forced to come and fight by the Quraysh. See: Bayhaqi 9:89; Ibn 'Abd al-Barr, *al-Isti'āb* 2:810

[16] Ibn Hanbal 3:421; Bukhāri (al-Isti'dhān 9); Muslim (al-Adab 37); Ibn Mājah (al-Adab 13); Abu Dāwud (al-Adab: 91); Tirmidhi (al-Isti'dhān 2 & 11)

[17] Zuhri: 52; Ibn Hishām 3:325; Ibn Hazm: 208; Kalā'i 1:127

[18] Wāqidi 2:822; Ibn Sa'd 2:98; Suhayli 4:101; Kalā'i 1:139

[19] This person, Sa'd ibn 'Ubāda al-Khazraji, was the ruler of the Khazraj tribe. This was one of the tribes that were always engaged in war and fighting in order to take control of Yathrib. As there was also enmity between the Qahtānis of Yathrib and the 'Adnānis of Makkah, the people of Madina accepted Islām and decided to help the Prophet (s) against the 'Adnānis. For this reason, when Makkah was conquered, many of the people of Madina who still held a grudge against their arch enemies thought of it as an opportunity to exact revenge. Sa'd took to chanting 'Today is the day of vengeance!' but when the Prophet heard about this, he took the flag away from Sa'd and raised the chant of 'Today is the day of mercy!' instead. (Tr.)

[20] Sirāj al-Deen, *Sayyidinā Muhammad Rasulullah* (s): 84

SCOPE OF RESEARCH

My method of research about the proposed subject is scientific and relies on fully documented evidence along with undisputed facts. It is based firstly on primary sources which form the foundation of the discussion and then secondarily turns to the more recent studies and views of contemporary scholars. In this research, differing viewpoints on military management (with the aim of finding the best one), the principles of war, the fundamental role of ideology (and motivation) and the art of war in its new form are discussed alongside each other. This paper comprises of six sections and one preface - wherein the most important available sources on this subject are mentioned.

Section One:
In this section, the traits and distinctions of the Arab military before Islām have been mentioned and the most important points that are related to their military management like: the purpose of battle, number of combatants, means of transport etc. have been discussed.

Section Two:
This section consists of the important discussion on 'Military Command' in which issues like moral qualities of a commander are discussed. These include: heightened intelligence, foresight and prudence, awareness of matters that he is faced with, understanding the rules and principles of war such as defensive warfare, sudden warfare, revolutionary warfare, offensive warfare and psychological warfare.

Section Three:
This section aims to explain the workings of the military bases and under this heading, details are given about staff headquarters and management issues pertaining to it are discussed, including:
1. Department of planning: this department deals with the general policies of the army, the enumeration of soldiers, arming them, understanding the enemy and related issues.
2. Department of consultation: this is the consultative body or the command post of the war and its members are all recognized for their knowledge, acumen and understanding of issues pertaining to warfare.
3. Department of spiritual guidance: this department is responsible for increasing the zeal of the fighters, studying the assignments and tours of duty.

Section Four:
This section discusses the branch and department of 'Security and Intelligence' that is responsible for gathering information and intelligence from the enemy and

analyzing it, and in the event of the intelligence being true, passing it to the supreme commander so that he may issue the correct orders.

Section Five:
In this section we discuss about the 'Base of Operations' which makes arrangements for the required equipment for planning, execution, training, creation and perfection of weaponry and all the other supplies for warfare and includes the following departments:
1. Department of operations: this is the department that is responsible for selecting the commander who leads the army in the battlefield, studying the assignments and sending troops and contingents.
2. Department of training: this department is responsible for training the fighters in the handling of all the tools used in battle including bows and arrows, hand to hand combat etc.
3. Department of armament: this department is in charge of securing all the supplies of war, weapons, military equipment etc.

Section Six:
This section deals specifically with the department of munitions that has the responsibility of securing munitions, sending support, transport, feeding the soldiers, providing army uniforms, overseeing booty and its distribution and handling medical issues. This department consists of the following sub-departments:
1. Department of munitions and relief support: this department has the task of providing support to the troops by means of providing supplies and fulfilling their other needs such as drinking water, tents, clothes and also removing the injured and dead from the battlefield.
2. Department of booty: its responsibility is gathering the war booty and categorizing, arranging and distributing it, and identifying those who should be permitted to use it.
3. Department of medical services: the aim of this department is protecting the wellbeing of the forces, providing medical treatment for those who are injured and incapacitated in battle, and burying the dead.
In this section, the role of women in providing assistance is also discussed.

Conclusion:
In the end, we shall discuss the 'growth of Islāmic Governance' after the migration of the Prophet (s) to Madina, the formation of the Islāmic Government under his leadership. The details of his role in nurturing the military forces during wartime and the beginning of the creation and training of the corps will also be discussed. We will examine how this army gained the ability of entering into battle and achieving decisive victory. In this regard, we find the causes of victory in the Muslim army to be the implementation of the principles and rules of war by their commanders – which the enemy was unaware of at that time and is more

in line with the principles and rules of war of today. Similarly, the organization of the army in such a way that a strong spiritual ethos existed among the commanders and the troops, must be considered one of the greatest factors of the Prophet's (s) success. When one studies the conquests that took place after the era of Prophethood, one finds that the Prophet (s) was considered the first conqueror of Islām, because he laid the groundwork and raised the primary pillar (of these conquests) through his own battles.

A CHRONOLOGICAL INTRODUCTION AND DESCRIPTION OF THE MOST IMPORTANT SOURCES

Despite the fact that the wars of the Prophet (s) were fought over a relatively short period (10 years), his method and style of command and military leadership lasted for a long time; because Muslims and others, within the military and without, have discussed, studied and analyzed this subject from the beginning of the first century A.H. up to this day and have not neglected it.

The Glorious Qur'ān is the most important source that speaks of these wars and battles, and we find a lot about this subject in its commentaries. The most important of these commentaries are: Tabari's Commentary, Nayshāburi's *Asbāb al-Nuzul*, Qurtubi's *al-Jāmi li Ahkām al-Qur'ān*, Baydhāwi's *Anwār al-Tanzil wa Asrār al-Ta'wil* and Suyuti's *al-Itqān fi 'Ulum al-Qur'ān*. Among these, Tabari's commentary, which describes the details of what takes place in the battles and also Nayshāburi's commentary, which records the occasion of revelation of specific verses in relation to the battles, are especially important.

Material about these issues can [also] be found in various books of history and biography, the most important among which include: Ibn Shihāb al-Zuhri's *al-Maghāzi al-Nabawiyya*, Ibn Is'hāq's *al-Siyar wa al-Maghāzi*, al-Wāqidi's *al-Maghāzi al-Nabawiyya,* Ibn Hazm al-Andalusi's *Jawāmi' al-Sirah*, al-Kalā'i's *al-Ihtifā'* and Ibn Sayyid al-Nās' *Uyun al-Athar*. Wāqidi was more precise in his historical recordings of all the wars than the others, and by describing the affairs of war and its management, he has been able to tackle the subject better. We cannot find complete references to the organization of the military except in his treatise. After him, Ibn Sa'd continues his work in the book *al-Tabaqāt al-Kubrā* and presents a picture of that which Wāqidi had not recorded.

However, the most important books of history about this subject are: *Tārikh Ibn Khayyāt*, Bukhāri's *Tārikh al-Kabir*, *Tārikh Tabari*, *Tārikh Ibn 'Asākir*, Ibn Atheer's *al-Kāmil fi al-Tārikh*, Ibn Katheer's *al-Bidāya wa al-Nihāya*, and also some biographical commentaries like Suhayli's *Rawdh al-Unf* have also set out to give details of such issues.

Books of Hadith and Jurisprudence have also devoted specific chapters and sections for these matters. The primary ones among these are: *Sahih Bukhāri* (Chapter 9 – The Book of Battles), *Sahih Muslim* (Chapter 3 – The Book of Jihad and Expeditions), *Sunan al-Tirmidhi* (Chapter 2 – The Book of Jihad), *Sunan Ibn Dāwud* (Chapter 2 – The Book of Jihad and Expeditions), *Sunan al-Nasā'i*

(Chapter 6 – The Book of Jihād), *Sunan al-Dārimi* (Chapter 2 – The Book of Jihād and Expeditions), *Sunan al-Dārqutni* (The Book of Expeditions), *Musannaf San'āni* (Chapter 5), Ibn Hanifa's *al-Maghāzi wa al-Musnad* (The book of Jihād and Expeditions), Shāfi'i's *al-Umm* (Chapter 6 – The Book of Willful Injury), Humaidi's *al-Musnad* (The Book of Battles and Jihād), Abi Sulaymān al-Khitābi's *Ma'ālim al-Sunan* and Ibn Qayyim al-Jawzi's *al-Tahdhib*.

In this context, *Sahih Bukhāri* is important both historically and militarily as the author has narrated the accounts chronologically and recounts the battles in the order in which they took place, starting from the Battle of al-'Ashirah to the Battle of Tabuk. Similarly, when he explains the battles, he takes all the angles into account, mentioning numerous narratives about it, such that the reader is able to come to a complete and correct understanding of these battles.

Aside from the books that discuss this subject separately, there are various books of history and annals of nations that have also been beneficial in this research. The most important among these are: Arzaqi's *Akhbāru Makkah*, Qutb al-Din's *Tārikh Makkah al-Musharrafah*, Fāsi's *al-'Aqd al-Tamin*, Bakri's *Mu'jam Mastu'jam* and Yāqut al-Hamawi's *Mu'jam al-Buldān*.

The most important feature of these histories and chronicles is that they mention the economic situation [at the time], military resources and battle expeditions and similarly give a clear representation of the economic life, which in this age was considered one of the more important issues, and for every discussion on the military it is a necessary factor that needs to be taken into account.

Books about the character of the Prophet (s) also consist of many points about his 'military management' and 'qualities of leadership' the most important among which include: Ibn Sa'd's *Tabaqāt al-Kubrā* (vol. 1 Chapter 2), Tirmidhi's *Shamāil*, Faryabi's *Dalā'il al-Nubuwwah*, Abu 'Ali Ansāri's *Sifāt al-Nabi* (s), Qādhi 'Ayyādh's *Shifā*, Suyuti's *al-Khasā'is al-Kubrā*, Ibn Hajar 'Asqalāni's *al-Mawāhib al-Daniyya*, al-Dhahabi's *Tārikh al-Islām* (vol. 1), Ibn Qayyim al-Jawzi's *Zād al-Ma'ād fi Hudā Khayril 'Ibād* (vol. 1 & 2) and his *Furusiyyat al-Muhammadiyyah*.

Books of biography are also not empty of material on this subject, rather, in many instances provide detailed accounts about the commanders of battles and wars and about the companions who had the responsibility of commanding the armies. Some of these (books) are: Ibn Habib's *al-Muhbir*, Ibn 'Abd al-Barr's *al-Isti'āb fi Ma'rifat al-Ashāb*, Ibn Atheer al-Jazari's *Usd al-Ghāba fi Ma'rifat al-Sahābah* and Ibn Hajar 'Asqalāni's *al-Isāba fi Tamyiz al-Sahābah*.

The Islāmic conquests at the time of the Prophet (s) and the companions were studied by those who came later and the various aspects and details were presented in a well organized fashion by them. Books of geography and history expound on the conquests within and without the Arabian subcontinent and also talk of the events after the spread of Islām from Madina al-Munawwarah to Damascus, Baghdād, Madā'in, and on the east to India and to Alexandria, Constantinople, Tarablus and Tunis. It could be said that the most important of these works are Ibn Khardāba's *al-Masālik wal-Mamālik* [vols. 3,4,5 and 6], Ibn Rusta's *al-A'lāq al-Nafsiyya* [Chapter 8] which talks about Madina, Makkah, Haramayn and the southern lands of Arabia.

Ibn Faqih's *al-Buldān* [Chapter 10 and 11] talks of Makkah and Alexandria while Ya'qubi's *al-Buldān* [Chapter 17 and 18] mentions the Maghreb, Baghdad and their historical importance. Balkhi's *Suwar al-Aqāleem* is the first book on geography written in Islām and Istakhri's *al-Masālik wal-Mamālik* is also the first book that describes the 'Islāmic World'.

In Ibn Hawqal's *al-Masālik wal-Mamālik* [Chapter 3, 4 and 24] the maps of Egypt, Syria, Iraq and the Arabian Peninsula have been drawn and the economical and social situation of Libya has also been portrayed. Muqaddasi has also given a description of Palestine and Syria in his *Ahsanu al-Taqāseem fi Ma'rifatil Aqāleem* [Chapter 32 and 34].

Mas'udi's *al-Tanbih wal-Ashrāf* [Chapter 37] speaks of the life of the Prophet (s), battles and expeditions in which he was the commander, military units, horses and mounts, and all that is related to the military transport. Mas'udi's recording of the 'Historical Geography of Battles', is considered an original source whose narrations can be relied upon, however, unfortunately most of his writings are lost.

Another source is Qazwini's *Athār al-Bilād wa Akhbār al-'Ibād* which discusses geographical history and related issues including the situations and conditions of different lands and their inhabitants. After this, we must mention the *Muqaddima* of Ibn Khaldun and Qalashqandi's *Subh al-A'shā*. These two books record geographical and historical information about different kingdoms, especially Egypt and Syria.

It is noteworthy that more recently books and research works, in both Arabic and English, have been written about the life of the Prophet (s) and his battles with the disbelievers. The most important works in Arabic include: *al-Rasul al-Qā'id* (S. Khattāb), *al-Rasul al-'Arabi wa Fann al-Harb* (General Mustafa Talās), *al-*

'Abqariyya al-Askariyya fi Ghazawāt al-Rasul, *'Ali Hāmish al-Sirah* (Tāhā Hussain), *Hayātu Muhammad* (Muhammad Hasanain Haykal), *al-'Abqariyyāt al-Islāmiyya* ('Aqqād) and *al-Anwār al-Muhammadiyya* (Nabhāni).

The foreign books that have been translated into Arabic and discuss the same subject, we can mention: *Muhammad in Makkah and Madina* (Montgomery Watt), *Muhammad, the Prophet of Allah* (Dianna), *The Heroes* (Thomas Carlayle), *The First Hundred* (Michael Hart) and others.

Many of these works are only limited to military, institutional or ethical issues that form part of the *seerah*. Because 'military management' encompasses all these issues, it is necessary that we discuss all these matters together, taking into consideration their correlation with each other. It is through this that the importance of this subject and its role in revealing the secret of the success of the Holy Prophet (s) and those whom he chose as army commanders, becomes evident.

Now we will take a look at the most important authors and researchers in history who have written on this subject and have left behind important works on the battles and expeditions, and since their importance in relation to this subject varies, we will first study the oldest writings that are relevant and have practical implications and thereafter we will mention others according to their chronology and relevance; in this order: Wāqidi, Ibn Is'hāq, Ibn Shihāb al-Zuhri, Kalā'i and Ibn Sayyid al-Nās.

THE MOST IMPORTANT HISTORIANS
(CHRONOLOGICALLY)

1. **Abu Bakr Muhammad Ibn Muslim Bin 'Ubaydallah Bin Shihāb al-Zuhri** (51-124 A.H.):

There is a difference of opinion about his date of birth and death. He was a learned scholar, a memorizer of the Qur'an[1] and an author who knew how to use the various expressions and idioms and he would use these in his works.[2] He was a poet[3] and a genealogist[4] who would look for the chains of narrators in the traditions.[5] He would strive in the quest for knowledge and would guard it. He kept aloof from the events and turmoil of his time.[6] He believed in the dissemination of knowledge among the people and used to say: 'In the spread of knowledge there is the strengthening of religion and worldly life and in the path of knowledge all this comes together.'[7] He studied about the seerah from Sa'eed bin al-Musayyab, 'Urwa bin Zubayr and 'Ubaydallah bin 'Abdullah bin Utbah, and in his attitude towards his teachers, he displayed exemplary ethics and morals. He would accompany them, serve them and show the utmost reverence to them.[8] Zuhri made efforts to author some works. He would write down what he heard. When his works became known, people turned to him and benefitted greatly from his knowledge.

Zuhri started with Hadith, History and Expeditions. He wrote so much that his writings had to be carried on the backs of animals. When he died, he was in such a position that there was none more learned than him in history.[9] His knowledge was disseminated through his narrators. The most famous of them who lived in Haramayn and Hijāz included: 'Umar bin Dinar, Yahya bin Sa'eed al-Ansāri, Musa bin 'Uqba and others. From those who lived in Iraq, the most important ones included: 'Abdullah bin 'Umayr, Ismā'il bin Abi Khālid, 'Atā ibn Sā'ib; and from the other places like Syria and Egypt, there were Mansur bin Sādhān, 'Abd al-Karim Jazari, Thawr bin Yazid and others.[10]

The merits of Zuhri's accounts of the expeditions over other works are as follows:

a) They were written with sincerity, honesty, clarity and eloquence. Zuhri had met some of the companions who participated in battles with the Prophet (s) and he has narrated from them about the wars and the strategies of the Holy Prophet (s). The most important of them are: Abdullah bin 'Umar, Anas bin Mālik, Suhayl bin Sa'd and others.[11] Similarly, in *al-Musannaf* (vol. 5, the chapter on expeditions), we find numerous traditions that Zuhri has narrated from 'Umar ibn Rāshid. He too, was truthful in narration and reliable in transmission.

b) Many of the scholars[12] have praised and criticized the narrators of expedition accounts like Ibn Is'hāq and Wāqidi, however Zuhri has been praised by all[13] and has been hailed as the most truthful and highly learned of his time. Therefore, we can rely upon what he has recorded or narrated about the battles of the Prophet (s).

c) Zuhri had a longstanding experience in recording expeditions.[14] He is the oldest writer to formulate a systematic and clear method in this field, therefore his recordings are well-grounded, clear and reliable and have been systematically categorized and are far off from the politics of authorship and other various discrepancies.

2. **Abu 'Abdillah Muhammad Ibn Is'hāq Bin Yasār al-Mutallabi** (85-151 A.H.)

Ibn Is'hāq was born in Madina and was buried in Baghdād after his demise. There is a difference of opinion regarding the date of his death.[15] His most important works include: *Kitāb al-Khulafā* and *al-Siyar wal-Maghāzi wal-Mubtadā*.[16] He was trustworthy and knowledgeable about expeditions and history and was also a memorizer of prophetic traditions.[17] Great scholars have narrated from him and Ibn Shihāb al-Zuhri, Ibn Hanbal and others have praised him.[18] Mālik called him a Dajjāl[19] and accused him of following the Qādiriyya sect[20] and also deemed him to be one who narrates ahādith with improper and incomplete chains.[21]

The Seera of Ibn Is'hāq has only come down to us through the recorders of seera, the most important of whom were: Ibn Hishām, Tabari, Kalā'i, Ibn Sa'd and Ibn Atheer. All of these [people] have not presented the seera of Ibn Is'hāq in the same manner as the original, rather they have mentioned a summary of his statements and recordings. Ibn Hishām has himself acknowledged this in the introduction of his *al-Seera al-Nabawiyya*[22], so it would be correct to say that this work is actually a summary and a selection of Ibn Is'hāq's narrations. He is one of the leaders of those who were involved in recording the seerah [of the Holy Prophet][23] and is the first person to collect the accounts of the expeditions and record them.[24] His works are a source of reference for researchers today. The great recorders of expeditions like 'Aāsim bin Umar Qatāda who wrote *al-Siyar wal-Maghāzi* gave the following testimony about him: 'The knowledge that Ibn Is'hāq placed at the disposal of the people through his narrations will never disappear.'[25] When Zuhri was asked about Ibn Is'hāq's accounts of expeditions, he said 'he is the most learned of all people about the expeditions'.[26]

Today, the narrations of Ibn Is'hāq that have been passed on by many reliable recorders of the seera like 'Aāsim and Zuhri have reached us.[27] It can be said that Ibn Is'hāq is from those scholars who recorded the accounts of the expeditions based on old methods. One day this point was raised in front of him, he said: 'I am only a safe keeper and recorder of the knowledge of expeditions.'[28]

The Merits of Ibn Is'hāq's Seera

a) He is the only person who has narrated the expeditions of the Holy Prophet (s) in its totality,[29] because the other Seera recorders have narrated the expeditions in an incomplete and disjointed fashion. Maybe their lifetimes were not enough for them to complete the work and their students did not expound on the details of their expedition accounts and sufficed with mentioning only a number of battles and wars.

b) The Seera of Ibn Is'hāq is detailed and contains numerous long narrations and includes mention of dates.[30] Shāfi'i says: 'Anyone who wishes to gain expertise about the expeditions needs (to study) Ibn Is'hāq.'[31] Through lengthy odes, he has highlighted the narratives of what transpired on the battlefields.[32] All this points to the vastness of the Seera of Ibn Is'hāq. These odes have immortalized the victories and give important information about works, situations and personalities. Even though it is not possible to give exact details about what takes place on the battlefield, all the military strategies and skills employed, some of the particulars about the battles of the Prophet (s) have been directly reported.

3. **Abu Abdillah Muhammad Ibn Umar al-Wāqidi** (130-207 A.H.)

Wāqidi was born in Madina and died in Baghdād.[33] He is buried in the Khayzarān graveyard. He was an author and used to pay special attention in writing [about] the seerah and expeditions (of the Prophet (s)), to such an extent that he became one of the foremost authorities in this field. His most important works are: *al-Maghāzi al-Nabawiyya, Fath Afriqiyya, al-Radda, Fath al-'Ajam, Fath Misr wa Iskandariyya, Akhbār Makkah, Tabaqāt, Futuh al-Iraq, Seerat Abi Bakr*, The Battle between the Aus and Khazraj and others.[34] The merits of Wāqidi's works can be outlined as follows:

a) Precise Information: He has given detailed and precise information about those who participated in the battles, the route taken by the armies, the weapons and modes of transport used, provisions, descriptions of battlefields, the factors that helped in gaining victory or led to them facing difficulties in battle, the location of the martyrdom of soldiers, and anything related to warfare.

b) Extensive Information: He wrote and recorded everything that was related to the battles,[35] such that through his narrations, we learn many of the specifics regarding the military, because he has reported all the different aspects of issues pertaining to warfare and leadership. In this way, the information provided by Wāqidi in the areas of the circumstances of war, its location, the type of ground on which it was fought etc. is of great importance. If his writings about the battles were collected together, it would in itself have been a source for the principles of war and battle at the time of the Prophet (s).

c) Recording of Exact Times[36]: In military management, for a commander, time and its determination is of the essence and can make all the difference in the result of the battle; whether it be victory or loss.

d) Recording of Exact Locations[37]: Wāqidi also recorded the exact locations of the battles and through this he gave value to the battlefields where the Prophet (s) fought. Many like Ibn Sa'd, Tabari and Ibn Katheer have narrated from Wāqidi about the birth and Prophethood of the Holy Prophet (s) and also his battles and conquests.[38] Ibn Sa'd's *Tabaqāt al-Kubrā* stands out in its military reporting because it has been written according to Wāqidi's style, meaning he has similarly paid a great deal of attention to the recording of exact times and locations and sometimes describes the locations in which the battles took place and adds on to the narrations of Wāqidi and then, in another place, he discusses the principles of warfare.[39] From his writings it can be deduced that he is truthful and his narrations are authentic.[40] Many of the important aspects of Wāqidi's narrations and works were revealed and expounded by his student Ibn Sa'd.

4. Abu al-Rabi' Sulaymān Bin Musā Ibn Sālim al-Kalā'i al-Himyari

Kalā'i was born in Balans and grew up there and he died in enemy territory (in battle).[41] He has narrated from Ibn Qāsim Hubaysh, Ibn Zarqum, Ibn al-Waleed bin Abi al-Qāsim and others.[42] He was famous for his eloquent oratory and writings[43] and gave great importance to recording and narrating ahadith. His most well known works are: *al-Iktifā bimā Tadhammanhu 'an Maghāzi al-Rasul (s)*, *Maghāzi al-Khulafā* (4 volumes), *al-Musalsalāt 'an al-Ahādith* and *al-Athār wal-Ishārāt*.[44]

When his works were published and his message was spread, people came towards him and sought to benefit from him and many attended his teaching sessions. The most famous of these was Abdullah ibn al-Abārid who has eulogized him after his martyrdom.[45] With regards to the importance of his writing 'al-Iktifā' it must be said that its chain of transmission is strong and it describes the battles and their various aspects in detail, because Kalā'i himself was a military person and had tasted the hardships of war. So if he has recorded something in the seera, he has done so truthfully and with total regard of his responsibility and questionability. Furthermore, in his books one senses an enlightening spirituality that none of the previous writers displayed.

Kalā'i al-Balansi was a leader and a courageous commander who was steadfast in battle and in one of the battles he is said to have addressed one of the fleeing soldiers thus: 'Do you flee from Paradise?'[46] He was martyred while he still held the standard in his hand[47] and was encouraging and urging the soldiers to go forth against the enemy. Aside from this, Kalā'i was a great poet who would compose epics and rouse the emotions of the people.[48]

5. **Abu al-Fath Muhammad Ibn Muhammad Ibn 'Abdillah Ibn Sayyid al-Nās**[49]

He was popularly known as Ibn Sayyid al-Nās. There is a difference of opinion regarding his date of birth and death. He died in Cairo. He studied under his father and a group of scholars, the most famous of whom was Ibn Daqiq al-'Eid.[50] This scholar tutored him in religion, Arabic grammar and poetry.[51] He gained precedence over his contemporaries in the fields of Seera and history. His most important works include: *'Uyun al-Athar fi Funun al-Maghāzi wa al-Shamāil wa al-Siyar, Nur al-'Uyun, Bushrā al-Labib fi Dhikrā al-Habib* and *Tahsil al-Isāba fi Tafsil al-Sahāba.*[52]

Many scholars like Qādhi 'Izz al-Deen Sharif, who has mentioned him in his *Wafayāt* and Ibn Katheer, Ibn Nāsir al-Deen, Suyuti and others have testified to his great knowledge.[53] He compiled the seera in two volumes by narrating what the recorders of the seera before him had written. That which makes his accounts of the expeditions stand out includes:

a) Precision and Depth: He would select authentic narrations and leave aside the weak ones. He would take this matter very seriously and would do it very well.[54] An example of this precision of his can be seen when he summarized his own book *'Uyun al-Athār* and named it *Nur al-'Uyun*. In this way it became easy for him to refer to previous works and to present his writings on the seera in a well-documented manner. One of the great scholars has said: "Ibn Sayyid wrote, compiled and corrected a lot in his beautiful handwriting and he created principles for this [also]."[55]

b) Following the Method of Zuhri: Ibn Sayyid al-Nās in his book *al-Siyar wal-Tārikh*, has followed Zuhri's method and has compiled all that which relates to the military. His *'Uyun al-Athār* is an example of the *Maghāzi* of Ibn Is'hāq which has shadowed the *Seera* of Ibn Hishām and is formed of a selection from the *Maghāzi* of Wāqidi and a selection from scholars of history such as Tabari and Ibn Khayyāt. That which assisted him in this was his great knowledge of the sources of the seera.

Ibn Sayyid al-Nās was also a specialist in jurisprudence and would benefit from the scholars of his time and gain knowledge from them. Ibn Zubayr says: "He gained the permission [to narrate traditions] from four-hundred scholars or more."[56]

c) Organization, Sequence and Reference: Ibn Katheer has described him thus: "He occupied himself in the pursuit of knowledge and was better in this than everyone else. After he learnt the seera and history, he compiled them in two volumes... grand poetry, well written prose, complete eloquence and proper writing is what he had and he was attributed with kindness and good morals. He was loyal to the principles and practices of the previous scholars that relied on the traditions of the Holy Prophet (s)."

NOTES AND REFERENCES

[1] Dhahabi, Tadhkirat al-Huffadh 1:108-113; Ibn Khallikān, Wafayāt al-A'yān wa Anbā'I Abnā'iz Zamān 4:177-178; Ibn Hajar 'Asqalāni, Tahdhib al-Tahdhib 9:488, 450

[2] Abu Na'im al-Isfahāni, *Hilyat al-Awliyā wa Tabaqāt al-Asfiyā* 3:371

[3] Marzbāni, *Mu'jam al-Shu'arā*: 345

[4] Abu Na'im al-Isfahāni 3:272

[5] *Ibid.* 3:365

[6] Ibn Khallikān 4:177; Abu Na'im al-Isfahāni 3:364

[7] Abu Na'im al-Isfahāni 3:369

[8] *Ibid.* 3:371

[9] *Ibid.* 3:161. Unfortunately all his works and writings are non-extant. However, his narratives were used by later historians and thus can be found in these secondary sources. (Tr.)

[10] Abu Na'im al-Isfahāni 2:372-373

[11] Khateeb Baghdadi, *Tarikhu Baghdād* 3:13-14; al-Dhahabi, *Mizān al-I'tidāl fi Naqd al-Rijāl* 3:470; Ibn Sayyid al-Nās 1:7

[12] Abu Na'im al-Isfahāni 3:361 onwards; Ibn Shihāb al-Zuhri: 27

[13] Ibn Shihāb al-Zuhri: 30

[14] Abu Na'im al- Isfahāni 3:369 onwards

[15] Khateeb Baghdādi 1:232; Ibn Khallikāk 4:277; Yāqut Humayri, *Mu'jam al-Udabā'* 18:8

[16] *Ibid.*

[17] Khateeb Baghdādi 1:215, Ibn Hajar 'Asqalāni, *Tahdhib al-Tahdhib* 9:43 onwards

[18] Al-Dhahabi 3:469

[19] Khateeb Baghdādi 1:223

[20] Khateeb Baghdādi 1:225; al-Dhahabi 30:470

[21] Ibn Sayyid al-Nās 1:7

[22] Ibn Hishām 1:7

[23] Al-Dhahabi, *Tadhkirat al-Huffādh* 1:173

[24] Yāqut Humayri, *Mu'jam al-Buldān* 5:18; Marghliyuth, *Dirāsāt 'an al-Muwarrikheen al-'Arab*: 998

[25] Khateeb Baghdādi 1:220; Yāqut Himayari, *Mu'jam al-Udabā'* 6:18; Ibn Khallikān 4:276

[26] Khateeb Baghdādi 1:219

[27] Yāqut Himyari 6:18, Khateeb Baghdādi 1:225

[28] Khateeb Baghdādi 1:223

[29] *Ibid.* 1:214

[30] Ibn Hajar 'Asqalāni 9:46

[31] Al-Dhahabi, *Mizān al-I'tidāl* 3:472; Khateeb Baghdādi 1:219; Ibn Sayyid al-Nās 1:9

[32] Al-Jumhi, *Tabaqāt Fuhul al-Shu'arā* 1:8; Marghliyuth: 73

[33] Ibn 'Asākir 15:395; al-Dhahabi, *Tadhkirat al-Huffādh* 1:348

[34] Yāqut Himyari, *Mu'jam al-Udabā'* 8:281; Ibn Khallikān 4:348; Ibn al-Nadim, *al-Firhrist* 1:144. Unfortunately most of Wāqidi's works are non-extant today. (Tr.)

[35] Khateeb Baghdādi 3:6

[36] Marghliyuth: 18

[37] Ibn Sa'd 5:315

[38] Tabari, *Tārikh al-Tabari* 1:942,980

[39] Ibn Sa'd 2:1-137

[40] Khateeb Baghdādi 5:321, al-Dhahabi, *Mizān al-I'tidāl* 3:560. With regards to Ibn Sa'd's reliability, there is a difference of opinion among the various sects of Islām. (Tr.)

[41] Ibn 'Imād Hanbali, *Shadharāt al-Dhahab fi Akhbār man Dhahab* 5:164; al-Katāni, *al-Risāla al-Mustadhrafa*: 198

[42] Al-Nabāhi, *Tārikh Qudhāt Andalus*: 119

[43] Ibn 'Imād Hanbali, *Ibid.*

[44] Al-Katāni, *Ibid.* He also wrote an important work called *Futuh al-Radda* (Tr.)

[45] Al-Nabāhi: 120

[46] *Ibid.* 119

[47] *Ibid.* Ibn Shākir al-Katbi, *Fawāt al-Wafayāt* 1:366

[48] Kalā'i was one of the great commanders in the war against the crusaders under Salāh al-Deen Ayyubi. (Tr.)

[49] Ibn Hammād Hanbali 6:108; Suyuti, *Tabaqāt al-Huffādh*: 52

[50] Al-Dhahabi, *Tadhkirat al-Huffādh* 4:1481

[51] Ibn 'Imād Hanbali 6:108; Ibn Ilyās, *Tārikh Misr* 1:171

[52] Al-Dhahabi 4:1451

[53] *Ibid.* Suyuti: 52

[54] Suyuti: 520

[55] Ibn 'Imād Hanbali 6:108

[56] Al-Dhahabi 5:1451

SECTION II

CHAPTER ONE
THE ARAB MILITARY BEFORE ISLĀM

The methods of war among the Arabs were different from that of all the other races. In their battles they relied on offence and attack[1] and their motivation was limited to: defending their idols,[2] bloodlust,[3] raiding and stealing cattle,[4] and increasing the status and position of their own tribes.[5] Their most important weapon was the sword.[6]

The role of Islām was changing the implements and their employment in battles and making appropriate use of them. The principles and beliefs through which Islām was manifested caused an increase in the spiritual and emotional uplifting of the soldiers and encouraged them to participate. Previously, an Arab soldier would be motivated by courage,[7] display of force,[8] a sense of loyalty[9] and selfish motives.[10]

The most important mode of transport that were used was the camel,[11] as it was capable of going for long without water and was able to bear the dryness and sandstorms of the desert. The most important qualities of the 'Arabian wars' were as follows:

1) **The Objectives of War**
   The Arab tribes were naturally linked to and reliant upon the economical and social status of their individual members. Because their land consisted of dry deserts lacking sufficient water, their objectives were:
   a) Gaining water and control over the pastures and cattle[12]: Often times, wars would be fought in order to gain control over watering holes or springs and one of the sides would gain control either through a peace treaty or by force. During times of drought and famine, intense battles took place. When wars were fought for water, inhabitants of the dry lands were forced to migrate to other places that had sufficient water.[13]
   When one tribe was envious of the wealth and prosperity of another, they would engage them in battle in order to loot their wealth and cattle.[14] The strong tribe was one that was able to overpower the weaker tribes and take their wealth. They would take all they wanted as booty. They would steal away their cattle and then return home victorious. Some of the Arab tribes even went so far as to march towards neighboring kingdoms[15] and cities that had plenty of food stocks.[16] During the age of Jāhiliyya, wars and raids were one of the primary source of sustenance, possession of livestock and booty in times of drought and famine.

b) Bloodlust and revenge: This was caused by social events like marriage and divorce,[17] social interactions among the members of a tribe,[18] jealousy, malice and competition,[19] or because of the establishment of relations by the allies with other tribes.[20]

c) Increasing the status and power of the warring tribe: The fundamental principle was, 'One who does not kill is killed and one who does not fight is fought'.[21] Also, once one tribe loses a battle, their power will never be regained and they are destined to destruction and annihilation and become incapable of defending themselves.[22]

d) Increasing the number of forces and soldiers in the army: The sources have not mentioned the size of the pagan Arab armies but they have noted that every tribe, with all its warriors, was considered one 'army block'[23], and these were the people who would engage the other tribes in battle. When the tribes would join forces, a large army would be formed.[24] The number of tribes that came together in a battle against the Greeks numbered 218 and consisted of more than ten thousand soldiers. When we refer to the compendiums, lexicons and books of literature, we find that some Arabs paid much attention to the organization and creation of armies while some even independently[25] joined their tribes and entered the battle. Nu'mān bin Mundhir had formed numerous organizations including the battalions called *al-Shubhā'*, *al-Dawwasar*[26] and *al-Radhā'i'*.[27]

The following names indicate the number of forces of the various groups of fighters and the types of weapons they used:
Al-Raht – 3 to 10 people.[28]
Al-'Usbah – 10 to 40 people.[29]
Al-Miqnab (*al-Minsar*) – 30 or 40 up to 300 on horseback.[30]
Al-Jumrah (*al-Qabilah*) – 300 to 1,000 on horseback.[31]
Al-Sariyah – 40 to 500[32] and at the very least 5 to 300 people.[33]
Al-Kutayba – 100 to 1,000 people or from 400 to 10,000 people.[34]
Al-Jaysh (*Faylaq* or *Juhfal*) – 100 to 4,000 people.[35]
Al-Khamis – from 4,000 to 12,000 people.[36]

All these groups or units would be strengthened by the backing of another group. In this case, it would be called *Kutaybah wa Jarrajah*[37] or *Jarradah*, *Jayshin Lujab* and *Khamisin 'Armum*.[38] The person who commanded a force of more than a thousand would be known as *Jarrarayn*.[39]

The Kutayba (the group with between 100 and 1,000 people) and Jumrah (300 to 1,000 riders) were two of the most important groups in the wars of the Arabs before Islām. However, during the time of the Holy Prophet (s) the Sariyah (consisting of between 50 and 400 people) became the only important group in battle and this name can be found in many of the narrations from the companions[40] because this number was also employed before the Hijrah.

The Sariyah was the smallest section of the army[41] and could be formed even by only ten people. For this reason, it was also called 'Asharatu Rahtin (a group of ten).[42] The Prophet (s) would also send these groups with fewer or greater numbers. They have said: the best companions are four, the best Sirāya (pl. of Sariyah) is made up of four hundred, the best army consists of four thousand and at the most, not exceeding twelve thousand soldiers.[43]

e) Weapons: By going through the narratives and poetry of the Age of Ignorance (Jāhiliyyah) we find that there is frequent mention of weapons, and especially the 'sword'[44]. Other weapons like the arrow, dagger, spear, spearhead, club, bow and the sling[45] that were considered offensive weapons and were used in attacks are also found in their poetry. As for the defensive weapons, they included the armor, shield, helmet and the armor that was worn beneath the helmet.[46] These weapons would come from Syria, Yemen and India and some were also made locally.

The Arabs would also use some heavy weaponry like the catapult. The first person to use it was Judhayma al-Abrash.[47] Another weapon known as *al-Dabbābah*[48] was first employed by 'Abdullah ibn Ju'dah.[49] Later the Muslim Arabs modified this weapon and used its improved version in their wars.[50]

At that time, an Arab soldier would either fight on foot or on horseback. The most important mode of transport at wartime were horses,[51] and the forces would ride on them. Horses had some distinct advantages in war, especially speed and agility.

f) The Relationship between the Commander and the Soldiers: Affairs of war and military leadership of a tribe would be in the hands of the head of the tribe, a person who would have the qualities of forbearance, clemency, co-operation, patience, kindness etc.[52] All the soldiers, be they freemen or slaves, volunteers or those who have been forced to participate, hired or otherwise, all have to respond to the call for war by the commander and none of them are allowed to disobey him, whether they like it or not, except those who are excused because of being too young or sick. Of course, at times some of the wealthy would disobey the command to participate in battle and would in return pay the fine and penalty for not joining the battle.[53]

One of the commanders would draw up the plans for battle, allot commanders for each section, define the assignments, identify the goal and arm the forces. The responsibility for these tasks rested on his shoulders because of his superiority over the others and in the end he would take command over the forces.[54] Many of the Arabs in the age of Jāhiliyya were known for their training in archery and their expertise in it. They were able to hit small targets[55] and would also train those who did not know archery.

g) Mobilization of forces and Recruitment: It was incumbent and obligatory [to fight] when the tribe needed to be defended or a general command had been issued. So in times of danger, all the people were mobilized. The men, old and young, small children and women too, would prepare and participate in the battle as much as they were able to.[56] Here we should mention two groups of fighters: (i) A group that was hired for an agreed sum. (ii) Another group that consisted of slaves who had to fight in the battle without any compensation and would have to stay and serve till the end of the battle. Those who would fight with all their might in order to defend themselves fought with strong will and determination whereas those who were forced to fight and were not paid anything, especially in times of hardship, would flee from the battle.

Conscription was not compulsory and would take place on an individual basis, not collectively. It would be carried out during attacks or in order to join the commander.[57]

h) Dealing with Prisoners: Prisoners (of war) would be dealt with harshly and with cruelty.[58] At times they would cut off their noses or tear out their ears from the roots or sever their limbs.[59]

Because of this torture, some prisoners would die while others would remain in their service as slaves, or alternatively a ransom could be given to secure their freedom[60] or they would be granted a favor for which they would remain obliged.[61]

They would also use hostages[62] to exact revenge for the deaths of those taken as prisoners. Just as the 'Aus did with the Khazraj – they killed three of the slaves who had been taken as hostages (in retaliation for three killed prisoners).[63]

i)   Material Support and Backup: This consisted of the collective measures that an army would put in place for its troops including weapons, provisions, food, water etc. The goal behind making these arrangements and providing munitions that were necessary for long drawn-out wars was gaining victory over the enemy and this was achieved by using different means. The most important factors that assisted in sending support were:

- Roads: The roads and paths that the pagan Arabs traversed in times of war have been not been clearly mentioned in historical records and some writings after the coming of Islām only give general indications about them. For example: in Ibn Kharadādibah's *al-Masālik wal-Mamālik*, Ibn Hawqal's *al-Masālik wal-Mamālik*, Mas'udi's *al-Tanbih wal-Ashrāf*, Qazwini's *al-Bilād wa Akhbār al-'Ibād* and all the other books of battles and expeditions.

  Similarly, the roads that were traversed by the armies of Islām in their conquests and battles have not been mentioned in detailed except in very few sources. Most of the paths that were used by the Muslim armies were the well known main roads and the most important among these were:
  (i)   Paths near the coasts and borders where water was plentiful and wells were many.
  (ii)   Roads that ran parallel to the Euphrates River that flowed from Iraq to Syria.
  (iii) The routes between Yathrib (Madina) and Makkah or between Makkah and Iraq.
  (iv)   Roads that linked the cities and villages of the Arabian Peninsula.[64]

- Weapons of War: In the age of Jāhiliyya, weapons of war constituted the most important part of munitions. In the beginning, a soldier would get armed before he went out to war, because no help would reach him during the battle. If, during the heat of battle, his sword broke or his arrows ran out, if he had extras he would exchange them, otherwise he would be unable to continue the fight.
- Water and Food: The most important foods that were used in sending support to the fighting soldiers were dates and grapes that were

grown in parts of Yemen and Tā'if. Fruits from the trees of Sidr and Miswāk, fish, barley bread and other foods were also sent. Dates were the staple food and Yathrib was known for its plentiful fresh dates. The Arabs were accustomed to eating less and would make to with a few dates for an entire day. When they were very hungry, they would eat animal hide, porcupines, lizards and meat of hunted animals.[65]

However, water was considered of strategic importance, because the routes chosen and roads taken would be determined by it and efforts would be made to secure drinking water and prevent the enemy from having access to it. This liquid of life was of great importance for the army that wished to set camp in a specific location and they would need to be near a source of water at all times. For this reason, they would take all the necessary measures to store as much water as possible. Ten guards would be posted at wells and springs[66] and in front of man-made water storages large boulders would be placed.[67] These reservoirs would become even more important in times of war, and especially defense, when besieged, or in the hot summer months.

- Clothes and Military Uniforms: The Arab soldiers of Jāhiliyya wore different varieties of clothes,[68] so fighters were indistinguishable for non-combatants, and the soldiers would look alike because of their similar turbans, armor, swords and other military equipment.[69] Turbans or caps were worn on the heads and the *Jubba* or a hooded garment, a shirt or a two-tone robe, trousers, a woolen cloth and striped Yemeni cloth would be worn and feet would be covered with shoes or sandals.

- Tents: The tents were made of skin, wool, hair and fur.[70] The Arabs would only use tents at the start of battles, because their fighting style was that of 'charge and attack' and this was highly disorganized. For this reason, the army did not need to remain outside its area for long periods of time. The Muslim armies during the time of the Prophet (s) also did not use tents frequently for this very same reason.[71]

- Modes of Transportation: The most important modes of transport were the horse and camel.[72] The horse was used because of its speed and control at all times and in different situations, be it during attacks, laying siege, face to face combat, ambush, night raids etc. Mares were especially used in night raids, attacks, chases, maneuvers and difficult tasks, and were more effective than stallions.[73] Khālid bin Walid used to fight battles while riding on a mare.[74] Similarly, mules were used in sieges and ambushes.

Many of those who fought on horseback were well known,[75] and they would observe the principles of combat to the letter. They did this by using the horses and concentrating their efforts on the weak points of the enemy's defenses or on the weak and timid people.[76] As a result, they would be successful in opening up fissures in the line of defense, penetrating their ranks and creating terror and fright in their hearts.[77] Camels were not useful for battle[78] but they could be used for transporting soldiers, weapons, munitions and provisions from place to place. This animal was known for its ability to bear hunger and thirst, move through the harsh desert and carry heavy loads over long distances.

- Booty: All that was taken over by the army or tribe after it was victorious over its enemy was known as booty.[79] War booty became the property of the overpowering forces who could use it as they wished.[80] In the age of Jāhiliyya, one fourth of the booty[81] was separated by the commander.[82] All that was acquired without war (*al-Nashitah*)[83] and the booty that could not be divided (*al-Fudhul*) was reserved for the commander.[84]

A poet has described the booty in this verse:
Laka al-Rubā'u wal-Safāya
Wa Hukmuka wal-Nashitah wal-Fudhul[85]

In the same way, the killer would take possession of what the one who was killed had with him [on the battlefield]. With the advent of Islām, Khums was prescribed.[86] The law of *Salab* (that which was taken from one who was killed in battle) was left as it was.

2) Wars of Arabs against the Sassanids

The pagan Arabs fought wars with the great neighboring kingdoms and they would raid the bordering areas. These kingdoms would also use some tribes as a barrier against the invaders so that they could hinder them as much as possible.

During the advent of Islām, the Sassanids had control over some areas at the edge of the Arabian Peninsula, including the lands of Yemen, Bahrain and some areas to the east of the peninsula. Because they were neighbors with the Arabs,[87] they had no option but to deal with each other and each of them would take necessary measures to prevent the incursions of the other, whether through peace pacts or war. Some of the steps taken by the Sassanids to this end included: pleasing members of some tribes,[88] making pacts[89] and treaties of friendship with them, strengthening the borders,[90] building fortresses, creating forts and protective barriers around the cities, creating canals from rivers and seas and keeping patrol ships in order to prevent the incursion of the enemy, creating points of defense along the border and repelling the threats of attacking tribes. Aside from this, guard units were formed by the tribes in return for payment and compensation that was given to the heads of the tribes so that they would protect the borders. These tribes were used to protect some of the more remote areas and they would establish their repositories for storing weapons and food in their land.

It can be said that the Sassanids would utilize the Arabs in their wars. When the Arabs saw the oppression and cruelty of the Sassanids against their own people, they would break the pacts. Udhaynah[91] the king of Tadmar rose up against the Sassanids (under Shāpur the First), fought a war against him and was victorious. However, the kings that came after Shāpur the First were able to gain victory over the Arabs, especially during the reign of Shāpur Dhul Aktāf[92] the person who later made a peace treaty with the Arabs.[93]

By studying the wars of the Arabs against the Sassanids, we find that they were not united under the leadership of one commander;[94] because every tribe had its own head and it was not possible for him to give up his leadership. Disagreements among them was the norm and therefore they were not able to unite with other tribes. As a result, each one of them would rise up to defend itself without the assistance of another. Jealousy, malice and hatred was rife among them;[95] to such an extent that the Sassanids would incite some of the tribes to fight against others.[96] It is obvious that this had a tremendous impact in the wars that were fought against the enemies.

The Sassanids were always afraid of fighting in the desert, and they were unable to stand the lack of water and harsh conditions of these lands. When the Arabs fought against their ally, they would arrange to transfer water, camels and all that was necessary for war in the desert, to the army.[97] The enemy was never able to defeat the Arabs in their own land, because they were fully aware about the conditions of their land. The Arabs would sometimes take recourse to guerilla warfare[98] and would attack the supply routes, stores and armories.

3) Civil Wars in the North

Intense battles between Arab tribes, and especially the 'Adnānis[99] - who were more inclined to combat and war[100] - was commonplace; because they were nomads and were accustomed to the harshness of the desert and this made them rougher and more intrepid.[101] Many battles were fought between the Qahtānis[102] and the 'Adnānis,[103] between the Taghlub and Bani Hakr, and others[104] and also between the Arabs and the Iranians.[105] The most important of these were:

- Yawm al-Awārat al-Awwal[106] that took place between Mundhir ibn Imra' al-Qays and Bakr bin Wā'il.
- Yawm al-Dahnā[107] between the tribe of Bani Asad.
- Yawm al-Kilāb al-Thāni.[108]
- Yawm al-Baydhā'.[109]
- And others like Yawm Bi'āth that took place between the Aws and the Khazraj.[110]

By studying the details of these wars and battles, we find that the Arabs never used to fight for goals and purposes that were sensible and that had resulted from careful thought and consideration, rather their wars would have other motives, including tribal ones.[111] These types of war were continuous and never-ending, and as such, they would always be practicing [and preparing] for war. It was as if they were habituated to war or that they liked it and were inclined to it. During the advent of Islām, some of the warriors joined the army that was formed after the migration [to Madina] with the intention of defeating the enemy, who were living under harsh conditions and were able to establish themselves in other places.[112]

The distinguishing factor of the Arabs in their wars against the external enemies was that they would unite with other tribes in some battles, like in the battle of Dhi Qār[113] that took place after the event of Yawm 'Ayn Abāgh and in which they were victorious. However, they would [then] separate and fight internal battles against each other and this made them weak and led to their defeat.[114]

NOTES AND REFERENCES

[1] Ibn Khaldun, *Muqaddimat al-'Ibar* 2:645

[2] Kalbi, *al-Asnām*: 100; Jawād 'Ali, al-*Mufassal fi Tārikh al-'Arab qabl al-Islām* 1:609

[3] Al-Azhari, *al-Nafhat al-Mulukiyya*: 85

[4] Refer to the event of *Yawmu 'Ayni Abāgh* in Ibn Atheer, *al-Kāmil*, 11:540; Ibn 'Abd Rabbih, *al-Iqd al-Fareed* 5:260

[5] Tabrizi, *Sharh al-Qasā'id al-'Ashar*: 121

[6] Ibn al-Shajari, *Hamāsat al-Shajariyya* 2:793 onwards; Tartusi, *Tabsirat Arbāb al-Albāb*: 11

[7] Ibn Khaldun 2:286 onwards

[8] Ibn Sa'd 2:7; Qalqashandi, *Qalā'id al-Jummāl* 7:12 & 2

[9] Ibn 'Abd Rabbih 1:244 & 252

[10] Ibn Sa'd 1:1-157; Wāqidi 1:41

[11] Ibn Qutayba, *'Uyun al-Akhbār* 2:161

[12] Refer to *Yawm al-Baydā* in Ibn Habib, *al-Muhbir*:246 and *Yawm al-Zuwayrin wa Yawm al-Shaytin* in Ibn Atheer, al-*Kāmil* 1:604-654

[13] This is due to the fact that most of the Arabian Peninsula is made up of dry desert and many areas lack sufficient water. (Tr.)

[14] Ibn 'Abd Rabbih 5:260, Ibn Atheer 11:54

[15] Ibn 'Abd Rabbih: 244; Ibn Atheer 1:62

[16] Jawād 'Ali 2:602

[17] Ibn Atheer 1:544, 566

[18] Ibn 'Abd Rabbih 5:345; al-Bakri, Mu'jam Mastu'jam 2:496

[19] Ibn 'Abd Rabbih 5: 224; Ibn Atheer 1:620

[20] Ibn 'Abd Rabbih 5:248; Ibn Atheer 1:578, 671

[21] Maqrizi: 121

[22] Ibn Khaldun, Muqaddimah 2:451

[23] Ibn 'Abd Rabbih 5:250 onwards

[24] Ibn Atheer 1:482

[25] Jawād 'Ali 1:575 and 2:21

[26] Ibn Sayyidah, al-Mukhassis 6:204; Ibn Hishām 2:254, 347; Zubaydi, Tāj al-Arus 1:327, 3:207

[27] *Ibid.*

[28] Al-Sikkeet, *Mukhtasar Tahdhib al-Alfādh*: 19; Ibn Mandhur, *Lisān al-'Arab* [under Ra Ha Ta] 6:305

[29] Al-Sikkeet, *Ibid.*

[30] *Ibid.* 27-28; Ibn Sayyidah 6:200

[31] Zubaydi [under *Ja Ma Ra*] 3:107

[32] Shaybāni 1:69; Tha'ālibi, *Fiqh al-Lughah*: 229

[33] Ibn Sayyidah 6:199; Zubaydi [under *Sa Ra Ya*] 10:174

[34] Al-Sikkeet: 27; Tha'ālibi: 229

[35] Tha'ālibi: 40 and 229; Abu Dharr al-Khashni, *Sharh Seera Ibn Hishām* 2:273 & 347

[36] Al-Sikkeet *Ibid.* Tha'ālibi: 229

[37] Al-Sikkeet: 28

[38] Al-Sikkeet: 30; Tha'ālibi: 229; Nuwayri, *Nihāyat al-Urub fi Funun al-Adab* 6:190

[39] Al-Sikkeet: 27; Ibn Habib: 246-552; Tha'ālibi: 230

[40] Bukhāri (*al-Adhān, al-Imān, al-Tayammum, al-Ahkām, al-Jihād*); Muslim (*al-Jihād, al-Siyar*); Abu Dāwud (*al-Jihād, al-Tahārah*); Tirmidhi (*al-Manāqib, al-Jihād, al-Jumu'ah*); al-Nasā'i (*al-Jihād, al-Bay'ah, al-Sayd*)

[41] Abu Dāwud 3:46

[42] Bukhāri 5:26

[43] Shaybāni 1:67; al-Dārimi 2:215; Abu Dāwud 3:36

[44] Al-Bakhtari, *al-Hamāsa*: 9-42; Ibn Shajari, al-*Hamāsa al-Shajariyya* 2:286 & 799; Tartusi, *Tabsirat Arbāb al-Albāb*: 11

[45] Ibn 'Abd Rabbih 1:179 onwards; Suhayli 1:9 & 2:212; Tartusi: 6-15

[46] Ibn Shajari 2:786 onwards; Ibn 'Abd Rabbih 1:179 onwards

[47] Suhayli 4:162; Tartusi: 16

[48] The Dabbābah was something like what is today known as a tank. All its sides were covered with metal and someone would sit inside and shoot arrows. (Tr.)

[49] Abul Faraj Isfahāni, *al-Aghāni* 5:24; Tartusi: 18

[50] Lord Monister, *Risāla fi Fann al-Harb 'indal 'Arab*: 75,77

[51] Mu'ammar bin al-Muthannā, *Kitāb al-Khayl*: 16 onwards; Ibn 'Abd Rabbih: 152 - 178

[52] Ibn 'Abd Rabbih 2:286 & 3:104

[53] Zubaydi [under *Ja 'A La*] 7:257

[54] *Ibid.* [under *Ha Ka Ma* and *Qa Dha Ma*] 8:252, 10:207

[55] Ibn 'Abd Rabbih 1:176 onwards

[56] Jawād 'Ali 5:405. 418

[57] 'Amir bin Tufayl, *Deewān*, Riwāyat Ambāri: 11, 98, 100

[58] Whoever took a prisoner would be consider his owner and would be able to treat him however he pleased. See Jawād 'Ali 5:631

[59] Abu al-Faraj Isfahāni 11:114 & 15:155

[60] Tabari, *Tafseer Tabari* 6:262; Abu al-Faraj Isfahāni 11:114

[61] Abu al-Faraj Isfahāni 11:158 onwards – this meant that they were set free.

[62] Zubaydi [under *'A Qa La*] 8:27 and [*Ra Ha Na*] 9:229

[63] Ibn Atheer 1:675

[64] Jawād 'Ali 7:331-365

[65] Zubaydi [under *Fa Sa Da*] 2:453; [*Ba Ja*] 2:5; [*Ra Ma La*] 7:350; [*'A Qa Da*] 2:425; [*Ta Fa Fa*] 6:260; Jawād 'Ali 5:58-63

[66] Zubaydi [under *Qa Ru Ba*] 1:423

[67] Balādhuri, Futuh al-Buldān: 23-25; Zubaydi [under *A Za Ba*] 1:147; [*Ba Ra Ka*] 7:106; [*'A Dha Ra*] 3:441

[68] Al-Sikkeet: 407 – 408; Ibn 'Abd Rabbih 2:225

[69] Tha'ālibi, *Thimār al-Qulub*: 159; Lord Monister, *Risāla fi Fann al-Harb 'ind al-'Arab*: 52

[70] Zubaydi [under *Bat a*] 1:529; [*Bu Ni Ya*] 10:46; [*Dha Ra Ba*] 1:340; [*Qa Ba Ba*] 1:419; [*Dha La La*] 7:425; [*Fa Sa Ta*] 5:199

[71] Wāqidi 7:825; Tabari 2:568

[72] Tim Quraysh, *Kitāb al-Khayl*: 16 onwards; Ibn 'Abd Rabbih 1:152-178

73 See: Yazbak, *Jud al-'Arabi*: 78-81

74 Nuwairi 9:365

75 Ibn 'Abd Rabbih 1:116; Zubaydi 3:335

76 Jawād 'Ali 5:460

77 An example of how they did this can be seen in the battle of Uhud. See: Uhud in History in the *Miqātu Hajj* Magazine vol. 7

78 Nuwayri 10:103 onwards; Zubaydi [under Ha Ma La] 7:263

79 Zubaydi [under *Gha Ni Ma*] 9:7

80 Jawād 'Ali 5:262, 264

81 Zubaydi [under *Kha Ma Sa*] 4:139

82 *Ibid.* [under *Sa Faa*] 10:211

83 *Ibid.* 5:231

84 *Ibid.* 8:63

85 Asma'i, *al-Asma'iyāt*, from the verses of the poet Abdullah ibn Ghunmah: 37

86 Ibn Qayyim al-Jawzi, *Zād al-Ma'ād fi Hudā Khayril 'Ibād* 2:172

87 Ibn Atheer 1:223 onwards; Umar Farukh, *Tārikh al-Jāhiliyya*: 64,65

88 Jawād 'Ali 2:626

89 Al-'Adwi, *al-Dawlah al-Islāmiyya wa Imperāturiyyat al-Rum*: 14

90 Jawād 'Ali 2:628

91 Jawād 'Ali 2:635

92 Mas'udi, *Muruj al-Dhahab wa Ma'ādin al-Jawhar* 1:215

93 Tabari, *Tārikh Tabari* 2:69 onwards

94 Ibn Khaldun, *Muqaddimah* 2:456

95 Ibn 'Abd Rabbih 2:319-326

96 Jawād 'Ali 2:641

97 Ibn Qutaybah, *'Unwān al-Akhbār* 2:161

98 Watt, *Muhammad fi Makkah*: 16; Sayyid Hanafi, *al-Farusiyyat al-'Arabiyyah fi al-'Asr al-Jāhiliyya*: 32

99 They were known as the 'Adnānis because they were descendents of 'Adnān, the ancestor of the Holy Prophet (s). They were natives of the Arabian Peninsula and

were from the lineage of Prophet Ismā'il ('a). They were known traders and merchants and were in charge of the Ka'ba (Tr.)

[100] Ibn Khaldun 2:409-413

[101] *Ibid.* 2:414-418 onwards

[102] The Qahtānis are the descendents of Qahtān ibn Ya'rab. They were one of the native Arab tribes who were not originally from the Arabian Peninsula, rather they were from Yemen and other Southern areas. The later migrated to the North and settled in Yathrib and Ghassān. Unlike the 'Adnānis, they came from an ancient civilization and were more inclined to life in cities and villages. (Tr.)

[103] Qalqashandi, *Subh al-A'shā* 1:390 onwards

[104] Ibn Is'hāq, *Harb Bakr wa Taghlub*: 8 onwards; Ibn 'Abd Rabbih 5:213, 249; Nuwayri 15:356, 316

[105] Ibn Atheer 1:482; Ibn 'Abd Rabbih 5:224; Nuwayri 15:407,413

[106] Ibn Atheer 1:552

[107] Ibn Atheer 1:626

[108] Ibn 'Abd Rabbih 5:224; Nuwayri 15:407

[109] Ibn Habib: 246

[110] Abu al-Faraj Isfahāni 3:39,154-156; Ibn Atheer 1:655 onwards; more about the wars between these two tribes of the Qahtānis can be seen here: Ibn Sa'd, Tabaqāt 3:604; Ya'qubi, Tārikh 2:27. We find that because of their internal strife and battles, these two tribes were never quite able to stand up against the 'Adnānis. Killings that took place between the Aus and Khazraj was something so common that it was like a daily occurrence. With the advent of Islām, the Prophet (s) was able to bring peace among these tribes and eventually end their bitter enmity. (Tr.)

[111] Ibn Is'hāq, *Harb Bakr wa Taghlub*: 8 onwards

[112] Mas'udi 1:112; 'Umar Farukh: 30

[113] Ibn 'Abd Rabbih 5:224

[114] Ibn Khaldun 2:453 onwards

CHAPTER TWO
LEADERSHIP AND COMMAND

Etiquettes of Leadership

The Noble Prophet (s) was the commander in many battles[1] and he sent forth numerous *Sariyah* missions. As far as good leadership, which necessitates certain conditions and characteristics such as good etiquette and lofty morals that are obviously required to be found in the individual, it is undisputable that the Holy Prophet (s) had the greatest morals, such that he was praised by Allah thus: *And indeed you possess a great character.*[2] His having such a character made him a successful commander who was able to attain the goals and gain momentous victories in many of his battles.

His most praiseworthy traits were:
He was kind to everyone[3] and was courteous with the soldiers and his people in all circumstances.[4] He was trustworthy and truthful,[5] loyal to his covenants and pacts.[6] When he got angry, he would swallow his anger and when he had the power (to exact revenge), he would turn a blind eye.[7] A prime example from the instances when this can be witnessed was the conquest of Makkah[8] - when there was an opportunity to take revenge against those who persecuted him and his followers, he forgave them all.

He was sincere in the actions he performed for God and in the service of the people. He brought peace between the people and established friendship between the opposing factions of the Aus and Khazraj, and even the Muhājirs and Ansārs. He removed malice, enmity, hatred and sedition from them and gave everyone their rightful position.[9] He would enjoin people to do good and forbid them from evil through struggle and the expounding of its importance, [and through] patience in hardships, tribulations, hopelessness and persecution of the people [the disbelievers].[10] Indeed these lofty characteristics were a sign of his greatness as a leader. Patience became the cornerstone of his leadership by which he would persevere against the enemies. Kindness and courtesy were the ornaments of his command and his respect, veneration, love and humility among the troops brought about a sense of brotherhood and love among them and gave them a feeling of closeness to their leader. His other qualities were forbearance and forgiveness. All these qualities of the Prophet (s) presented him as the light of guidance for all those who would be given the responsibility for leadership.

(A) INTELLECTUAL TRAITS

One: Reflection, Contemplation and Far-sightedness
When the Noble Prophet (s) was sent, the people were immersed in superstition, idol worship, magic and sorcery. Their values were materialistic and their thoughts were lowly. They would say: *There is nothing but the life of this world; we live and we die.*[11] The Prophet forced them to apply their intellects in thought and contemplation, invited them to worship One God and purified them of the vileness of idol worship and depravity and got rid of it.[12] He then took them towards greatness and glory. The Almighty chose the Prophet (s) so that he could be a messenger and a teacher to them. Whenever the Creator of the Universe chooses someone to bring His message, He selects the person who has the greatest intellect of all people.[13] *Allah knows best where to place His Message.*[14] Therefore there is no doubt that the Prophet (s) had a perfect intellect by which he was able to lead an entire nation and take them to the highest level of religious and worldly achievement.

By thinking and pondering about the situation of his community, we come to the conclusion that the Holy Prophet (s) was the wisest person in the world. This is because he was able to reform a community that was accustomed to harshness and violence and had ingrained [in themselves] the qualities of vainglory and callousness. He trained them and took their affairs in hand and led them out of ignorance into knowledge and guidance; in such a way that despite their past, they became his fervent supporters. They carried on his message and spread it throughout the world and stood up to fight by his side.[15]

The Noble Prophet (s), by his own acumen, devised new methods in the 'art of warfare', 'government', 'administration', 'politics', 'economics', 'social order' etc. On this basis, in the Battle of Badr,[16] he initiated battle formations. In the Battle of Ahzāb[17] he dug a trench around the city. In the expedition of Hudaybiyyah[18] he negotiated with the Quraysh and made a pact with them, the great benefits of which were only seen later. In the same way, he would use new strategies in the battlefields that assisted him in gaining victory over the enemies and they were stunned and perplexed by the [new] tactics.

The greatest and most important intellectual traits of the Holy Prophet (s) were: reflection, contemplation and far-sightedness. These attributes were deduced from his many feats in the battles, the most important of which was his choice and selection of the first soldiers from among the Quraysh and the Muhājirin without the participation of the Ansār. The wisdom behind this was that the Ansār has made a vow in the Second Pledge of 'Aqabah[19] that they would help and support the Prophet in Madina and for this reason it was evident that the

Muhājirs would have to play the main role in battles and wars. However, after some time, without making any reference to the pledge, the Holy Prophet (s) informed the Ansār and made it clear to them that their participation and assistance in the battles was required. From the other instances where the wisdom and prudence of the Prophet we can cite the treaties that he would make with neighboring tribes;[20] because through this he would gain access to various desert routes that were frequented by the caravans of the Quraysh on their way to Syria.[21] In the Battle of Uhud he ordered a group of archers to position themselves on the mountain side[22] and to remain there until they were allowed by him to leave their post and it was seen how those archers disobeyed the order of the Holy Prophet (s). When they thought that victory had been gained, they abandoned their post in order to take their share of the booty, thereby granting the enemy easy access and enabling them to overturn the outcome of the battle.

The Holy Prophet (s) wanted the archers to remain in their positions on the mountain so that after the victory is achieved in this fight, the forces could increase in their strength through peaceful means and the awe and glory of the Muslim army may be elevated both within and outside the borders. About this Zuhri says: 'There was no bigger victory that was gained in Islām before this.'

The Noble Prophet (s) would deal cautiously[23] with the Jews and hypocrites who lived in the neighboring areas.

A good commander also needs a creative and an innovative mind with superior intelligence and the Prophet (s) was distinguished with these very attributes. He manifested this in certain instances, the most important of which were:

The creation and establishment of a state[24] and the selection of warriors who would be harsh against their enemies and merciful and kind with their friends.[25] With these principles, the Holy Prophet (s) would fight battles against the Quraysh, the Jews and the hypocrites.[26] He planned the stages of battle and begin studying the strategies of war with the Quraysh and the possibility of gaining control of Madina and its surrounding areas. He was the one who envisioned the war with the Romans[27] which was later realized by the army of Islām and this was another prime example of his far-sightedness and vision.

The Prophet, with his vision and insight, foresaw that the Jews of Khaybar would soon rebel against the Muslim army just as the Jews of Bani Nadhir and Bani Quraydha has done, so he made all the necessary preparations for such an occurrence. In the meantime, he forbade the tribe of Bani Asad from helping the Jews of Kahybar[28] in any way and prevented the pact of unity that was about to be made between them. As a result, he made it possible to weaken the Jewish forces and then send an army the likes of which they had never faced to fight them.

During the Expedition of Bani Mustalaq,[29] he married Juwayrah the daughter of Hārith. Not long thereafter, the tribe of Bani Mustalaq accepted Islām group by group. At the same time, the mission carried out by Usāma bin Zayd[30] was also successful and resulted in a great victory.

Even though many of the commanders of the Muslim army lacked the vision and far-sightedness of their great leader, the Holy Prophet (s), they would nonetheless turn to themselves and accept these obvious and evident truths. The greatest reflections of the Prophet (s) and his superiority of intellect were manifested in the following matters:

1. **Planning and Organization:**
Planning and organization are considered two of the primary elements in the establishment of a state, a society, an army and all affairs related to these.[31] Before the Prophet created an army and groups and delegations turned to him, he formulated a plan to set up a new state in Madina. One of the manifestations of this planning was that he met with some people from Madina during the period of Hajj and made a 'quasi-military'[32] pact with them and presented a new religion for them to accept and accepted the responsibility of ending the conflict between their two tribes of the Aus and Khazraj. He advised them to be the representatives for the propagation of Islām in Yathrib. The next year, before the commencement of the Hajj rituals, a group that was bigger than the first group, came to meet with the Prophet (s) and pledge allegiance to him, and this was the first official pledge of allegiance of the people of Madina.[33] After the pact, the Prophet (s) send Mus'ab ibn 'Umayr[34] to teach the people of this newly 'converted' city. He should therefore be considered the first emissary of the newly founded Islāmic state.

Thirteen years after the appointment of the Prophet, a group comprised of 73 men and women from the chiefs and nobles of the Aus and Khazraj came for Hajj and make a pact with the Holy Prophet (s) in which they vowed to defend him just as they would defend their honor and their children. This pact became known as the 'Second Pledge of 'Aqaba'.[35] From the outcomes and consequences of this planning was the spread of the Islāmic faith and the securing of the basic material and security needs of the Muslims in Madina and support for them against the persecution [of the enemies] and the formation of an army to face the threat of the Quraysh and their allies.

The Prophet (s) organized an army comprising of the Muhājirin and the Ansār. The Ansārs were made up of the Aus and Khazraj while the Muhājirs consisted of all the different tribes and were considered among the foremost experts of warfare in the army. The Holy Prophet (s) appointed a commander for each tribe and also appointed one general commander over them all.

In every battle,[36] he would organize them according to the needs, natural resources, enmity, friendship and terrain. His soldiers were arranged and divided into the front-line, the rear, the right flank, the left flank and the heart of the army. The Prophet gave a lot of importance to military intelligence and information [about the enemy].[37] In the same way, he would send some soldiers in martyrdom-seeking *Sariya* missions, like the *Sariya* of Muhammad ibn Maslamah that was given the mission of assassinating Ka'b ibn Ashraf[38] because of his insolence and malice against Islām, the leadership [of the Prophet] and all the Muslims. Or like the *Sariya* of 'Abdullah ibn 'Ateek[39] who was given the mission of killing Salām ibn Abi al-Huqayq, and other similar missions that were sent.

2. Taking Decisions and Issuing Clear Orders

The Prophet (s) never used to issue firm and clear orders except after he had got the complete information about the conditions of the battle and was able to make decisive judgments and issue the best orders accordingly while remaining steadfast in the face of the changing situations of battle.[40] The most important qualities that distinguished the commands of the Holy Prophet (s) were:

a) Studying the different aspects before making a decision and consequently issuing the command.[41]

b) Not reverting or turning back after the command has been issued.[42]

c) Changing the commands in accordance with the changing circumstances of the battle.[43]

d) Maintaining the ability of making intellectual decisions and offer continuous guidance and leadership even during the most difficult times in the battlefield.[44]

e) He would decide on the realization of victory.

Two: Skill and Intellectual Brilliance in Executing the Duties of a Commander
With certainty, the sagacity an intellectual brilliance of the Holy Prophet (s) in commanding and controlling the army during war was clearly manifested.[45] He would test people and then select the strongest and most capable person to give the command to. For example, he chose Hamza ibn 'Abd al-Muttalib as the commander of one of the first *Sariya* missions.[46] He appointed 'Abdullah ibn Jahash[47] to lead a *Sariya* mission to gather intelligence about the Quraysh.[48] He made Abā Dujāna[49] the head of the sword-fighters and selected Usama bin Zayd

as the commander of an army that comprised of some of the great companions.[50] He put some of the Ansār and Muhājirin under the command of 'Amr bin 'Aās and send them to fight the tribe of Bani Qudhā'ah.[51] All these examples show that all these people who were given the responsibility of leadership in important missions were more capable and skilled than others and had the vision and insight required to overcome the enemies they had to face.[52]

Another example of the intellectual brilliance of the Prophet (s) in times of war was his focus, at the start of battle, on the points which would secure victory and attain the desired goal. For instance, in the battles of 'Dhi Amr' and 'Bani Salim'[53] he put the focus on the right flank[54] and in all the other battles like Uhud, would identify the weaknesses in the enemy army and focus on it.[55] Transferring and moving the command post during battle was necessary in order to maintain a control over the forces and urge them to remain strong and move forward. In order to protect the forces and organize them in specific formations, the Holy Prophet (s)[56] would shift his command post depending on the changing circumstances during battle.

In the Battle of Uhud, the Prophet (s) chose a juncture and a means of shifting[57] the command post to a new location. In the Battle of Khaybar, he set up four command posts.[58] He positioned the central command post at the uppermost corner of the fortress *al-Natāh* and stationed the furthermost post in *Rajee'*[59] and later ordered that the central command post should be moved to a new location that was better suited strategically.

One of the most important traits and strategic acumen of a commander is the ability to face new scenarios that may be encountered in battle. He needs to be creative and resourceful and should be well aware of the realities that would enable him to reach the road of liberation [from the enemy's grasp] and victory. It is in this way that experiential knowledge in examination is a way which follows the intellect in order to arrive at correct decisions.[60] The Noble Prophet (s), with his far-sightedness, vision, skill and intellectual brilliance, understood this and applied it to solve all the problems and execute all the missions that the commander was responsible for.

Three: Sagacity and Perspicacity
Sagacity and perspicacity actually refer to deep insight and discernment that are able to clear up ambiguities and discover the reality of hidden secrets and a means of reaching it.[61] It is evident that from the people, those who are distinguished for their perspicacity are the ones who have insight and ingenuity. Ostensibly, sagacity depends upon observing, listening, moving or all of these combined. The Noble Prophet (s) would take guidance from the Glorious Qur'ān[62] that was revealed to him, or from the intellectual ability and sagacity

that God had bestowed upon him.[63] He has even spoken about the cleverness of a believer.[64]

As for his perspicacity in matter of warfare, [this is seen in] the fact that he invited Suhayl ibn 'Amr,[65] the spokesperson for the Quraysh, to accept Islām. He did great service to the community and foresaw the fall of the Roman and Persian empires[66] and the spread of Islām throughout the Arabian Peninsula.[67] After the killing of Mundhir bin 'Amr al-Sā'idi's[68] forces in the *Sariya* that was sent to Bi'r al-Ma'unah,[69] the Prophet (s) also hid his concern from the inhabitants of Najd[70] and only after the Battle of Khandaq did the he announce that the Muslim army would change to an attacking army.[71] The sagacity of the Holy Prophet (s) was also witnessed in the Treaty of Hudaybiyya[72] which turned out to be a great victory for the Muslims.

In the Battle of Muta, he informed of the impending martyrdom of three commanders in his speech.[73] In the Expedition to Tabuk, he dismantled the borders of the Byzantine Empire[74] in order to open the way for the Muslim army to enter their lands.[75] All these decisions were made by the far-sightedness and perspicacity that the Prophet (s) had in politics, economics, sociology, matters pertaining to warfare and his ability to gauge individuals and groups both within and without in issues of this world and the hereafter.

(B) PRACTICAL TRAITS

1. Principles of Warfare

The principles of warfare that were instituted by the Noble Prophet (s) were the foundational principles [that were necessary] for 'attaining victory'. Therefore his call was clear[76] and his war was based on the following principles: (i) recruiting forces[77] (ii) deploy them sparingly[78] (iii) using surprise attacks[79] at the appropriate time and place[80] (iv) relying on speed[81] that would enable battle strikes. (v) continued pressure[82] during continuous and consecutive battles against the enemies that take place without any break (vi) implementing maneuvers[83] using the resources and forces that were at hand (vii) giving importance to maintaining security for the forces[84] (viii) reliance on acquisition of intelligence and information (ix) organizing the forces[85] (x) Establishing a form of synchronization and a co-operation between the various fighters of the cavalry, infantry and all the other ranks as well as between the right and left flanks and the center of the army (xi) Not dispersing the forces[86] because it was not appropriate to do so given the weapons and resources that were available, and this is [also] a practice of the new form of warfare (xii) Strengthening the morale of his own soldiers[87] in such a way that they would not fear death (xiii) Creating an atmosphere of security in all the various battlefields; and all of these were from the great principles of warfare of the Holy Prophet (s).

Just as the Noble Prophet (s) was aware of the principles of war, he was also skilled in the use of both defensive and offensive warfare. He would use defensive warfare when constrained and execute attacks when necessary. When the threat was averted, he would have no need for either.

It is for certain that when the Prophet (s) had weak forces and few resources, he would take up defense.[88] For this reason, in the beginning of his mission,[89] his defensive stance was evident, because at this time he was prey to the persecution and harassment and was forced to migrate; an affair that brought nothing but good for him. In Madina, his intention and goal, except in a few cases when he had no choice but to take up defense,[90] was to attack.[91] When he had a strong and complete army, he turned to offensive warfare.[92] This method is one of the more advanced styles of war – which he used when sending the *Sariya* missions and laying the groundwork for battle[93] before the great Battle of Badr, which was an offensive battle. The methods and means by which this offensive warfare would be carried out were:
1. Killing[94] the people who were in the way of the Islāmic revolution.
2. Swift reprisal[95] for those who were always ready to oppress and tyrannize.

3. Making pacts of unity[96] with the neighboring tribes.
4. Focusing the [army's] strength[97] on some of the more important fights against the enemies.

When the Battle of Uhud took place, he was forced to temporarily take up a defensive position, but this defensive war was again changed back into an offensive war in the Battle of Hamrā al-Asad[98] and the Muslim army was able to retake the victory from the enemy with its attacking forces and overturn the outcome.[99] The Prophet (s) continued to face the enemy and conduct pre-emptive strikes[100] until the Battle of Khandaq took place in which he also came out victorious. After the Battle of Khandaq, he used offensive warfare continuously and endlessly. He would say: Now it is we that must take the initiative to fight the enemy while they cannot fight us, and we should take the initiative to go towards them.[101]

2. Pre-emptive Warfare (*Harb al-Wiqāyah*)

The Noble Prophet (s) founded the basis of pre-emptive warfare,[102] which required fewer fighters and resources as was seen in the first Sariya mission which comprised of thirty fighters, but this number was increased to 313 plus two on horseback in the Battle of Badr. The Holy Prophet (s) would always attack the enemy before they could rise up [and launch an attack on the Muslims].[103]
The most important principles of this type of war that the Prophet (s) relied upon were: swiftness, stealth, surprise attacks, moving the war to the enemy's area at the right time and place, acquiring of precise information, increasing the morale of the attacking fighters, deploying the forces sparingly and minimizing loses. With these principles, he opened up the way of attaining greater victory over the enemy.

The Prophet started pre-emptive war in the Battle of Bani Saleem.[104] He marched his forces towards the tribes of Ghatfān and Saleem who had gathered at the waters of Qarqarat al-Kadar.[105] He carried out a surprise attack on them which lead to a greater victory over them. This was the same strategy applied in the Battle of Dhi Amr against the Bani Tha'labah, Ghatfān and Muhārib tribes to overpower them.[106] In this case, he obtained information[107] and then carried out a perfect *Sariya* mission[108] wherein he did not utilize all the forces he had, rather he only deployed those whom he needed in every battle, in accordance with the forces of the allies and enemies, and in this way, he put the principle of 'deploying the forces sparingly' into practice.

In the aforementioned battle (of Dhi Amr), the number of soldiers were four hundred and fifty[109] whereas in the next battle (the Battle of Bahrān) the number was reduced to three hundred.[110] The Prophet (s) appointed Salamah bin 'Abd al-Asad al-Makhzumi[111] as the leader of the mission and ordered him to march quickly,[112] day and night, so that he can reach the Bani Asad before they could recruit their forces.[113] In order to carry out the surprise attack, the commander would move stealthily, march by night[114] and use routes that were not common. He would take advantage of the time and place when the enemy is most vulnerable, just as was done in the Battle of Bani Mustalaq[115] where an attack was carried out while they were busy watering their animals[116] at a place known as al-Marisee' near the shore.[117]

3. Lightning Strikes and Blitzes

The Holy Prophet (s) would order the carrying out of lightning strikes and blitzes and for this he would rely on the following: (i) the psychological effect it would have on the enemy[118] (ii) swiftness[119] in movement and maneuvering (iii) training in advanced archery skills[120] (iv) competition (v) resistance (vi) carrying out surprise attacks[121] (vii) establishing the morale of attack[122] in his own army[123] (viii) Keeping the preparations for a surprise attack secret (ix) reducing the load of munitions and equipment that is carried by the troops.

Here we can mention the battles of Badr and Uhud under defensive and the Conquest of Makkah, Hunayn and Tabuk under offensive battles. In each case the speed of the troops was in accordance to what was appropriate [for the type of battle].[124] Lightning strikes and blitzes needed dominance and superiority[125] and could be changed in relation to defense and offence.[126] It also reduced human and material losses; because it terrified the enemy and made him continuously come under intense hardships and tribulations. In this state, in the face of lightning attacks, they would be forced to hesitate and end up surrendering without putting up any resistance. As a result, the number of martyrs and wounded [in this type of warfare] would be reduced.

In offensive battles, the Holy Prophet (s) would always try to have a greater number of forces [than the enemy]. In the Battle of Bani Quraydha, the number of forces in the Muslim army was three thousand compared to seven hundred and fifty from the Bani Quraydha. In the Battle of Khaybar 1,500 fighters were sent to face one thousand Jews of Kahybar, and in the Conquest of Makkah, ten thousand men faced the entire city of Makkah; and similarly this superiority was seen in most of the *Sariya* missions that were sent.[127]

In battles where it was not possible to gain superiority as far as the number of forces was concerned, like in the Battle of Hunayn,[128] he implemented lightning strikes. In this battle, the number of soldiers in the Muslim army was twelve thousand against the twenty thousand from the Hawāzin, the Watheeq and other tribes. This attack was commanded by people who were distinguished for caution, resistance,[129] utilizing the time and place,[130] swiftness that was greater[131] than the speed of the enemy,[132] changing and adapting quickly in the face of changing circumstances and making choices[133] based on them, focusing the attention on the enemy and obtaining strong intelligence[134] about them. All this factors made the Muslim army superior and enabled them to gain victory.

4. Pursuing and Chasing After Fleeing Enemy Soldiers

Chasing the enemy and pursuing him after carrying out a successful attack is known as 'al-Mutāradah' and the aim behind it is to annihilate and destroy the defeated forces of the enemy.[135] The Holy Prophet (s) never allowed this in any of the battles he fought and was victorious. He would [after gaining victory] set the enemy captives free and allow them to go wherever they wished. He also instructed the commanders of Sariya missions not to pursue the fleeing enemy because this was not helpful in realizing any of the military and political goals. When we look carefully at the Battle of Dhāt al-Suwayq[136] we find that the Prophet (s) was not keen to pursue Abu Sufyān, because if he would have reached the Quraysh in Makkah while the Muslim army was pursuing him, the polytheists would quickly prepare and gather for war, and thus this would end in an outcome that was not favorable for the pursuing forces.[137]

In the Battle of Dhāt al-Ruqā',[138] after the Noble Prophet (s) gained victory over the Bani Mahārib, the Bani Tha'labah and the Ghatfān, he never pursued their fleeing fighters, because it was possible for them to regroup with the Ghatfān and recruit more forces and in such a case it would be difficult to gain the upper hand over them. In the Battle of al-Ghābah[139] also, the Muslim army caught up with the fleeing enemy army at Dhi Qirad[140] but was forced to return back from the same route. After this, the Prophet (s) sent out many missions[141] to fight against the enemy, but he would always command them not to pursue the enemy if they were victorious. When he sent Abi Salamah ibn 'Abd al-Asad al-Makhzumi to fight the Bani Asad, he instructed him: Go towards the land of the Bani Asad and carry out an attack on them before they can gather together against you.[142] Similarly, in the other missions like the Sariya of Usāmah ibn Zayd[143] that was sent to (fight) the Abnā, there was no effort to pursue the defeated and fleeing soldiers.

5. Attacks and Onslaughts

The Prophet (s) was fully aware of this tactic, because it has been narrated that he would use offence and attacks whenever the situation called for it[144] in such a way that if it is used [in the present], by an elite commander – meaning someone who is courageous, brave, sound, intelligent and with a great personality who can execute attacks successfully – it would not match up to the way it was done at the time of the Prophet (s).

The attacks and onslaughts that were carried out by the Prophet (s) had the following distinguishing features:

a) Camouflage and Stealth: Like what took place in the Battle of Bahrān[145] against the tribe of Bani Saleem.

b) Silence and Quietness: This was seen in all the offensive missions and battles, especially the Battle of Bani Saleem, Bani al-Mustalaq and Badr, as well as other battles.[146]

c) 'Surprise' was a constituent of all the offensive battles and military missions, especially Badr, and was part of the foray. Just as seen in the Battle of Bani Quraydha, Khaybar, the Sariya of 'Ali ibn Abi Tālib ('a) against the Banu Sa'd and the Sariya of Usāma bin Zayd.[147]

d) Speed: as witnessed in the battle against the Bani Muhārib and the Bani Tha'labah in the Battle of Dhāt al-Ruqā'[148] and in other Sariya missions.[149]

e) Deception in Time and Place: this was another distinguishing feature of the military operations conducted by the Muslim army that was used in the Battles of Khandaq and Khaybar.[150]

The commander who was given the task of carrying out an attack was someone who was physically strong, had good hearing, strong sight and was free from any ailment or malady that could impede him during the operation. Similarly, the Prophet (s) would take into consideration the goal and the time [together] - like in the Battle of Khaybar,[151] the place - as in the Battle of Khandaq,[152] and all three i.e. time, place and the objective – as in the Sariya of Usāma bin Zayd to Abnā,[153] so that the enemy could be attacked when they were least prepared for battle.

The Noble Prophet (s) prevented the fighters from raising their voices or shouting and screaming, and in the Battle of Badr he ordered that the bells of the camels should be removed from their necks.[154] He would always encourage his troops to use new ways and methods for carrying out attacks.

6. Deception and Trickery

Some of the military tactics that are necessary and important in the battlefield are deception and trickery. Deception is the art of hiding and concealing the truth and involves doing things that would mislead the mind of the enemy away from the fight, while at the same time being alert about the resources and operations [of one's own army].[155] The Holy Prophet (s) knew about the importance of deception and trickery in war and would plan it and then execute it perfectly. He counted deception as part of warfare and would say: War is deception.[156] In the first battle that was fought against the enemy at Badr, he replied to the question of Habāb bin Mundhir about this tactic and reaffirmed that indeed, war is deception, cunning and trickery.[157]

The Prophet (s) also gave Muhammad bin Maslamah,[158] who had taken the responsibility of killing Ka'b ibn Ashraf, the permission to deceive the enemy[159] and say anything that will enable him to carry out his mission. Similarly, after his accepting Islām, Na'eem bin Mas'ud was ordered to trick the enemy in the battle of Khandaq in the same way. So he was told: You are from the tribe of Ghatfān. When you go to them, if you are forced to display hatred for us then do so for this will be more beneficial for us than if you openly help us. So go forward, for war is deception and cunning.[160] In this mission, he successfully dispersed the enemy and this resulted in a victory for the Muslims.

In the war of Bani Lahyān, the supreme commander portrayed the type of battle, the time and the route taken in a different way [to what he actually intended].[161] In the Battle of Khaybar, he used trickery and deception against the Ghatfān[162] and they were not able to join with the forces at Khaybar and thus returned to their homeland. In the Conquest of Makkah,[163] the Prophet (s) misled the Quraysh by sending Abi Qatāda ibn Rabi' towards the direction of Najd, thus misdirecting and distracting them from his real target (which was Makkah), and by equivocation[164] and trickery, he cut off all the routes in and out of Makkah.[165] In the Battle of Muta also, Khālid bin Walid used this tactic.[166] And in this way, by increasing the movements of the army, the enemy was tricked into believing that a large number of reinforcements had come to the aid of the Muslim army, so they became frightened and turned back.

7. Superiority in Battle

The Prophet (s) would always be careful about superiority over the enemy in battle, so he would gather all the needed forces and resources for the important battles. He sent Sariya missions towards the coastal regions and also to face the Quraysh, like the Sariya of Hamza and the later missions, or the battles like Waddān, Bawāt and al-'Asheera; and also towards the eastern regions after the battle of Badr.[167] The Prophet (s) gained an upper hand in the following ways:
1. Inventing new ways of warfare: like in the Battle of Badr, the battle of the fortresses and the lightning strikes.[168]
2. Focusing the forces at the appropriate time and place,[169] as in the Battle of Uhud and Hunayn.
3. Being swift as was required by the conditions of battle,[170] like in many of the battles and Sariya missions.

4. Destruction of most of the enemy forces,[171] like in the Battle of Badr, Hunayn and Bani Quraydha.
5. Restricting the freedom of the enemy, like in the battles of Badr, Quraydha and Khaybar.[172]
6. Putting the enemy forces in hardship and difficulty,[173] just like cutting off any reinforcements from the Bani Quraydha and besieging them.
7. Burning down the date palms of Bani Nadhir and the gardens of Tā'if.[174]
8. Gaining access to the backup forces of the enemy and restricting or destroying them,[175] such that the Prophet (s) would make his forces reach the enemy and take their horses as booty.

The Holy Prophet (s) did not always seek to have a larger army than the enemy.[176] For instance, in the Sariya of Hamza, the number of soldiers was thirty as opposed to the three hundred Makkans. In the Battle of Badr, 313 [Muslim] fighters went up against one thousand polytheists. In the Battle of Uhud, seven hundred came to face three thousand polytheists, and in the Battle of Ahzāb, three thousand faced ten thousand infidels. However, he mostly sought to gain superiority as far as the excellence of the forces were concerned[177] just as in the battles of Hamrā al-Asad, Badr al-Aākhar and Bani al-Mustalaq. In some of the battles, despite the greater number of enemy forces and weapons,[178] he would gain decisive victories over them for which the battles of Badr and Hunayn are perfect examples. Nonetheless, he would change the number of forces sent in every different situation. In the Battle of Bani Quraydha, there was a relatively large number of forces as compared to the enemy[179] as was also the case in the War of Bani Lahyān.[180]

The Prophet (s) would not attack one tribe or one group in a single strike.[181] Rather, he would divide the enemy in order to gain complete victory and dominance of them materially and spiritually. For example, he divided the Jewish forces into the following: Bani Qaynuqā, Bani Nadhir, Bani Quraydha and [the Jews of] Khaybar. He attacked each of these groups separately. For instance, in the Battle of Ahzāb, he attacked the Jews separately from the Quraysh[182] and the Bani Ghatfān separately from them both[183] and in the Battle of Hunayn, he also divided the enemy i.e. he separated the front-line from the soldiers who were behind and then launched an attack on them.

8. Swiftness and Speed in Battle

The Noble Prophet (s) was steadfast about the importance of speed in battle, because this tactic made it possible for him to carry out surprise attacks. The number of fallen soldiers would not be known [when the attacks were swift] and this would weaken the resolve of the enemy while strengthening the morale of the attacking army such that the enemy was unable to launch a counter attack.[184] In order to achieve the desired swiftness, the Prophet embarked on training the forces[185] and made them practice it in all the consecutive battles[186] and missions[187] that would be carried out to face the enemy. In this way, the soldiers became accustomed[188] to move swiftly and fight in the battles without making mistakes.

The modes of transport used by the Prophet played an important role in attaining the desired speed. These consisted mainly of horses and camels. The Muslim army also relied on being quick in getting ready for war[189] and in order to instantaneously face the enemy and recruit forces, they needed material resources and manpower.

In order to achieve this, the Prophet (s) used the following methods:
a) Swiftness in defense and attack[190]: In defense, like in the battles of Uhud and Khandaq and in attack, like in the battles and Sariya missions of Bani Saleem, Dhi Amr, Bahrān, Dhāt al-Ruqā', Dumat al-Jundal, the Sariya of Abi 'Ubayda ibn al-Jarrāh, Abi Salama and al-Khabt, this was clearly seen.[191]
b) Speed in besieging[192]: Like in the battles of Bani Qaynuqā, Bani Quraydha and Khaybar.
c) Quickness in marching forward: In the battles and missions like Badr, when the enemies were heading towards al-Udwat al-Dunyā, they overtook them and also in the battles of Bani Saleem, Dhāt al-Ruqā', Bani Quraydha, Bani Lahyān, the Sariya of Muhammad ibn Maslamah to kill Ka'b ibn Ashraf, the Sariya of Zayd bin Hāritha to attack the caravan of the Quraysh and the Sariya of Abi Salamah where he journeyed by day and night in order to reach the enemy.
d) Speed in acquiring information and intelligence: Like in the battles of Badr, Dhāt al-Ruqā', Bani al-Mustalaq, Khaybar, the Conquest of Makkah and the Sariya of Muhammad bin Maslamah to destroy the Bani Bakr, (the Sariya of) 'Akāsha bin Mahsan against the Bani Asad and Ghālib bin 'Abdillah al-Laythi against the Bani Murrah.[193]
e) Swiftness in counter attacks: Like in the Battle of Uhud[194] and in lightning strikes[195] like in the Battle of Hunayn.
f) Speed in [carrying out] other missions[196]: Including in the Sariya missions of 'Umayr ibn 'Uday to kill 'Asmā', of Sālim bin 'Umayr to kill Ibn Abi 'Ifk, of Muhammad bin Maslamah to kill Ka'b ibn Ashraf, Of 'Abdullah bin Anees to kill Sufyān ibn Khālid al-Hadhali and of 'Abdullah ibn 'Ateek in order to kill Abi Rāfi'.
g) Swiftness in attack[197]: In battles and Sariya missions like Dumat al-Jundal, Bani al-Mustalaq, Ibn Quraydha, Bani Lahyānm the Sariya of

'Ali ibn Abi Tālib ('a) [who was sent] towards the Bani Sa'd, Bashir ibn Sa'd Ansāri who was sent to the Bani Murrah and Usāma bin Zayd towards the Abnā.

h) Speed in preventive war: Like in the battles and Sariya missions of Dhi Amr, Bahrān, Dhāt al-Ruqā', Dumat al-Jundal, Bani al-Mustalaq, the Sariya of Abi Salamah, Abi 'Ubaydah ibn Jarrāh for revenge from the Bani Tha'labah, and al-Khabat.[198]

i) Swiftness in Lightning Strikes[199]: Like in the battles of Dhāt al-Ruqā', Bani Quraydha, Dhi Qirad and the Sariya of Zayd ibn Hāritha against the tribe of Judhām.

j) Quickness in raids[200]: In the battle of Dhāt al-Ruqā' and other Sariya missions.

9. Revolutionary and All-inclusive War

This type war was based on rising up against injustice and tyrannical forces with all the might and resources available and it relied on the power of the people who have been inspired and are driven by the force of spiritual, political or religious motivations, and is actually a first step in destroying the might and awe of the enemy and gaining victory over him.[201]

In 'revolutionary and all-inclusive war', the Holy Prophet (s) would spiritually and mentally prepare the forces and the inhabitants of the city.[202] In turn, they would be ready to sacrifice all their lives and property[203] for the cause, because they believed and trusted in the fairness, the instruction, the authority, the love and the command of the Prophet (s).[204] It is undeniable that the spiritual aspect[205] played an important role in strengthening the resolve of the revolutionary forces and weakening the enemy, and as such it was employed in all the battles and was also accompanied by material means[206] in order to strengthen it. The Holy Prophet (s) used this to the utmost in the weak points of the enemy so that he could make them internally and externally weakened and perplexed.[207]

That which distinguished the Islāmic revolution of the Noble Prophet (s) and gave the Prophet (s) a special status as a knowledgeable and spiritual leader included:

a) Selecting appropriate agents.[208]
b) The people were content with his fairness and justice.[209]
c) Preparing all the people completely.[210]
d) Establishing of affinity and affection between them.[211]
e) Guiding both armed and unarmed forces towards a common goal.[212]
f) Acquiring new friends and allies.[213]

g) Humiliating the tyrants and despots.[214]

h) Demonstrating how the Islāmic system is superior to polytheism and other systems.[215]

i) Teaching and propagating the new ideology.[216]

j) Making others love faith and hate disbelief.[217]

k) Being the best role model as a leader.[218]

10. Psychological Warfare

This is a collection of actions that are undertaken to influence the enemy or the rival[219] with the aim of weakening the enemy's determination, resolve and material and spiritual power. Psychological warfare was considered the most important type of war in the strategy and planning of the Noble Prophet (s) and he made it the focal point in his battle against the enemy. He would leave them stunned and gain control over their spirits and minds, and as a result, he would take away their ability to fight back and resist. The Prophet (s) has himself said about this: *I have been assisted by creating a fear in the hearts of the enemy.*[220]

One who is frightened begins imagining things that are far from reality. For example, in the Battle of Khaybar, the tribe of Ghatfān imagined that their lands were under attack by the Muslim army, so they turned back and returned out of fear[221] but when they reached their land they found nothing of what they had imagined. The same thing that happened to the Ghatfān happened to the Jews of Khaybar also and this made them ready to surrender and seek peace and conciliation.[222] An army that becomes frightened and scared is unable to benefit from their weapons and fight in battle, and even if they fight, they would be very weak and disorganized in battle and this would result in nothing but [loss or] surrender to their enemy.

Because of being overcome by fear, the commander of the army of the inhabitants of Khaybar was unable to shoot the arrows from his bow even after readying them for firing, and his forces had become weary and weak.[223]

The level of fear can be clearly seen in the words of one Jewish person who was granted amnesty by the Prophet (s): *The inhabitants of this place have been destroyed out of fear of you.*[224]

From the first time that the Holy Prophet (s) sent a Sariya mission[225] to fight against the enemy, he relied on psychological warfare. After the first battle, all this changed[226] and he began to use it against the Quraysh and ended it against the Romans. Through this practice, a number of enemies would flee before coming face to face with the Muslim army[227] just like what happened in the Battle of Bani Saleem and in other battles.

Some of the enemies like the inhabitants of Akeedar, Jurbā' and Yuhannā would seek [to make] peace pacts.[228] Many groups from Arab tribes would frequently come to him to sign peace treaties while others would fight with fear and weakness,[229] like the tribes of Hawāzin and Thaqeef in the Battle of Hunayn and the people of Makkah during the Conquest of Makkah. Other groups would also be on the watch for this [Muslim] army and would be frightened of it, like the fear of the Romans in the battles of Dumat al-Jundal and Tabuk.[230]

The Prophet (s) was able to put fear in the heart of the enemy even in the smallest of battles, from a single mission to a large contingent, in such a way that they would fear even coming face to face with him and would become unable to face any army, small or big. The Jews of Bani Nadheer, because of the fear that had entered their hearts, destroyed their houses by their own hands and the hands of the Muslim army,[231] and the Banu Lahyān[232] chose to flee and disperse when the army of the Prophet (s) approached them.

However, the Sariya mission would create fear in the enemy as well. Just as the Sariya of 'Ali ibn Abi Tālib ('a)[233] with the Bani Sa'd had done - to such an extent that they loaded their belongings on their camels[234] and fled along with their leader who said: *The army of Muhammad is coming towards us and we are incapable of facing them.*[235]

A psychological war was also fought with the tribes of Ghatfān through the Sariya of Sa'eed ibn Sa'd al-Ansāri,[236] and 'Uyayna ibn Mihsan[237] and his companions were routed in this battle. When Hārith ibn 'Auf al-Muriy, who had an allegiance with them called them to stand up and fight, he heard nothing but this response: *How strong are the companions of Muhammad who are on our trail!* Harith ibn 'Auf says: *I went on the side of the route followed by the army of Muhammad (s) so that I could see them from a distance while they would not see me. I stayed from evening until late in the night but I saw nobody, it was as if nothing was following my allies but fear.*[238] Similarly, the Quraysh got scared and took to their heels when they just came face to face with 'Utbah ibn Aseed (Abu Baseer) al-Thaqafi.[239] Even the kings and emperors to whom the Prophet (s) sent emissaries[240] were fearful of the messengers and emissaries.

The most important tools of psychological war that were used by the Prophet of God (s) were intelligence agents and spies whom he would send towards the enemy. These spies would spread rumours that would enervate the enemy and force them to flee. The Prophet (s) sent Ma'bad al-Khuzā'i towards the Quraysh in the Battle of Hamrā' al-Asad.[241] He began talking to them about the huge number of forces in the Muslim army and their intense urge for revenge and thirst for blood, thereby influencing the minds of the Quraysh and paralyzing them.

In the Battle of Khandaq, he (s) send Na'im ibn Mas'ud[242] so that he could divide and disperse the confederates and weaken the enemy forces. The Holy Prophet (s) would send Sariya missions in order to fulfill the objectives of psychological war[243] and would at times, like in the expedition to Tabuk, send the entire army for this purpose[244] and at other times he sent only a section of the army[245] like in the Battle of Bani Lahyān where he sent Abu Bakr with a section of the army and ordered him to march towards the Quraysh. The Prophet (s) arranged all this in order to attain the goals of psychological war and would also in turn seek to destroy the information and intelligence of the enemy. He would achieve this through complete sagacity[246] and by arresting the enemy spies,[247] like the shepherd who was arrested on the way to the Battle of Bani Saleem, or the arresting and imprisoning of a spy until the end of the Battle of Bahrān, as well as killing the spy of the Bani Mustalaq because of his not giving up the intelligence, and the interrogation of the spies of Khaybar where the Prophet (s) himself asked them questions.

As for the second instrument [for attaining the objectives of psychological warfare], it was displaying the might of the forces that were under the command of the Prophet (s). The features of these forces included:

a) Being invisible: Meaning the divine power that put fear into the hearts of the enemy like the battle of the angels [who participated] in the Battle of Badr[248] and the blowing of storms and [falling] hailstones in the battle of Khandaq,[249] until even the commanders of the army of polytheists and their council of chiefs pointed to the invisible force and would say: *The God of Muhammad will soon take revenge.* And so they turned back.

b) Being undefeatable: As the enemy themselves emphasized this saying: *Standing up against him yields no results.*[250] This transpired with 'Uyayna ibn Mihsan who had tried numerous times to rise up with his people against the Muslim army. After this happened, he became a Muslim and even led a Sariya mission against the Bani Tamim. In the same way, the Arab tribes who realized that there was nothing to be gained by their enmity with the Muslims saw it prudent to surrender and submit themselves to the Holy Prophet (s) and would thus come to him. As such, the Bani Qaynuqā', Bani Nadheer, Bani Quraydha and the Jews of Khaybar, all gave a suggestion of peace when they lost hope in their rebellion.

c) They had the spirit [and zeal] of attack.[251]

d) They would invent new ways and methods of warfare.[252]

It is undisputable that this [military] management took on a new form in the Battle of Hamrā al-Asad. During this battle, the Prophet (s) took the wounded and handicapped along with his army[253] and ordered that many fires be lighted[254] so that the enemy would think that the Muslim army was large and powerful.[255] In the Battle of Hudaybiyya, he pulled his cloak and his garment to one side and left his right arm openly visible and ordered the Muslims to do the same, saying: *May Allah bless the one who displays the strength of his arm.*[256]

(C) PHYSICAL AND SPIRITUAL TRAITS

From the most evident spiritual traits of the Holy Prophet (s) was that he was never overcome by pride from his victories.[257] This was clearly seen when he returned from the Battle of Badr and the Conquest of Makkah. He also never became disheartened by loss,[258] just as the loss in the Battle of Uhud did not affect him, rather he quickly prepared for the Battle of Hamrā' al-Asad soon after. The breach of the treaty by the Bani Quraydha, who joined with the confederates [in the Battle of Ahzāb] also did not affect the Prophet (s) in the least, rather it strengthened his resolve and made him steadfast.

Another one of his traits was 'precaution and restraint', and he would assess the enemy in this way and would begin preparing and readying the resources and weaponry required to face them. Even during the time of prayer he would not leave precaution, rather he was careful and cautious. Another trait of his was 'softness accompanied with firmness' which would be seen in the different circumstances of battle and because of the quickly changing conditions, he would issue new commands and orders. 'Speed in (issuing) command(s)'[259] was considered important by him in order to tackle the new circumstances [that came up in battle] and was a necessary condition for the 'centralization of command'[260] which the Prophet (s) stressed upon and of which he was the protector in its essence and foundation. This was considered one of the loftiest personal traits of his command; because all of the struggles and military resources that were spent for attaining the goal would be recruited and organized by himself and in this way his renown as a commander spread both internally and externally and this was sufficient to cause the enemies to flee before having to march towards them.

1. Physical Traits

In modern science it has been proven that parts of the body of an individual have specific features which show their 'strength and courage', 'beauty and appeal', 'ethics and intentions' and 'habits'. For example, a round face[261] shows wisdom and dignity; a wide mouth[262] shows strength; big black eyes[263] show beauty, intelligence, eloquence, humility, forbearance and dignity; arched and separated eyebrows[264] indicate awe, courage and might; and plenty of hair[265] on the body, chest, chin and head indicate might and intensity in combat. When we do a detailed and complete study we find that the Holy Prophet's body had all these features that spoke of his ability and genius in leadership, and all this also agrees with what has been mentioned by the scholars of modern science.[266]

2. Spiritual Traits

As the extent of the scope of a person's kindness gets larger and encompasses all human beings equally, it makes him a leader who is close to the hearts of the people and gives him greater control of different aspects of leadership and makes him more powerful as a commander.

The life of the Holy Prophet (s) had a completely humanitarian face and approach.[267] He (s) grew up as an orphan[268] and faced poverty and deprivation,[269] and had to bear patiently with the persecution and harassment of some of his relatives and community members.[270] The Prophet (s) addressed all the people and called them towards right guidance and urged them towards the advancement of humanity.[271] In this task, he began with his near relatives[272] and then gave the message to others[273] and finally addressed it to the entire world.[274] He bestowed honor on the Children of Adam[275] and his dealings with his friends and community members was based on affinity[276] and reconciliation between them.[277] He strengthened the bond of trust and harmony among them[278] and inculcated the feeling of mercy for all human beings in their hearts.[279] He would be merciful to the young[280] and would show respect to the elderly.[281] He would take away some of their burdens and hardships[282] and forbade their killing in wars.[283] He would please the orphans and grant them refuge. He would show kindness to the poor and needy[284] and instructed the people to be good to their servants.[285] He even showed mercy to animals[286] and forbade the people from harming them.[287]

The attention and consideration of the Noble Prophet (s) would also include (inanimate) things such that he named his sword 'Dhul Fiqār', his shield 'Dhāt al-Fudhul',[288] his spear 'Mathwā',[289] his bow 'al-Katum',[290] and his quiver 'Kāfur'.[291]

One of the most important examples of his humanity was that when the Holy Prophet (s) sent forces to battle or for Sariya missions against the enemy, he would advise them to be friendly with the people[292] and not to carry out raids or night assaults on them. He always preferred to come to a compromise with the enemy instead of killing their menfolk and leave their women and children [without guardians].[293] He (s) always instructed that the elderly, the children and the women[294] were not to be tortured and the bodies of the dead[295] must not be disfigured.[296]

From his greatest humanitarian traits in war was that when the Quraysh had sought refuge with him, he ended the 'economic blockade'[297] against them and accepted their request for importing grain from Yemen.[298] Despite what they had done to him, he freed the women and children prisoners of Bani Tamim.[299] The Noble Prophet (s) called for universal peace[300] in the world and avoided war except in cases where there was no other option.[301] The letters that he sent to the neighboring kings and rulers were adorned and embellished with calls for peace and conciliation.[302] And this is what he instituted as the start of conversation between the Children of Adam.[303]

The Holy Prophet (s) gave a new and specific meaning to leadership.[304] In some of the battles he appointed more than one commander.[305] He outlined the criteria for a befitting commander of the army and its strengthening and he established a bond between the principles of politics and the military.[306] He made obedience the secret of discipline, submission and compliance.[307] He laid the foundation of new planning, exemplary organization and better leadership.[308] He made the soldiers steadfast in [the quest for] good morals and knowledge[309] and put in their hearts the love for death and disinclination towards the life of this world.[310] He (s) would select the commanders and leaders based on their merit and ability.[311] He brought the army and the people together equally under his leadership[312] and would grant them as much of the resources as were available.[313] In these matters, he included the young and old, the strong and weak, the men and women. He invited them to [follow his] leadership and the ideology of equality and made these two complementary counterparts to each other.[314] He always tried to elaborate these ideas and transform them so that he could arrive at his desired goal.[315]

NOTES AND REFERENCES

[1] Wāqidi 1:7; Ibn Sa'd 2:1 onwards; Ibn Atheer 2:203 onwards

[2] Al-Qalam: 4

[3] Q9:128; Bukhāri (*al-Janā'iz, al-Tawhid, al-Adab*); Muslim (*al-Janā'iz, al-Fadhā'il, al-Tawba, al-Nudhur*); Sanā'i (*al-Janā'iz, al-Tahārah, al-Hajj*); Ibn Māja and Tirmidhi (*al-Ahkām*)

[4] Bukhāri (*al-Adab, al-Nafaqāt, al-Istinābah*); Muslim (*al-Imāra, al-Birr, al-Jihād*); Tirmidhi (*al-Ahkām*).

[5] Bukhāri (*al-'Ilm, al-Adhāhi, al-Imān, al-Maghāzi*); Muslim (*al-Imān*); Dāwud (*al-Adab*)

[6] Bukhāri (*al-Jizya, al-Adab, al-Imān, al-Sayd, al-Maghāzi*); Ibn Māja (*al-Sadaqāt, al-Janā'iz, al-Jihād*)

[7] Q3:34; Bukhāri (*al-Nikāhm Fadhā'il al-Sahābah*); Muslim (*Fadhā'il al-Sahābah*)

[8] Bukhāri (*al-Istindhān, al-Buyu'*, Tafseer Surah 59: 65, *al-Adab, Fadhā'il al-Sahābah*); Muslim (*al-Jihād, al-Zakāh, al-Eimān*); Abu Dāwud (*al-Wasāyā, al-Hudud, al-Diyāt, al-Ada*); Tirmidhi (*al-Libās, al-Birr, al-Manāqib*); Nasā'i (*al-Qadhā', al-Qasāmah, al-Janā'iz*)

[9] Aāl 'Imrān: 103, 110; A'rāf:157, 199; Tawba:112; Bukhāri (*al-Fitan, Badw al-Khalq, al-Shurb*); Muslim (*al-Uqdhiyyah, al-Zuhd*); Ibn Māja (*al-Fitan*)

[10] Ibn Māja (*al-Fitan*)

[11] Al-Mu'minun: 37

[12] Bukhāri 3:2

[13] Dārimi, *al-Muqaddimah*: 34, 57; Bodyle, *al-Rasul* (The Life of Muhammad), translated into Arabic by 'Abd al-Hamid Judah: 54

[14] Al-An'ām: 124

[15] Al-Nubhāni, *al-Anwār al-Muhammadiyya min al-Mawāhib al-Daniyya*: 22; Jād al-Mawlā, *Muhammad al-Mumathil al-Kāmil*: 20; Cobold, *al-Bahth 'an Allah*: 51; Carlyle, *Muhammad Rasul al-Hudā wa Shari'at al-Khālidah*, translated into Arabic by Muhammad al-Sabā'i: 49

[16] Ibn Hishām 2:58; Ibn Sa'd 2:6

[17] Al-Zuhri: 79; Wāqidi 2:44; Suhayli 3:276; and see also: Muhammad Rawās Qal'echi, *Dirāsāt al-Tahliliyyah li Shakhsiyyat al-Rasul Muhammad* (s): 226-232 (Tr.)

[18] Ibn Hazm: 207; Ibn Sayyid al-Nās 2:13; Kalā'i 1:127

[19] A group of people from Yathrib met with the Prophet (s) in Minā and made two pacts with him (that later became known as the first and second pledge of 'Aqaba) in which they promised to support and protect him. When the first battle between the Muslims and the polytheist took place, only the Muhājirs participated in it, meaning

that the Prophet did not involve the Ansār in battle before the Battle of Badr, because they had agreed to protect the Prophet only in Madina. For this reason, in the Battle of Badr, out of the 313 fighters, more than 240 were from the Ansār. (Tr.)

[20] Ibn Khayyāt, *Tārikh Khalifah ibn Khayyāt* 1:15; Tabari 2:403, 405

[21] The Quraysh would travel for trade twice a year. In the winter they would go to Yemen and the southern areas of the Arabian Peninsula, and in the summer they would go towards the north. (See: Jawād 'Ali, *al-Mukhtasar fi Tārikh al-Islām*, under the section about Makkah) (Tr.)

[22] This refers to the Mountain of 'Aynayn. This was the same place where the Prophet (s) had ordered the Muslims to keep watch in the battle of Uhud. (Tr.)

[23] Ibn Sa'd 2:41

[24] See Haydarabādi, Majmu'ah *al-Wathā'iq al-Siyāsiyyah lil 'Ahd al-Nabawi wal Khilāfa al-Rāshidah*: 15-21 (Tr.)

[25] Al-Fath: 29

[26] Ibn Sa'd 2:136

[27] Wāqidi 1:402, 2:755, 3:989; Tabari 3:100; Ibn Hazm: 220.249

[28] Ibn Sayyid al-Nās 2:41

[29] Wāqidi 1:404; Ibn Hishām 3:302; Ibn Sa'd 2:45; Ibn Hazm: 203; Kalā'i 1:124; Ibn Sayyid al-Nās 2:91; Ibn Katheer 4:156

[30] Wāqidi 3:112; Ibn Sa'd 2:137; Tabari 3:185; Ibn Sayyid al-Nās 2:281

[31] Ibn 'Abd Rabbih 1:7, 11, 19, 22, 32, 43; Ibn Khaldun, *Muqaddimah* 2:711 onwards; M. Watt, *Muhammad fi al-Madina*: 4; in this pact, five people from the Aus tribe gave allegiance to the Prophet (s). (Tr.)

[32] Ibn Sa'd 1:147; Ibn Atheer 2:94

[33] Tabari 2:355; this pact is also known as Bay'at al-Harb. 11 people from the Aus and Khazraj pledged allegiance to the Prophet (s). This pact laid the groundwork for the migration of the Prophet to Madina. (Tr.)

[34] Ibn 'Abd al-Birr 4:1473; Ibn Atheer, *Usd al-Ghāba fi Ma'rifat al-Sahāba* 4:370; Harawi, *al-Hiyal al-Harbiyya*: 75

[35] Ibn Sa'd 1:148; Tabari: 356

[36] Ibn Sa'd 2:1; Suhayli 2:252

[37] Zuhri: 63; Wāqidi 1:182, 194, 203, 337, 395, 404 onwards; Ibn Hishām 2:268

[38] Ka'b ibn Ashraf was one of the heads of the Jews and was a staunch enemy of the Muslims and especially of the Holy Prophet (s). He would compose poems mocking the Prophet and would encourage the disbelievers to rise up against the Muslims. The Prophet (s) asked his companions if anyone from among them would be willing to take up the mission of assassinating him. Muhammad ibn Maslamah took up the challenge. In order to accomplish the mission, he tricked Ka'b into leaving his companions and coming with him to a remote place and after talking with him for some time, he suddenly took out his sword and killed him. When the Prophet (s) heard the news he was very happy and embraced Ibn Maslamah and praised him. (See Wāqidi 1:90) (Tr.)

[39] Abdullah's mother used to live among the Jews and hid her faith from them. At night he and some others entered into Khaybar and took refuge at his mother's house. They hid their weapons and once they had found out where Abi al-Huqays's mansion was, they sought to meet with him on the pretext that they had brought him some gifts. Once inside, they killed him with their swords. In this way, in the month of Ramadān, in the year 6 A.H. one of the greatest enemies of Islām was assassinated. However it should be noted that, contrary to what the author has mentioned, the Prophet (s) did not sent 'Abdullah ibn 'Ateeq on this mission, rather, when he heard how Abi al-Huqayq was insulting and mocking Islām and the Prophet, he felt a sense of responsibility and thus took the initiative himself to do away with him. (See Wāqidi 1:391; Ibn Sayyid al-Nās 1:120) (Tr.)

[40] Ibn Sa'd 2:6, 25, 34, 40, 44, 53

[41] Wāqidi 1:97, 2:440, 3:885 onwards; Ibn Hishām 3:64, 224, 4:80; Ibn Sa'd 2:25, 47, 108; also see Rawāw Qal'echi, *Dirāsah Tahliliyyah lishakhsiyyat al-Rasul Muhammad (s)*: 228-229

[42] In the battle of Uhud, the Prophet wanted the Muslims to remain in Madina but because of the insistence of the young zealous fighters, he was forced to move out. After a short while, the same people came to the Prophet (s) and told him they were

ready to remain in Madina and wait for the enemy. The Prophet replied that it was inappropriate to change the decision as everything had already been prepared. (Tr.)

[43] When the Muslims began losing in the battle of Uhud, the Prophet quickly transferred the command post of the army to the mountain and assumed a defensive position. (Rawās Qa'ehchi: 29) (Tr.)

[44] For example, when the Prophet (s) was injure in the battle of Uhud, this did not prevent him from playing his role as the leader of the army. (Tr.)

[45] Al-Uqqād, *al-'Abqariyyat al-Islāmiyyah*: 220, 250; M. Watt, *Muhammad fi al-Madina*: 511; Cobold: 121

[46] Wāqidi 1:1; Kalā'i 1:57

[47] Wāqidi 1:13; Ibn Hazm: 105; Ibn 'Abd al-Birr, *al-Istee'āb* 3:878; Ibn Katheer 3:248

[48] In the month of Rajab in the first year of Hijra, the Prophet (s) send 'Abdullah ibn Jahash with seventeen men on a mission to Wādiyu al-Nakhlah. There he was to launch an attack on the caravan of the Quraysh. After some fighting, 'Abdullah returned to Madina victorious (see: Ibn Sayyid al-Nās 1:359) (Tr.)

[49] Tabari 2:512; Ibn Hazm: 160; Ibn Sayyid al-Nās 2:6; Kalā'i 1:101, 102

[50] Usāma bin Zayd ibn Hāritha was a young man of about nineteen who was appointed as the commander by the Prophet (s) because of his ability and leadership skills. He was given the authority above the older companions (like Abu Bakr). His appointment came in the last days of the Holy Prophet's life. Many of the companions complained to the Prophet (s) because of his young age. The Prophet became angry and said that he was chosen because he was a capable commander like his father was. (see Wāqidi 20:769; Ibn Hishām 4:272) (Tr.)

[51] Wāqidi 1:12; Ibn Sa'd 2:4; Tabari 2:408

[52] It is worthy to note here that the author has unfortunately fallen prey to sectarian bias as is evident in his selection of personalities. Though, it is a known and acknowledged fact that 'Ali ibn Abi Tālib ('a) was one of the most effective commanders in battle, he has neglected to even mention his name. Even though the

author has made an effort to remain impartial, it is in instances such as these that the lack of impartiality becomes clear. When the main sources from both the sects are studied, it can be seen that 'Ali ('a) was the driving force in some of the major battles and without his participation in them, victory would not be forthcoming. He was among the first warriors to participate in the Battle of Badr and was the first to kill an enemy of Islām (see: Ibn 'Abd Rabbih, *al-Iqd al-Fareed* 5:96). When the life of the Holy Prophet (s) was in danger, it was 'Ali ('a) who stood by him and courageously defended him in the Battle of Uhud (see: *Usd al-Ghābah fi Ma'rifat al-Sahābah* 1:154; Ibn Jawzi, *Tadhkirat Khawās al-Ummah*: 16). The historians are also in agreement that he played a primary role in the Battle of Khandaq wherein he killed the giant 'Amr bin 'Abd Wudd (see: Ba'lami, *Tārikhnāme Tabari* 1:205). His victory over the Jews in Khaybar was a feat that many other companions failed to accomplish and this is recorded in many sources such as Ibn Hishām 2:334; Balādhuri 2:93; Ibn Jawzi: 16. In the Battle of Hunayn, where many of the 'great' companions fled from the battlefield, 'Ali ('a) stood next to the Prophet (s) and fought with valor (see: Ibn Sa'd 2:151; Ya'qubi, *Tārikh al-Ya'qubi* 2:47). In fact the instances of great courage and leadership displayed in battle are greater for 'Ali ibn Abi Tālib ('a) than for any other companion. Unfortunately, we cannot elaborate on all of these here. (Tr.)

[53] Wāqidi 1:194; Ibn Sa'd 2:24; M. Watt: 130

[54] Wāqidi 1:195; Ibn Sa'd (*Ibid.*); Ibn Hishām 3:50

[55] Zuhri: 76; Ibn Sa'd 2:25; Tabari 3:9; Dhahabi, *Tārikh al-Islām* 1:183

[56] Ibn Hishām 2:58, 64, 199, 224, 633

[57] Wāqidi 1:220; Ibn Hishām 3:69; Kalā'i 1:102, 103, Ibn Qayyim Jawzi, *Zād al-Ma'ād* 2:241

[58] Wāqidi 2:649

[59] *Ibid.* 2:645

[60] Hakeem, *Masā'il Manhajiyyah 'Ilmiyyah fi Nadhariyyah al-Harb wa Tatbiqihā min Wihjat al-Nadhar al-Sufitiyyah*: 121 onwards

[61] Ibn Saydah, *al-Mukhassas* 13:25; Rāzi, *Jumal Ahkām al-Firāsah*: 8; Carlyle, *Muhammad Rasul al-Hudā wa...*: 29

[62] Al-Hijr: 75; al-'Ankabut: 38; Qāf: 22; Qasas: 80

[63] Al-An'ām: 124; See also: Abu Na'im al-Isfahāni 4:26

[64] Bukhāri (*al-Ta'beer*); Tirmidhi (*al-Ru'yā*)

[65] Ibn 'Abd Rabbih 2:669; Ibn Atheer 2:371; Suhayl ibn 'Amr was the representatives of the Quraysh in the Treaty of Hudaybiyya. During the Conquest of Makkah, the Prophet invited him to accept Islām and he did so. In this way, the polytheists lost one of their most valued people. (Tr.)

[66] Ibn Mājah (*al-Fitan*); Abu Dāwud (*al-Jihād*); al-Dhahabi 1:227

[67] Al-Baqarah: 125; Qasas: 57; Nur: 55

[68] Ibn 'Abd al-Birr 4:449; Ibn Atheer 4:418

[69] In the 4th year of Hijrah, Abu Barrā' sought permission to take 70 Qurrā' (Qur'ān reciters) with him to propagate the religion among the people of Najd. The Prophet (s) advised him against this move, but he was insistent. When they reached a place known as Bi'r Ma'unah, they were surrounded by some members of the tribe of Saleem and were all martyred. (Tr.)

[70] Wāqidi 1: 348; Ibn Hishām 3:194; Ibn Sa'd 2:36; Ibn Khayyāt 1:42

[71] Bukhāri (*al-Maghāzi* 29); Ibn Hanbal 2:262; Ibn Hishām 3:243

[72] Zuhri: 52; Ibn Hishām 3:325; Ibn Sa'd 2:70; Kalā'i 1:127

[73] Wāqidi 2:756; Ibn Sa'd 2:39; Ibn Khayyāt 1:56; Suhayli 4:80; Kalā'i 1:176. In the year 8 A.H. the Prophet (s) dispatched a contingent to fight the Romans in the Battle of Muta. He made Zayd bin Haritha the commander saying that if he will martyred, the command would go Ja'far bin Abi Tālib and if he too was martyred then the command would go to 'Abdullah bin Rawāhah. This is exactly what happened. First Zayd was martyred, then Ja'far became the commander but after some time, he too was martyred, and finally 'Abdullah became the commander, but in the end he was also martyred. By this time the reinforcements had arrived under the command of Khālid bin Walid who then took the remaining troops back to Madina (Tr.)

[74] Wāqidi 3:996, 990; Ibn Hishām 4:161, 169; Ibn Sa'd 2:119, 120; Ibn Atheer 2:280

[75] In the year 9 A.H. the Prophet (s) was informed by the Nabtis that Roman forces had gathered in Syria, so he led an army of thirty thousand towards Tabuk. When they

arrived in Tabuk there was no sign of the Romans. Either the information they had been given was false or the Romans had fled after hearing about the approaching Muslim army. So in the end, the Prophet (s) was forced to return to Madina – for more details see Wāqidi, Futuh Shām (Tr.)

[76] Zuhri: 252; Wāqidi 1:344; Ibn Hanbal 3:351; Tabari 2:356; Kala'i 1:127

[77] Wāqidi 1:193; Ibn Hishām 3:342; Ibn Sa'd 2:25; 47, 118; Ibn Hazm 3:27

[78] Wāqidi 2:670, 673; Ibn Hishām 3:344, 347; Ibn Sa'd 2:2, 5, 18, 21, 39, 64

[79] Ibn Sa'd 2:6, 25, 44, 45, 53, 56, 77; Ibn Hazm: 201

[80] Zuhri: 71, 79, 84; Kala'i 1:122, 134; Ibn Katheer 4:264, 247, 344

[81] Wāqidi 1:2-8, 2:444; Ibn Hishām 3:70; Tabari 2:512; Kala'i 1:101

[82] Zuhri: 79; Wāqidi 2:974; Ibn Hishām 4:159; Ibn Sa'd 2:118; Qurtubi, *al-Jāmi' al-Ahkām al-Qur'ān* 14:133

[83] Wāqidi 2:796; Ibn Sa'd 2:2, 3; Kala'i 1:138

[84] Saff: 4; Wāqidi 2:825-828; Ibn Sa'd 2:1, 9, 98; General Akram, *Sayfullah Khālid bin Walid*: 114

[85] *Majmu'ah al-Ta'lif fi Akadimiyyah Frunza al-'Askariyya (al-Takteek)*: 103 onwards

[86] Ibn Sa'd 2:6, 26, 47, 66, 77, 93, 136; Tabari 2:421, 499

[87] Zuhri: 66; Wāqidi 1:22, 26, 32, 96, 100, 2:644, 666, 670, 680, 685, 700; Ibn Hishām 2:276, 313, 320, 3:344, 347, 358; Tabari 2:644, 3:10 & 16

[88] Ibn Sa'd 1:133-150; Tabari 2:298-387; Dhahabi 1:139, 146, 166, 168, 188

[89] Hajj: 39-41; al-Tawba: 11,191,193; al-Nisā: 75; Ibn Hishām: 147, 150; Suhayli 2:252

[90] Zuhri: 76, 79; Wāqidi 1:97, 2:440; Ibn Hishām 3:64, 224; Ibn Sa'd 2:25, 47; Ibn Hazm: 156, 158; Kala'i 1:104,114; Tabari 2:9

[91] Wāqidi 1:2-8; Ibn Sayyid al-Nās 1:122, 223

[92] Wāqidi 1:9-19; Ibn Hishām 2:241, 257; Ibn Sa'd 2:1-6; Ibn Khayyāt 1:15-16; Tabari 2:408-421; Ibn Sayyid al-Nās 1:224-241

[93] See Wāqidi 1:173, 147, 184; Ibn Hishām 5:54

[94] Wāqidi 1:181, 363, 2:552; Ibn Sa'd 2:20,40; Ibn Sayyid al-Nās 1:296, 2:48

[95] Wāqidi 1:121; Ibn Hishām 2:241; Ibn Khayyāt 1:15; Ibn Hazm: 100

[96] Wāqidi 1:9-19, 182, 193; Ibn Hishām 3:46, 49, 50; Yāqut Hamawi 1:152, 341

[97] After the Battle of Uhud, in order to uplift the spirits of the Muslim army and to show the enemy that they were prepared, the Prophet (s) immediately sent the same soldiers who had participated in Uhud to pursue the enemy, and he even prevented the recruitment of new forces and also took along the injured and wounded. This was very effective in strengthening the morale of the forces and putting fear in the enemy. (See: Ibn Hishām 3:128; Ibn Sa'd 2:34) (Tr.)

[98] Wāqidi 1:335; Kalā'i 1:105

[99] See: Zuhri: 72 onwards; Wāqidi 1:342; Ibn Hishām 3:192; Ibn Sa'd 2:35-47; Ibn Khayyāt 1:139; Tabari 2:546; Ibn Hazm: 178

[100] Ibn Hanbal 4:91, 262; Bukhāri (*al-Maghāzi* 29); Ibn Mājah (*al-Fitan* 35); Abu Dāwud (*al-Jihād* 156)

[101] Wāqidi 1:9, 27; Ibn Sa'd 2:7

[102] Wāqidi 1:182, 194, 195; Ibn Hishām 3:46; Ibn Sa'd 2:21,23,24; Ibn Khayyāt 1:27

[103] Wāqidi 1:182; Ibn Hishām 3:46; Ibn Sa'd 2:21; Ibn Khayyāt 1:27; Ibn Hazm: 152

[104] Seven days after the Battle of Badr, the Holy Prophet (s) got the news that a number of men from the Bani Saleem and the Ghatfān were gathering at the watering hole of the Bani Saleem which was known as 'Kadar' with the aim of launching an attack on the Muslims. He ordered a contingent to march there but when they arrived they found no one. There was only a young shepherd who was taken captive and then released. (Tr.)

[105] See: Wāqidi 1:193, 2:23; Suhayli 3:136; Yāqut Hamawi, *Mu'jam al-Buldān* 1:252

[106] Wāqidi 1:182, 194, 395, 404

[107] Wāqidi 1:196, 2:563

[108] Wāqidi 1:194; Ibn Sa'd 2:24

[109] *Ibid*. The Sariya of Bahrān was conducted in 3 A.H. but there was no combat involved. (Tr.)

[110] Ibn 'Abd al-Birr 4:1682; Ibn Atheer 5:219

[111] Wāqidi 1:342; Ibn Sa'd 2:35; Ibn Sayyid al-Nās 2:39; Yāqut Hamawi 4:374

[112] It was in the 4th year of Hijra when the Prophet (s) sent Abu Salamah al-Makhzumi along with 125 men to the tribes of Bani Asad. They travelled by night and would hide during the day in order to conduct the surprise attack. Three men were taken as captives, one was killed and the rest fled. (Tr.)

[113] Wāqidi 1:403; Ibn Sa'd 2:44

[114] Wāqidi 1:404; Ibn Hishām 3:302; Ibn Sa'd 2:45; Ibn Hazm: 203; Kalā'i 1:124; Ibn Sayyid al-Nās 2:91; Ibn Qayyim al-Jawzi 3:278

[115] Ibn Hazm: 203-204

[116] Ibn Hishām 3:302; Ibn Sa'd 2:45; al-Bakri, *Mu'jam Masta'jam* 4:1220; Yāqut Hamawi 5:118

[117] The Bani al-Mustalaq had united with other tribes in order to fight against the Holy Prophet (s). In Sha'bān, 6 A.H. a fierce battle took place in which ten infidels were killed and the rest were taken captive. A lot of booty was acquired by the Muslims, including two thousand camels and five thousand sheep. (Tr.)

[118] Wāqidi 1:194, 338, 391, 402

[119] Wāqidi 1:396; Ibn Sa'd 2:53; Kalā'i 1:123; Ibn Sayyid al-Nās 2:106; Ibn Katheer 4:246; 'Azmi: 230; Miksha: 118

[120] Ibn Hishām 3:64; Ibn Sa'd 2:25; Tabari 2:268; Polātof, *al-Mufājāt al-Taktikiyya*: 5

[121] Ibn Hanbal 4:262; Bukhāri (al-Maghāzi 29); Kalā'i 1:114

[122] Wāqidi 2:796; Ibn Sa'd 2:24; Tabari 3:75; Ibn Sayyid al-Nās 1:304; Ibn Qayyim al-Jawzi 2:299; *'Azmi, Dirāsāt fi Harb al-Khātifah*: 234

[123] Zuhri: 62,76,92, 106, 111; Azraqi, *Akhbār Makkah*:4, 198; Yāqut Hamawi, *Mu'jam al-Buldān* 5:83; Jawād 'Ali 1:196, 221; *Majmu'ah al-Ta'lif fi Akadimiyyah Frunza al-'Askariyya* (*al-Takteek*): 335; Miksha, *al-Harb al-Khātifah*: 118

[124] Mishān, *Tārikh al-Jaysh al-Aālmāni*: 547; 'Azmi: 9, 88

[125] Miksha, *al-Harb al-Khātifah*: 60, 65, 82

[126] Liwā' Hamawi, *Matālib al-Harb al-Haditha*: 76 onwards; 'Azmi: 233

[127] Zuhri: 86; Wāqidi 2:510, 522, 574, 637, 642, 650; Ibn Hishām 4:42, 63

[128] Wāqidi 3:889, 893; Ibn Hishām 4:83

[129] Dhahabi 1:267

[130] Ibn Sa'd 2:109

[131] Wāqidi 3:903

[132] Ibn Katheer 4:237

[133] Ibn Hishām 4:85

[134] Kalā'i 1:143

[135] *Majmu'ah al-Ta'lif fi Akadimiyyah Frunza al-'Askariyya – al-Takteek*: 437; Mujmu'ah Muhādharaat alqayt fi al-Akadimiyyah al-'Askariyyah al-'Ulyā fi al-Jumhuriyyah al-'Arabiyyah al-Suriyyah, Mawri Bek; *Ghāyat al-Aāmāl fi Fanni al-Harb wal-Qitāl* 2:50

[136] Wāqidi 1:181; Ibn Khayyāt 1:128; Tabari 2:483; Suhayli 3:136; Ibn Sayyid al-Nās 1:296

[137] These days pursuing the enemies is considered 'taking advantage of the victory' to finish off the enemy completely. (Tr.)

[138] Wāqidi: 395; Ibn Hishām 3:231; Ibn Sa'd 2:43; Muslim 2:142 (Ghazwat Dhāt al-Ruqā' 50); Tabari 2:556; Ibn Hazm: 182; Kalā'i 1:112; Ibn Sayyid al-Nās 2:52; Ibn Qayyim 2:275

[139] Wāqidi 2:537; Ibn Hishām 3:293; Ibn Sa'd 2:58; Ibn Khayyāt 1:43; Tabari 2:601; Ibn Hazm: 201; Kalā'i 1:123; Ibn Sayyid al-Nās 2:84; Ibn Qayyim 2:294

[140] Wāqidi 2:546, 547; Ibn Sa'd 2:58; Hamawi 4:321; Elward (Monister), Risālah fi Fann al-Harb: 74

[141] Wāqidi 2:546; Ibn Sayyid al-Nās 2:39, 103; Ibn Sa'd 2:35

[142] Ibn Sa'd 2:35

[143] Zuhri: 151; Wāqidi 3:117; Ibn Hishām 4:191; Ibn Sa'd 1:136; Tabari 3:184; Ibn 'Abd Rabbih 1:99; Ibn Sayyid al-Nās 2:281

[144] Wāqidi 3:117; Ibn Sa'd 2:56, 61, 62, 65, 85; Ibn Katheer 4:61

[145] Wāqidi 1:195; Ibn Hishām 3:50; Ibn Sa'd 2:24; Ibn Sayyid al-Nās 1:304

[146] Wāqidi 1:182, 404; Ibn Hishām 3:46, 302; Ibn Sa'd 2:21, 45; Ibn Hazm: 152; Kalā'i 1:124; Ibn Sayyid al-Nās 1:94; Ibn Katheer 3: 278, 344

[147] Wāqidi 2:496, 562, 633, 3:117; Ibn Hishām 3:244, 342, 4:291; Ibn Sa'd 2:53, 65, 77, 281; Muslim: 1357; Tabari 2:181, 3:9; Ibn Hazm: 18; Ibn Sayyid al-Nās 2:68,

109, 130; Ibn Qayyim al-Jawzi 2:299; Ibn Katheer 3:206, 4:116; Polātof, *al-Mufājāt al-Taktikiyyah*: 13, 27, 37

[148] In the 4th year of Hijra, after the Battle of Bani Nadheer, the Prophet (s) was informed that the Bani Muhārib and the Bani Tha'labah from the tribe of Ghatfān had started gathering in Dhāt al-Ruqā' and were preparing to launch and assault on the Muslims. The Prophet (s) made Abu Dharr his deputy in Madina and led the Muslim army until the Valley of Nakhla and it was here that he faced the large army from the tribe of Ghatfān, but no war took place. In this battle, the moment the Prophet got the information (about the enemy troops), he quickly proceeded towards them before they could get the opportunity to launch an attack. (See: Ibn Hishām 3:214; Ibn Sa'd 2:61) (Tr.)

[149] Wāqidi 1:395; Ibn Hishām 3:213; Tabari 2:55

[150] Wāqidi 2:652; Ibn Hishām 3:344; Muslim 3:1361; Ibn Qutayba, 'Uyun al-Akhbār 2:114; Ibn 'Abd Rabbih 1:122; Ibn Qayyim al-Jawzi 2:292

[151] Wāqidi 2:670; Nādhif, al-Tāj 4:422

[152] Wāqidi 2:652; Ibn Hishām 3:344

[153] Wāqidi 3:117; Muslim 3:1357

[154] Wāqidi 3:1117, 1122; Ibn Katheer 3:261

[155] Shaybāni, Sharh Kitāb al-Sayr al-Kabir 1:119 onwards; Ibn 'Abd Rabbih 1:122 onwards; Majmu'ah Muhādharāt Alqaytu fi Akādimiyya al-'Ulyā fi al-Jumhuriyyah al-'Arabiyyah al-Suriyya

[156] Shaybāni 1:119; Nāsif, *al-Tāj* 4:372

[157] Wāqidi 1:53; Ibn Sa'd 2:9; Muslim (*al-Birr*); Tirmidhi (*al-Birr*)

[158] Ibn 'Abd al-Birr 3:1377; Ibn Atheer 4:330; Ibn Hajar 6:63

[159] Ibn Is'hāq: 319; Ibn Katheer: 704

[160] Bukhāri (*al-Jihād*); Muslim (*al-Jihād*); and see also the chapters on Jihād in Sunan Abi Dāwud, Ibn Mājah and Tirmidhi, and the use of trickery and deception by Na'im bin Mas'ud against the enemy tribes and bringing about divisions among them in the Battle of Khandaq to such an extent that they were unable to attain their objectives and lost all hope, forcing them to turn back. (Tr.)

[161] Bukhāri (*al-Jihād, Maghāzi*); Muslim (*Tawba*)

[162] Wāqidi 2:651, 652; Ibn Hishām 3:344

[163] Wāqidi 2:796; Ibn Sa'd 2:96. When the Prophet set out for the Conquest of Makkah, he did not let anyone know that his intention was to conquer Makkah and even sent a contingent towards another place in order to deceive the enemy (see: Ibn Sa'd 2:296) (Tr.)

[164] Wāqidi 2:796; Ibn Sa'd 2:96; Ibn Sayyid al-Nās 2:161

[165] Wāqidi 2:815; Ibn Hishām 4:39

[166] Wāqidi 2:764; Ibn Hishām 4:21; Kalā'i 1:136

[167] Wāqidi 1:11, 12, 56; Ibn Hishām 2:245, 248, 251; Ibn Sa'd 1:1; Tabari 2:259; Ibn Hazm 100-102; Ibn Sayyid al-Nās 1:226

[168] Wāqidi 1:56, 2:583; Ibn Hishām 4:85; Ibn Sa'd 2:2; Ibn Qutaybah 2:114; Tabari 2:853; Kalā'i 1:143; al-Dhahabi, *Tārikh al-Islām* 1:167

[169] Wāqidi 3:903; Ibn Hishām 3:69; Tabari 2:507 onwards; Ibn Hazm: 239

[170] Wāqidi 1:395; Ibn Hishām 3:213; Ibn Sa'd 3:43; Ibn Sayyid al-Nās 2:79, 104, 147

[171] Wāqidi 1:54; Ibn Sayyid al-Nās 1:25; Ibn Katheer 4:237

[172] Wāqidi 2:496, 633; Ibn Hishām 3:244, 342; Ibn Hazm: 18

[173] Wāqidi 2:499; Kalā'i 1:111; Ibn Sayyid al-Nās 2:201

[174] Unfortunately the author has not given any reference for this (Tr.)

[175] Wāqidi 1:13, 343, 2:35; Ibn Sa'd 2:41; Ibn Sayyid al-Nās 2:50

[176] Wāqidi 1:9; Ibn Hishām 3:68; Ibn Sa'd 1:7, 47

[177] Wāqidi 1:81 onwards, 3:901 onwards; Ibn Sa'd 1:10 onwards, 2:109 onwards

[178] Wāqidi 2:496, 499; Ibn Hishām 3:244 onwards; Ibn Sa'd 2:53 onwards

[179] Ibn Hazm: 200; Suhayli 3:305; Kalā'i 1:122; Ibn Sayyid al-Nās 2:83

[180] Ibn Sa'd 2:3, 19, 20, 23, 25, 40, 43, 44, 53, 77; Tabari 2:408, 487, 583 onwards

[181] The Prophet (s) fought many battles against individual Jewish tribes and managed to defeat them and curtail their evil from Madina. The battles of Bani Nadhir, Bani Qaynuqā', Khaybar and Bani Quraydha are examples of these. The Prophet would always try to keep these tribes divided and attack them separately, not allowing them to come to the aid of one another (Tr.)

182 Ibn Sa'd 2:19, 40, 53, 77; Tabari 2:479, 581, 3:9, 234; Ibn Hazm: 239 onwards

183 *Majmu'ah al-Ta'lif fi Akadimiyyah Frunza al-'Askariyya – al-Takteek*: 400 onwards; Miksha, *al-Harb al-Khātifah*: 237, 239; 'Azmi, *Dirāsāt fi Harb al-Khātifah*: 230 onwards; General Fuller, *Idārat al-Harb*: 70

184 Ibn Hanbal 4:23; Bukhāri 5:27, 71, 74; Abu Dāwud 3:28; Tirmidhi (al-Adab 78)

185 Zuhri: 71, 79, 84; Ibn Sa'd 1:2, 4:19, 23, 34, 40, 56, 77, 108, 118

186 Ibn Hishām 2:245, 4:260, 290; Ibn Sa'd 1:2, 19, 35, 56, 85, 94, 117, 136

187 One of the most important facets of the military forces is their training and exercise which is one of the surest ways to achieve success in war. By continuously sending contingents to different battle zones, the Prophet (s) prepared and trained them in new strategies and maneuvers. (Tr.)

188 Zuhri: 79, 151; Wāqidi 1:121, 2:496, 537, 3:1117, 1122; Ibn Hishām 2:251, 3:224, 4:291; Ibn Sa'd 2:1, 53, 58, 186; Ibn Khayyāt 1:43; Tabari 2:181, 601, 3:184; Ibn Qayyim al-Jawzi 2:291, 294

189 Wāqidi 2: 445, 464, 493; Ibn Hishām 2:230, 360; Tabari 1:511, 568; Ibn Hazm: 16; Kalā'i 1:15

190 Ibn Sa'd 2:21, 35, 43, 62, 95; Ibn Sayyid al-Nās 1:294m 203, 2:38, 91, 158, 105; Ibn Atheer: 174, 192, 232

191 Wāqidi 1:177, 496, 499; Ibn Qutayba 2:111; Kalā'i 1:116; Ibn Atheer 2:217; Nāsif 4:422

192 Wāqidi 1:190, 196, 198; Ibn Hishām 1:264, 265, 271; Ibn Sa'd 2:7, 9, 21, 43; Ibn Sayyid al-Nās 1:251; Ibn Atheer 2:188

193 Zuhri: 63; Wāqidi 1:19, 295, 406, 2:534, 550, 640, 802, 808; Ibn Hishām 4:271; Ibn Sayyid al-Nās 2:167

194 Ibn Is'hāq: 328; Ibn Hishām 3:71; Tabari 2:507

195 Wāqidi 3:902, 903; Ibn Hishām 4:85; Ibn Sa'd 2:109; Tabari 3:75; Ibn Hazm: 239; Kalā'i 1:143; Ibn Sayyid al-Nās 2:193

196 Wāqidi 1:173, 184, 391; Ibn Sa'd 1:18, 19, 20

197 Wāqidi 2:445, 492; Ibn Hishām 2:220, 231, 265; Ibn Sa'd 2:44, 56, 64, 86, 136; Tabari 2:566

[198] Wāqidi 1:342; Ibn Sa'd 2:21,35,43,62, 95; Ibn Sayyid al-Nās 2:39

[199] Wāqidi 1:396, Ibn Sa'd 2:53; Kalā'i 1:123; Ibn Sayyid al-Nās 2:39

[200] Wāqidi 1:395; Ibn Hishām 3:213; Ibn Sa'd 2:43; Tabari 2:556; Kalā'i 1:113; Ibn Sayyid al-Nās 2:39, 79, 102, 145, 146

[201] *Majmu'ah min al-Mu'allifeen al-'Askariyyeen* 1:581 onwards

[202] See Q2:74 and Q2:154; Q3:157; Q4:36, Q4:74; Q9:111; Q22:39, Q22:58; Bukhāri (*al-Jihād, al-Maghāzi*); Muslim (*al-Amārah, al-Eimān*); Ibn Mājah (*al-Jihād*); Tirmidhi (*al-Eimān*); and see al-Sa'eed, *Fusul fi 'Ilm al-Nafs al-Askari*: 94 onwards

[203] Q8:72, Q8:88; Q9:41, Q9:79; Ibn Is'hāq: 328; Muslim (*al-Jihād, al-Maghāzi, al-Riqāq, al-Amārah*); Abu Dāwud (*al-Jihād*); Nasā'i (*al-Zakāt*)

[204] Wāqidi 1:211, 360; Ibn Hishām 3:181; Muslim (al-Eimān 8)

[205] Zuhri: 87; Wāqidi 2:479, 3:1123; Ibn Hishām 4:46; Ibn Sa'd 2:28, 49, 79, 97, 137; al-Sa'eed: 26 onwards

[206] Q8:60; Bukhāri (*al-Jihād* 38); Ibn Mājah (*al-Jihād*: 3, 5, 71); Abu Dāwud (*al-Jihād* 17); Ibn Sa'd 2:119

[207] Zuhri: 86, 87; Wāqidi 2:780 onwards; Ibn Hishām 4:31, 46; Ibn Qayyim al-Jawzi 2:386, 390; al-Sa'eed, *Shakhsiyyah al-'Askariyyah*: 12 onwards

[208] Bukhāri (*al-Jihād* 122); Muslim (*al-Masājid* 3); Tirmidhi (*al-Seerah*); al-Sa'eed: 99 onwards

[209] Q2:190-192, Q2:246; Q4:75, Q4:90; Q22:39; Suyuti al-Rahibāni, *Matālib al-Nuhā fi Sharh Ghāyat al-Muntahā* 2:50 onwards

[210] Wāqidi 3:990-996; Ibn Hishām 4:161; Tabari 3:101; Kalā'i 1:155; Haydarābādi, *Majmu'at al-Wathā'iq al-Siyāsiyyah lil 'Ahd al-Nabawi wal-Khilāfat al-Rāshidah*: 15-20

[211] Bukhāri (*al-Adab* 127); Muslim (*al-Eimān* 93, *al-Amārah* 47, *al-Jihād* 133, *al-Birr* 68); Nasā'I (*al-Qisāmah* 10-14); Ibn Sayyid al-Nās 1:197-199

[212] Wāqidi 1:13, 534, 2:757, 868, 3:1117; Muslim 3:1357; Kalā'i 1:161

[213] Zuhri: 88; Ibn Hishām 1:205-245; Tabari 3:61; Ibn Qayyim al-Jawzi 1:51 onwards

[214] Zuhri: 52; Ibn Hishām 3:322; Ibn Sa'd 2:41, 70; Tabari 2:552, 573, 575; Ibn Hazm: 208; al-Zahili, *Athār al-Harb*: 149

[215] Q3: 19, 83, 85; Q5:3; Q9:33, 36; Q48:28; Q61:9; Zuhri: 55; Bukhāri (*al-Diyāt* 6, al-'Ilm 29); Muslim (*al-Amārah* 173); Tirmidhi (Tafseer Surah 33; *al-Manāqib* 32); Ibn Mājah (*al-Rahun* 5, *al-Fitan* 33, al-Talāq 27); Abu Dāwud (*al-Amārah* 26, *al-Malāhim* 14)

[216] Q2:115; Q5:67; Q6:19; Q55:2; Q15:94; Wāqidi 1:347; Ibn Hishām 3:178, 194; Bukhāri (*al-'Ilm* 1:23, 24, 34, 40, 42) Ibn Mājah (*al-Zuhd, al-Muqaddimah*); Tirmidhi (*al-Zuhd*)

[217] Q2:121; Q3:173; Q5:5; Q15:5; Q16: 106; Q23:1; Q49:11; Wāqidi 2:215, 216; Bukhāri (*Maghāzi* 46, *al-Adab* 42); Muslim (*Fadhā'il al-Sahāba* 161); Ibn Mājah (*al-Fitan* 23); Nasāi (*al-Talāq*)

[218] Q9:129; Q33:6, 21; Q48:29; Q68:4; Zuhri: 92; Wāqidi 1:74 onwards; Bukhāri (*al-Kifāyah* 5); Muslim (*al-Farāidh* 16); Tirmidhi (Tafseer Surah 44); Nasāi (*al-Eidayn* 22); Tabari 3:75

[219] Majmu'ah min al-Mu'allifeen al-'Askariyyeen 1:767; Harawi: 111 onwards; al-Sa'eed, *Fusul fi 'Ilm al-Nafs al-Askari*: 26

[220] Bukhāri (al-Salāh 438)

[221] Ibn Hishām 3:344

[222] Wāqidi 2:670

[223] Wāqidi 2:666; Ibn Katheer 4:198

[224] Wāqidi 2:670

[225] Wāqidi 1:9; Ibn Hishām 2:245; Ibn Sa'd 2:2

[226] Wāqidi 1:11; Ibn Hishām 2:241; Ibn Sa'd 2:3; Ibn Khayyāt, *Tārikh* 1:7; Ibn Hazm: 100; Ibn Sayyid al-Nās 1:224

[227] Wāqidi 1:182, 395; Ibn Hishām 3:46, 213; Ibn Sa'd 2:21, 43; Ibn Khayyāt 1:27; Tabari 2:556; Ibn Hazm: 152, 182; Kalā'i 1:111

[228] Ibn Hishām 4:169, 205-245; Ibn Sa'd 2:120

[229] Wāqidi 2:780, 3:885; Ibn Hishām 4:31, 80; Ibn Sa'd 2:96, 108; Ibn Hazm: 223, 236, 187; Ibn Qayyim 2:384, 438

[230] Wāqidi 3:1091; Ibn Sa'd 2:44; Suhayli 4:196

[231] Q 59:2; Tabari 2:557; Ibn Katheer 4:76

232 Wāqidi 2:535; Ibn Hishām 3:292; Ibn Sa'd 2:65; ibn Hazm: 200; Ibn Atheer 2:188

233 Ibn Sayyid al-Nās 2:109; Ibn Atheer 4:16; Ibn Qayyim 2:299; ibn Hajar 4:299; Wāqidi 2:562; Ibn Sa'd 2:65; Ibn 'Abd al-Birr 3:1089

234 Wāqidi 2:563; Ibn Sa'd 2:65

235 Wāqidi 2:563

236 Wāqidi 2:727; Ibn Sa'd 2:87; Ibn 'Abd al-Birr 1:171; Ibn Atheer 2:226; Ibn Sayyid al-Nās 2:147; Ibn Qayyim 2:361

237 Ibn 'Abd al-Birr 3:1249; Ibn Atheer 4:166

238 Wāqidi 2:729

239 Zuhri: 57; Wāqidi 2:627, 628; Ibn 'Abd al-Birr 4:1612; Suhayli 4:37; Ibn Atheer 3:360; Ibn Qayyim 2:308

240 Ibn Hishām 4:254, 255; Ibn Katheer 2:262

241 Wāqidi 1:338; Ibn 'Abd al-Birr 3:1314; Ibn Atheer 4:390

242 Ibn 'Abd al-Birr: 1508; Ibn Sayyid al-Nās 3:62; Ibn Atheer 5:33; ibn Qayyim 2:292. Na'im was successful in causing a rift between the Quraysh and the Jews and without the help of the Jews the siege of Madina lost its strength and the Quraysh were forced to return to Makkah without accomplishing their objective (Tr.)

243 Wāqidi 1:9-19; Ibn Sa'd 2:2-5; Kalā'i :58; Ibn Sayyid al-Nās 1:224, 227

244 Zuhri: 106; Wāqidi 3:989; Ibn Hishām 4:159; Ibn Sa'd 2:118; Ibn Khayyāt 1:64; Tabari 3:10; Ibn 'Asākir, *Tārikh* 1:107; Ibn Qayyim 3:3

245 Wāqidi 2:536; Ibn Hishām 3:293; Ibn Sa'd 2:57; Kalā'i 1:122; ibn Sayyid al-Nās 2:83

246 Bukhāri (*al-Jihād – al-Khawf, al-Adab, al-Dhabā'ih*); Ibn Mājah (*al-Jihād, al-Iqāmah*); Abu Dāwud (*al-jihād, al-Safar, al-Sawm*); Muslim (*al-Imārah, al-Musāfirin, al-Siyām*); al-Nasā'i (*al-Isti'ārah, al-Khawf, al-Jihād*)

247 Wāqidi 1:182, 196, 406, 2:460; Abu Dāwud (*al-Jihād* 100)

248 Q3:123

249 Wāqidi 2:563, 666, 7:29; Ibn Hishām 2:285, 3:243; Ibn Sa'd 2:17

250 Wāqidi 2:563, 729; Ibn Katheer 4:198

251 Wāqidi 1:9, 99; Ibn Sa'd 2:1, 6; Tabari 2:546-565; ibn Hazm: 175; Kalā'i al-Balansi 1:104, 105; Ibn Sayyid al-Nās 1:296, 2:48, 105, 110, 207

252 Wāqidi 1:56, 177, 368, 2:499; Ibn Hishām 3:244; Ibn Sa'd 2:47, 48; Tabari 2:583, 3:9, 75; Ibn Hazm: 239; Dhahabi, *Tārikh al-Islām* 1:267

253 Wāqidi 1:335

254 *Ibid.* 1:338

255 Ibn Hishām 3:107; Kalā'i 1:105; Ibn Katheer 4:49

256 Ibn Hanbal 1:229; Bukhāri (al-Hajj 80). The Prophet (s) did this in order to frighten the enemy and show the strength of the Muslims (Tr.)

257 Zuhri: 66; Wāqidi 1:96; Ibn Hishām 4:56, 69; Tabari 2:466, 3:61; Kalā'i 1:139

258 Wāqidi 1:199, 334, 464; Ibn Hishām 2:64, 128, 3:232; Ibn Sa'd 2:25, 34; Tabari 3:9, 29, 2:586; Ibn Hazm: 156; Kalā'i 1:104 onwards

259 Tabari 3:26, 70; Suhayli 3:168

260 Wāqidi 2:800, 819; Ibn Hishām 4:42; Ibn Sa'd 1:147; Ibn Atheer 2:303

261 Abu Tālib Ansāri, *al-Siyāsah fi 'Ilm al-Firāsah*: 41; Hakam, *al-Firāsah*: 16

262 Rāzi: 23; Abu Tālib Ansāri: 30

263 Rāzi: 2 onwards; Ibn 'Abd Rabbih 2:104; Nuwayri, Nihāyat al-Urub 2:111

264 Ibn 'Abd Rabbih 6:108; Abu Tālib Ansāri: 21

265 Rāzi: 2; Nuwayri 2:102; Abu Tālib Ansāri: 20 onwards

266 Al-Balāyā, *al-Mujaz fi Mabādi al-Tashrih wal-Gharā'iz al-Bashariyyah*: 16 onwards; Mahmud al-'Aqqād, *'Abqariyyat al-Islāmiyyah*: 483; Boudley, *Hayātu Muhammad*: 53

267 Ibn Hishām 1:167; Ibn Sa'd 1:287 onwards; Ibn Qutaybah 1:150; Tabari 1:39; Dhahabi 1:18 onwards

268 Q93:6; Ibn Hishām 1:166, 177

269 Ibn Hishām 1:177; Ibn Sa'd 1:73; Ibn Sayyid al-Nās 1:37; Dhahabi 1:35; Nuwayri, *Nihāyat al-Urub* 16:87

270 Q11:49; Q46:35; Q52:48; Q76:24; Ibn Hishām 1:380 onwards

271 Ibn Hishām 4:54; Bukhāri (*al-Jihād* 102); Muslim (*al-Amārah* 117); Ibn Mājah (*al-Iqāmah* 25, 14, *al-Zuhd* 28); See also Q2:21; Q4:170; Q10:108; Q35:5

[272] Q26:214; Ibn Hishām 1:280; Ibn Sa'd 1:132; Ibn Atheer 2:60

[273] Ibn Hishām 2:63, 73, 86, 4:205 onwards; Ibn Sa'd 1:45, 2:39; Ibn Atheer 2:94; Nuwayri 16:302 onwards

[274] Q6:19; Ibn Hanbal 5:257; Abu Dāwud (Sunan 10); ibn Atheer: 210

[275] Q17:70; Q49:13; Ibn Hanbal 2:277; Abu Dāwud (al-Adab 101)

[276] Bukhāri (al-Fitan 1); Muslim (32, 40); Ibn Mājah (al-Akhām 23); Tirmidhi (al-Qiyāmah 3); Tabari 3:49

[277] Wāqidi 1:7; Ibn Sa'd 2:116; Ibn 'Abd al-Barr 3:1249

[278] Wāqidi 2:756; Ibn Katheer 2:238, 4:248, 253

[279] Ibn Hanbal 3:112; Muslim (al-Fadhā'il 63); Abu Dāwud (al-Adab 58); Tirmidhi (al-Birr 12, 15)

[280] Muslim (al-Fadhā'il 63); Abu Dāwud (al-Adab 58); Tirmidhi (al-Birr 12,15)

[281] Bukhāri (al-Adab 89); Tirmidhi (al-Birr 75)

[282] Bukhāri (al-Adhān 45); Ibn Mājah (al-Manāsik 43); Abu Dāwud (al-Sawm 3, 35, 58, al-Jihād 30)

[283] Ibn Hanbal 4:24, 3:425; Dārimi (al-Siyar 25); Q93:9; Ibn Mājah (al-Adab 6, 12)

[284] Dārimi (al-Riqāq 118); Tirmidhi (al-Manāqib 46, al-Qiyāmah 48); Sanā'i (al-Janā'iz 43)

[285] Bukhāri (al-'Itq 15, al-Kaffarāt 6, al-Jihād 145); Muslim (al-'Itq 22, 23); Ibn Mājah (al-Adab)

[286] Bukhāri (al-Adab 37, Bad' al-Khalq 16, al-Hanbalā' 45, al-Madina 4, al-Dhabā'ih 4)

[287] Bukhāri (al-Adhān 90, Bad' al-Khalq 16); Muslim (al-Birr 135); Ibn Mājah (al-Zuhd 30)

[288] *Ibid.*

[289] Ibn Sa'd 1:174; Tabari 3:176; Dhahabi 1:291

[290] Ibn Sa'd 1:174; Tabari 3:176; Ibn Sayyid al-Nās 2:318; Dhahabi 1:291

[291] Dhahabi 1:291

[292] Wāqidi 1:391, 2:560; Ibn Hishām 3:287; Ibn Sa'd 2:56; Ibn Atheer 2:209

293 Shaybāni, *Sharh al-Siyar al-Kabeer* 1:38, 79; Bukhāri (al-Adhān 17, al-Adab 27, 38); Muslim (al-Qadr 8); Abu Dāwud (al-Eimān 21, al-Salāh 167); Tirmidhi (al-Qiyāmah 48); Sanā'i (al-Adhān 8)

294 Shaybāni 1:42; Wāqidi 2:534, 778; Ibn Hanbal 1:224, 2:91, 3:435, 4:24; Ibn Mājah (al-Jihād 30); Abu Dāwud (al-Jihād 82)

295 Ibn Hanbal 3:403; Muslim (al-Bill 117); Abu Dāwud (al-Amārah 33)

296 Ibn Hanbal 4:264; Bukhāri (al-Madhālim 30, al-Dhabā'ih 25, al-Maghāzi 36); Abu Dāwud (al-Jihād 110, al-Hudud 3)

297 Muslim 3:1386

298 Ibn Hishām 4:287 onwards; Ibn 'Abd al-Barr 1:215; Ibn Atheer 1:247

299 Wāqidi 1:7; Ibn Sa'd 2:116; Ibn Sayyid al-Nās 2:203

300 Q4:94; Q5:16; Q6:54; Q8:61; Bukhāri (a;-Iqāmah 1, al-Salāh 56); Muslim (al-'Itq 16)

301 Wāqidi 3:1117; Ibn Hishām 2:241, 245, 251; Ibn Sa'd 2:6; Ibn Hazm: 235

302 Ibn Hishām 4:454; Ibn Sa'd 1:152; Tabari: 2:644 onwards; Ibn Atheer 4:210 onwards

303 Bukhāri (al-Isti'dhān 9, al-Ashribah 28); Muslim (al-Adab 37, al-Libās 12); Ibn Mājah (al-Adab 13, 18); Abu Dāwud (al-Adab 91); Tirmidhi (al-Isti'dhān 2, 11); Sanā'i (al-Tatbiq 100)

304 Shaybāni 1:60, 156; Bukhāri (al-'Itq 17, al-Nikāh 90, al-Adhan 54); Muslim (al-Amārah 20); Abu Dāwud (al-Imārah 504); Tirmidhi (al-Fitan 77); Nasāi (al-Amārah 3, 5, 11)

305 Shaybāni 1:61; Zuhri: 150; Bukhāri (al-Ahkām 22, al-Jihād 164, al-Maghāzi 60); Muslim (al-Masājid 279, 291); Q2:261; Q8:28, 60, 65; Ibn Hanbal 1:46, 229, 3:475, 4:23; Dārimi (al-Jihād 14); Ibn Mājah (al-Jihād 19); Abu Dāwud (al-Jihād 14, 23); Nasāi (al-Khāyl 8); As the Prophet (s) appointed three commanders in the Battle of Muta. (Tr.)

306 Wāqidi 2:800, 801, 812, 819, 820; Ibn Hishām 2:42; Haydarābādi: 15-21

[307] Q3:132; Q4:13, 59, 69, 80; Q5:92; Q8:1, 20, 46; Q24: 54, 56; Zuhri: 54; Bukhāri (al-Ahkām 4); Ibn Mājah (al-Muqaddimah 6); Abu Dāwud (al-Imārah 9, al-Yabu' 31); Nasāi (al-Eimān 45, al-Bay'ah 27)

[308] Wāqidi 1:7 onwards; Ibn Sa'd 1:147; Suhayli 2:525; Ibn Atheer 3:303; Haydarābadi :15-21

[309] Bukhāri (Manāqib al-Ansār 33, Fadhā'il al-Sahāba 27, al-Adab 39); Ibn Mājah (al-Jihād 19, 25, al-Muqaddimah 17); Tirmidhi (al-'Ilm 19, al-Birr 71); Nasā'I (al-Tatbiq 100)

[310] Bukhāri (al-Jihād 110, al-Maghāzi 35, al-Ahkām 43); Muslim (al-Amārah 80-81); Tirmidhi (al-Siyar 34)

[311] Zuhri: 150; Wāqidi 2:142; Ibn Hishām 4:15; Ibn Sa'd 2:92; Tabari 3:36; Muslim 4:1884; Ibn 'Asākir, *Tārikh Dimishq* 1:92

[312] Wāqidi 2:443; Ibn Sa'd 2:47, 48; Bukhāri (al-Jihād 68, al-Ahkām 49, al-Janā'iz 39); Muslim (al-Amārah 89); Ibn Mājah (al-Jihād 43)

[313] Q9:20, 41, 88; Q8:74; Q61:11; Bukhāri (al-Riqāq 34, al-Jihād 13, 31, al-Adab 100, al-Maghāzi 53); Muslim (al-Amārah 116); Abu Dāwud (al-jihād 12); Tirmidhi (Fadhā'il al-Jihād 22); Sanā'i: 20, 45

[314] Zuhri: 150; Wāqidi 1:21, 2:43; Ibn Hishām 4:272; Ibn Sa'd 2:47, 48

[315] See how the stance of the army changed from defensive to offensive (Ibn Hishām 3:266) and how it transformed from internal battles to external wars, like the Battle of Tabuk (al-Zuhri: 106 onwards; Wāqidi 3:989 onwards). And see the transformation of the army after the passing away of the Holy Prophet (s) (Tārikh Ibn Khayyāt 1:103; Ibn Atheer 2:342, 349, 372; Ibn Katheer 6:316)

CHAPTER THREE
STAFF HEADQUARTERS

The [Army] Staff Headquarters was responsible for organizing the affairs pertaining to recruitment of soldiers and encouraging them [to join the army], as well as personal matters [of the individual soldiers] like strengthening the spirit of the combatants etc. The following departments fell under their command:

1. The Department of Planning and Scheduling

This is the department that is responsible for:
  a)   Planning the overall policy
  b)   Drawing out maps for war
  c)   Finding out the number of combatants in the army (and)
  d)   Their weaponry
  e)   Instituting regulations and rules of military service
  f)   Preparing the senior commanders
  g)   Establishing the procedure of selection[1]
Now we will explain each of the above in turn.

a)   Planning the policy for the participation of the Ansār in battle
The Ansār were obliged by their agreement in the Pledge of 'Aqaba to protect the Holy Prophet (s) inside Madina.[2] This had made the Quraysh angry and infuriated them so they began making preparations quickly to wage war on those who had granted refuge to and helped the Muhājirin.[3] In the beginning, the Muhājirin took up the flag of charge and attack on their shoulders[4] and carried out the first military mission without the participation of a single person from the Ansār, under the command of Hamza ibn 'Abd al-Muttalib, the Master of the Martyrs ('a),[5] and in this way numerous consecutive missions and minor battles were fought by the Muhājirin themselves until the Battle of Badr.[6] After the Prophet (s) informed the Ansār about the threat that they were all faced with, he sought their view about participation in war and assisting him inside and outside Madina. The Ansār were ready to cooperate and participate in battle and expressed their decision to fight alongside the Muhājirin with their own volition. In this way, they diverted from the Pledge of 'Aqabah and the allegiance of Wādi Dhafarān[7] and participated in the Battle of Badr and other battles alongside the Muhājirin.[8] From this time onwards, the Muslim army consisted of these two groups.

b) Methods of Negotiation
Negotiations with the enemy after the end of battle and the agreement that was reached between the two parties was, depending on the circumstances,

conducted by the supreme commander (s) who would take full control.[9] When the Jews sought negotiations, he (s) dealt harshly with them, to such an extent that he banished some of them from their lands[10] and after disarming them, he let their wives and children go,[11] however he ordered the killing of some others who has broken their covenant and had cooperated with the enemy.[12]

The Prophet (s) displayed forbearance and leniency with the Quraysh in the Treaty of Hudaybiyya.[13] He accepted their conditions and even accepted some of the conditions that his companions and commanders deemed to be against the interest of the Muslims,[14] and went ahead to sign the treaty.[15] In this way and in order to attain the actual goals, the Prophet (s) would obtain victory through harsh measures at certain times and through leniency and tolerance in other situations.[16]

c) Designing a Program in order to Know the Enemy

The Prophet (s) would, at the outset, study the enemy and ways of countering them. The Quraysh were people who had forced him to leave his home and were determined to fight against him uncompromisingly.[17] The Prophet (s) also began preparing forces and weapons in order to counter them[18] and faced them in a number of battles,[19] and in the end he eventually gained victory and they submitted to his wishes.

However, with regards to the Jews, when they showed their enmity by breaking the covenant [they had made with him][20] and took up arms against him, he was forced to fight them or banish them from their lands.[21] It was at this time [and for this reason] that the first battle against them took place.

With regards to the other Arab tribes, however, he only entered into battle against them when they were the instigators[22] or when they attempted to wage war against Madina and invade it with their armies.[23] Taking this into consideration, he only faced the enemy tribes and dealt with them the way they deserved to be dealt with.[24]

As for Rome, he (s) saw it as a grave threat in the way of the Islāmic Revolution, especially since they possessed vast resources and had a lot of political influence in the Arabian provinces.[25] Despite this, the Prophet (s) delayed military action against them until an appropriate time and enough preparations had been made to come face to face with the Roman army. For this reason, he did not enter into intense and decisive battles with them as he had done with his previous enemies [i.e. the Quraysh and the Jews], rather he launched minor assaults on them[26] and, in order to develop the Muslim army and increase their military might, he embarked on small battles with them.

d) Creating a Plan to Gain Control of the Most Important Routes and Courses

The most important routes and courses that the Holy Prophet (s) studied and planned on controlling were the 'coastal routes'[27] which would be a sure means of cutting off the primary reinforcements of the enemy, and he was successful in doing this.[28] Then he turned his attention to the 'eastern route'[29] that the Quraysh had begun using after the first route was blocked, and by taking control of this route also, he completed his siege of the enemy from all the directions. The Prophet (s) was victorious in all the battles that were subsequently fought in order to regain control of these routes.[30]

In the same way, the supreme commander successfully planned and took control of the 'northern route' of Arabian Peninsula – in the border of Syria[31] – and of Dumat al-Jundal,[32] because of their strategic locations militarily, politically and economically, for the war with the Romans.[33]

e) Appointing a Deputy in Madina

Whenever the Holy Prophet (s) went for any battle, he would always appoint a deputy and representative in Madina,[34] and he would change the appointee from battle to battle.[35] Sometimes two representatives would be selected[36] and each one of them would be given specific tasks. The functions of the Prophet's deputy would normally consist of leading the congregational prayers for those who remained behind and did not participate in battle for some valid excuse,[37] and protecting and safeguarding the status and respect of the members of the household of the Holy Prophet (s).[38] After the Conquest of Makkah, the Prophet (s) also appointed a deputy to manage the important affairs of that city.[39]

f) Reviewing of the Supreme Commander of the Army

The supreme commander would review the 'mobilization and stationing' of the army.[40] He would inspect the army[41] and arrange it for marching or battle. He studied their capability for war,[42] sent back the sick, young and weak,[43] lifted the spirits of those who fought in battle[44] and gave the necessary orders and instructions to the commanders (of the army).[45] If he sent them for a Sariya or a mission, like the Sariya of 'Abd al-Rahmān ibn 'Auf to Dumat al-Jundal, and his sending of Zayd bin Haritha for war with the Romans [in the Battle of Muta], he would personally bid them farewell and pray for their success.[46] When the army was getting organized, he would join them and take over the command himself.[47] The Prophet (s) would organize and arrange the forces for parades and processions, just as he had done before the Conquest of Makkah and during their entry into the city. In this organization, the 'cavaliers' would be in the fore and were made up of three groups. Then followed the units of the Muhājirin and Ansār and then came the units of the Ghaffār, Aslam, Bani 'Umar, Bani Ka'b,

Mazinah, Jahinah and Bani Hamzah. Is was after this that the Green Column was positioned.[48]

The manner of stationing of the forces was in such a way that the Bani Saleem were in front, the Jahinah were in the middle and the Green Column was placed at the back.[49] The course of the army's movement with this arrangement[50] in front of Abu Sufyān and other observers and the station of the supreme commander – which was located in the Green Column – was determined and the soldiers marched in front of them in this order.[51]

The carrying of flags[52] was in such a way that in every contingent and unit, a number of flags were hoisted and the main banner was with 'Ali ibn Abi Tālib ('a) at the central command post in the last unit. The parade and procession of the army was conducted in full military attire[53] in such a way that from the Green Column, nothing but the pupil of their eyes could be seen. The vanguard and the cavaliers marched in front.[54] The Banu Saleem were in the front-line with one thousand horsemen and the commander of the paraded columns was selected by the supreme commander.[55] Khālid bin Walid was chosen as the commander of three columns of the vanguard:

First: The column under the command of 'Abbās bin Maradās al-Salami
Second: The column under the command of Khafāf ibn Nudbah
Third: The column under the command of Hajjāj ibn 'Alāt
Then Zubayr ibn 'Awām was appointed as the commander of the column of the Muhājirin and Ansār and Abu Dharr al-Ghaffāri was made in charge of the column of the tribe of Ghaffār and others.

g) Placing the Capable Individuals in Appropriate Positions

Military skills and expertise in the Muslim army were numerous and varied,[56] like intelligence, combat on horseback, fighting on foot, archery etc. In order to assign posts for every responsibility conditions were placed that were different for every individual. The Holy Prophet (s) would assign the task of intelligence operations[57] to such an individual in whom the ability of protecting and hiding secrets was strong, who was well informed, trustworthy, patient and forbearing in [times of] pain, hunger and thirst, like 'Abdullah ibn Jahash, Habbāb ibn Mundhir, Zubayr ibn 'Awām, Hudhayfa ibn al-Yamān and others.
In the same way, he would appoint a commander of a contingent[58] who was aware about the topography of the land and the enemy that he would face, like Zayd ibn Hāritha, 'Amr ibn 'Aās, Khālid ibn Walid and others.

As for the flag-bearer,[59] a steadfast and courageous person was chosen such as 'Ali ibn Abi Tālib, Hamza ibn 'Abd al-Muttalib and Mus'ab ibn 'Umayr. From

106

the archers[60] also, someone highly skilled like Sa'd ibn Abi Waqqās was selected. The [head] swordsman[61] was someone who used his sword well in the thick of war. The [head] horseman[62] was one who fought steadily and unfalteringly on the horse, like Khālid bin Walid.

These individuals and others would be given charge of these responsibilities without any regard for their relationship[63] [to the Prophet (s)]. The supreme commander chose Zayd ibn Hāritha as the first commander of the army, whereas he made Ja'far bin Abi Tālib, who was a close relative of his, second in command. Sometimes the selection was not based solely on his past [military] record,[64] because the Prophet (s) appointed Usāma bin Zayd, a young commander, as the leader of the army that was sent to Abnām and some of the other great commanders were placed under his command.[65] Similarly, one's previous record [with regards to accepting Islam] was not a consideration;[66] because 'Amr ibn 'Aās was given the charge of a Sariya mission in which great companions like Abu 'Ubayda ibn Jarrāh and other great commanders participated, while it had only been a few months since 'Amr ibn 'Aās had accepted Islam.[67] Similarly, the rank and status of a person[68] was not a criterion for being appointed a commander. The Holy Prophet (s) made Abu Salama ibn 'Abd al-Asad Makhzumi the commander of a Sariya mission wherein others who [according of their rank and status] were more deserving, were present.[69]

h) Preserving the Unity and Integration of the Army

The supreme commander forbade disputes and quarrels among the members of the army. He established friendship and camaraderie among them and made them like a single body.[70] The Prophet (s) prevented the killing of the known hypocrite 'Abdullah ibn Ubay and instructed that he should be dealt with kindly.[71] In this way, he (s) was able to quell the disturbance that was about to obliterate the unity and harmony of the Muslim army after the Battle of Bani al-Mustalaq[72] because of a verbal confrontation between the Muhājirin and Ansār.[73] Similarly, the Holy Prophet (s), in another instance, forgave the lapse of Abu Lubāba when he took the wrong course in consultation with the Bani Quraydha.[74] He forgave Hātib bin Abi Balta'ah for his a mistake when sending letters to the enemy before the Conquest of Makkah[75] and this was because of his illustrious track record in the Muslim army. He (s) also ordered Abu 'Ubayda ibn Jarrāh to cooperate with 'Amr ibn 'Aās [who as the commander of the army in Dhāt al-Salāsil] in order to preserve unity.

The Prophet (s) also took it upon himself to 'refine and purify the souls' of the Ansār, who constituted a large part of the army. He did this during the distribution of the booty of Hunayn when he saw[76] anger and rage on their faces.[77] In the same way, he instilled affection and brotherhood in their hearts[78] and in the end he would be pleased with all the good qualities and merits of his armed forces.[79] It is for this very reason that the politics of 'wisdom and planning', 'far-sightedness and judging the character of the army soldiers', 'giving greater importance to expediency', 'ending quarrels and arguments that lead to listlessness and defeat, before they spread through and pervade the army', were required.

i) Discipline

'Discipline' was the honest and sincere execution of the commands that were issued by the supreme commander in order to achieve the aimed objectives.[80] Discipline in the Muslim army was centered around the belief in God, the Prophet,[81] his evenhandedness,[82] and unconditional loyalty to one commander.[83] Among the most important foundations of discipline was the complete obedience in difficulty and ease, war and peace, likes and dislikes.[84] The most evident signs of this were: 'absolute obedience',[85] 'contentment',[86] 'acceptance of responsibility',[87] 'the strength to come face to face with dangers',[88] 'acting with one's own volition',[89] 'innovation by the executors',[90] 'the profundity of the meaning of discipline and its practice by the commander himself (as well)' and 'his method and ability in action', which he would strive in for the attainment of the required goal.[91]

Discipline in the Muslim army meant that following the commander and emulating him was compulsory for the executive officers.[92] It was never permitted, under any circumstances, for them to act on their whims, without thinking, with complete ignorance or rigidity.[93] Rather they were bound by the spirit of obedience and doing that which was necessary and what they were able to in order to realize the goal.[94]

The strength of discipline was clearly seen in the Battle of Hamrā al-Asad, when the order was given for the enemy to be pursued, before returning to Madina, [immediately] after the Battle of Uhud. At this time, despite the fact that the soldiers were tired and wounded as a result of war, and were mourning their martyrs, they still all obeyed the order and none of them contravened the command of facing the enemy.[95] Similarly, the affection for the commander and belief in him made the army submit to [what were perceived as] the harsh and unpalatable conditions of the Treaty of Hudaybiyya.[96]

An example of the belief in the evenhandedness of the commander in his orders was that he compelled 'Abdullah ibn Rawāha to enforce discipline when he gave him instructions during the fight against the Romans in the Battle of Muta.[97] The supreme commander would warn against lack of discipline which would lead to listlessness, defeat and hardship in the battlefield.[98]

j) Determining the Number of Soldiers in the Army

In the first Sariya that the Holy Prophet (s) sent to fight against the enemy, he started by be sending thirty fighters[99] and in the second Sariya, he increased the number to eighty.[100] With the passing of time and the sending of more groups and missions, this number increased, until the Battle of Badr where it reached three hundred and thirteen[101] and in the last battle that was fought, there were over thirty thousand [Muslim] soldiers.[102]

In the beginning, the organization of the army was limited to the Muhājirin,[103] but after some time, the Ansār[104] and eventually a number of other Arab tribes joined the army.[105] The most important of these were: Muzayna, Aslam, Juhayna, Banu Sulaym, Banu Ghifār, Kināna, Ashja' and Banu Layth.

Women also constituted a small part of the armed forces and would help in the treating the wounded and providing assistance to the soldiers.[106] The supreme commander would endeavor to promote the growth and expansion of this army, and for this very reason, he would protect the soldiers – meaning that he would not send them towards their death or destruction - to such an extent that the total number of martyrs in all the nine years under his command did not exceed three hundred and seventeen.[107] This number is divided as follows:

Badr – 14 martyrs, Uhud – 70 martyrs, Bi'r Ma'unah[108] – 70 martyrs, al-Rajee' – 10 martyrs, Khandaq – 6 martyrs, the Sariya of Muhammad ibn Maslama against the Bani Tha'laba – 10 martyrs, Bani al-Mustalaq – one martyr, Khaybar – 15 to 19 martyrs, the Sariya of Bashir ibn Sa'd al-Ansāri towards the Bani Murrah – 30 martyrs, the Sariya of Abi al-'Awjā' al-Sulami towards the Bani Saleem – 50 martyrs, Ka'b ibn 'Umayr al-Ghifāri to the Bani Qudhā'ah – 15 martyrs, the Battle of Muta – 8 martyrs, the Conquest of Makkah – 2 martyrs, Hunayn – 4 martyrs and Tā'if – 12 martyrs.

The people, from the time they accepted Islām, displayed their courage in joining this army and would try to outdo each other.[109] The Prophet (s) would not send the entire army against the enemy, rather he selected an appropriate number to [send in] each battle depending on the available resources and the number of soldiers in the enemy's army.[110] For example, he entered the battle against the Bani Saleem with a section of the forces[111] and the battle of Dhi Amr with a larger number of forces.[112] In the Battle of Tabuk and some other battles, he brought the entire army to fight.[113] Based on this, one of the most fundamental principles of war, meaning 'economizing with the forces', was always taken into consideration by the Prophet (s).[114]

k) Organization and arrangement of the troops

Organization included the division of the troops into units [and contingents], outlining the hierarchy of command, type of battle, where it will be fought, the army's military might, the enemy's strengths and weaponry, and the modes of transport used by both sides.[115] The Prophet's goal from this organization was facilitating ease of command and control over the troops during the battle, motivation and stabilization.[116] It was for this reason that he put different units under the command of one person[117] and put different types of weapons at their disposal.[118] This is precisely what he did in the Conquest of Makkah where he rearranged the tribes according to the prevailing conditions.[119]

In the battle of the Conquest, he arranged the Muhājirs into three columns consisting of two hundred soldiers each, the Aus into six columns of 350 soldiers and the tribe of Aslam into one column consisting of two hundred fighters, and he did the same with different groups and new contingents,[120] just as he had arranged the column of archers in the Battle of Uhud.

The Prophet (s) would at times arrange the army based on 'new battle equipment',[121] this is why the arrangement of the army in the Conquest of Makkah was very different from the arrangement of the army in the Battle of Hunayn. He (s) would bring together various distinct qualities and talents during the formation of each contingent in order to make them able to fight independently;[122] like the groups of four who entered Makkah. The Prophet organized the troops in pyramidal forms in a single group and in groups of two, three and four depending on the number of tribes. The single pyramidal contingent was led by Abu Wāqid al-Laythi and was made up from the tribes of Kanānah, Bani Hamzah, Bani Layth and Sa'd bin Bakr. The group of twos were made up of troops from the tribe of Ashja' and the groups of three consisted of members from the tribe of Muzaynah while the groups of four were from the tribe of Juhaynah. This formation made it easier to attain the best speed and movement during battle.[123] In the present day and age also, armed forces are organized into pyramidal groups of three and four.[124]

The organization for battle was different from the arrangement of troops who were marched in front of Abu Sufyān before the Conquest of Makkah. The Holy Prophet (s) would try to give the command of an entire column to the leader of the tribe whose troops were present in that column.[125] Whenever the numbers of the tribe did not match with the column, he would include other groups in it and would select a commander from a tribe that was present in that column.[126]

2. The Administrative Council

The Administrative Council was a body whose responsibility was to advise the supreme commander about all affairs related to the military. This council consisted of military commanders from the Muhājirs, the Ansārs and other tribes.[127] The Holy Prophet (s) always consulted with this council about issues related to war and he would take the opinion of its members about the following matters:

a) Declaring war on the enemy
b) Benefitting from the participation of the Ansār (in battle)
c) Centralization of the troops like in the Battle of Badr[128]
d) Remaining in Madina or coming out to face the Quraysh in the Battle of Uhud[129]
e) Digging the ditch in the Battle of Ahzāb
f) Creating a peace treaty with the Ghatfān for one third of the dates of Madina[130]
g) Whether to make peace or war in the expedition of Hudaybiyya[131]
h) The fixity and change of command in the Battle of Khaybar[132]
i) Whether to remain steadfast or move and launch an attack on the Roman empire
j) Return to Madina[133]
k) The battle between the Roman army and the troops of Zayd bin Hāritha where, when consulted, most of the commanders, and especially 'Abdullah bin Rawāhah, the deputy commander, gave the opinion that they should fight against the Romans[134]

After studying the progress of the various battles it must be said that the situation would be different from place to place and in different military zones, and the study and deliberation about this issue can be considered clear evidence of the aptitude and soundness of opinion of the Holy Prophet (s) in these matters.[135]

In this council, the Prophet (s) had one vote just like the other members and he would listen carefully to the opinions and views of the other members. For the Battle of Uhud,[136] due to the fact that the majority had given the opinion that they should come out of Madina, even though he himself thought it would be more prudent to remain in the city, he supported the view of the council.[137] This was the beginning of 'democracy', something that most of the countries in today's world are calling for.

The Holy Prophet (s) would refrain from imposing his opinions and insisting on his views.[138] Therefore, he would respect the commanders and sit with them and take their advice on various issues, just as he accepted the advice of Habāb bin

Mundhir, Salmān al-Fārsi, Sa'd bin Mu'ādh, Sa'd bin 'Ubādah and 'Umar bin Khattāb in different situations in battle.[139] He would always show tolerance and leniency to those who offered advice and would respect their views. He would never accuse them of being ignorant. With his kind words and clear statements,[140] he would assist them to remain free of pretence and flattery[141] and to acquire good characters and remain truthful.[142] In the end, after listening to the advice, he would issue his orders. Because he was determined to carry out the decision of the council,[143] nobody would dare to oppose the orders he gave.[144] Members of the council were attributed with higher intelligence, prudent judgment and a greater awareness and understanding of military affairs, and were deemed trustworthy and reliable by the supreme commander.[145]

One of the most important results of forming an administrative council was that the experience of war which was the cause of the Muslim army's victory were revealed, the morals and characters of the participants were improved and strong bonds of friendship between them were formed. At the same time the full responsibility and accountability fell on their shoulders[146] and any matter that was put before the administrative council was discussed and debated by its members, the pros and cons were highlighted[147] and an appropriate conclusion was drawn.[148]

The Holy Prophet (s) would request the views of the council in matters such as warfare,[149] selecting a representative[150] and deputy[151] and other matters, and he would stress on the important role played by its members in leadership, because if they were suitable then the commander would also be good[152] otherwise the leadership will be corrupted and they will lead the commander to destruction and will act as hindrances and impediments in his path. The commanders who came after the passing away of the Holy Prophet (s) would also seek advice from the trustworthy leaders of the army.[153] 'Umar bin al-Khattāb gave more importance to this than anyone else,[154] to such an extent that he would also listen to the advice of children.

3. The Department of Doctrinal Guidance

This department was responsible for 'the spiritual and doctrinal development of the troops, its preservation and strengthening and at the same time, for weakening the morale of the enemy and destroying it', and was divided into various sections, each carrying out specific functions that were different from state to state, but overall it had a common spiritual goal that it tries to fulfill.[155]

The Prophet (s) would continuously strengthen the morale of the army[156] using various means, the most important of which included: training and continuous guidance of the troops,[157] putting the supreme commander (i.e. himself) at the same level as the soldiers,[158] sharing in their sorrows[159] and happiness,[160] defending the soldiers, steadfastness in battles,[161] [fair] distribution of war booty,[162] upgrading the weapons and equipment used by the troops in battle,[163] caring for the families of those who were martyred,[164] carrying out training for different battle strategies[165] so as to break down the wall of fear among the troops, and bringing them face to face with the different battle scenarios.[166]

The Holy Prophet (s) also used various techniques to maintain this spirit, the most important among which were: expulsion of weak soldiers and those who have been defeated [spiritually] from among the troops,[167] wiping out false rumours,[168] hiding information that could weaken the spirit and resolve of the people,[169] habituating the forces to adherence to strict discipline at all times[170] and creating a bond of mutual trust and friendship between the commander and his troops.[171]

An example of the strength in spirit was the presence and participation of some fighters in the army to face the enemy without any weapons whatsoever,[172] some would come to fight despite being young in age,[173] and another group would be ready to face hoards of enemy soldiers despite their few numbers.[174] Others would pull their horses behind them and would continue doing so throughout the battle.[175] Yet others would make it their mission to assassinate those who had said or done anything against the supreme commander and who had ill will against the Islāmic revolution.[176]

He (s) would instill faith and belief in the Muslim army in such a way that their spirit would never wane and would provide them the energy and strength to carry out all the missions that required self-sacrifice and struggle.[177] The distinguishing feature that impelled the soldiers to strong spirituality[178] was the hope in the life hereafter and [the fact that] they were faced with two options which both led to success, either victory with honor or martyrdom and entrance into everlasting bliss.[179] In this way, the father and son would keep their relationship aside and would strive to surpass one another in the hope of paradise.[180] In the Battle of Uhud, despite the rumour that the Prophet (s) had been killed, they continued to fight bravely. And this bravery was a testament to their strong faith and conviction.[181] Some of the forces would [try to] outdo each other in fighting for the supreme commander and would even kill their own relatives in defense of their faith.[182] Khubayb bin. 'Uday when forced to return to his previous faith preferred death.[183] Therefore the spirit in the Muslim army was aimed at protecting the faith and it was one of the most important goals of the Prophet (s) to strengthen this very spirit.

The supreme commander would also, on the other side try to weaken the spirit and resolve of the enemy, causing them to waver, and instill fear and terror in their hearts[184] to such an extent that they were not capable of coming out to fight against him. The most important ways in which he accomplished this included: displaying their strength and might,[185] using intelligence agents, taking precaution in employing counter-intelligence measures[186] and scrutinizing them,[187] arresting enemy spies,[188] carrying out attacks using offensive strategies[189] especially in the battles of Bani Quraydha and Khaybar and some of the Sariya missions like the Sariya of Muhammad bin Maslamah against the Bani Bakr, and that of 'Amr bin 'Aās against the Qudhā'ah, all of which were missions in which swift attacks were used. This was similarly the case, the attacks against the tribe of Bani Mahārib and Bani Tha'labah in the Battle of Shāt al-Ruqā'. Another way was by propagation of the renown and reputation of the leadership and bravery of Muslim army,[190] especially in the battle against the Bani Nadhir which was the cause of the Jews destroying their homes and strongholds by their own hands. In the battle against the Bani Lihyān, when the enemy heard that the Holy Prophet (s) had set out [with his army] to wage war against them, they fled, as did the Banu Sa'd when they got the information that 'Ali ibn Abi Tālib ('a) had started marching towards them. Similarly, being quick in defense and repulsion of any incursion by enemy forces,[191] especially in the Battle of Badr al-Kubrā and al-Ghābah, was another of the Prophet's tactics for weakening the resolve of the enemy.

The Holy Prophet (s) would awaken and enliven the spirit of the troops before the commencement of battle in order to attain the highest level of commitment and zeal[192] and would always try to preserve this throughout the war while removing anything that could cause a weakening in their spirits.[193] Whenever the soldiers started feeling disheartened, the Prophet (s) would strive to lift their spirits. This can be seen in the Battle of Ahzāb when the Bani Quraydha broke their covenant with the Muslims, where after the siege was taking its toll, he utilized clever trickery to cause disharmony in the ranks of the enemy's army thereby lifting the spirits of his own troops.[194]

The spirit and zeal of the Muslim fighters would increase and decrease in accordance with the varying situations in every battle, but on the whole, the Muslim army would be in high spirits until the final stages of the battles, and in order to achieve victory, they would remain steadfast and ready to attack,[195] even in situations where they had faced shocking events, the army would come out with their heads held high and would carry through till the end. The Battles of Uhud and Khandaq were two examples of this, because the Prophet (s) lifted the spirits of the army after the Battle of Uhud by initiating the Battle of Hamrā al-Asad and during the Battle of Khandaq by causing disharmony and division in

114

the ranks of the enemy. As a result, the confederates lost the victory and had to turn back humiliated.

NOTES AND REFERENCES

[1] Wāqidi 1:98; Ibn Hishām 2:266; Ibn Hazm: 208; Haydarābadi: 15-21

[2] Ibn Sa'd 1:11 Tabari 2:255; Because they had made a pact to protect the Holy Prophet (s) inside Madina, the Ansār did not participate in the first battle against the disbelievers. (Tr.)

[3] Q8:74

[4] Wāqidi 1:10, Ibn Hishām 2:241, Ibn Sa'd 2:1-5; Tabari 2:259

[5] Ibn Hishām 2:245; Ibn Sa'd 2:2; Ibn Sayyid al-Nās 1:224

[6] Wāqidi 1:48; Ibn Hishām 2:266; Ibn 'Abd al-Barr, *al-Durar fi Ikhtisār al-Maghāzi wal-Siyar*: 121 onwards

[7] Wāqidi 1:48; Ibn Hishām 2:266; Ibn Sa'd 2:8; Bakri, *Mu'jam Mastu'jam* 2:613; Yāqut Hamawi, *Mu'jam al-Buldān* 3:6

[8] Wāqidi 1:23; Ibn Hishām 2:333; Ibn Sa'd 2:13; Tabari 2:552; Kalā'i 1:136

[9] Wāqidi 1:177, 2:501; Ibn Hishām 3:201; Ibn Sa'd 2:19; Tabari 2:552; Kalā'i 1:134

[10] Wāqidi 1:374; Ibn Hishām 3:200; Ibn Sa'd 2:19; Ibn Hazm: 154, 182. After the victory over the Bani Nadhir, the Prophet (s) left it to the Khazraj, who had a covenant with them, to decide what should be done to them. The Khazraj decided that they should be banished from their land but their women and children should be released. (Tr.)

[11] Wāqidi 1:80; Ibn Hishām 3:210; Ibn Sa'd 2:19

[12] Wāqidi 2:517; Ibn Hishām 3:251; Ibn Sa'd 2:56; Tabari 2:588. After defeating the Bani Quraydha, the Prophet (s) left it upon the Aus, who had a covenant with them, to decide their punishment. The chief of the Aus, Sa'd ibn Ma'ādh, decided that their men should be put to death for their treason and their families and wealth should be taken. (Tr.)

[13] Zuhri: 54; Ibn Hishām 3:325; Ibn Sa'd 2:70; Ibn Sayyid al-Nās 2:116

[14] Zuhri: 55; Ibn Sa'd 2:76; Ibn Sayyid al-Nās 2:114. In the Treaty of Hudaybiyya where Suhayl ibn 'Amr was appointed as the representative of the Quraysh, there were many conditions that were made which the Muslims found to be one-sided and unfair, however,

the Prophet (s) gave in to their demands because he knew that it was in the interest of the Muslims to do so. (Refer to Bihār al-Anwār 20:335)

[15] Zuhri: 52; Ibn Sa'd 2:77; Kalā'i 1:130

[16] Wāqidi 1:76, 2:496; Ibn Hishām 3:50; Ibn Sa'd 2:19; Tabari 2:479, 3:9; Kalā'i 1:130; Ibn Sayyid al-Nās 1:294

[17] Zuhri: 50; Wāqidi 2:571;Ibn Hishām 3:321; Ibn Sa'd 2:69; Ibn Khayyāt 1:48; Tabari 2:620; Kalā'i 1:127; Ibn Sayyid al-Nās 2:113

[18] Ibn Hishām 1:281; Ibn Sa'd 1:134; Ibn Sayyid al-Nās 1:102; Dhahabi 1:91, 168

[19] Zuhri: 76; Tabari 2:259; Ibn Hazm: 104; Ibn Sayyid al-Nās 2:225, 2:106

[20] Wāqidi 1:176, 2:510; Ibn Sa'd 2:77; Tabari 2:552; Suhayli 3:137; Ibn Sayyid al-Nās 2:48

[21] Wāqidi 1:176; Ibn Hishām 3:50; Ibn Sa'd 2:19; Ibn Khayyāt 1:27; Ibn Sayyid al-Nās 1:294; Atanin Dianna, *Muhammad Rasulullah* (s): 277

[22] Wāqidi 1:404; Ibn Hishām 3:302; Ibn Sa'd 2:21, 62, 117; Razqāni, *Sharh al-Mawāhib* 2:166

[23] Wāqidi 2:562; Ibn Hishām 3:213; Ibn Sa'd 2:65; Kalā'i 1:112; Ibn Sayyid al-Nās 2:109

[24] Wāqidi 1:395; Ibn Sa'd 2:43; Tabari 3:27; Kalā'i 1:112; Ibn Sayyid al-Nās 2:83

[25] Tabari 2:6 onwards; Mas'udi, *Muruj al-Dhahab* 1:215; Jawād 'Ali, *al-Mufassal fi Tārikh al-'Arab qabl al-Islām* 2:635

[26] See Wāqidi 1:402, 2:755, 3:989; Ibn Hishām 3:244, 4:15; Ibn Sa'd 2:44, 92, 118, 136; Ibn Hazm: 184

[27] Wāqidi 1:11; Ibn Hishām 2:245, 251; Ibn Sa'd 2:1; Tabari 2:259; Ibn Sayyid al-Nās 1:226

[28] Wāqidi 1:10, 13; Ibn Hishām 2:245; Tabari 2:259; Ibn Sayyid al-Nās 1:225

[29] Wāqidi 1:182, 197; Tabari 2:492; Suhayli 3:142; Yāqut Hamawi 4:212; Ibn Sayyid al-Nās 1:305

[30] Wāqidi 1:199, 384, 440; Ibn Hishām 3:64, 224; Ibn Khayyāt 1:29; Tabari 3:9; Kalā'i 1:104, 113; Ibn Sayyid al-Nās 2:2, 55, 53

[31] Wāqidi 3:990; Ibn Hishām 4:169; Ibn Sa'd 2:119; Bakri 1:203

[32] The Battle of Dumat al-Jundal took place in Rabi' al-Awal, 5 A.H. and the reason for this battle was the Christian ruler of the Dumat al-Jundal (an area near Syria) called Akidar ibn 'Abd al-Malik Kindi, who was loyal to the emperor of Rome, Heracleus. Because his land was in the center of the trade route that ran from Arabia to Syria, he would create hindrances and obstacles and would harass the Muslim travelers. When the Holy Prophet (s) heard about this, he sent a large contingent of a thousand men to Dumat al-Jundal, but by the time they got there, the people had fled and they returned without fighting. (See: Wāqidi 1:402; Ibn Hishām 3:224; Ibn Sayyid al-Nās 2:54, 108) (Tr.)

[33] Wāqidi 1:404, 3:1026; Ibn Sa'd 2:44, 120; Suhayli 4:196, 201

[34] Wāqidi 1:12, 2:573, 3:995; Ibn Hishām 2:401, 3:220, 4:32

[35] Wāqidi 1:182; Ibn Hishām 3:220; Ibn Sa'd 2:21, 45; Ibn Hazm: 184

[36] In the Battle of Tabuk, 'Ali ibn Abi Tālib ('a) was initially appointed as the deputy of the Prophet (s) in Madina and later Muhammad ibn Maslamah was also chosen as a representative. (See: Wāqidi 3:1047; Ibn Hishām 4:162; Ibn Sa'd 4:112) (Tr.)

[37] Wāqidi 1:277; Ibn 'Abd al-Barr 3:1198

[38] Wāqidi 3:1047; Ibn Hishām 4:136; Tabari 3:104

[39] Ibn 'Abd al-Barr 3:1023

[40] Wāqidi 1:20, 56, 2:642, 819; Ibn Hishām 2:257, 3:218, 4:46; Ibn Sa'd 2:25

[41] Wāqidi 3:1117; Ibn Hishām 2:257; Ibn Sa'd 2:25; Ibn Sayyid al-Nās 2:121

[42] Wāqidi 1:13, 56, 217; Ibn Sa'd 2:96; Tabari 3:75; Ibn Hazm: 239

[43] Wāqidi 1:20, 87; Ibn Hishām 2:279; Ibn Sa'd 2:26; Ibn Hanbal 1:117

[44] Ibn Hishām 3:70; Ibn Sa'd 2:6, 27; Tabari 2:505; Ibn Sayyid al-Nās 1:257

[45] Wāqidi 1:13, 2:560, 3:1117; Ibn Hishām 4:49; Ibn Sa'd 2:35, 98; Kalā'i 1:144

[46] Wāqidi 2:560, 755; Ibn Hishām 4:15; Ibn 'Asākir 1:92; Ibn Sayyid al-Nās 2:108. In some locations in Madina, meaning near the *Thaniyāt,* the Prophet (s) would bid farewell to the army, that is why these places would be known as *Thaniyāt al-Wadā'* and the Prophet would come to these places in order to bid farewell to the army and welcome them back. (Tr.)

[47] Zuhri: 86, 92; Ibn Sa'd 2:96, 108; Ibn Khayyāt 1:56

[48] Wāqidi 2:819; Ibn Hishām 4:46

[49] Wāqidi 2:819; Ibn Hishām 4:46

[50] Wāqidi 2:823

[51] Wāqidi 2:819; Ibn Hishām 6:46. One of the examples of the psychological war of the Prophet (s) was that he paraded his troops in front of Abu Sufyan and when the latter saw the strength of the Muslim army, he realized that they would not be able to fight them. Thus he was left with no choice but to submit and it was at this point that he accepted Islām. (Tr.)

[52] Wāqidi 2:819 onwards

[53] Wāqidi 2:821; Ibn Hishām 4:46; Ibn Sa'd 2:98; Tabari 3:54

[54] Wāqidi 2:819

[55] Wāqidi 2:819; Ibn Hishām 4:46, 47

[56] Wāqidi 1:218, 2:457; Ibn Hishām 2:278; Ibn Sa'd 2:45; Ibn Hanbal 5:420; Tabari 2:446

[57] Wāqidi 1:13; Ibn Hishām 2:268, 3:243; Ibn Sa'd 1:207; Ibn 'Abd al-Barr 3:878

[58] Wāqidi 1:198, 2:553, 564, 769, 3:883; Ibn Hishām 4:15, 272; Ibn Sa'd 2:24, 63, 92; Tabari 3:108, 126; Ibn 'Abd al-Barr 2:427, 3:1184; Harawi, *al-Hiyal al-Harbiyya*: 90

[59] Ibn Hishām 2:241; Ibn Khayyāt 1:29; Ibn 'Abd al-Barr 3:1090, 4:1473

[60] Wāqidi 1:10, 67; Ibn Hishām 2:278; Ibn al-Atheer, *Usd al-Ghābah* 2:291

[61] Bukhāri (al-Jihād 54, 82,165); Muslim (al-Fadhā'il 48); Ibn Mājah (al-Jihād 9); Tirmidhi (al-Jihād 15); Ibn 'Abd al-Birr: 1644; Kalā'i 1:101

[62] Wāqidi 2:541; Ibn Hishām 3:296; Tabari 2:598; Ibn Sayyid al-Nās 2:84; Dhahabi, *Tārikh al-Islām* 1:267

[63] Wāqidi 2:757; Ibn Hishām 4:15; Ibn Sa'd 2:92; Kalā'i 1:135

[64] Zuhri: 150; Ibn Hishām 4:291; Ibn Sa'd 2:136; Ibn Atheer 1:65. It should be noted that Tabarsi has narrated from Imam al-Sādiq ('a) that the Prophet (s) first appointed Ja'far ibn Abi Tālib as the commander and then, if he was martyred, Zayd ibn Hāritha and finally 'Abdullah ibn Rawāha (Refer to A'lām al-Warā: 62) (Tr.)

[65] In the month of Safar, 11 A.H. (during the last days of the Prophet's life), the Holy Prophet (s) prepared an army in order to avenge the blood of the martyrs of the Battle of Muta and appointed Usāma bin Zayd, whose father had been killed in the said battle, as

the commander. Usama was a young man of 18 or 19 years and all the older and more experienced companions, aside from 'Abbās (the uncle of the Prophet) and 'Ali ibn Abi Tālib, were placed under his command. When the army was about to leave, some of the older companions voiced their discontentment about the fact that their commander was a young lad. 'Umar ibn Khattāb took this message to the Prophet (s) who in turn expressed his intense displeasure. Despite his sickness, the Prophet (s) put one hand on 'Ali's shoulder and one hand on the shoulder of 'Abbās and came to the Masjid where he delivered a fiery sermon in which he cursed those who opposed the army of Usāma. The army was stationed outside Madina when the news of the Prophet's demise came and when Abu Bakr took over the Caliphate, he sent the army to fight against the Romans. (See: Wāqidi 3:1117; Ibn Sa'd 2:190; Ibn Atheer 2:317) (Tr.)

[66] Zuhri: 150; Wāqidi 2:769; Ibn Hishām 4:272; Ibn Sa'd 2:94; Ibn 'Abd al-Barr 3:1184; Ibn Sayyid al-Nās 2:157

[67] In the 8th year of Hijra, the Prophet (s) received information that a group of disbelievers had gathered at Dhāt al-Salāsil behind Wādi al-Qurā with the intention of launching a night raid on the Muslims. The Prophet (s) initially sent 'Amr ibn 'Aās with an army to fight against them but he returned unsuccessful and expressed his fear to the Prophet (s). Immediately, the Prophet (s) sent 'Ali ('a) to the same place and after their rejection of his invitation to accept Islām, he fought against them and even took some booty back as he returned to Madina victorious (See: Shaykh Mufid, *al-Irshād*: 51) (Tr.)

[68] Wāqidi 1:34; Ibn Sa'd 2:35; Ibn 'Abd al-Barr 4:1682; Ibn Sayyid al-Nās 2:39; Harawi: 99

[69] In Muharram of the fourth year of Hijra, the Holy Prophet (s) sent Abi Salamah ibn 'Abd al-Asad in order to fight the tribe of Bani Asad. Great companions like Abi 'Ubaydah ibn Jarrāh, Arqam ibn Abi Arqam and Abu Qatāda ibn Nu'mān were present in his army. (Wāqidi 1:343-345) (Tr.)

[70] Bukhāri (al-Adab 27); Muslim (al-Birr 66)

[71] Zuhri: 77; Wāqidi 1:219; Ibn Hishām 3:68, 305; Kalā'i 1:24; Ibn Sayyid al-Nās 2:59

[72] Wāqidi 2:415; Ibn Hishām 3:303; Ibn Sa'd 2:46; Tabari 2:605; Ibn Sayyid al-Nās 2:95

[73] 'Abdullah ibn Ubay was the leader of the Hypocrites of Yathrib. When the Prophet (s) migrated there, his plans to take over the leadership of the city were thwarted, and for this reason he held a deep rooted hatred for Islām and the Muhājirin, but because he had no other option, he openly professed his belief in Islām. He was always on the lookout for opportunities to weaken the Muslims and bring about differences among them. In the Battle of Uhud, he was instrumental in turning back three hundred soldiers. He never participated in any battles and when he did, he would weaken the spirits of the Muslims. In the Battle of Bani al-Mustalaq, when the Muslims returned victorious, a misunderstanding came about between a Muhājir and an Ansār. The servant of 'Umar ibn Khattāb and a man from the Ansār were quarrelling about who should take water out of a well. The disagreement was about to turn violent. 'Abdullah ibn Ubay took this opportunity to start spreading hatred for the Muhājirin among the Ansār. When the Prophet (s) heard about this, he called 'Abdullah ibn Ubay but the latter denied what he had done. Some of the companions sought permission from the Prophet (s) to kill Ibn Ubay for what he had done but the Prophet (s) did not allow them to do this. (Wāqidi 2:415) (Tr.)

[74] Wāqidi 2:506; Ibn Hishām 3:247; Ibn Sa'd 2:54; Tabari 2:546; Kalā'i 1:117; Ibn Sayyid al-Nās 2:70. In the Battle against the Bani Quraydha, the Prophet (s) sent a companion called Abu Lubāba to the Jews in order to get them to surrender, but when Abu Lubāba met the chiefs of the Jews, he was affected by the sounds of weeping from their women and children and thus made a sign with his hand towards his neck meaning that 'if you surrender you will be killed'. When Abu Lubāba left the Bani Quraydha, he realized his mistake and felt remorse for his treachery against the Prophet (s), so he made a vow and tied himself to one of the pillars of the Masjid of the Prophet (s) and began praying to Allāh for forgiveness. Early in the morning the Prophet (s) came to Abu Lubāba and untied him from the pillar saying that Allāh had forgiven him. Henceforth this pillar was known as the pillar of Abu Lubāba. (Tr.)

[75] Bukhāri (al-Maghāzi 2:46); Muslim (Fadhā'il al-Sahāba 161). Hatab bin Abi Balta'ah was one of the Muhājirs who, because the weakness of his faith, acted treacherously. Before the Conquest of Makkah, he secretly sent a letter to some of the heads of the

Quraysh to inform them about the intention of the Holy Prophet (s) to conquer Makkah. No sooner had he sent the letter that Jibra'il descended to the Prophet (s) and informed him of this. The Prophet (s) sent Imam 'Ali ('a) to stop the messenger and take the letter. Then the Prophet (s) called Hatab and sought to know his reason for doing this. Ibn Abi Balta'ah said that he was still a Muslim and had not given up his faith, but it was only because of his fear for his family who were in Makkah that he did what he had done. When the companions heard this they sought permission from the Prophet (s) to kill him but the Prophet refused and spared his life. (Tr.)

[76] Zuhri: 150; Ibn Hishām 4:272; Ibn 'Asākir 1:104; Ibn Sayyid al-Nās 2:157; Ibn Hajar 5:3

[77] The Holy Prophet (s) was sent to guide a people who were living in the depths of ignorance. People would fight wars in order to gain booty and gain possession over the other's property, as well as to show their valor or secure their 'honor'. The Prophet (s) came to these people as an exemplary role model, with perfect morals and an infallible character. But some people were not able to do away with their old habits and we see, for example, in the Battle of Uhud, that the archers who were commanded not to leave their post disobeyed the direct order of the Prophet (s) just so that they could get a portion of the war booty. Another example is what took place after the Battle of Hunayn when the Ansār were given a lesser portion of the booty they began to protest. When the Prophet (s) got angry and explained the reason for this allotment, the Ansār began to cry and said that they do not wish for anything more than the Prophet's pleasure with them. (Tr.)

[78] Bukhāri (Maghāzi 56); Muslim (al-Zakāh 139); Tirmidhi (al-Zakāh 29); Nasā'i (al-Zakāh 79)

[79] Zuhri: 77; Wāqidi 2:415; Ibn Hishām 4:47; Tabari 3:61; Ibn Qayyim 2:444

[80] Ibn Hanbal 3:67; Bukhāri (al-Ahkām 4); Majmu'ah min al-Mu'allifeen al-'Askariyyeen, *al-Mawsu'ah al-'Askariyya* 1:131

[81] Q4:136; Q24:62; Q48:9,13; Q49:15; Q61:11; Bukhāri (al-Jihād 4); Abu Dāwud (al-Ashribah 7); Tirmidhi (Fadhā'il al-Jihād 230)

[82] Zuhri: 52; Wāqidi 2:760; Kalā'i 1:127

[83] Q7:157; Q48:9; Bukhāri (al-Eimān 8, Maghāzi 53); Muslim (al-Eimān 69); Nasā'i (al-Jihād 14)

[84] Q2:285; Q3:32, 172; Q4:13, 59, 69, 80; Q5:7; Q8:1; Q24:51, 54; Q64:16; Bukhāri (al-Ahkām 4, al-Jihād 109); Muslim 3:1391; Nasā'i (al-Bay'ah 5)

[85] Q3:172; Q13:18; Q42:38; Muslim 3:1433

[86] Q9:59; Ibn Hanbal 2:310; Muslim (al-Masājid 279, al-Salāh 13, al-Fadhā'il 63); Ibn Mājah (al-Iqāmah 147); Abu Dāwud (al-Jihād 118); Tirmidhi (al-Zuhd 57)

[87] Ibn Sa'd 2:2-5, 24, 35, 56, 61

[88] Wāqidi 1:347, 355; Ibn Hishām 3:194; Ibn Sa'd 2:36, 39; Ibn 'Abd al-Barr 4:1449; Ibn 'Asākir 1:92; Ibn al-Atheer 4:344

[89] See examples of this in Wāqidi 2:552, 506; Ibn Sa'd 2:62, 122; Tabari 3:126; Ibn Sayyid al-Nās 2:105, 108; Ibn al-Hajar, *al-Isābah* 1L98, 4:11, 176

[90] Wāqidi 1:10, 67; Ibn Hishām 4:21; Tabari 2:512; Kalā'i :136

[91] Zuhri: 52; Bukhāri (al-Jihād 82); Muslim 4:1804

[92] Q2:153; Q3:31; Q33:21; Shaybāni 1:118; Tabari 3:75

[93] See how the army took sensible measures to choose a new commander after the martyrdom of three commanders in the Battle of Muta in al-Maghāzi 2:756, 763; Ibn Hishām 4:21; Ibn Sa'd 2:94

[94] Zuhri: 150; Wāqidi 2:769; Ibn Hishām 4:272; Ibn Sa'd 2:94; Tabari 3:31

[95] Q3:172; Wāqidi 1:335; Ibn Sa'd 2:34; Kalā'i 1:105

[96] Zuhri: 55; Ibn Hishām 3:327; Ibn Sa'd 2:70; Ibn al-Atheer 2:204. In the Treaty of Hudaybiyya there were numerous conditions that seemed unfair to the Muslims and for this reason many companions voiced protests against the signing of this treaty but at the same time, they submitted to the will of the supreme commander and had to accept the treaty in the end. (Tr.)

[97] Wāqidi 2:760; Ibn Hishām 4:17; Tabari 3:37

[98] Ibn Hishām 3:71; Tabari 2:507; Ibn Hazm: 160; Kalā'i 1:102, 103

[99] Wāqidi 1:9; Ibn Hishām 2:245; Ibn Sa'd 2:2; Tabari 2:402; Ibn Sayyid al-Nās 1:224

[100] Ibn Hishām 2:241; Ibn Sayyid al-Nās 1:224

[101] Wāqidi 1:152; Ibn Sa'd 2:6; Tabari 2:431; Ibn 'Abd al-Barr: 121

[102] The first battle was the Battle of Waddān which took place in the month of Safar, 2 A.H. against the Bani Khumra and Quraysh, after which a peace treaty was signed. The last battle was the Battle of Tabuk against the Romans, where the forces numbered thirty thousand and ten thousand on horseback. (Tr.)

[103] Wāqidi 1:10 – 13; Ibn Hishām 2:241, 251; Ibn Sa'd 2:1-5; Tabari: 259

[104] Wāqidi 1:48; Ibn Hishām 2:266; Ibn Sa'd 2:8; Tabari 2:434; Ibn Sayyid al-Nās 1:247

[105] Wāqidi 2:800, 812, 819

[106] Wāqidi 1:218, 2:685; Tabari 3:77; Suhayli 4:37; Kalā'i 1:145

[107] Wāqidi 1:45, 300, 2:495, 705, 723, 741, 825, 3:922, 938; Ibn Hishām 3:357, 4:129; Ibn Sa'd 2:36, 61, 89, 92

[108] It should be noted that Bi'r Ma'unah and al-Rajee' were not battles or military missions, rather they were unarmed missions sent for propagation of the faith who were attacked and killed by the enemies. (Tr.)

[109] Ibn Hishām 4:205-245; Ibn al-Atheer 2:283 onwards

[110] Wāqidi 2:670; Ibn Hishām 3:344, 347; Ibn Sa'd 2:502

[111] Ibn Sa'd 2:21

[112] Wāqidi 1:194

[113] Wāqidi 2:454, 800; Ibn Hishām 3:231, 4:23, 63; Ibn Sa'd 2:47; Tabari 3:100; Ibn Sayyid al-Nās 2:215

[114] The issue of economizing on forces is something that is given importance and taken into consideration even today (Tr.)

[115] Wāqidi 1:220, 2:800 onwards; Dhahabi 1:267

[116] Ibn Hishām 4:85; Ibn Sa'd 1:44, 77, 109; Tabari 3:9; Yāqut Himyari 2:487; Ibn Sayyid al-Nās 2:193

[117] Zuhri: 76, 84; Wāqidi 1:199, 2:440, 633; Ibn Hishām 3:64, 224, 342; Ibn Sa'd 2:25, 47, 77; Ibn Khayyāt 1:29; Kalā'i 1:104, 114, 130

[118] Wāqidi 2:800, 812, 819; Ibn Hishām 4:42

[119] Wāqidi 2:800 onwards; Ibn Hishām 4:42

[120] Ibn Hishām 3:96 onwards; Tabari 2:507; Ibn Hazm: 160; Kalā'i 1:102

[121] Wāqidi 3:895 onwards; Ibn Sa'd 2:108; Suhayli 4:96

122 Wāqidi 2:802; Ibn Hishām 4:94; Ibn Sa'd 2:98; Ibn Hazm: 231

123 Wāqidi 2:800, 812

124 *Majmu'ah al-Ta'leef fi Akadimiyya Farunzi al-'Askariyya – al-Takteek*: 464

125 Wāqidi 2:800, 812 onwards

126 Wāqidi 2:820; Ibn Hishām 4:41

127 Zuhri: 50; Wāqidi 2:643; Ibn Hishām 2:266, 272; Qurtubi 2:1493; Ibn Katheer 3:262, 267

128 Wāqidi 1:53; Ibn Hishām 2:272; Ibn Sa'd 2:9; Tabari 2:440; Ibn 'Abd al-Barr 1:316

129 Wāqidi 1:209 onwards; Ibn Hishām 3:67; Ibn Sa'd 2:26; Tabari 2:503

130 Wāqidi 2:445, 478; Ibn Hishām 3:234; Ibn Sa'd 2:47, 53; Tabari 2:566, 573; Ibn 'Abd al-Barr 2:594, 601, 634; Ibn al-Atheer 2:283

131 Wāqidi 2:580; Tirmidhi (al-Jihād 34)

132 Wāqidi 2:644

133 Wāqidi 3:1019

134 Wāqidi 2:760; Ibn Hishām 4:17; Ibn Sa'd 2:93; Tabari 3:37; Ibn Sayyid al-Nās 2:154; Ibn al-Qayyim 2:375

135 Zuhri: 50; Wāqidi 2:580, 643, 3:1019; Tabari 3:37; Ibn Sayyid al-Nās 2:154; Ibn al-Qayyim 2:375

136 Wāqidi 1:209; Ibn Hishām 3:67; Ibn Sa'd 2:26; Tabari 2:503; Ibn Sayyid al-Nās 2:4

137 Ibn Hishām 2:67; Ibn Sa'd 2:26; Ibn al-Atheer 2:150; The youth were enthusiastic about leaving Madina and they felt that if they remained behind and fought defensively, the enemy would become bolder and would take them as cowards. For this reason they insisted that the army go out of Madina, and the Prophet (s) agreed to this even though it was against his own opinion. In the end, the Muslims suffered a defeat in this battle. (Tr.)

138 Ibn Hanbal 2:231; Muslim (al-Jannah 64); Ibn Mājah (al-At'imah 6, 30); Abu Dāwud (al-At'imah 17); Tirmidhi (al-Jumu'ah 43); al-Nasā'i (al-Istisqā' 3)

139 Dārimi (al-Muqaddima 34); Ibn Mājah (al-Fitan 71); Abu Dāwud (al-Malāhim 17)

140 Ibn 'Abd al-Barr 1:316; 2:594, 634; Ibn al-Atheer 1:364, 2:283, 338

141 Ibn Hanbal 5:230; Dārimi (al-Ru'yā 13); Bukhāri (al-Munāfiqun 10); Abu Dāwud (al-Aqdhiya 11); Tirmidhi (al-Ahkām 3); al-Nasā'i (al-Hajj 49)

142 Bukhāri (al-Jihād 195); Muslim (al-Fadhā'il 140, al-Salāh 178); Abu Dāwud (al-Sunnah 12) al-Nasā'i (al-Qudhāt 11)

143 Dārimi (al-Ru'yā 13); Bukhāri (al-I'tisām 28); Abu Dāwud (al-Jihād 37)

144 Q33:36; Wāqidi 1:53 onwards; Nasā'i (al-Ashriba 36)

145 Q3:159; Ibn Hanbal 1:30, 3:105, 4:10; Bukhāri: 79; Abu Dāwud (a;-Adab 88); Harawi: 73

146 Ibn Hanbal 3:729; Bukhāri (al-Hudud 71, al-Muhāribun 16); Abu Dāwud (al-Adab 114); al-Nasā'i (al-Jihād 6)

147 Wāqidi 1:53, 209, 2:445, 478, 760; Ibn Hishām 2:272, 3:67, 4:17; Abu Dāwud (al-Buyu' 5); Harawi: 74

148 Ibn Sa'd 2:9, 26, 47, 53, 93; Tabari 2:440, 503, 566, 3:37; Ibn 'Abd Rabbih 1:63 onwards; Harawi: 74

149 Wāqidi 1:53; Ibn Hishām 3:234; Ibn Sa'd 2:26; Tabari 2:566, 573

150 Q42:38; Ibn Hanbal 1:48; Muslim (al-Masājid 78); Abu Dāwud (al-Adab 114); Tirmidhi (al-Fitan 78)

151 Tirmidhi (al-Manāqib 37); Bukhāri (al-'Ilm 2); Muslim (al-Imārah 22)

152 Bukhāri (al-Ahkām 42, al-I'tisām 28); Nasā'i (al-Bay'ah 32); Ibn 'Abd Rabbih 1:32 onwards

153 Ibn Hanbal 5:274; Bukhāri (al-I'tisām 28); Abu Dāwud (al-Adab 114); Tirmidhi (al-Zuhd 39, al-Adab 57)

154 'Umar ibn al-Khattāb would constantly seek advice from the close companions of the Holy Prophet (s) like 'Ali ibn Abi Tālib ('a). In more than one occasion, the Muslim army achieved victory because of this advice. (Tr.)

155 Q8:65; Bukhāri (al-Jihād 110); Nasā'i (al-Jihād 30)

156 Q4:84; Bukhāri (al-Maghāzi 17); Muslim (al-Imārah 117); Nasā'I (al-Zakāh 85; al-Buyu' 98)

157 Q6:19, Q17:106, Q18:54, Q73:20, Q96:1; Wāqidi 1:347, 3:1057; Ibn Hishām 3:178; Ibn Sa'd 2:36, 39

[158] Examples of this was when the committee was discussing whether to leave Madina in the Battle of Uhud and during the digging of the trench in the Battle of Khandaq (see: Ibn Hishām 2:226)

[159] Dārimi (al-Jihād 18); Abu Dāwud (al-Jihād 25); Tirmidhi (Fadhā'il al-Jihād 13); Nasā'i (al-Qisāmah 18)

[160] Bukhāri (al-Nikāh 71, 72); Muslim (al-Nikāh 98, 101, al-'Eid 19); Nasā'i (al-'Eidān 36)

[161] Bukhāri (al-Jihād 82); Muslim 3:1401, 802; Tirmidhi (al-Jihād 15)

[162] Q8:41; Zuhri: 93; Wāqidi 1:96, 407, 2:535, 3:943; Ibn Sa'd 2:61, 95, 120

[163] Wāqidi 1:78, 377, 2:540, 648; Ibn Hishām 4:122; Ibn Sa'd 2:174; Tabari 3:73

[164] Muslim (al-Imārah 139); Ibn Mājah (al-Nikāh 36, 53); Nasā'i (al-Jihād 47)

[165] Shaybāni 1:58; Ibn Hishām 2:245, 278; Tabari 2:181

[166] Ibn Hishām 3:71; Ibn Sa'd 2:61; Bukhāri (al-Jihād 80)

[167] Dārimi (al-Siyar 53); Muslim (al-Jihād 150); Abu Dāwud (al-Jihād 142)

[168] Wāqidi 1:338, 2:729, 803; Ibn Hishām 3:304; Ibn Sa'd 2:56; Ibn Sayyid al-Nās 2: 167

[169] Look at how the Prophet (s) wanted to keep the information about the breaking of the pact by the Bani Quraydha confidential and also told Habbāb ibn Mundhir not to let anyone know about the number of enemy forces in the Battle of Uhud (Wāqidi 1:207)

[170] Ibn Hanbal 5:321; Bukhāri (al-Ahkām 4); Nasā'i (al-Bay'ah 5)

[171] Bukhāri (al-Eimān 8, al-Maghāzi 53); Muslim (al-Eimān 69); Nasā'i (al-Jihād 14)

[172] Wāqidi 1:258; Ibn Hishām 2:280, 3:39; Ibn Sayyid al-Nās 1:257

[173] Wāqidi 1:21, 88; Ibn Hishām 3:70; Tabari 2:505; Ibn Sayyid al-Nās 2:6

[174] Wāqidi 1:152, 2:457, 755; Ibn Hishām 3:231; Ibn Sa'd 2:47; Tabari 2:431

[175] Ibn Hishām 4:19-21; Tabari 3:37; Ibn Qayyim 2:375

[176] Wāqidi 1:173, 184, 391; Ibn Hishām 3:54, 287; Ibn Sa'd 2:21; Ibn Hazm: 184, 198

[177] Q8:65, Q9:19, 20, 41, 89; Bukhāri (al-Maghāzi 53, al-Jihād 110); Tirmidhi (al-Eimān 8, Fadhā'il al-Jihād 22); Nasā'i (al-Jihād 18)

[178] Q2:154, Q3:169, Q4:73; Bukhāri (Fadhā'il al-Sahābah 5); Nasā'i (al-Jihād 19, al-Bay'ah 37)

[179] Q9:52; Ibn Hanbal 3:483; Nasā'i (al-Jihād 19, al-Buyu' 98)

[180] Wāqidi 1:212

[181] Ibn Is'hāq: 309; Wāqidi 1:208; Ibn Hishām 3:88; Tabari: 517; Ibn 'Abd al-Barr 1:108; Ibn Sayyid al-Nās 2:12; the brother of Anas bin Mālik would cry out: life after the death of the Holy Prophet (s) has no value for us (Tr.)

[182] Wāqidi 1:69, 112, 257; Ibn Hishām 3:305; Ibn Sa'd 2:10, 46

[183] Wāqidi 1:360; Ibn Hishām 3:185; Tabari 2:541; Ibn 'Abd al-Barr 2:440; Khubayb was one of the teachers of the Qur'ān who was martyred in the tragedy of 'al-Rajee'. The polytheists tried to force him to turn away from Islām before killing him when they were unable to do so (Tr.)

[184] Zuhri: 79; Wāqidi 2:353, 563, 729; Ibn Hishām 3:292; Tabari 2:554

[185] Ibn Hishām 4:13; Ibn Hanbal 1:229; Tirmidhi (al-Hajj 30); Nasā'i (al-Manāsik 84); in today's terminology this is known as 'psychological warfare' and it is carried out to weaken the spirits of the enemy's army (Tr.)

[186] Wāqidi 1:203, 338; Ibn 'Abd al-Barr 3:1473

[187] Wāqidi 1:99; Ibn Sa'd 2:70; Ibn 'Abd al-Barr 4:1473

[188] Wāqidi 1:404, 2:550, 640, 802; Abu Dāwud (al-Jihād: Ba'th al-'Uyun 84)

[189] Wāqidi 1:395, 2:496, 633; Ibn Hishām 3:244, 342; Ibn Sa'd 2:53, 77; Tabari 2:556; Ibn Sayyid al-Nās 2:39, 105 onwards

[190] Wāqidi: 535; Ibn Hishām 3:292; Ibn Sa'd 2:56; Ibn Sayyid al-Nās 2:109

[191] Wāqidi 1:12, 2:537; Ibn Hishām 2:315, 3:293; Ibn Asad 2:1, 58; Tabari 2:601; Kalā'i 1:123

[192] Ibn Hanbal 4:354; Bukhāri (al-Jihād 110); Abu Dāwud (al-Jihād 24)

[193] Shaybāni 1:118; Wāqidi 1:207; Tabari 3:75; Kalā'i 1:144

[194] Zuhri: 79; Muslim 3:1361

[195] Zuhri: 79; Wāqidi 1:337 onwards and 2:440; Ibn Hishām 3:129 onwards; Ibn Sa'd 2:36, 47; Tabari 3:29, 565; Kala'i 1:104, 114; Watt: 57

CHAPTER FOUR
THE DEPARTMENT OF INTELLIGENCE AND SECURITY

The Intelligence Department

The department of Intelligence is a department which is responsible for acquiring and collecting all the information in matters pertaining to the enemy. This information especially covers: intention [of war], amassing [of forces], land where the enemy will fight, a detailed study of the acquired information and ensuring its accuracy – and different methods and tools of intelligence were employed to this end.[1]

The Holy Prophet (s) would, more than anything else before the battle, try to acquire intelligence [about the enemy] because gaining intelligence and complete information about the enemy was a requirement for the issuance of appropriate orders and commands. In order to get intelligence about the Quraysh, he (s) send numerous Sariya missions[2] to different places.[3] These missions were charged with acquiring information about the number of enemy tribes,[4] and also [in preparation for the battles with non-Arabs] the Roman forces.[5] The forces who were sent kept an eye on the points of entry into and exit from Makkah.[6]

The supreme commander made various peace pacts with some of the tribes[7] and sought their assistance against the enemy and at the same time commissioned them to keep watch over the borders of the neighboring state (i.e. Rome),[8] just as he had done in the Battle of Dumat al-Jundal when he sent 'Abd al-Rahmān ibn 'Auf to that area to gain the friendship of the Bani Kalb – a tribe that lived in on the border area – and also in the case of the peace treaty with Akeedar and others. The Prophet (s) would send troops to the sensitive areas[9] and would himself meet with the traders and travelers[10] and would get information from them and from those who lived there.[11]

Interrogating the prisoners,[12] settling intelligence gathering forces in enemy territory,[13] studying their movements and transferring them at the appropriate time, were all other methods for acquiring intelligence. The Prophet (s) would never be heedless of any means of obtaining information about the enemy, and at times he would personally undertake to find out the latest information about them.[14] The goal of this was to achieve victory and gain accurate information.
One of the examples of success in the Holy Prophet's information gathering was that he (s) would keep all the plans secret[15] like in the case with the Sariya of 'Abdullah bin Jahash[16] and the Conquest of Makkah and more than this, even the

intelligence officers and those charged with information gathering were unaware about some of these plans.[17] Just as in the Sariya of Abi Qatādah ibn Rabi' al-Ansāri to the 'Batn Adham' he tried as much as possible to carry out this mission in total secret,[18] so he made only a few of his topmost commanders privy to the detailed planning of the mission.[19] In the Battle of Uhud, he kept the acquired information hidden from his own uncle 'Abbās and he did the same thing during the Conquest of Makkah.

The supreme commander prepared the intelligence outfit and personnel very well[20] and chose the most suitable people for such missions[21] as in the Battle of Badr where he sent Talha bin 'Abdillah and Sa'eed ibn Zayd to gather information from the trading caravan of the Quraysh; Ibn 'Amr al-Jahni and 'Uday bin Abi al-Za'bā' to gather information from the heart of the enemy's camp; 'Ali ibn Abi Tālib ('a) and Sa'd bin Abi Waqqās to find out about the number of enemy soldiers and Habbāb ibn Mundhir to get information about their movements and the number of reinforcements.

The Prophet (s) was fully aware of all issues pertaining to the organization and strategies of the enemy, their goal, weapons, commanders and plans.[22] He obtained this detailed information by sending a Sariya mission under the command of 'Abdullah bin Anees to assassinate Sufyān bin Khālid al-Hadhali[23] and other leaders of the Quraysh in the Battle of Badr and also displayed them (i.e. what he had acquired from the enemy) in front of Abu Sufyān during the Conquest of Makkah. When intelligence information was sent to the Holy Prophet (s), he would study and scrutinize it very carefully and would coordinate it with the reality of the current situations in the battle.[24] He showed this in the Battles of Badr and Uhud and also in the Battle of Ahzāb when the Bani Quraydha broke their allegiance and in the Conquest of Makkah when he gave permission to acquire information about the capabilities of the enemy, especially [about] their weapons etc.

He made a lot of effort to ensure that the intelligence division was highly active and dynamic and would always cooperate with the commander and those in charge.[25] For example in the Battle of Badr and the Conquest of Makkah, he used the intelligence to acquire every minor detail including the number of those animals slaughtered [for food][26] and when he sent secret missions, like the Sariya of Hamzah ibn 'Abd al-Muttalib, he did the exact same thing.

The Noble Prophet (s) would always give importance to acquiring information at all times, whether before, during or after battle, like in the Conquest of Makkah, and in all situations, however difficult they may be,[27] as in the Battle of Ahzāb

130

where he ordered Hudhayfah bin al-Yamān to go and gather intelligence [about the enemy] in cold weather and harsh conditions.

The Prophet (s) insisted that intelligence gathering be done from near and without keeping a distance from the enemy,[28] like in the Battle of Uhud when he sent Anas and Munis[29] to Dhu Hulayfah, the place where the Quraysh had encamped and ordered them to join the enemy's camp and remain with them. Then, when they arrived at Aqd, near Uhud, he sent Habbāb bin Mundhir and in this way he would use intelligence agents to transfer intelligence and information about the enemy and order them to penetrate within the enemy ranks and at the same time he would station guards and his intelligence agents at the northern borders of the enemy.

The intelligence activities that were carried out by the Holy Prophet (s) were not only for obtaining information about the enemy, but also to negate any intelligence they may have acquired about him, and this was one of the most imperative steps he took which was most necessary and of the utmost importance.[30] He (s) would do this in the following ways:

1. Through 'covert operations'[31] while marching through routes that are filled with vegetation and trees in Madina; namely al-Manqā, al-Khubayth, Dhi Qasr, al-Kutayb and Dhi Amr, that took place in the Battle of Dhi Amr (also known as Ghatfān). In the two battles of Dhi al-'Asheerah and Dumat al-Jundal the cover of darkness in the night was also benefitted from.[32] The Prophet (s) would advise the secret missions to take advantage of the darkness of night time, so they would mostly march at night, as is seen in the Sariya of Muhammad bin Maslamah against the Bani Bakr and that of Zayd ibn Hāritha against the tribe of Judhām and the mission of 'Abd al-Rahmān bin 'Auf against Dumat al-Jundal.

2. Speed and swiftness in movement, as was seen in the Battle of Dumat al-Jundal.[33]

3. Using shortcuts in order to arrive at the enemy's camp faster as in the Battle of Bani Lihyān and the commanders who were sent in the Sariya of 'Akāshah bin Muhsin to fight against the Bani Asad, and (the mission of) Qutbah ibn 'Aāmir against the Khat'am.

4. Ordering that bells should be removed from around the necks of camels[34] so that the forces could move unnoticed as in the example of the Battle of Muta and the Conquest of Makkah.[35]

5. Concealing the state of readiness and the initial mobilization of forces,[36] as was the case in the battles of Bani Saleem, Dhi Amr, Dhāt al-Ruqā'

and Bani Lihyān, and the Sariya of Abi Qatāda bin Rab'i al-Ansāri towards the Batn Adham.

6. Using secret codes and identification[37] as was employed in the Battle of Badr and the Sariya of Usāma bin Zayd from the commander of the group.

7. Instructions to ensure that no noise was to be made that could alert the enemy of the approaching army,[38] like in the Battle of Khaybar where one of the soldiers was prevented from going ahead of the army and advancing alone.

8. Preventing the shining of weapons during the march and not passing in front of the inhabitants of the area,[39] just as he did in the Battle of Badr, Bani Saleem and the Sariya missions of 'Abdullah bin Jahash and 'Ali ibn Abi Tālib ('a) against the Bani Sa'd.

9. Ordering the army to march through uninhabited areas[40] like the desert routes which were taken by the supreme commander in the battles of Bani Saleem and Bahrān and [the Sariya of] 'Amr ibn 'Aās in the fight against the Bani Qudhā'ah.

10. Issuing the command that secrets should be safeguarded and information about the battle-plan should be kept hidden,[41] like in the Conquest of Makkah and the Sariya missions of 'Abdullah ibn Jahash, Abi Qatāda and others.

11. Diverting the enemy from the targets of attacks. This was carried out in various ways which would put the enemy in doubt and misguidance until they would assume that the Holy Prophet (s) is not marching against them.[42] This is precisely what happened in the battles of Bani Lihyān and Dumat al-Jundal and also took the inhabitants on Makkah and their leaders by surprise in the Conquest of Makkah as they were unsure if Muhammad (s) was marching towards Najd, Hawāzin or another region, therefore they were completely baffled and the matter was unclear to them.

12. Arresting the spies and intelligence agents of the enemy and preventing them from sending information[43] as can be pointed out in the battles of Badr, Dumat al-Jundal and Bani al-Mustalaq. During the Conquest of Makkah, one of the spies of the Hawāzin was arrested before entry into Makkah and in the Battle of Khaybar, one of the bold spies of the enemy who had acquired a lot of intelligence was captured.[44]

The goals and objectives in terms of what the Holy Prophet (s) sought to learn about and concentrated on were:

First: Intention and Objective

He (s) would try to find out the goals and objectives of the enemy either through his intelligence agents who were always present among the enemies, like 'Abbās ibn 'Abd al-Muttalib,[45] or by means of trickery[46] and deception.[47] In the battles of Badr and Bani Lihyān, he kept the battle-plan, the time and the place secret and in the Battle of Khaybar, he deceived the tribe of Ghatfān in such a way that they returned back from whence they had come. In the battles of Uhud, Dhāt al-Ruqā' and Khandaq, he learnt of the enemy's goals by eavesdropping on the conversations of the [enemy] commanders and soldiers.[48] Sometimes information was gotten from the way the enemy conducted its exercises and the activities that is carried out openly,[49] or through allied tribes such as the Bani Dhumrah and Bani Mudlij. In the Battle of Dhāt al-Ruqā' he got information from members of the Najd tribe and in the Battle of Tabuk he got information from the Mudhar tribe.

Second: Assembly (of enemy troops)

In this matter, the Prophet (s) would acquire his information from allied tribes[50] or by means of his intelligence division.[51] Just like in the Battle of Uhud, he gave the responsibility to Habbāb ibn Mundhir to obtain information about the assembly and mobilization of the forces of the Quraysh. In the Battle of Khandaq, he used Zubayr ibn 'Awām to get detailed information about the assembly of the confederates, their headquarters, the places where they were stationed and their level of intelligence.[52] In the same way he got information from the intelligence gathering groups of Habbāb ibn Mundhir in the Battle of Uhud, Buraydah ibn Haseeb in the Battle of Bani al-Mustalaq and Busr ibn Sufyān in the Battle of Hudaybiyya.

Third: Terrain and the points of advancement

The Holy Prophet (s) would use the following ways to gain complete and detailed information:
1. Through the vanguard of the army[53] like the action taken by the front-line of the contingent of 'Abbād ibn Basheer in the Battle of Khaybar and of Khālid bin Walid in the Battle of Hunayn and others.
2. By using guides[54] like the employment of Jabbār the guide in the Battle of Dhi Amr, Abi Khuthaymah al-Hārithi in the Battle of Uhud, Madhkur from the tribe of Bani Udhrah in the Battle of Dumat al-Jundal and Haseel bin Mudhirah in the Battle of Hudaybiyya.

The supreme commander would instruct the commanders to make use of guides, especially on routes and in areas that were not well known to them and also in routes that were outside the regular paths; or to use the prisoners[55] who had valuable information as was done in the battles of Dumat al-Jundal, Bani al-Mustalaq, Khaybar etc. and in the various Sariya missions.

3. From the inhabitants of the area.[56] They would send people to them and by asking them questions, they would establish the movement patterns of the enemy and other issues, as was carried out in the battles of Badr and Khaybar. In the Battle of Tabuk too, they benefitted from the intelligence that the tribes who lived near the area where the enemy was marching had to share.

4. By sending patrols to far off areas to gather information.[57]

Fourth: Identifying the area of operations

The supreme commander would complete his 'identification' using various intelligence apparatuses[58] and would also personally get involved in this[59] like in the battles of Badr, Uhud, Khaybar and Khandaq. The most important ways that the Holy Prophet (s) used to obtain this information was using watchmen and eavesdroppers.

1. Watchmen: The lookout would be appointed in the intelligence gathering missions.[60] During this, they would keep watch over the enemy's movements inside and outside the points of interest[61] as well as possible areas in two tactical and strategic levels. Some of the sentries[62] or watchmen would keep an eye on the routes taken by the enemy's caravans,[63] just as was the case when one of the troops was posted at Nakhbār in order to keep an eye over the activities and movements of the enemy, or in the Sariya of Zayd bin Hāritha where they performed the duty of a lookout when he was encamped at 'Ayyis.[64] These forces would stand in a place from where they could carry out their duties as watchmen and spies in an effective manner.[65]

    In every situation, one sentry or spy was posted in a secret location, hidden from the eyes of the enemy[66] and would take advantage of his senses of sight and hearing.[67] No amount of hardship, tribulation or affliction would prevent him from carrying out his duties.[68] Anees ibn Abi Murthad al-Ghanawi who was the sentry appointed in the Battle of Hunayn, remained steadfast despite all the hardships that he had to face. He also remained firm in the Sariya of Ghālib ibn 'Abdullah al-Laythi despite having been shot and injured by an arrow.

2. Eavesdroppers: This was a method that the Holy Prophet (s) used during the night or in situations where visibility was low or when the weather was bad. In such cases, the intelligence agents and eavesdroppers would

move in complete secret until they arrived at the enemy's camp. They would eavesdrop on their conversations and then return and inform the Muslim army of what they had heard.[69] This is exactly what one of the members of a Sariya mission did for the Bani al-Maluh. Hudhayfa ibn al-Yamān also used eavesdropping against Abu Sufyān, the commander of the army of confederates.

What can be seen is that the responsibility of information gathering and eavesdropping needed to be given to men who had certain attributes and qualities, from bodily strength and courage to freedom from certain sicknesses such as coughing, being hard of hearing etc. that could prevent in their successfully carrying out the missions.[70]

The types of information that the Prophet (s) sought to obtain were:
1. General information, for which he would employ normal troops to gather the information such as the vanguard,[71] patrols,[72] guides,[73] locals[74] etc.
2. Urgent information, for which the special military patrols would be brought in.[75] Just as in the battles of Badr, Dumat al-Jundal, Bani al-Mustalaq and the Conquest of Makkah, and the Sariya of 'Akashah ibn Muhsin against the Bani Asad, that of Zayd bin Hāritha and other similar missions.

Sometimes this action would be carried out by those who were behind enemy lines as in the Battle of Uhud. The commander would turn to this when he did not have enough information about the enemy,[76] so he would capture some prisoners and would obtain the information from them.[77]

Reconnaissance would be carried out according to the different stages, meaning the Prophet (s) would conduct reconnaissance at the tactical level to make preparations for battle and during battle[78] when the field of operation for the intelligence agents was limited to the front lines of the enemy, however reconnaissance at the strategic level was carried out by his forces deep within the enemy territory and among the enemies.

Additionally, in order to protect the troops during movement and encampment, he would post his intelligence patrols for reconnaissance in front and on the sides of the army,[79] as he had done when marching from Madina to Badr and from Madina towards Uhud and from Makkah towards the valley of Hunayn. In the same way, he (s) would carry out reconnaissance of the territories and areas where the troops could camp with relative ease and their surrounding areas,[80] like in the battles of Badr, Uhud and Khaybar and would select those people to keep watch whose duties among other things, was to prevent the enemy from finding out their numbers, to protect their base from the approaching enemy, protecting the commander and the troops from being taken by surprise and giving warning about the nearing enemy while at the same time not giving any opportunity to enemy spies and saboteurs.[81]

This guarding and protection was either stationary,[82] which would protect in sensitive and dangerous areas, or mobile,[83] which would offer protection in some areas that were considered to be of special importance militarily and during battle; and normally the former type would require fewer numbers of troops.

NOTES AND REFERENCES

[1] Harawi, al-Hiyal al-Harbiyya: 79; al-Mawsu'ah al-Askariyya 1:62, 70; Majmu'at al-Ta'leef fi Akādimiyyah Farunzi al-'Askariyyah – al-Takteek: 179

[2] Wāqidi 1:11; Ibn Hishām 2:45; Ibn Sa'd 2:2; Tabari 2:259

[3] Wāqidi 1:9, 197; Ibn Sa'd 2:2, 23, 35

[4] Wāqidi 2:534, 550; Ibn Sa'd 2:61, 85; Tabari 3:29; Suhayli 4:252; Kalā'i 1:158

[5] Wāqidi 2:560, 755; Ibn Hishām 3:224; Ibn Sa'd 2:64, 92; Tabari 3:63; Ibn Sayyid al-Nās 2:108, 153; Ibn al-Qayyim 2:299

[6] Wāqidi 1:11, 196, 2:815; Ibn Hishām 3:53; Ibn Sa'd 3:24; Tabari 2:492; Ibn Hazm: 102

[7] Ibn Hishām 2:241; Ibn Sa'd 1:2, 38, 86; Tabari 2:408, 3:130-146; Ibn Hazm: 100; Ibn Sayyid al-Nās 1:224, 226; Mu'jam Qabā'il al-'Arab 1:216, 2:667, 3:1061

[8] Wāqidi 1:402; Ibn Hishām 3:224; Ibn Sa'd 2:44; Ibn Hazm: 253; Ibn Sayyid al-Nās 2:108; Ibn Katheer 5:17

[9] Wāqidi 1:218, 2:457, 461; Ibn Hishām 2:268; Ibn Sa'd 1:207; Tabari 2:436; Kalā'i 1:113; Ibn al-Katheer 4:103

[10] Wāqidi 1:395, 3:990; also see Ibn Sa'd 2:44, 119; Ibn Mandhur, Lisān al-'Arab 7:344

[11] Wāqidi 2:805, 808; Ibn Hishām 2:268; Ibn Sayyid al-Nās 1:224

[12] Ibid.

[13] Wāqidi 1:203; Kalā'i 1:139; Ibn 'Abd al-Barr 2:810 onwards

[14] Wāqidi 2:445; Ibn Hishām 2:267; Ibn Hazm: 226 onwards

[15] Wāqidi 1:11, 13, 2:796; Ibn Hishām 2:245, 4:39; Ibn Sa'd 2:5; Kalā'i 1:57; Ibn Sayyid al-Nās 1:226; Ibn al-Katheer 2:282, 283; Harawi: 79

[16] Wāqidi 1:13-15; Ibn Hishām 1:600-610

[17] Wāqidi 2:769; Ibn Hishām 3:292; Ibn Sa'd 2:96; Ibn Sayyid al-Nās 2:161; Ibn Atheer 4:81

[18] Wāqidi 1:13, 2:535, 3:1123; Ibn Hishām 4:15; Ibn Sa'd 2:56, 65, 136; Harawi: 89; 'Batn' was the word used to describe a group that was smaller than a tribe. (Tr.)

[19] Wāqidi 1:203; Ibn Hishām 4:36; Kalā'i 1:138; Ibn al-Katheer 4:82

[20] Ibn Hishām 2:268; Ibn Sa'd 2:3, 24, 35; Ibn al-Atheer 4:16; Ibn Hajar 4:22

[21] Wāqidi 1:19, 2:457; Ibn Hishām 2:268, 3:243; Ibn Sa'd 1:207

[22] Wāqidi 1:53; Ibn Hishām 4:64; Ibn Sa'd 2:36; Ibn Hanbal 4:325

[23] Wāqidi 2:532

[24] Wāqidi 1:207, 2:457, 805; Ibn Hishām 2:268; Ibn Sa'd 2:25 onwards; Ibn Katheer 4:103

[25] Wāqidi 1:19 onwards, 2:803; Ibn Hishām 2:268 4:37 onwards; Tabari 2:436; Kalā'i: 87 onwards; Ibn Sayyid al-Nās 2:167

[26] Wāqidi 1:11, 194; Ibn Hishām 4:160; Kalā'i 1:151

[27] Zuhri: 63; Wāqidi 1:19; Ibn Hishām 2:268, 4:37, 42; Tabari 2:436; Kalā'i 1:87 onwards

[28] Wāqidi 1:207; Ibn Sa'd 2:25; Tabari 3:378; Jawād 'Ali, al-Mufassal fi Tārikh al-'Arab qabl al-Islām 1:590

[29] Wāqidi 1:206

[30] Wāqidi 2:792, 803; Ibn Atheer 2:241; Ibn Sayyid al-Nās 2:167

[31] Wāqidi 2:636, Ibn Sa'd 2:4; Suhayli 2:142; Hamawi, Mu'jam al-Buldān 1:252, 4:428, 5:215

[32] Ibn Hanbal 5:153; Bukhāri (al-Maghāzi 28); Abu Dāwud (al-Jihād 57); Wāqidi 1:403, 2:557

[33] Wāqidi 1:403, 2:536; Ibn Sa'd 2:61, 117; Ibn Hishām 3:292; Ibn Sayyid al-Nās 2:103

[34] Ibn Hanbal 6:150; Ibn Katheer 3:261

[35] Wāqidi 2:755; Ibn Hishām 4:39; Kalā'i 1:138; Ibn Katheer 4:282

[36] Wāqidi 2:796; Ibn Sa'd 2:33, 43, 56; Tabari 2:555, 3:38; Ibn Sayyid al-Nās 2:161

[37] Wāqidi 1:71, 2:466; Ibn Hishām 2:287, 3:237; Ibn Sayyid al-Nās 2:282

38 Wāqidi 1:56, 2:636; Ibn Katheer 3:216

39 Wāqidi 1:13, 194; Ibn Sa'd 2:21; Ibn Hazm: 108; Ibn Sayyid al-Nās 2:109; Ibn Qayyim, Zād al-Ma'ād 2:299

40 Wāqidi 2:771, 1:195; Ibn Sa'd 2:21

41 Wāqidi 1:12, 2:796, 815; Ibn Sa'd 2:96; Kalā'i 1:138

42 Wāqidi 1:403, 2:536, 2:799-805; Ibn Hishām 3:292; Ibn Sa'd 2:44; Ibn Sayyid al-Nās 2:54

43 Wāqidi 1:404, 2:640, 808; Ibn Hishām 3:268; Harawi, al-Hiyal al-Harbiyya: 77

44 It should be noted that the enumeration of these points in such a manner has been undertaken by the translator for ease of understanding. In the original text the points were not numbered. (Tr.)

45 Ibn Sa'd 4:1 onwards; Ibn 'Abd al-Barr 2:810; Ibn Atheer 3:109

46 Trickery here is not used in the negative sense, rather it means keeping the truth hidden and mentioning something else which is neither true nor false. (Tr.)

47 Wāqidi 2:536, 651; Ibn Hishām 2:268, 3:292; Ibn Atheer 2:188

48 Ibn Hishām 3:243; Kalā'i 1:113

49 Wāqidi 1:207, 395, 2:464

50 Wāqidi 1:395, 3:1011; Ibn Hishām 2:241; Ibn Sayyid al-Nās 1:226

51 Wāqidi 1:207; 2:457

52 Wāqidi 1:207; Ibn Sa'd 2:45

53 Zuhri: 92; Wāqidi 2:640, 3:996, 1123; Ibn Sa'd 2:69, 109

54 Wāqidi 1:194, 218, 404, 2:639, 3:1117

55 Wāqidi 1:404-406, 550, 640; Abu Dāwud (al-Jihād 84)

56 Wāqidi 2:666, 3:1011; Ibn Hishām 2: 268

57 Wāqidi 1:19; Ibn Sa'd 2:25

58 Ibn Hishām 2:271, 3:69; Ibn Sa'd 2:9; Tabari 3:9

59 Wāqidi 2:445; Ibn Hishām 2:271; Tabari 2:507; Kalā'i 1:30; Ibn Sayyid al-Nās 2:131

60 Ibn Sa'd 2:2, 56, 63, 85, 95; Ibn Sayyid al-Nās 1:224, 2:103-112, 145

61 Wāqidi 1:11, 195, 443; Ibn Sa'd 2:63; Ibn Sayyid al-Nas 2:106

62 Wāqidi 1:217, 2:602

[63] Wāqidi 1:19 onward; Ibn Sa'd 2:63; Ibn Sayyid al-Nās 2:106

[64] Wāqidi 2:564, 3:894; Ibn Hishām 4:265; Ibn Sa'd 2:65; Ibn Sayyid al-Nās 2:110

[65] Wāqidi 1:217, 3:894; Ibn Hishām 2:265; Ibn Sa'd 1:63; Ibn Katheer 4:222

[66] Wāqidi 2:750, 3:894; Jawād 'Ali 5:436

[67] Ibn 'Abd al-Barr 2:764; Ibn Atheer 3:9

[68] Wāqidi 3:751, 894; Ibn Sa'd 2:90; Ibn Sayyid al-Nās 2:150

[69] Wāqidi 2:750; Ibn Hishām 3:243; Ibn Sa'd 2:89; Tabari 3:27; Kalā'i 1:113

[70] Ibn 'Abd al-Barr 1:113, 334; Ibn Atheer 1:390

[71] Wāqidi 1:19, 207; Ibn Sa'd 2:25, 45

[72] Wāqidi 2:194, 218, 404, 2:639, 3:1117

[73] Wāqidi 2:666, 3:1011; Ibn Hishām 2:268

[74] Wāqidi 2:406, 550, 805; Ibn Hishām 2:268; Ibn Sa'd 2:44, 62

[75] Wāqidi 1:203; Ibn Sa'd 2:25

[76] Wāqidi 1:404, 2:550, 805; Ibn Hishām 2:268

[77] Wāqidi 1:19, 194, 404, 2:640, 3:996, 1123; Ibn Sa'd 2:25, 45, 69, 109

[78] Wāqidi 1:204 onwards; Ibn Sa'd 2:25 onwards

[79] Zuhri: 92; Ibn Sa'd 2:61, 109; Ibn Hazm: 108, 109

[80] Ibn Hishām 2:271 onwards, 3:69; Ibn Sa'd 2:9; Tabari 3:9; Kalā'i 1:130; Ibn Sayyid al-Nās 2:232

[81] Wāqidi 1:217, 2:602

[82] Wāqidi 2:462, 734; Ibn Sa'd 2:48; Tabari 2:568; Suhayli 3:270

[83] Wāqidi 2:444, 464, 815

CHAPTER FIVE
OPERATIONS PERSONNEL

Operations personnel were all the units responsible for planning, command, training, upgrading weapons, equipment and war strategies and all matters related to these. We shall now proceed to give details about each one of these:

First: Department of Operations

The Department of Operations was a division that was responsible for planning, military command and securing backup from the military and administrative standpoint.[1]

a) Orders of operations: Before or during battle, the Holy Prophet (who was also the supreme commander) issued orders to the army either verbally or in writing,[2] as he had done with 'Abdullah ibn Jahash and Abi Salamah ibn 'Abd al-Asad al-Makhzumi when sending them to the tribes of Bani Asad, or to the commander of the groups during the Battle of Hunayn and during their entry into Makkah.

These orders included the following:
1. Objective:[3] In all the orders of all the battles and military missions, the objective was specified.
2. The necessary measures to be taken during war:[4] as in the Battle of Badr, digging the trench in the Battle of Ahzāb, or before the start of the war like in the Battle of Tabuk.
3. Choosing the specific location:[5] For each operation, the area where the forces would remain and from which they would not cross would be specified, as in the Sariya of 'Abdullah ibn Jahash towards Nakhlah and like the Battle of Dhi Amr towards the place where this tribe had settled and also in the 'conquest', towards Makkah.
4. Ways of reaching the goal:[6] It was necessary for the army to cross over certain points, lands and known areas, like in the battles of Badr, Saleem, Hudaybiyya and Khaybar.
5. Direction:[7] The Muslim army would march towards the places where the enemy had been mobilized or towards the areas where the supreme commander had specified for them, like in the Sariya of Hamza ibn 'Abd al-Muttalib towards the land of the Juhaynah, Abi Qatāda ibn Rab'i al-Ansāri towards Batn Adham and Kurz ibn Jābir Fahri towards the area where he could join the group of 'Ikl and

'Urayna, and also in the Battle of Bani Quraydha to the place where the Jews were living.

6. Locating the most appropriate place to set camp:[8] The most appropriate place for the army to set camp and create a base, where the required amenities were close by and from where administration and medical care could be given, was ascertained. Like in the battles of Badr, Uhud and Khaybar.

7. Guarding and protection:[9] The number of guards, their commander, their orders, their position and all related issues were specified.

8. Secret code and identification:[10] In order to identify the forces of the (Muslim) army, secret codes were used, which were changed from battle to battle and from mission to mission, as was done in the battles of Badr and Khandaq and the Sariya missions of Abu Bakr against the Bani Kilāb and of Usāma bin Zayd towards the Abnā.

9. Changing the flag-bearer:[11] The flag-bearer would be appointed by the supreme commander and would be changed from battle to battle. The responsibility of carrying the flag was given to one of the soldiers who was known for his trustworthiness and reliability.

10. Commanding the rear:[12] For the rear of the army, a specific commander was appointed who was in charge of all the administrative matters [of that portion of the army]. Some of these commanders would always be given this responsibility [in every battle].

11. Command of Sariya missions:[13] For separate and independent intelligence gathering or military missions, a leader was chosen over a group of forces.

12. Special conditions:[14] These special conditions called for special measures, like giving an immediate response to the enemy in the Battle of Dhāt al-Suwayq and other battles, carrying out attacks and assaults like in the battles of Bahrān and Bani Lihyān, the conducting of suicide missions by 'Umayr ibn 'Uday bin Kharshah in order to assassinate 'Asmā', by Sālim ibn 'Umayr in order to kill Abi 'Akf, by Muhammad ibn Maslamah in order to kill Abi Ashraf and by 'Abdullah ibn 'Ateek to assassinate Salām ibn Abi al-Haqeeq.

13. Securing different requirements in the battlefield:[15] like securing intelligence information and administrative requirements in the battles of Badr, Khandaq and Tabuk.

14. Increasing the zeal:[16] When the orders would be issued, effort would be made to ensure that the spirit and zeal of the soldiers should be lifted while at the same time disheartening the enemy. Like the orders that were issued in the battles of Badr and Uhud.

15. Insisting on the steadfastness of the troops:[17] This can be clearly seen from the words of the supreme commander in all the battles.

16. Seek recourse in patience:[18] Patience is the prerequisite of victory and many a group consisting of few individuals has been led to victory over a large army of soldiers through patience.

17. Sacrificing one's wealth and life:[19] These are the two prime ingredients of volitional warfare and for this reason, the Holy Prophet (s) put a lot of importance on these two factors in all his orders to the troops.

This was the summary of the orders given and we will now proceed to explain each one in detail:

1. Objective

Every war has 'objectives'. The objectives of the Holy Prophet (s) in the battles were:

a) Acquiring information.[20]

b) Invading the enemy caravans.[21]

c) Weakening the economic strength and cutting the lines of reinforcements[22] from the west and east for the Quraysh and the Jews of Khaybar.

d) Securing freedom for the propagation and spread of Islām[23] as was the case in the Sariya of Hamza ibn 'Abd al-Muttalib and Khālid ibn Walid against the Bani Hārith and also that of 'Ali ibn Abi Tālib ('a) against the Bani Mudhjah.

e) Displaying the strength and might of the Muslim army[24] as in the battles of Hamrā al-Asad, Hudaybiyya and Muta and that which was done against the Romans.

f) Instilling fear and terror in the hearts of those who allied themselves with the enemies of Islām or were preparing to do so.[25]

g) Enacting peace treaties with neighboring tribes:[26] like the Bani Dhumrah, Bani Juhaynah and Bani Mudlij as well as the treaty will Bani Kalb; meaning those who had come to fight in Dumat al-Jundal, Tabir and the outskirts of Shām. This was done in order to secure the success of the military operations.

h) Concentrating on the points and areas of tactical and strategic importance[27] like the areas around the coast and towards the east after the Battle of Badr against the Bani Saleem who were a threat to the revolution and also towards the north in order to survey the area of Dumat al-Jundal and invading upon the enemy who were waiting for opportunity or had already begun working against the Muslim army,[28] like the Jews and the Romans.

i)   Assassinating those who had evil intentions against the supreme commander, the army troops, the caretakers of the towns or the Islāmic revolution in general.[29]

j)   Punishing the Jews of Bani Qaynuqā'[30] because they broke their allegiance and their covenant for their own benefit, and similarly the Bani Nadhir,[31] Bani Quraydha[32] and the inhabitants of Khaybar.[33] The Prophet (s) destroyed the pact of these four groups[34] with each other as well as their pact with the enemy Arab tribes.[35]

k)   Giving a strong reaction against Abu Sufyān and his forces: this was when they had the intention to invade Madina and ransack it in the Battle of Dhāt al-Suwayq.[36]

l)   Dealing with the two tribes of Bani Saleem and Bani Ghatfān because they had declared their open enmity against Islām.[37]

m) Preventing other tribes from attacking Madina, such as the tribes of Bani Tha'labah and Muhārib and others.[38]

n)   Teaching and training the children of the Ummah and purifying their hearts from filth, doubts and falsehoods.[39]

o)   Creating fear against Rome and Persia:[40] The Prophet (s) made it his general policy in dealing with these two states and preparing for war with them before they launched an attack on the Muslim lands[41] or gain control over the northern borders.

p)   Taking the battle to the enemy territory:[42] The Prophet (s) would only fight against the enemy outside Madina and the moment he received information that the enemy intended to attack Madina, he would launch a pre-emptive strike on them before they could start marching from their own lands. This happened in many of the battles like Bani Saleem, Dhi Amr and Bahrān against the Arab tribes and in Muta and Tabuk against the Romans.

q)   Taking revenge and punishing those who killed innocents:[43] As was the case in the Sariya of Kurz ibn Jābir Fahri in order to teach the 'Ikl and 'Urayna a lesson. Or in order to punish those who were acting against the rules and regulations of the leader and ruler,[44] like the opposition of the Jews of Bani Quraydha to the agreements and conditions of the homeland pact.

r)   Realizing peace:[45] This was another objective. An example of this was the Battle of Hudaybiyya against the Quraysh and the Sariya of 'Abd al-Rahmān ibn 'Auf against the Bani Kalb.

s)   Coming to the aid of the oppressed:[46] as was the case in the Battle of Dumat al-Jundal which took place on the orders and instructions of the supreme commander.

t)   Belief in oneness and unity:[47] This was done by destroying the idols that were adorned and worshipped by the Arabs. An example was the Sariya of Khālid bin Walid in order to destroy the idol 'Uzzā', that of 'Amr bin 'Aās to destroy the idol Siwā', of Sa'd ibn Zayd al-Ashal to destroy the idol Manāt, Tufayl ibn 'Amr to destroy the idol Dhil Kiflayn and 'Ali ibn Abi Tālib ('a) to destroy the idol al-Filis and all the idols of the Ka'bah.

u) Collecting taxes from the tribes that had accepted Islām.[48]

2. Sending military missions and commanding the army in battle

The Holy Prophet (s) arranged a number of military missions[49] and battles[50] or personally took on the responsibility of commanding them. On the tactical and strategic level he did the planning and expounded the short and long term goals[51] and the primary and secondary objectives,[52] just as the primary objective of the Battle of Dumat al-Jundal was crushing the tribes of that area who were forcing the traders and travelers to pay a toll and the secondary objective was to instill fear in the hearts of the Romans. The primary objective in the Battle of Khaybar was also to bring down Khaybar and deal with its inhabitants while the secondary objective was to prevent the Arab tribes from allying themselves to the Jews and preparation for war against the Quraysh in Makkah and those enemies who were deemed more dangerous.[53]

He (s) also planned 'offensive' and 'defensive' operations[54] and would always use assaults and offense in every battle.[55] He made this something that was ingrained in the minds and hearts of the soldiers.[56] He would specify different stages of battle,[57] meaning he would not just attack the enemy at one go, rather he would launch assaults on them at different times. If the enemy did not launch an all-out attack against him,[58] he would launch successive and consecutive attacks on them and would fight each one independently while at the same time preventing others from joining forces with the enemy. This is precisely what he did in his battle with the Jews. He started with the Bani Qaynuqā' and ended with Khaybar. He employed the same tactic against the Arab tribes of Bani Tha'labah and Ghatfān in the Battle of Dhi Amr, Bani Saleem in the Battle of Bahrān and Bani al-Mustalaq in the Battle of Bani al-Mustalaq and others.

The Prophet (s) would command the troops using 'new techniques'[59] of warfare, including centralization of command, organizing the ranks, laying siege, mobile defense, pre-emptive, offensive and psychological warfare.

3. Studying what was important and necessary

The Holy Prophet (s) would define the primary and secondary objectives for his commanders[60] and would stress on the importance of achieving the primary objective.[61] His commanders would also adhere to this and issues of secondary importance would not deter them from their priorities. For example, when the supreme commander sent 'Umar ibn al-Khattāb[62] to fight the 'Ajz Hawāzin,[63] after doing this he refrained from invading the other related tribes saying, "The Prophet (s) only commanded me to fight against the Hawāzin.'[64]

Tufayl ibn 'Amr[65] also accomplished his primary objective[66] which was to join with the army that was sent towards Tā'if as well as his secondary objective[67] which was to break and destroy the idol Dhil Kiflayn and he never crossed over the limit that was determined for him. In the same way, he (s) specified the missions during the entry into Makkah by selecting the commanders of the different groups,[68] and in defining the priorities, he considered the personality of the commander, the type of enemy, the ordinances and the route to be taken.

4. Preserving the goal

The goals of the Holy Prophet (s) were numerous and various[69] and all of them were geared towards the complete annihilation of the enemy both materially and spiritually and the spread of the message of Islām, which he accomplished with complete freedom and total success.[70] The Prophet's enemies would always try to prevent him from attaining his goals, but they were not successful and he (s) was steadfast in guarding his goal.[71] The supreme commander would also require this from his commanders. For example, he sent 'Ali ibn Abi Tālib ('a)[72] to destroy the idol of the tribe of Tā'i[73] and also sent him in the second phase to spread Islām among the tribes of Yemen.[74] 'Ali ('a) arrived in their land. The tribes rose up in opposition to him, but he fought them and continued his important mission until he was able to secure his goal.[75] However, Khālid bin Walid[76] did not remain steadfast in his mission to invite the Bani Judhayma to Islām[77] and diverted from his goal. Despite not having been ordered to kill them, he slaughtered some of the men of the said tribe.[78]

5. Exhortation to fight

The Prophet (s) would exhort the soldiers and fighters towards dedication and self-sacrifice, to the extent of their ability, and would try to strengthen their spirits, resolve and readiness before they entered into battle.[79] He would call on them to be just and fair in their dealing with those whom they were fighting. He would also encourage his soldiers and urge them to be brave[80] and would recall the reward of those who were patient in the battlefield.[81] This yielded many results, because the soldiers would jump into the heat of battle and in order to combat the enemy, would try to overtake death.[82] Many of them came to the battlefield with complete courage. In one of the battles, a soldier who had a date in his mouth spit it out,[83] another threw away his armor and fought courageously.[84] The youth would keenly prepare for battle[85] and as a result, with a small force they were able to gain victory over large hoards.

6.   The flag and banner

The Liwā'[86] was one sign that was carried by the most courageous and strong soldier in the Muslim army under the command of the supreme commander.[87] The flag-bearers, who were personally selected by the Holy Prophet (s),[88] would be changed in every battle.[89] The color of the flag was white[90] and its shape was quadrangular.[91]

As for the Rāyah,[92] it too was held by the bravest and strongest soldier of each tribe[93] and depending on the number of tribes present at the time of organizing the army, it had various shapes and colors.[94] The Rāyah was normally smaller than the Liwā'. The flag was a means of strengthening the spirits of the forces, and as long as it was hoisted, the forces would continue fighting.[95] If the flag fell, the troops would be faced with defeat,[96] so the commander would insist on guarding the flag and self-sacrifice until death in order to safeguard it.[97] The flag-bearer would strive to keep the flag hoisted even if it meant having his hand chopped off or giving up his life.[98] If one of the brave-hearted soldiers saw in himself the ability to rescue the army from defeat, he would raise the flag again after it had fallen,[99] and it would not be long before the dispersed army would again assemble and prepare to fight.

7.   Code words and identification

These were words by which the soldiers would recognize each other when battling against the enemy. This code word was changed from battle to battle.[100] In the Battle of Badr, the code was 'Ahad... Ahad' (one... one). The code word of the Khazraj was 'O Bani 'Abdillah' and the code word of the Aus was 'Bani 'Ubaydillah'. In the Battle of Khandaq, the code word of the army was 'Hum La Yunsarun' and the code of the Muhājirs was 'Ya Khaylullah'. In the Conquest of Makkah, Hunayn and Tā'if it was 'O Bani 'Abdul-Rahmān'. The code word was used when the forces would communicate with each other and was especially necessary during the night, because the clothes were similar and there was the possibility of mistaking enemy patrols for friendly patrols.[101] Even today, code words are still used.[102]

These secret codes are always different in each war, and when they are found out by the enemy, they are immediately changed. The mentioned codes were not limited to battles, rather the commander of Sariya missions would also give his troops different codes when sending them out on missions.[103] Just like what happened in the Sariya of Abu Bakr against the Bani Kilāb and that of Usāma against the Abnā.

8. Being prepared for war

This took the form of giving a quick response to the incursions of the enemy and not giving them an opportunity to accomplish their intended goals.[104] It was required of the soldiers that they should quickly assemble at the call (of the supreme commander) with their weapons, armor and means of transport ready to launch counter-attacks.[105] It is obvious that the Muslim army was prepared for battle with Kurz ibn Jābir Fahri when Madina was attacked and the strong response of the army when the supreme commander declared war against the Bani Quraydha,[106] therefore they were able to get prepared for battle within a short period of time. The preparation included wearing armor, sharpening swords, carrying spears and getting the means of transport ready. After assembly, all the columns would move towards the enemy and would in the end come together. The Holy Prophet (s) was the first person who prepared for battle in this war (against the Bani Quraydha).[107]

In the Battle of al-Ghābah,[108] the soldiers quickly became ready with their battle gear, weapons and mounted their horses and joined 'Ayniyyah ibn al-Hisn.[109] The Muslim army displayed its mobilization and readiness in the Sariya of Usāma ibn Zayd.[110] At this time three thousand troops who were fully equipped[111] came together on the orders of mobilization and assembled in one day,[112] something that is not seen even in today's armies, because mobilizing such a large force cannot be done in less than three days. In reality, the zeal for war and martyrdom, discipline, sufficient training and constant preparedness for battle were the necessary pre-requisites for this higher level of readiness.

9. General mobilization

The general mobilization is the creation of a battle-plan and making the necessary preparations for the armed forces, mobilizing the human, material, psychological and spiritual resources for battle while at the same time being economically and materially prepared for it.[113] The Noble Prophet (s) would mobilize the people in groups or all together[114] depending on the available resources and the type of enemy. This is why he conducted a general mobilization[115] during the battles of the conquest and Tabuk, while in the Battle of Badr, he only ordered a partial mobilization.[116] In most of the wars and battles, this would take place in secret[117] but sometimes, as in the case of the Battle of Tabuk, it was conducted openly.

148

The armed forces would thus be prepared. When the order of mobilization reached the other Muslim tribes, they would all be called to prepare for battle.[118] Once the troops were organized, they would be ready for a new mission;[119] as had happened in the Conquest of Makkah and the Battle of Hunayn. The battle gear and weapons[120] were taken on loan from Safwān ibn Umayya before the battle and some more was bought to make it more complete, and the people would also assist in the preparation out of their fervor by contributing what was required, and they would be encouraged to do so.[121] The spirit among them would be strengthened[122] and the faith in the righteousness of the battle that they are fighting would be ignited in them,[123] the love for battle and combat[124] became intensified,[125] and when it was announced that certain equipment was required, it would be collected and sent to fight the battle against the enemy.[126] It was certain that the people would all answer the call to mobilize and none of them ever turned away,[127] and they would wear their battle armor in the quickest time possible.[128] In some of the battles, the speed of mobilization and preparation of the army was such that it was done in less than 24 hours.[129] The distinguishing feature of the mobilization of the Muslim army was that the forces would try to outdo each other in obedience (to the Prophet) and would act with complete love and devotion.[130]

10. Taking the appropriate counter-measures

The Holy Prophet (s) would retaliate against the enemy in various ways, among them were:

a) Preventive counter-measures[131] which would be taken when information about an impending enemy attack on Madina was underway. This was seen in the battles and missions such as Bani Saleem, Dhi Amr, Bahrān, Dhāt al-Ruqā', Dumat al-Jundal and Bani al-Mustalaq.

b) Disciplinary counter-measures:[132] These operations were conducted as a result of the breaking of pacts, heedlessness and impudence of the enemy against the rules and regulations of the Islāmic state. Of course it was normally the case that first warnings would be given, as in the case of the battles against the Bani Qaynuqā', Bani Nadhir, Bani Quraydha and Khaybar.

c) Decisive and conclusive counter-measures:[133] This was a more serious and firm response to the enemy's incursions, to such an extent that they should never again even think of carrying out similar attacks in the future. Like what was done to the Bani Quraydha after they broke their pact and mobilized themselves to fight against the Muslims in the Battle of Ahzāb, and as a result they were all killed, and also what transpired against Abu Sufyān, the commander of the enemy forces, when he tried to threaten the Muslims and the response to his threat was much stronger and more forceful.

d) Immediate counter-measures:[134] This would take place immediately and swiftly after the enemy's incursion and would be forceful and strong, to such an extent that it would weaken the enemy's base and inflict severe loss and casualties on them; like in the battles of Badr al-Awwal and al-Ghābah.

11. The routes taken by the forces

The Holy Prophet (s) would study and specify the routes (to be taken) from Madina to the enemy,[135] just as he had done in the Battle of Badr, Hudaybiyya and Khaybar, and he would also define the arrangement in which the forces would march,[136] and would also keep an eye over the main focal points[137] like the movement of the forces from Madina towards Tabuk and from Madina towards Makkah, and would also select the places where 'military parades' would be held in the areas of settlement and assembly.[138]

In the Battle of Badr, the parade and review of the army in the area where it was assembled and camped was carried out in al-Buq'a. In the Battle of Uhud, the Muslim army was reviewed in Shaykhayn and in the Sariya of Usāma bin Zayd it was carried out in Jaraf. The places of rest for the forces in the daytime and nighttime[139] and the places where the army should concentrate were also considered by him (s) as in the battles of Badr and Tabuk.[140] He (s) would select the shortest route to arrive at the goal and would keep it hidden from the view of the enemy.[141] At the same time, he would try as much as possible to choose routes that had wells and plenty of water supply throughout.[142]

The supreme commander would give the following instructions to the army when they set out:

a) To be careful not to make noise and avoid anything that would draw the attention of the enemy, like the bells worn around the necks of camels.

b) Not to use shiny and glittery tools.

c) Staying behind or moving ahead of the forces.[143]

d) Moving during the night in order to remain hidden from the enemy.[144]

e) Taking routes that would not bring them directly face to face with the enemy,[145] like in the Sariya of 'Abdullah ibn Jahash and the Conquest of Makkah.

f) Moving swiftly[146] in order to remain one step ahead of the enemy and arriving at the place of battle at the appropriate time.

At the same time, the movement of the forces would be such that a group of information gathering patrols would be kept at a distance in order to keep watch.[147] During this march, the forces were either on foot or on riding on camels.[148]

12. The area of assembly and mobilization

This was a place which the Prophet (s) had chosen to conduct the following matters: assemble the forces,[149] organize them,[150] review them,[151] carry out a selection of some soldiers and ask others to return,[152] prepare the battle gear, weapons,[153] conduct a final check,[154] arrange the necessary food and water provisions,[155] prepare (the soldiers) physically and mentally,[156] make the battle-plan by taking all the possibilities and different battle scenarios into consideration,[157] select and announcing his deputy in Madina,[158] review the flags and banners and select those who will carry them,[159] determine the tribes who will participate in the battle[160] and review the means of transport to be used by the forces.[161]

13. The area of encampment and setting up base

This was a place selected by the Prophet (s) for the army to set camp.[162] In the Battle of Badr it was in al-'Adwat al-Dunyā, in the Battle of Uhud it was in front of the Mountain of Uhud[163] and in the Battle of Khandaq it was near the Sala' Mountain. The camping of the troops in a suitable place,[164] like an area which is fortified in three directions and keeps the enemies at bay; as in the Battle of Khandaq where only the northern area was accessible, and also selecting suitable places in battle, such that this place is in accordance with all the required conditions of a base camp. For example in the Battle of Khaybar, the said places were chosen by the inspection of the commanders[165] and the decision was based on the following criteria:

a) Securing the ease of access and movement for friendly forces while at the same time making it hard to reach for enemy troops.[166]

b) Facing the direction which would cause the sun to be behind their own forces;[167] like in the Battle of Badr and other battles.

c) For the troops to be in front of a mountain or any other natural fortress;[168] as in the Battle of Uhud.

d) Keeping the base camp near sources of water and some major highways.[169]

e) Plentitude of grass and grazing ground in the area.[170]

f) Making sure the area is suitable medically and hygienically.[171]

g) Ensuring the ground is hard and with areas where the battle can be fought.[172]

h) Being far away from the reach of enemy arrows;[173] as in the battles of Bani Nadhir, Bani Quraydha and Khaybar.

i)   Having the possibility of moving away in case there are no reinforcements. [174]

j)   The ability to cut off the enemy supply routes and stopping them from obtaining it (supplies). [175]

k)   The possibility of securing the necessary cover and camouflage. [176]

l)   Being able to fully control their own forces. [177]

m) Ease of movement in order to keep watch over the enemy and spy on them. [178]

In this area, the Prophet (s) placed the command post at an elevated position, so that it would be possible for him to have complete control and ability to supervise the war. [179] He (s) would arrange the forces in ranks [180] according to their battle instructions; [181] like the cavalry, the infantry, the special forces, the vanguard, the archers, the rear and others.

The measures that were taken in the area when the base camp was set up included: review and assessment; [182] inspection of the troops; [183] assembling the troops and their accouterments; [184] organizing the ranks; [185] specifying the battle instructions, [186] and the necessary guarding and protection especially of the command post; [187] appointing the commanders of the ranks and contingents [188] including those responsible for the command post and its protection; preparing the troops psychologically and spiritually; [189] encouraging them to fight; [190] specifying the secret code words for identification; [191] issuing the command to start the war; [192] the mode of co-operation [193] between the forces as was done in the Battle of Badr - between the units like in the Sariya of Tufayl ibn 'Amr, between the commanders who marched towards Tā'if after the Battle of Hunayn and between the units and contingents, as in the troops who entered Makkah during the Conquest of Makkah; conducting training exercises on the principles of archery, [194] attack or the techniques that the soldiers should use when they come face to face with the enemy; [195] specifying the time and place for war [196] which would be before the enemy was well prepared and in the hours of twilight. Aside from these issues, in the command post the battle with the enemy would also be supervised. [197]

14. Keeping the operations secret and covert

The Holy Prophet (s) would try very hard to conduct the military operations in a covert and clandestine manner. Therefore he would take extra measures to attain this goal. For this reason, the mobilization and preparation for war would take place in secret; like in the Sariya of 'Abdullah ibn Jahash and the Conquest of Makkah etc. and aside from a select few who were known for their trustworthiness and their ability to keep secrets, nobody was aware what the intention and goal of the Holy Prophet (s) was.[198] The Holy Prophet (s) would then issue brief instructions for the commander of the operations[199] and would complete his orders to the commanders either by letter or verbally.[200] He (s) would also specify the time it should take for the mission to be conducted[201] and the direction and ways by which they should divert the enemy.[202] He would keep the missions and preparations for some of the battles hidden and would not do them openly.[203] Aside from this, he would give instructions that the secrets should be kept hidden and the goal should not be announced until the appropriate time.[204]

He would disperse spies and intelligence agents,[205] arrest enemy spies in order to prevent them from sending information to the enemy,[206] blockade the routes used by the enemy spies so that they could not take information back to the enemy base,[207] and would actually not permit any of these forces from entering or exiting the said area.[208] In order that the intelligence apparatus may function even better, the Holy Prophet (s) would personally oversee these operations and would stress on their importance.

15. Specification and assessment of the battle ground

The assessment and specification of the battle grounds was linked to the military, economic and political prowess of the commanders and personnel. Strategically, a more prudent and complete, and from the tactical viewpoint, the enemy, the land and the battle strategy a firm position was selected.[209] The Holy Prophet (s) would assess the battle readiness in all the ranks and would constantly seek information and updates about the enemy and his own forces in the battlefield[210] and was completely aware of all the other military and political conditions.[211] As a result, his orders would only be issued after being supported by strong intelligence and various other means of affirming their prudence and correctness.[212]

Other matters that were examined and looked into by the Holy Prophet (s) included:
a) With regards to the enemy: their strength, assembly, preparation and weaponry.[213]
b) With regards to the friend: Furnishing complete battle gear and military equipment and making them equally trained and motivated.[214]
c) With regards to the land: ensuring that it is suitable for setting up camp and carrying out military operations.[215]

16. Co-operation

The Holy Prophet (s) would encourage his forces to co-operate with each other when he was readying them for battle.[216] He asked the soldiers and all the people to assist the army materially.[217] In the same way, he would instruct the commanders to work with those who were under them, the soldiers to co-operate with each other, the units to collaborate with one another, the cavalry to support the infantry, the rear to work with the vanguard and the contingents to work with the army. In the same way he would himself, as the supreme commander, work with the soldiers[218] and in order to strengthen this bond,[219] he instituted a pact of brotherhood between the Muhājirs and the Ansārs[220] and placed all the believers as one entity and one body.[221]

17. Invasion and attack

'Invasion and attack' was one of the military strategies of the Holy Prophet (s) that he would implement against the enemy. He (s) employed a state of constant offense and would attack the enemy continuously, and as a result he left them with no choice but to do things that would make their goals and intentions clear.[222] The Prophet's goal in invading and attacking was displaying the strength and might of the Muslim army,[223] gaining the upper hand over the enemy[224] and continuously encountering them (and countering their intended attacks).[225]

The Sariya and military missions that he (s) would send was not for anything but invasion and attack,[226] the Battle of Hamrā' al-Asad[227] was only a show of strength and the Battle of Dumat al-Jundal[228] was only fought to get information, learn about and test the strength and capability of the Roman army. The Muslim army fought Badr al-Aākhar[229] only in order to gain the upper hand over the enemy and it was then that Abu Sufyān turned back on his promise of war and tried to give excuses (for not fighting).[230] However, the Prophet (s) had decided to launch an attack and said: 'I swear by He in whose hand my life is, even if nobody accompanies me, I will come out to fight.'[231]

18. Display of strength and might

One of the manifestations of attack is 'psychological warfare' which is actually an indirect type of warfare[232] whose goal is instilling fear in the enemy,[233] weakening his spirits[234] and preventing him from many of his aggressive plans.[235] The Noble Prophet (s) used various methods to gain information in order to create fear in the enemy.[236] In the battles of Hamrā' al-Asad, Khandaq and the Conquest, by burning the dry date palms and plantations of the enemy,[237] he created a large fire[238] and paraded the large number of troops and weapons[239] he had in front of the enemy commander i.e. Abu Sufyān, before entering Makkah. Before the Battle of Badr, while performing the Hajj al-Tamatu', he slaughtered the camel that was linked to Abu Jahl.[240] During the Conquest, he performed the Sa'ee between Safā and Marwa quickly,[241] with his followers carrying sheathed swords,[242] he performed the circumambulation while riding on a camel.[243] Then he turned his cloak on the side and left his right arm open,[244] ordering the whole army to do just as he had done.[245] He praised those of them who displayed their strength to the enemy.[246] These tactics were quite successful and assisted in destroying the resistance of the enemy, to such an extent that he had made them certain that they would by no means be capable to come face to face with the Muslim army.[247]

19. Forewarning prior to battle

The supreme commander would commence war in the following manner:[248]

a) In a direct manner[249] i.e. he would normally remain in a condition of continual war with the enemy, and would use it as a preventative measure.[250]

b) Giving the enemy an choice between accepting Islām and war.[251] He would send this type of warning through a messenger, and if he did not get a response he would commence the war; like in the Sariya of 'Abd al-Rahmān ibn 'Awf and Khālid bin Walid to Dumat al-Jundal and against the Bani al-Hārith.

c) Nullification and breaking of pacts:[252] When the enemies would break their peace pacts, the Prophet (s) would send some people to warn them and remind them of their treachery and betrayal; just as he had done in the 'four battles' against the Jews.

The Holy Prophet (s) would fight three types of battles. One was the battle fought without any warning or notice,[253] like the battles that he fought against the hostile Arab tribes or the Quraysh and external foes. In these cases, he would launch surprise attacks on these groups in their own territories. Another type was preceded by forewarning,[254] so he would mostly give the enemy an option and try to reason with them kindly as he wanted all the people to accept Islām.

However, nullifying the pact[255] was dealt with in a different way when it came to the Jews who lived in Madina and its outskirts. The Prophet (s) created a pact of defense with them as 'citizens' and had acknowledged them as fellow compatriots. Despite this they broke their pact and turned into a center for plotting and ambush (against the Muslims). He (s) also sent a representative[256] to the Bani Qaynuqā'[257] and the Bani Nadhir[258] and gave them a notice that they should leave their lands in ten days,[259] but they did not pay any attention to the warning reacted with disdain.[260] The Prophet (s) was left with no option but to wage war against them.

20. The order to commence the war

The order to start the war was issued by the supreme commander[261] or by the commander of any independent unit[262] and would usually be marked by the sounding of "Allahu Akbar"[263] which would be repeated loudly so that all the soldiers could hear.[264] In the Battle of Hunayn, the Holy Prophet (s) took advantage of the loud voice of his uncle 'Abbas for this.[265] The soldiers would be asked to remain silent (after the battle had begun). No loud sound was heard from any soldier, except the movement of their lips and whisperings of 'Takbir' and 'Dhikr'.[266] In the Battle of Badr, during the heat of battle, someone (from among the enemy) said: Don't you see them? It is as if they are all mutes; they don't say anything but they are alive and are benefitting from life.[267]

In the new battles, the command to commence the war was issued by sounds that were made from behind trenches or fortified areas or by fires that were thrown up in the air or by other means of communication.[268]

The command to begin the battle with Takbir and other similar slogans would heighten the bravery and courage of the troops and would remove the fear of battle from their hearts.[269]

21. Combat

Battle and combat between the two sides would start in such a way that first one or a few brave soldiers from the Muslim army, and from the enemy's army, would come forward.[270] These combatants would use various weapons including swords. They would either be on foot or horseback and would be in full armor and would move to fight each other in single one-on-one combat.[271] Each one of them would kill one or more of his opponents.[272] It is then that the other soldiers rush in and the full scale battle starts with complete intensity.[273]

In the Battle of Badr, three fighters from the Muslim army stood to face three soldiers from the polytheists and ended up (successfully) killing their opponents.[274] In the Battle of Uhud, one person from the Muslims went to face one person (from the polytheists) and caused him to fall to the ground by one strike of the sword.[275] This (one-on-one) combat would be observed by the supreme commander and the soldiers of both sides.[276] So if they would kill their opponents, the spirit and courage of the troops would be strengthened while weakness and a sense of defeat would prevail over the enemy.

22. Organization of the battle

The Assembly of the troops and arrangement of their encampment was done in spaced out columns which would be organized in one line or more. The arrangement of the soldiers in form and depth, was dependent on the type of war, enemy forces, military facilities, the number of forces, battle gear and equipment available, the type of weapons used and the terrain. The aim of this organization was creating a readiness for launching the main strike on the enemy, gaining freedom to maneuver, co-operation and assistance, preventing the strikes of the enemy and reducing losses.[277] The Arabs of the Age of Ignorance would employ the 'Karr wa Farr' (strike and flee) tactic in their wars.[278] But the Holy Prophet (s) invented a new form of arrangement and organization of the ranks[279] with a specific order, and this technique has also been used in more recent wars and especially in World War II. The arrangement of ranks was either in the form of a single column or many columns.

In the Battle of Badr, the Holy Prophet (s) arranged the troops in two columns,[280] in such a way that he placed the archers in the first column[281] and in the second column he positioned the spearers and the infantry,[282] and behind this column he put the rear of the army.[283] Later, he changed this arrangement and organization and transferred the first column to the heart of the army and reorganized the right flank, the left flank and also the infantry.[284] When the soldiers would be arranged into two columns, a section of the cavalry would remain behind the second column and in the rear i.e. behind the infantry and the second column.

The women, munitions, preserves, the commander's camp, the place for prayer, food and other provisions were placed at the rear of the army.[285] The place of the commander was in the heart and the first column of the army,[286] the lookout post was at an elevation[287] from where he could get an overview and control the battle, just as the Holy Prophet (s) had done in when commanding the battles of Badr and Uhud.

Organization and arrangement of the troops in battle

First scenario

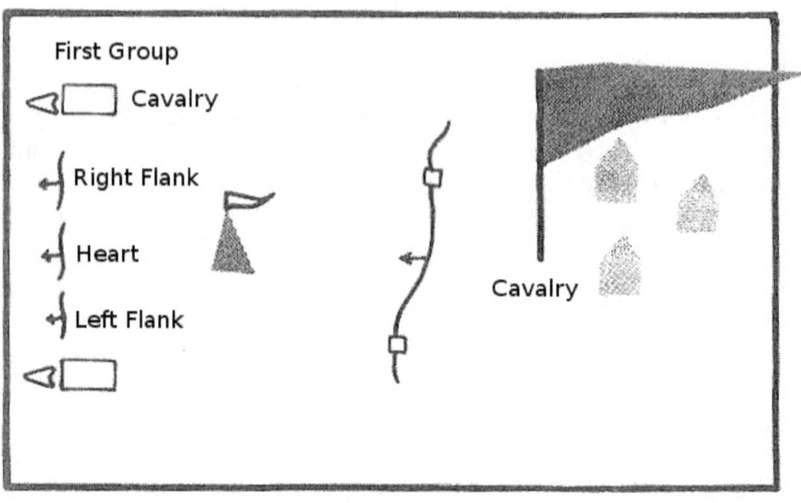

Second scenario

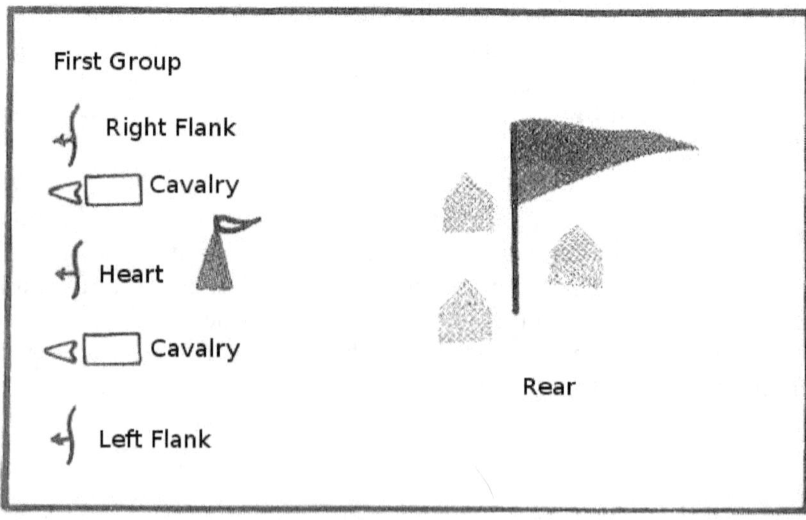

Third scenario

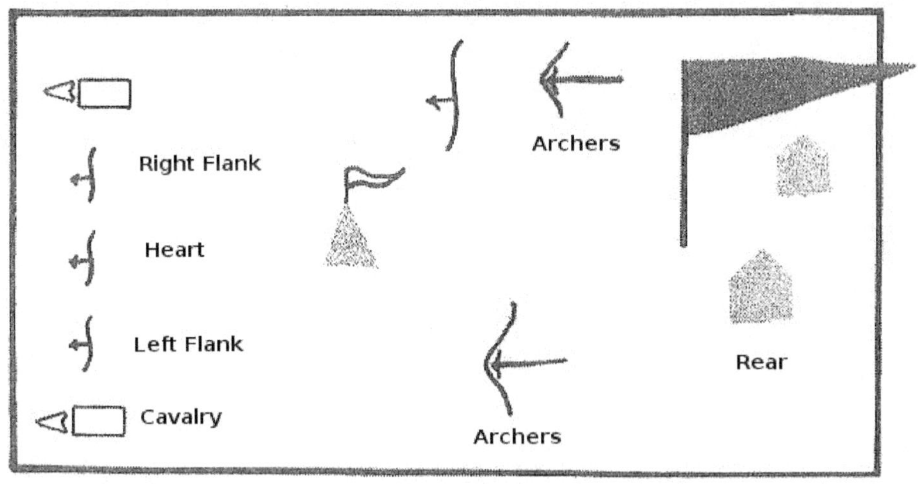

Fourth scenario

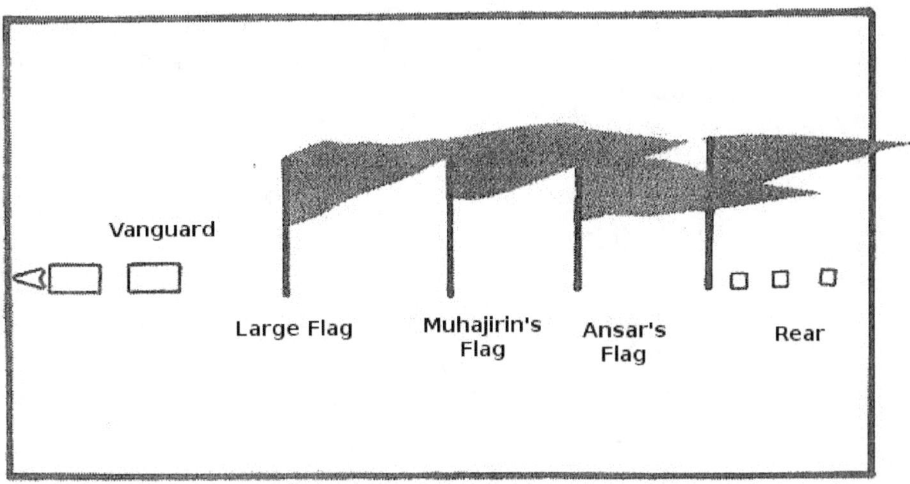

The situation on the ground in the Battle of Uhud and its results

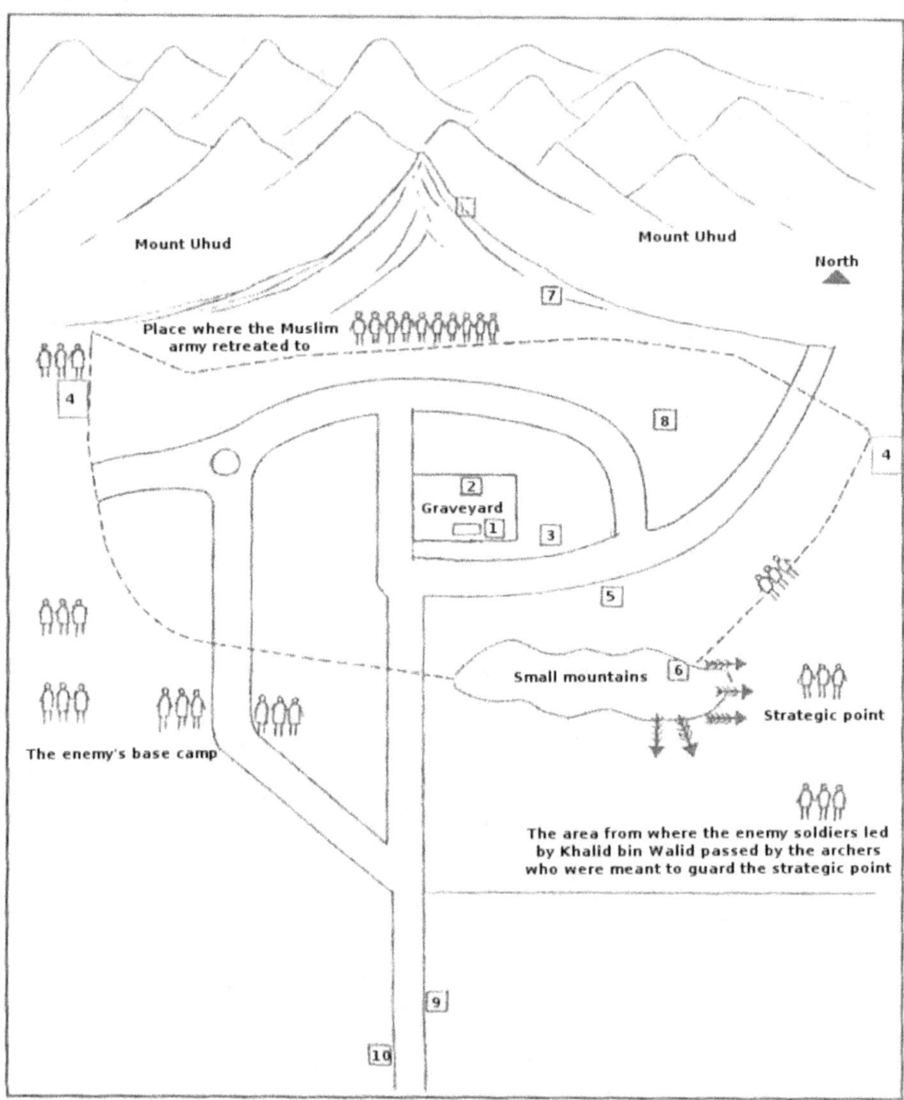

KEY

1. The place where Hamza the uncle of the Prophet (s), 'Abdullah ibn Jahash and Mus'ab ibn 'Umayr have been buried.
2. The place where the martyrs of Uhud have been buried.
3. The area where there Muslim army fought with the army of the polytheists.
4. The last borders of the battle in the east and west.
5. The place where Hamza ibn 'Abd al-Muttalib (r) was martyred.
6. The place where archers from the Muslim were positioned to guard the pass on the small Mountain of al-Rummāh.
7. The place where the Holy Prophet (s) was hidden after he had been injured – it was inside a fissure in the side of Mount Uhud.
8. Masjid al-Fasah.
9. Masjid al-Mustarāh (where the Holy Prophet (s) rested with his army before entering into Uhud).
10. Masjid al-Dir' (where the Prophet (s) stopped briefly when returning from Uhud).

23. Battles fought in order to capture forts (*Harb al-Husun*)

The Holy Prophet (s) employed the tactic of 'siege' in order to capture forts[288] and aside from Khaybar and Tā'if, he never used 'direct attack and assault',[289] because this type of warfare led to many casualties. Using heavy weaponry on a wide scale as in the Battle of Tā'if was not common practice for the Muslim army.[290] Many military operations would be carried out while laying siege on the fortresses, the most important among which included: completely cutting off any aid and support to the enemies who were besieged inside the fortresses,[291] distancing one's own forces from the reach of the enemy's arrows,[292] deceiving the besieged enemy using different means[293] in order to get them to come out of their fortress.

The Bani Qaynuqā' surrendered after fifteen nights of siege[294] and the Bani Nadhir had also been besieged for fifteen days after which they lowered their heads in surrender on the command of the Prophet (s).[295] The Bani Quraydha were also dealt with in the same manner.[296] After this, the inhabitants of Khaybar came to the Prophet (s) and agreed to obey his commands, thus they were exiled to Syria.[297] The Holy Prophet (s) also besieged Tā'if and after a while the caused them to come out of the siege.[298]

The Noble Prophet (s), in his orders, limited the attack on the Fortress of Khaybar to the eastern direction, just as the present day armies do. He made the priority of the mission was to gain control over the primary fortress[299]

161

and then he gained control over all their forts one after another.[300] Once their fall and defeat was complete, he gave the order for them to attack the secondary fortress.[301] They gained control over that too and captured (the forts) one after the other[302] until they achieved their goal completely and then proceeded to conquer the main defense fortress[303] which was another of the orders the army had been given. The Muslim army turned its focus on the first defensive fort,[304] and especially on the Fort of Nā'im[305] and once that had fallen, they moved towards the other forts. Before carrying out any attack on these forts, he (s) obtained the required information[306] and surveillance on them,[307] then he positioned his forces in the area of al-Rajee'[308] thereby separating the Ghatfān[309] (who were allies and helpers of the enemy) with the inhabitants of Khaybar and through this tactic he gave the advantage to the Muslim army, because he was able to prevent these tribes from working with the Jews of Khaybar thereby making it easy to attack the forts from all sides[310] and conquer them[311] while also being free to maneuver[312] and divide the enemy.[313] The supreme commander started with the Fort of Nā'im[314] and conquered it. Then he attacked the other forts[315] and in this way he conquered the forts gradually, one by one.

24. Battles with barriers (and impediments)

Using barriers in battle has been an age-old practice that started with the very first battles.[316] For example, the Romans and Persians would use trenches in their battles.[317] However, we do not have any evidence that the Arabs used such barriers before the advent of Islām.[318] The Holy Prophet (s) ordered that a trench be dug in order to prevent the army of confederates from gaining access into Madina from the north and west,[319] and selected the suitable ground for this purpose,[320] and personally specified its dimensions for the army i.e. the length of the battlefront which was from Mudhād up to Dhubāb Rātij[321] was dug by the Muslim army.[322] In order to remove the gravel, they used metal tools, pickaxes and large buckets[323] and the removed gravel was poured outside to hide the front-line that would counter the enemy[324] and the remaining areas were concealed using rocks that were brought from Mount Sala'.[325] Then passageways from which their own troops could pass from the trench were made.[326] In order to dig through hard ground and rock, water was first poured over it and then it was struck with the pickaxe continuously until it eventually broke up.[327]

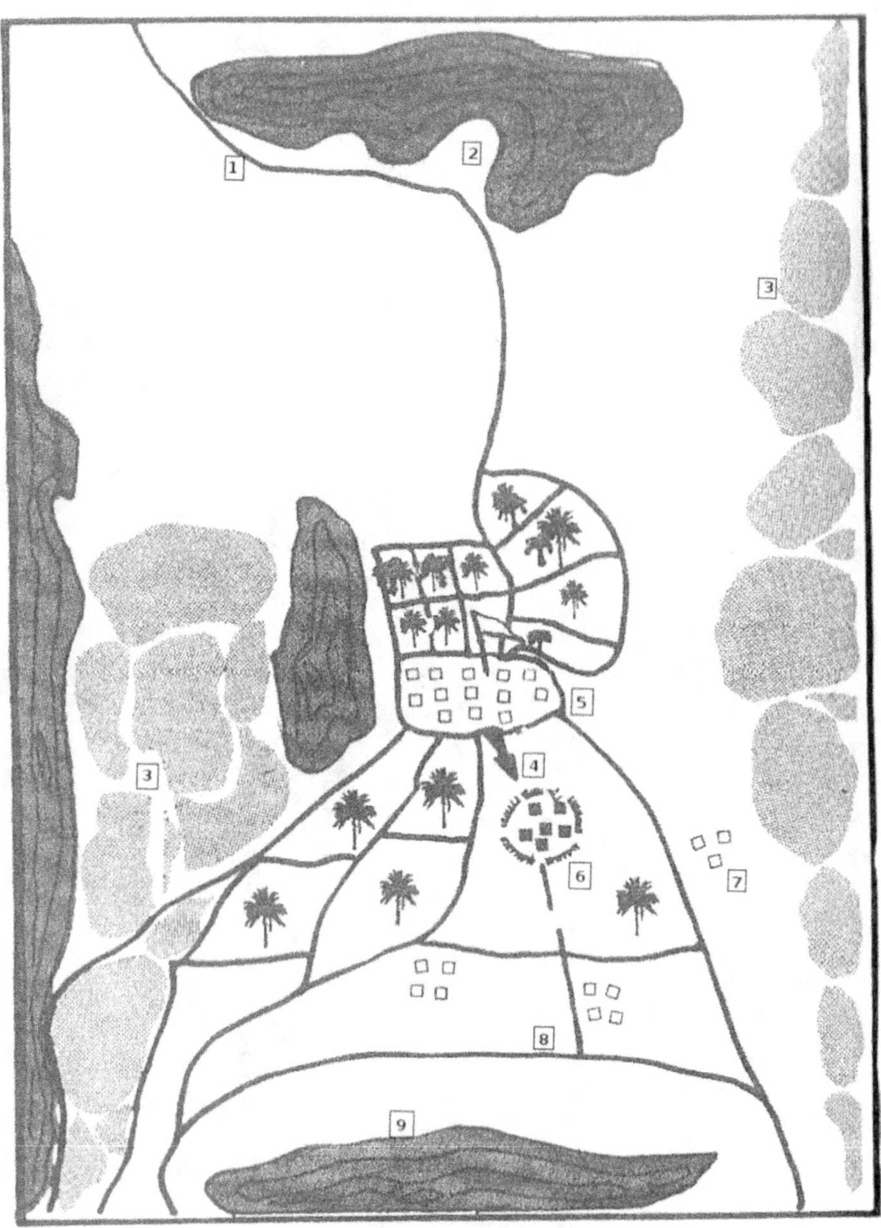

The Battle of Bani Qaynuqā' (fig. 1)

The Battle of Bani Nadhir (fig. 2)

KEY (fig. 1 & 2)

1. **The route from Basra to Damascus**
2. **Mount Uhud**
3. **Volcanic rock**
4. **Route taken by the Muslim army (fig. 1) & Mount Sala' (fig. 2)**
5. **The city of Madina**
6. **The Jews of Bani Qaynuqā'**
7. **The Jews of Bani Quraydha**
8. **The Jews of Bani Nadhir**
9. **Mount 'Aseer**

The length of the ditch was five thousand cubits, which is equivalent to two kilometers and its width was nine cubits, which is equal to four meters, while its depth was between five and seven cubits which comes up to about three meters.[328] Digging the trench took between six to ten days.[329] The Muslim army spread out along the border of the trench to face the enemy. They carried with them the weapons that were required and stood right behind the trench.[330] They would remain on constant watch and guard the areas where there was a possibility that the enemy could pass through.[331] When the soldiers of the two armies came face to face, they began shooting long arrows towards each other.[332] If the enemy came near the trench and crossed over it, they would use their swords,[333] and when this was happening to some of the enemy soldiers, and in the process 'Amr ibn 'Abd Wudd[334] was killed, the other soldiers retreated and rejoined their forces behind the trench. In this battle, the Muslim forces used stones abundantly[335] and had gathered them along the line of the trench.

The trench that was dug was quite helpful to the Muslim army and acted as a barrier between them and the enemy. In the end it must be said that the Battle of Khandaq is not much different from the present-day battles, and aside from different weaponry, there is very little else that is dissimilar.

25. Battles in cities and towns (*Harb al-Mudun*)

After he had concealed all his might and strength and military prowess from the inhabitants of Makkah, the Holy Prophet (s) conquered this city.[336] In this battle, he also: used psychological warfare;[337] entered the city from all four directions;[338] divided the operations according to the arrangement and formation of the troops;[339] explained the route, direction, goal, force and other matters;[340] asked them to be careful to refrain from bloodshed.[341]

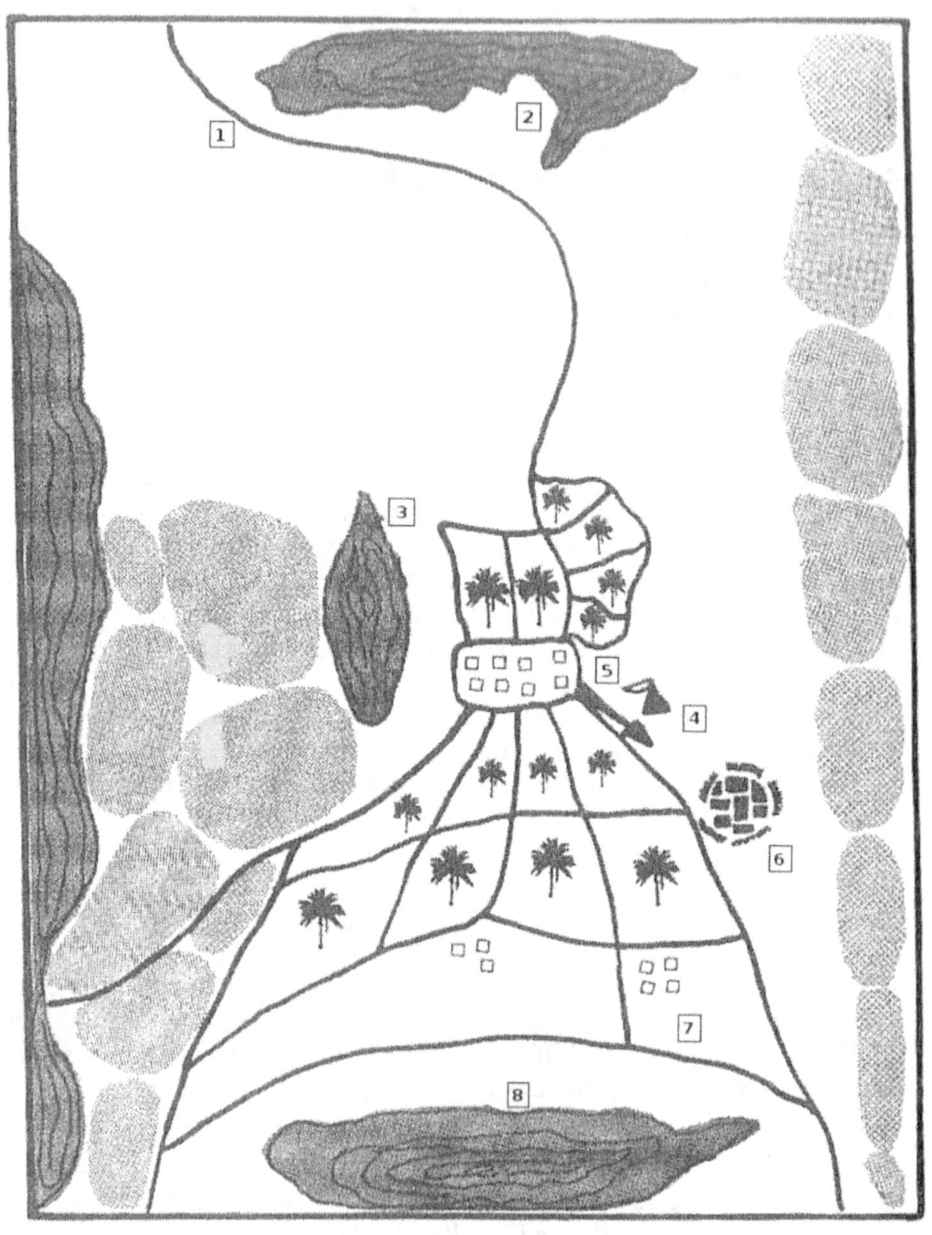

The Battle of Bani Quraydha (Ref. KEY 2.1)

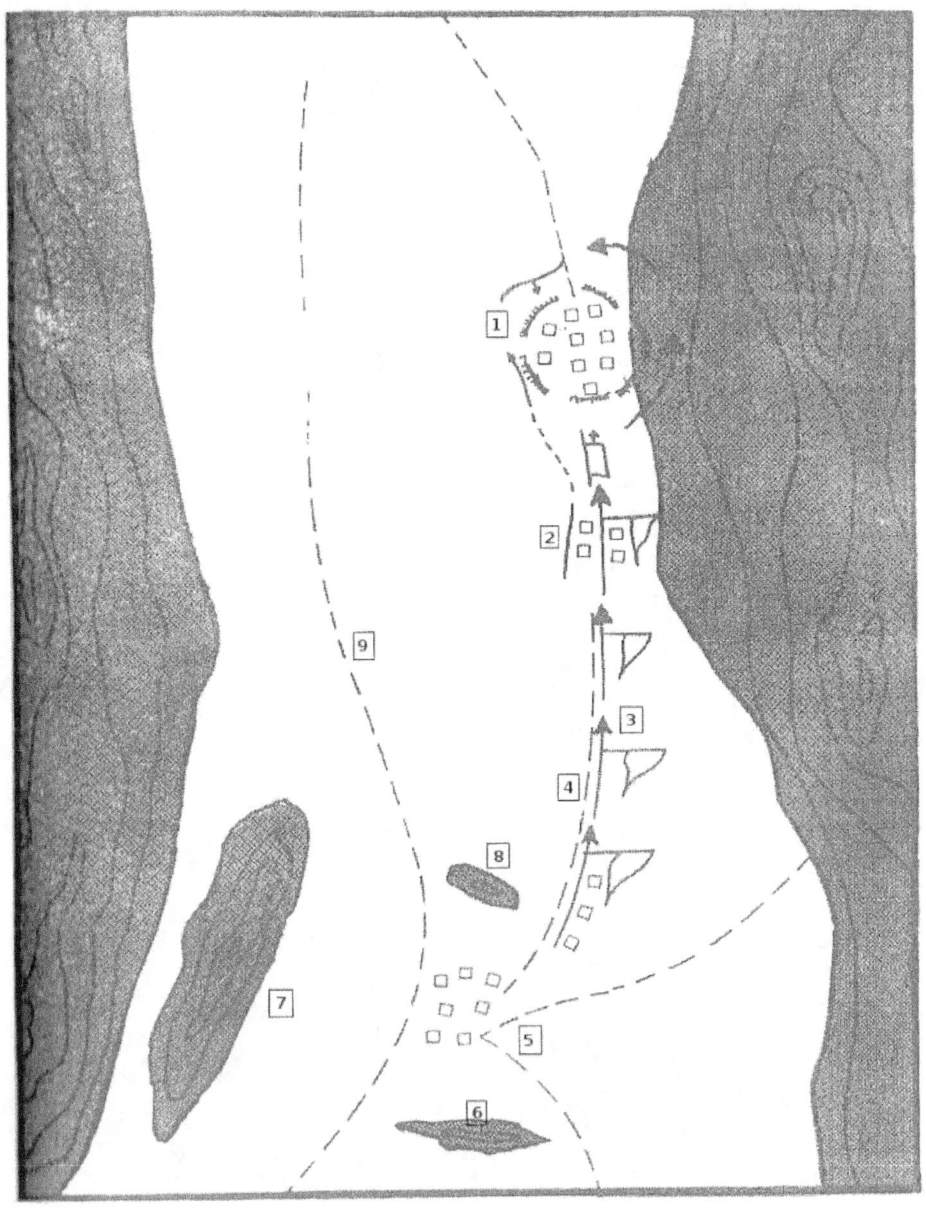

The Battle of Khaybar (Ref. KEY 2.2)

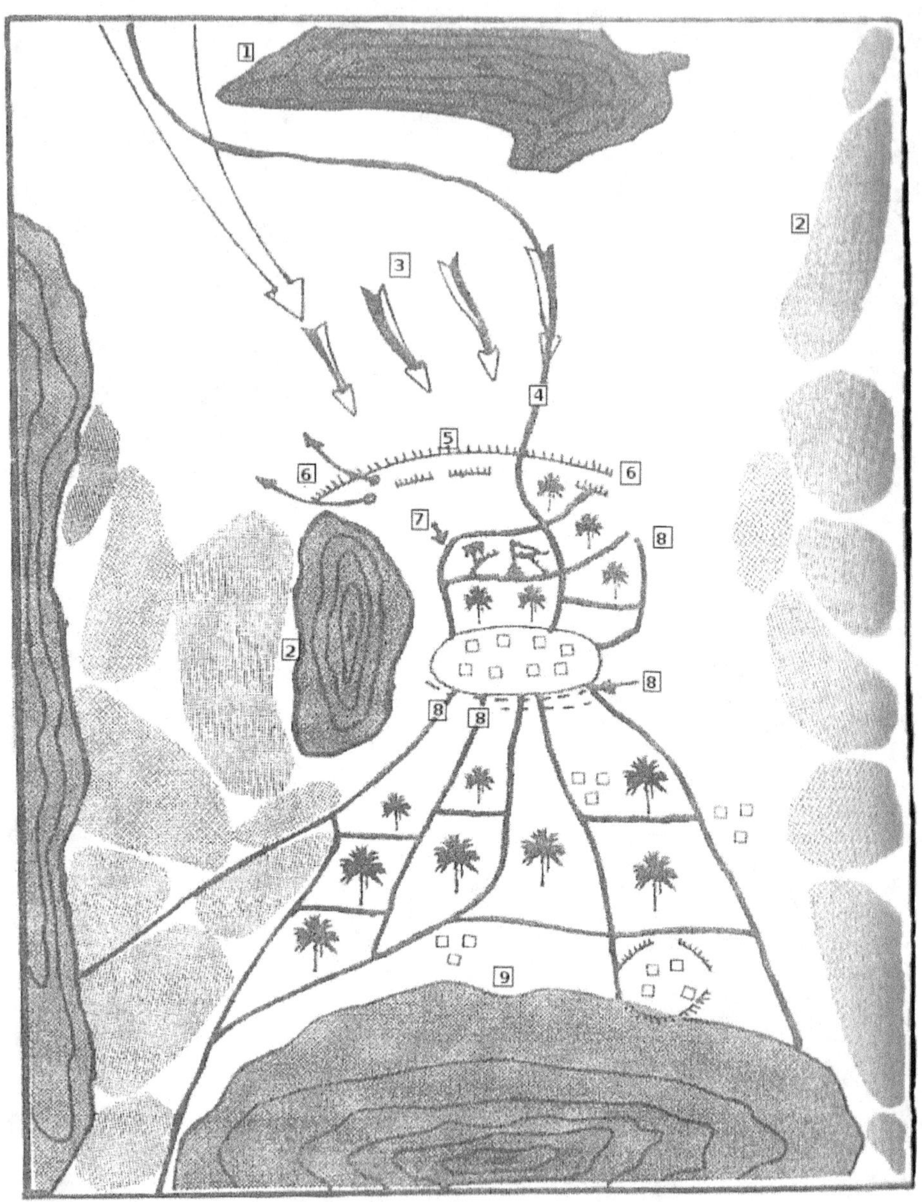

The Battle of Khandaq (Ref. KEY 2.3)

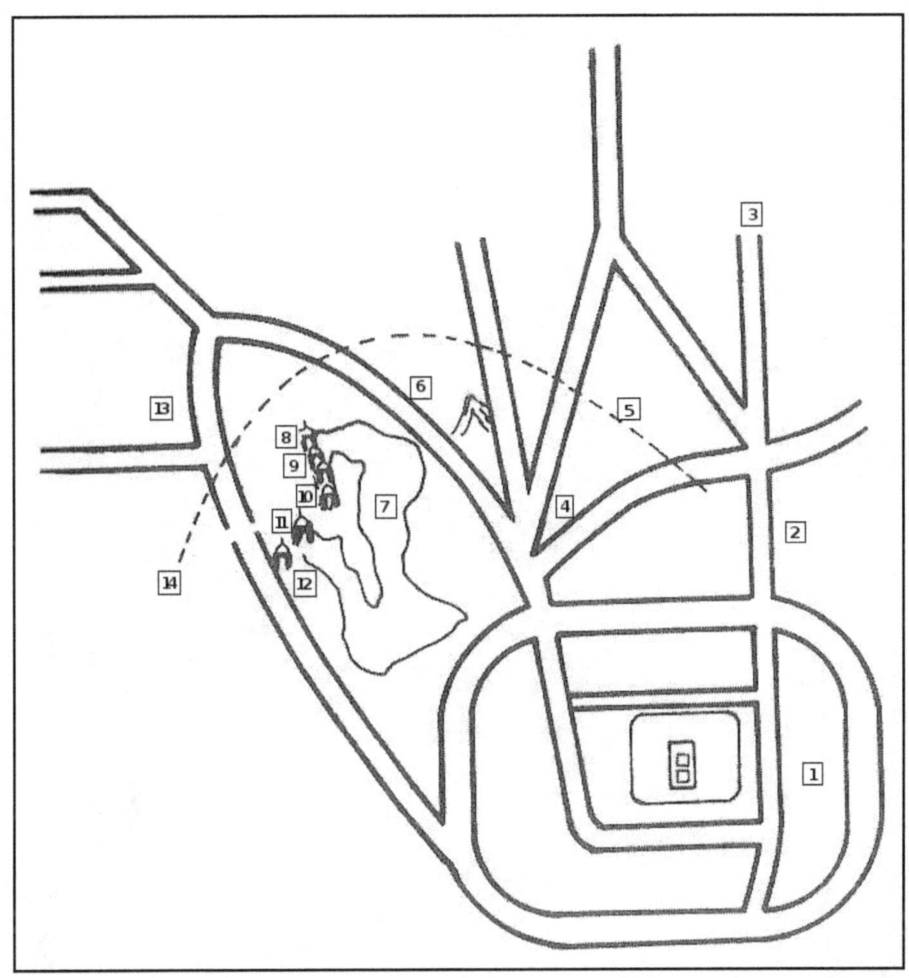

Current map of Madina with the place where the Battle of Khandaq took place and the location of the al-Masājid al-Sab'ah or 'seven mosques' (Ref. KEY 2.4)

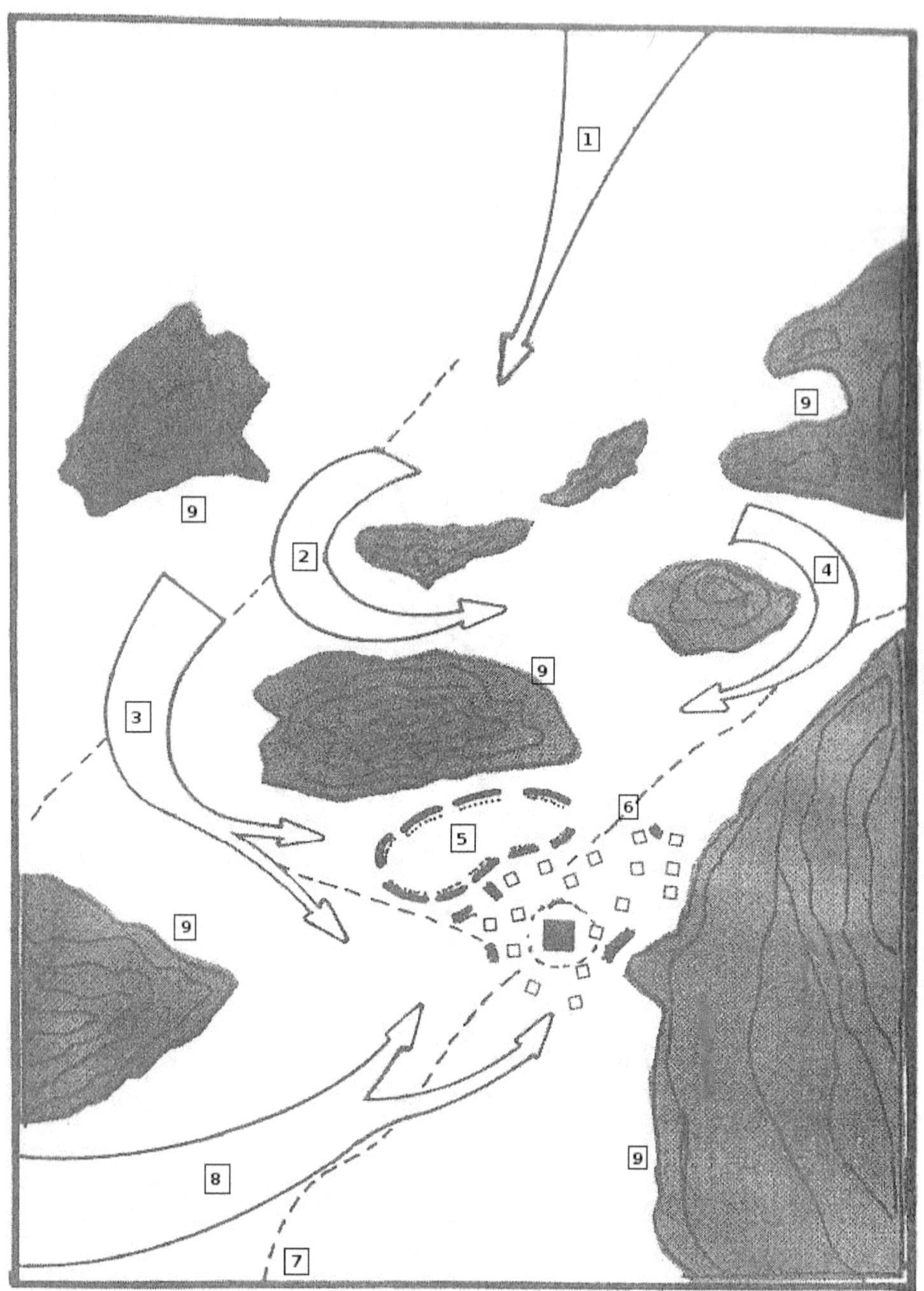

The Conquest of Makkah (Ref. KEY 2.5)

KEY 2.1: Battle of Bani Quraydha
1. The route from Basra to Damascus
2. Mount Uhud
3. Mount Sala'
4. The Muslim army
5. The city of Madina
6. The Jews of Bani Quraydha
7. The Jews of Bani Nadhir
8. Mount 'Aseer

KEY 2.2: Battle of Khaybar
1. Khaybar
2. Fadak
3. The Muslim army
4. The route traversed by the army (in eight days)
5. The city of Madina
6. Mount 'Aseer
7. Mount Sala'
8. Mount Uhud
9. The route to Madā'in

KEY 2.3: Battle of Khandaq
1. Mount Uhud
2. Volcanic rocks
3. The confederate army (Ahzāb)
4. The place where the enemy was blocked
5. The defensive trench (2 km long)
6. Permanent guard-posts
7. The Muslim Army
8. Moving guards
9. Mount 'Aseer

> **KEY 2.4: Present-day Madina**
> 1. The graveyard of al-Baqee'
> 2. Abu Dharr al-Ghaffāri Street
> 3. The area of Uhud
> 4. Sayyid al-Shuhadā Street
> 5. Path of the trench (that was dug in the Battle of Khandaq)
> 6. Abu Bakr Street
> 7. Mount Sala'
> 8. Masjid al-Fath
> 9. Masjid Salmān al-Fārsi
> 10. Masjid 'Umar ibn al-Khattāb
> 11. Masjid Abu Bakr
> 12. Masjid 'Ali ibn Abi Tālib ('a)
> 13. Masjid Dhul Qiblatayn
> 14. Masjid Fātimah bint Muhammad (s)

> **KEY 2.5: Conquest of Makkah**
> 1. The Muslim army – 10,000 strong
> 2. The forces of Abi 'Ubaydah ibn Jarrāh
> 3. The forces of Qays ibn Sa'd ibn 'Ubādah
> 4. The forces of Zayd ibn 'Awām
> 5. The place where the Muslim army encamped
> 6. The city of Makkah al-Mukarramah
> 7. Entrance into Makkah
> 8. The forces of Khālid bin Walid
> 9. Mountainous areas

He instructed the inhabitants of Makkah to throw down their weapons, close their door and windows,[342] and show no resistance whatsoever.[343] It was after these orders and instructions that he set up camp for the army in Hajun,[344] and after conquering Makkah, he again prepared them for the next important mission.

Indeed, the supreme commander was highly capable in carrying out all these measures. Among other things, he made it clear to the people of Makkah that they were incapable of resisting the mighty Muslim army,[345] and in this way he entered Makkah peacefully and enacted a peace treaty without any bloodshed or war.[346]

26. Daily reports

These reports contained details about the state of the battle, the munitions, the spirit and zeal of the forces, the requirements and the objectives, and would usually be compiled and sent to the supreme commander daily.[347] The Holy Prophet (s) told all his commanders to chronicle the objectives and important developments of the battles and send them to him,[348] so that he was fully aware of what was going on at their end. This was something that was not done verbally[349] and it was not necessary to send it in the day, as the military do these days, rather, depending on the need, it would be sent after the mission or battle was over[350] by means of a messenger on horseback or on foot.[351]

The most important issues that were contained in these reports were: the missions of the units[352] and especially the sentinels, intelligence information,[353] the method of attack on the enemy,[354] the results that were seen from that battle[355] – especially the losses, booty[356] and the measures that needed to be taken to strengthen the troops.[357]

An analysis of the battles on the various front-lines

The Holy Prophet (s) would simultaneously battle on many front-lines, against the Quraysh, the Arab tribes, the Jews and the Romans. Therefore, he would prepare for numerous wars and in the end, he achieved victory in all of them. These front-lines included:

a) The front-line against the Quraysh

Before preparing for any war,. the Holy Prophet (s) would send Sariya missions or numerous military missions[358] to gather intelligence from the enemy forces and also to dishearten them or he would send them to attack their trading caravans - in order to display the might of the Muslim army. In this way, he established a somewhat new base of command in Madina. When the Quraysh came to learn of this change and technique, they decided that to destroy this army and were searching for an opportunity to annihilate the Muslim army before it could grow and develop into and unstoppable power, and this is why they prepared for the Battle of Badr.[359] Badr was the first full-fledged battle where the

Muslim army displayed its readiness and capability for war[360] especially by choosing the appropriate place for setting up camp,[361] innovation, organizing the battle-formation into columns in depth,[362] training,[363] zeal,[364] faith and a new belief,[365] discipline and following orders,[366] the necessary organization and hierarchy of command[367] and by these military tactics, they strengthened their soldiers.

As for the Quraysh, they were stronger in terms of numbers and battle gear,[368] and just as we will demonstrate, the victory is for the side that is better in terms of quality, not quantity; that is why the Prophet (s) astounded the enemy by his victory in Badr. After their defeat, the Quraysh became worried about the loss of their profits and trade and responded with a weak blow to this victory,[369] and this was when Abu Sufyān launched an incursion into Madina and killed two civilians and then quickly returned towards Makkah. At this point, the Holy Prophet (s) sent soldiers to follow him as he was fleeing, but they did not catch up to him.[370]

The supreme commander of the Muslim army would use economic sanctions and other means to put pressure on the Quraysh.[371] For instance, he sent Zayd ibn Hāritha to al-Qurdah in order to attack the trading caravan of the Quraysh and he too was successful in overpowering it.[372] In order to take revenge and gain freedom from sanctions and other pressures, the enemy assembled a large army and prepared for the Battle of Uhud.[373] In the first phase, the Muslim army was victorious,[374] but in the second phase,[375] because of the disobedience of the archers to the orders of the supreme commander and their abandonment of their positions in order to take the spoils of war, the result turned in favor of the Quraysh.[376] In the end, however, the final result was in favor of the Muslim army[377] i.e. when the Holy Prophet (s) was able to gather a large number of troops,[378] and remain steadfast[379] despite his injuries and losses, was able to launch a counter-attack in the Battle of Hamrā' al-Asad.[380] In this way, by being a prudent,[381] determined and courageous[382] commander, and by using psychological warfare[383] through which he instilled fear in the hearts of the enemy, he caused their forces to fall down helplessly. The string of consecutive victories that were achieved by the Prophet (s)[384] against the Quraysh, the Jews and the enemy Arab tribes, made it evident that there was a serious threat that was forming against them[385] and they had no choice but to annihilate this Muslim army. For this purpose, they came together, joined hands and made covenants with each other so that they could assemble a united army to fight against the Muslims. As a result, some Arab tribes and Jews joined with the Quraysh and launched what was to be known as the Battle of Confederates (Ahzāb).[386]

The confederates came into the field with a large force, numbering almost ten thousand strong,[387] and proceeded towards Madina. However, they were stopped in their tracks by the large trench[388] that was dug by the Muslim army.[389] Although they made many attempts to cross over it, but all in vain[390] and because of the differences that arose between them, they returned without having realized their military objective.[391] From the ingenuity and innovation of a new strategy in warfare i.e. digging the trench[392] and also due to the leadership of a continent,[393] steadfast commander,[394] using deception[395] and having high spiritual values,[396] the Muslim army gained victory over the Quraysh and their allies. The consequence of this was that the reverence that the Arab tribes felt for the Quraysh was greatly reduced[397] and they lost their position as central political and military figures.[398] The respect of Abu Sufyān was lost because of this,[399] he failed as a commander and his pivotal role was demeaned in the eyes of his allies. This was because the severe loss he faced was caused by a trench[400] and by the fleeing of the tribes of Ghatfān and their partners, the Quraysh were put to shame[401] and it became established that they are totally incapable of gaining a victory over this (Muslim) army.[402]

After this battle, the Jews got worried and became sure that they would be annihilated because they broke their pledges and pacts with the Muslims.[403] The Prophet (s) immediately besieged the Bani Quraydha and was successful in removing them from Madina.[404] It must be said that this battle was the point of change for the Muslim army, from a defensive state to an offensive one.[405]
News of the pressure and hardships that came upon the Quraysh because of their loss in this battle reached the Holy Prophet (s), so he sent Zayd ibn Hāritha[406] with a mission to cut off their supply routes and prevent their caravans from travelling outside, and he successfully carried out this mission.[407]

This victory was followed soon after by the Treaty of Hudaybiyya[408] which was to tantamount to another victory for the Muslim army, however the Quraysh reneged on the agreement,[409] and were looking for an opportunity to come out of it and stand up against to the Muslim army. As a result, the Prophet (s) hastened his preparation for the Conquest (of Makkah)[410] and marched against their city and homes. In order to enter Makkah, he made a secret plan[411] and this plan was to carry out a surprise invasion.[412] After he had bewildered the Quraysh and left them with no choice but to surrender to this army,[413] he entered Makkah and gained victory over his enemies.[414] After this victory, the Quraysh also acknowledged the Holy Prophet (s) as their leader and accepted the religion of Islām.[415]

b) The front-line against the other Arab tribes

The Holy Prophet (s) fought many battles against these tribes, either commanding them personally[416] or sending contingents and Sariya missions to fight against them.[417] Aside from this, he would send individuals and small groups[418] to assassinate the leaders of these tribes and those who were opposed to the Islāmic revolution and had evil intentions against its leader or had plans to carry out invasions (against them). The tribes that were fought by the supreme commander were: Bani Saleem,[419] Kadar,[420] Bahrān,[421] al-Jumūm,[422] the tribes of Bani Tha'labah,[423] Ghatfān and Mahārib in Dhi Amr,[424] the tribes of Sirār,[425] Bani al-Mustalaq[426] in al-Muraisiya',[427] the tribe of Bani Lihyān[428] in Gharrān,[429] Bani Hawāzin[430] and the Thaqeef in Hunayn.[431]

The Holy Prophet (s) also carried out Sariya and other military missions against the following tribes: Bani Asad[432] in Qatan,[433] al-Ghamr[434] and Bani Bakr ibn Kilāb,[435] Dhiryah,[436] Bani Tha'labah[437] and 'Awāl in Dhi al-Qassah,[438] al-Tarāf[439] and Bani Judhām[440] in Husmā,[441] Bani Fuzārah[442] in Wādi al-Qurā,[443] Bani Sa'd[444] in Fadak,[445] 'Ajz wa Hawāzin[446] in Turbah,[447] Bani Kilāb[448] in Najd,[449] al-Zajj[450] and Bani Murrah[451] in Fadak,[452] Bani 'Abd ibn Tha'labah[453] in al-Mayfa'ah,[454] Bani Ghatfān[455] in Yemen and Jabbār,[456] Khadhrah[457] and Bani al-Malūh[458] in al-Kuryah,[459] Bani Qudhā'ah[460] in Dhat Ittilā',[461] Bani Hawāzin[462] in al-Sayy,[463] Bani Tamim[464] in al-Suqyā[465] and Bani Khath'am[466] in Batn Musjā'.[467]

The Holy Prophet (s) would carry out pre-emptive wars[468] against these tribes, meaning that he would launch an attack on them first before they could march towards Madina.[469] More often than not, the enemy would flee in fear the moment they heard that the Muslim army was on its way;[470] to such an extent that they would also leave their animals behind as war booty (for the Muslim army to take).[471]

The number of troops in these military missions would vary from battle to battle.[472] In the Battle of Bawāt, the number of soldiers reached two hundred strong whereas in the Battle of Badr, they numbered three hundred and a few. Similarly, the numbers would change from Sariya mission to Sariya mission.[473] For example, in the Sariya of Muhammad ibn Maslamah against the Bani Bakr, the soldiers numbered thirty, whereas in the Sariya of Zayd ibn Hāritha against the tribe of Judhām, there were fifty. In the Sariya of Usāma bin Zayd to fight against the Romans, the number of forces reached three thousand. In this way, the supreme commander would send the appropriate number of forces depending on the number of enemy soldiers and the type of mission.

Because of the fact that the enemy tribes that have been mentioned were spread out throughout the Arabian peninsula,[474] from far and near they were affected by the Muslim army[475] and were never able to launch raids, invasions or attacks on Madina.[476] The attacks of the Muslim army on these tribes were based on swiftness,[477] surprise attack,[478] marching at night,[479] secret missions,[480] gathering new and important intelligence;[481] and this is why they would always attain victory. The priorities in dealing with these tribes and making them submissive were specified in such a way[482] that they would first concentrate their efforts on gaining control over the tribes in the coastal regions,[483] then they would move on to those in the east (of the Arab peninsula)[484] and finally the other tribes would be attacked.[485] In the same way, they would start with tribes that were nearer and then proceed towards those that were further.[486] They were also precautious of the threat posed by the tribes of Bani Saleem, Ghatfān and Tamim.[487]

c) The front-line against the Jews

After the Holy Prophet's migration to Madina, he (s) created a 'civil pact' with those who lived in that city.[488] However, not long after this pact was created, the Jews of Bani Qaynuqā'[489] were waiting for an opportunity to break away from the conditions of the pact they had made and bring defeat to the Muslim army, which had since developed and grown after the many battles it had fought. For this reason, they broke their pact and manifested their enmity for the Muslims, and continued to do so despite the warning given to them by the Holy Prophet (s).[490] In response, the Prophet (s) besieged them in their fortress and gained victory over them.[491] From that day, all the Jews were waiting for the same thing to happen to them that had happened to the other Jews. Ka'b ibn Ashraf, Salām bin Abi al-Haqiq and other Jewish leaders[492] who had gone against and fermented opposition to the supreme commander and the Muslims,[493] had seen their end and were killed in suicide missions.[494]

The Jews of Bani Nadhir[495] also did not hesitate to betray the Prophet (s) after the Muslims lost the Battle of Uhud, and even made plans to assassinate him.[496] This was when the Holy Prophet (s) sought to take the blood-money for the two Muslims killed by 'Amr ibn Umayyah al-Dhumri and had gone to their land for this purpose.[497] Because of this treachery, the Prophet (s) besieged them and took over their lands.[498]

The Jews of Bani Quraydha also joined hands with the Quraysh to work against the Muslim army in the Battle of Khandaq.[499] Their attempts and struggles were to no avail and because they broke their allegiance to the Muslims, they returned back afraid and worried.[500] That which they had thought of did not transpire and now they saw themselves under threat of being besieged.

After the Battle of Khandaq, the Holy Prophet (s) himself led the army,[501] marching towards the area of the Bani Quraydha.[502] He fought a battle with them and put them all to death.[503] Despite this, the Jews continued in their enmity with the Muslims and again began inciting and encouraging the Arab tribes to fight against the army of the Prophet (s). This is why the Battle of Khaybar took place.[504] In this war also, the victory belonged to the Muslim army[505] and as a result the greatest opposing force and enemy was done away with, and all the Jews surrendered.[506]

The battles against the Jews were different from other battles because they were in fortresses[507] and secure shelters and were able to store the needed supplies and weapons for a long period of time.[508] They used to construct their buildings in elevated locations so as to prevent the archers and lookouts, keep the enemies at bay by the strength and fortification of their fortresses,[509] dig moats just outside the and filling them with water.[510]

The Jews would store a lot of other weapons and armaments in the fortress and would use them when needed.[511] At the same time, they would be well trained and would possess all the battle gear that was required.[512] The number of Jews was many times more than the soldiers in the Muslim army.[513] In the Battle of Bani Qaynuqā' they numbered seven hundred as opposed to the four hundred in the Muslim army. In the Battle of Bani Quraydha, three thousand Jews fought against only seven hundred Muslims and in the Battle of Khaybar, there were ten thousand strong against an army of 1,500 fighters. Aside from this, they had a lot of wealth[514] and wielded a lot of economic, political and military influence;[515] but despite all this, they were still divided[516] and each group would fight on its own without the help of the others. In the Battle of Qaynuqā', nobody joined forces with them and this was the case with the other battles against the Jews also.

In the battles against the Jews, the Muslim army had the following distinct characteristics:
1. Laying siege:[517] this was a technique where all the aide and military assistance was completely blocked from reaching the enemy.[518]
2. Remaining far away from the reach of enemy arrows.[519]
3. Carrying out frontal and side attacks on their fortress,[520] as they did at Khaybar.
4. Using psychological warfare.[521]
5. Heightening the spirits of their own forces.[522]
6. Selecting a suitable place to set camp.[523]
7. Creating a split between the Jewish forces.[524] This was done using the superior battle strategy of the Muslims. Once this was achieved, the

Prophet (s) was able to gain separate victories over the Bani Qaynuqā',[525] Bani Nadhir,[526] Bani Quraydha[527] and the residents of Khaybar.[528] Aside from this, the Muslim army was distinguished by its unity of command, concentration, obedience, persistence and swiftness;[529] all of which made it possible to attain victory and overpower the Jews.

d) The front-line against the Rome

The Holy Prophet (s) fought the first battle at the border with Rome (Dumat al-Jundal),[530] and this was because of the importance of this location,[531] because this place was the gateway for the future invasions of the Muslim army on Rome[532] and the base of security[533] and also was considered a secure barrier between Rome and the Muslims.[534] By sending 'Abd al-Rahmān ibn 'Awf on a Sariya mission,[535] the supreme commander completed his gathering of intelligence and information from the tribes who lived near the area[536] in order to learn about the Roman forces and how to invade them.[537]

The Battle of Muta was the first full-fledged battle between the Muslim army and the Roman troops.[538] It can be said that the goals of this battle were to display the might of the Muslim army[539] and test the capability of the enemy.[540] However the vast difference between the forces of the two sides made this war one-sided.[541] The supreme commander came face to face with the Romans for a second time in the Battle of Tabuk.[542] One of the goals of this battle was the avenging of the Martyrs of Muta[543] and launching an attack on the enemy and their allies.[544] In this battle, no combat was seen, however a large part of its objectives were fulfilled. The pressure against the Romans continued and in the end, an army under the command of Usāma bin Zayd was send against them.[545] He attained victory in this battle and in this way the first victory over the Romans was established. After this the Muslims continued in their war against them.[546]

The Romans had become worried from the time when the first battle against them was fought near their borders[547] and they turned their attention towards this growing Muslim army whom they expected to face again. However, the Holy Prophet (s) dispelled the fear of this enemy from his forces[548] and he put the idea in their minds that conquering the lands of Shām is not difficult or impossible.[549] He (s) would train his troops to bear the hardships of travelling the long and arduous routes, and endure the difficulties and tribulations of the desert.[550] Having subjugated some of the neighboring tribes,[551] he made several pacts with them[552] so that they could act as a refuge and a leading force in this army against the Romans and open up the way for the Battle of Muta.[553]

The Roman soldiers were known for their military outfits and great adornments.[554] Their forces, weapons, equipment and armaments were plenty[555] for this reason they became heavy and their maneuvers became sluggish and slow.[556] The Roman foot-soldiers would use bows in situations where they had not been trained for battle.[557] Aside from this, the Roman forces and the Arabs (who were in their service) had no co-operation with each other, and because they were all mixed together,[558] they did not have an opportunity to conduct well planned maneuvers together. Aside from this, they had a weak system of command which greatly reduced their efficiency and speed in battle.[559]

As for the Muslim army, it was distinguished by its continuous attacks on the enemy,[560] psychological warfare,[561] securing of the northern borders and strategic locations,[562] taking the battle away from its own land,[563] remaining steadfast against an enemy that was stronger,[564] and employing the principles of war in different ways.[565] This was accompanied by practice, maneuvering[566] and ease of movement.[567] When a soldier would shoot arrows while moving, his stability and poise would increase. It was as if he was not carrying any weapon or battle gear such as would impede on his swiftness or cause him to remain behind and become weary.[568]

Second: Department of Training

This was the department that was responsible for preparing the armed forces and their various units in order to carry out battle operations.[569] In the Muslim army, training was common to all and included individuals,[570] communities,[571] groups,[572] large organizations[573] and all the armed forces[574] and would be conducted in all the situations that arise in battle. This included: recognition,[575] archery,[576] combat,[577] fighting when being attacked,[578] running,[579] carrying out surprise attacks,[580] onslaught,[581] moving covertly and camouflage,[582] conducting ambushes and patrols,[583] marching at night,[584] covering long distances on foot,[585] the principle of concentration,[586] assistance and co-operation,[587] pre-emptive warfare,[588] taking advantage of the enemy's negligence,[589] mass attacks,[590] psychological warfare,[591] remaining patient[592] and steadfast against the enemy,[593] bearing all the hardships of securing resources and reinforcements,[594] battling to overcome fortresses,[595] war using trenches[596] and fighting battles in the cities.[597]

The supreme commander paid special attention to training the cavalry.[598] That which separated the training of this army from those of other armies was that training took place in real-life situations and in the battlefield, during battle.[599] One of its distinguishing features was that it gave skills to individuals, groups and contingents, preparing and polishing them for every different battle scenario and taught them about all the intricate details. It did away with mistakes and error or greatly reduced them. It made the troops precautious when facing the enemy, to the extent of necessity, just as the armed forces today conduct training exercises so as to gain experience and remain free from fear, sluggishness or laziness.

Military training in the Muslim army was something that was conducted on a continuous basis.[600] Between one Sariya and another or between one battle and the next there was not a long gap.[601] For example, after the completion of the Sariya of Hamza ibn 'Abd al-Muttalib, a month later the Sariya of 'Ubaydah ibn Hārith was conducted. The Battle of Dhi al-'Asheera took place a month after the Sariya of 'Abdullah ibn Jahash and the gap between the battles of Dhi Amr and Bahrān was no more than two months. The Sariya of Muhammad ibn Maslamah against the Bani Tha'labah and 'Awāl took one month and the Sariya of Abi 'Ubaydah ibn Jarrāh came immediately after it. During these short gaps, the forces would prepare to march against the (next) enemy and some of the units would undergo training before battle;[602] just as they had done in the Battle of Badr and the Conquest.

The continuous training (of the troops) had the following results:

1. It would increase in the steadfastness of the individuals,[603] like in the Sariya of Zayd ibn Hāritha where his later missions were carried out with more steadfastness than his previous missions. Similarly, the 'battle of the fortress' that took place at Khaybar was better than the battles of Bani Nadhir and Bani Qaynuqā'.

2. The hesitation and fear of coming face to face with the enemy was removed.[604] In the Battle of Badr, the forces were more hopeful of taking over the caravan of the Quraysh without having to fight a battle and they were fearful of face to face combat. However, in the Battle of Uhud, they were competing with each other to go to battle and most of them gave the view that they should go out of Madina to face the enemy threat, because at this time fear and trepidation had totally disappeared from them.

3. It strengthened the spirits of the forces[605] and established the certainty of victory in them;[606] as in the battles of Hunayn and Ahzāb.

4. Swiftness in getting prepared for battle[607] was maintained with precision and quality as in the Battle of Dhāt al-Suwayq, the war against the Bani Mahārib and Tha'labah in the Battle of Dhāt al-Ruqā', and in the Battle of Bani Quraydhah. This made them stronger and more capable to quickly carry out orders, remain swift in the difficult circumstances of battle and able to change tactics;[608] in the same way as was witnessed after the army had dispersed and the forces had made blunders in the battles of Uhud and Hunayn.

Third: Department of Armament

This was the department responsible for securing the weaponry and battle gear, either by producing it, buying it or taking it from the spoils of war, and then distributing it and the issue of armament was done in conjunction with the department of munitions and the training of weapons-use was in co-operation with the department of training; and in the end the discharge, restore and stockpile the armaments.[609]

The most important weapons that were used by the Muslim army were:

1. Offensive weapons:[610] these included mainly the sword, spear and bow.
2. Defensive weapons: the most important of which were the armor, shield, helmet and the mail that was worn under it.

a) Offensive weapons

1) The sword was considered the most important weapon for offense and the Holy Prophet (s) also gave a lot of importance to it. He (s) had many swords that were either from war booty, gifts or inheritance of his father, and he had named each of them with specific names.[611]

2) The spear was another of the weapons of offense. The supreme commander had different types of spears and would use whichever one he wanted. In total they were of four types.[612]

3) The bow was of various types and each one had a specific name depending on its attributes, the type of action it would be used for and how it would be carried.[613] The most important types were the hand-held bow and the 'Hijāzi' bow. The Holy Prophet (s) had four bows: i) al-Safrā' (the Yellow) ii) al-Rawhā' (the Open) iii) al-Baydhā' (the White) and iv) al-Katum (the Secret-keeper).[614]

b) Defensive weapons

1) Armor was considered one of the most important weapons of defense which was worn to remain protected from the strikes of swords, spears or arrows.[615] Armors were of different shapes and types, each with a different name.[616] The supreme commander also had a number of armors, the most important of which were: Dhāt al-Fudhul, al-Sadriyya and al-Sird.[617]

2) Helmets would be made from iron and would be worn to protect the head from attacks by offensive weapons.[618]

3) 'Mighfar' was the armor or mail that a soldier would place under his helmet and would cover his head and face with it so that he does not get injured.[619] The Holy Prophet (s) and the soldiers who fought alongside him in battle would use this.[620]

182

4) 'Minjineeq' (catapult) was one of the 'heavy' weapons which was used to throw huge boulders or fireballs on the enemy.[621]

5) 'Dabbābah' (tank):[622] These two weapons (i.e. the catapult and the tank) were used in the Battle of Tā'if.

In the same way, the Muslim army would give importance to the arming of the cavalry[623] and would give it a priority over the other ranks. In the first battles, the soldiers on horseback were few. For example, in the Battle of Badr, there were only two soldiers on horseback.[624] This number reached two hundred in the Battle of Khaybar[625] and in the Conquest of Makkah there were more than two thousand soldiers on horseback.[626]

As for the sources from where weapons could be procured, these included:
1. By way of those who would engage in making them and selling them to the soldiers[627] but this small number was not enough for the whole army.
2. From the buyers who would buy from inside the Arabian Peninsula[628] and outside it.[629] The budget for buying the weapons from this source would be gotten from:
   a) The personal wealth and possessions of the soldiers[630]
   b) Those who were in charge of the army.
   c) The wealth that would remain after distribution.[631]
   d) The booty that was taken from the enemy[632] and especially the Jews.

The supreme commander would leave behind some of the wealth after making pacts of alliance with the defeated enemies, however he would never leave behind any of their weapons; because this was the main source of weapons and strengthening the army while at the same time weakening the enemy in order to prevent any future attacks and incursions.[633] There was also another source of weapons for the army and that was taking them on loan and then returning them to their owners after the battle.[634]

Training with weapons was one of the requirements of the Muslim army and the supreme commander would insist and encourage the fighters to train on how to carry the weapons,[635] the principles of their usage,[636] archery and gaining mastery over it,[637] training on the use of the catapult.[638] Many of the Muslims such as Talha ibn 'Abdillah al-Qarashi and Sa'd ibn Abi Waqqās[639] were well known for their skill in archery. At the same time, the Prophet (s) emphasized on training the riders who would fight on horseback.[640] He (s) also gave importance to the creation of weapons and encouraged and promised paradise to those who would undertake this task.[641] For this purpose, he sent a group to Jurash (Yemen) in order to learn how to make new weapons and acquire them before the siege of Tā'if.[642]

The importance given to making various light weaponry[643] was another of the goals of the supreme commander and for this he would give orders to the weapon makers in the area for different models of spears and bows.[644] When the weapons were distributed among the soldiers, those that were on loan would be taken back and those acquired from war booty would be kept by them. In this way, each soldier would get to use more than one type of weapon.[645]

As for supplies of weapons during battle, the situation was not as it is in the new age. A soldier would bring whatever weapon he had in his possession, and whatever he needed in the battlefield, he would have to carry himself. So if he were to lose one of his weapons or it were to break, he would exchange it and continue to fight.[646] With regards to the storing and stockpiling of weapons, each individual would store his own weapons in his home[647] and things were not as they are today i.e. there was no central repository where the weapons would be stockpiled. In the house of every soldier, a number of swords, spears and bows could be found, and he would pay due attention to their repair and maintenance.[648]

In times of 'peace', the weapons would be kept in a large warehouse that was strategically located and would be guarded.[649] The supreme commander would order that weapons must be carried at all times, in every situation, even when the enemies are not (apparently) present. He would forbid the forces who had returned from battle and were tired and weary, and intended to remove their weapons,[650] from doing so and he was always put the thought about the struggle (against the sworn enemy), whether in times of war or peace, in the present or future, despite the presence or absence of the enemy in their minds and would strengthen this idea in them.[651]

NOTES AND REFERENCES

[1] Wāqidi 1:220, 371; Ibn Sa'd 2:48

[2] Wāqidi 1:13; Ibn Sa'd 2:35; Ibn Hazm: 105; Kalā'i 1:144

[3] Ibn Sa'd 2:2 onwards

[4] Shaybāni, *al-Kabir* 1:58; Wāqidi 1:67, 3:996; Ibn Hishām 2:278, 3:260, 4:161; Ibn Sayyid al-Nās 2:216

[5] Zuhri: 86; Wāqidi 1:13, 193; Ibn Sa'd 2:5, 24; Tabari 3:42; Ibn Hazm: 105

[6] Wāqidi 1:11; Ibn Hishām 3:244; Ibn Sa'd 2:5, 24; Tabari 3:6; Kalā'i 1:162

[7] Ibn Hishām 3:69; Ibn Sa'd 2:9; Tabari 3:6; Kalā'i 1:130; Ibn Sayyid al-Nās 2:131

[8] *Ibid.*

[9] Wāqidi 2:445, 462, 734, 815

[10] Wāqidi 1:72, 2:466, 722; Ibn Hishām 2:287; Ibn Sa'd 2:85; Ibn Sayyid al-Nās 2:146

[11] Wāqidi 1:12; Ibn Hishām 2:248; Ibn Khayyāt, *al-Tārikh* 1:29; Ibn Hazm: 100

[12] Wāqidi 1:26, 300, 378; Ibn Hishām 2:264; Kalā'i 1:144

[13] Ibn Sa'd 2:2, 56, 61, 85, 95; Ibn Sayyid al-Nās 1:224, 2:103, 145, 150, 162

[14] Wāqidi 1:174, 184, 363; Ibn Hishām 3:292; Ibn Sa'd 2:56; Ibn Hazm: 155

[15] Zuhri: 63; Wāqidi 1:19, 207, 2:245, 450; Ibn Hishām 2:268; Ibn Sa'd 2:25

[16] Zuhri: 87; Wāqidi 1:88, 91; Ibn Hishām 4:64; Ibn Qayyim 2:386

[17] Bukhāri (al-Jihād 34, al-Maghāzi 29); Muslim (al-Jihād 123); Nasā'i (al-Jihād 29)

[18] Ibn Hanbal 2:340, 4:354; Bukhāri (al-Jihād 32); Abu Dāwud (al-Jihād 49, 130)

[19] Q8:74, Q9:20, 41, 88; Bukhāri (al-Riqāq 34, al-Jihād 2, 31, al-Adab 1)

[20] Wāqidi 2:534, 550; Ibn Sa'd 2:2, 35; Tabari 2:410, 3:36; Ibn Sayyid al-Nās 2:108

[21] Ibn Sa'd 2:2-5, 24; Ibn Sayyid al-Nās 1:224, 304

[22] Wāqidi 1:10-13, 197; Ibn Sa'd 2:2; Tabari 3:126; Ibn Sayyid al-Nās 1:224

[23] Wāqidi 1:11; Ibn Hishām 3:249; Ibn Sa'd 2:2; Tabari 3:126; Ibn Sayyid al-Nās 1:224

[24] Wāqidi 1:334; Ibn Hishām 3:128, 321; Ibn Sa'd 2:92; Ibn Hazm: 207, 220

[25] Wāqidi 2:666, 670; Ibn Hishām 3:245, 344; Ibn Sa'd 2:2; Ibn Hazm: 100

[26] Ibn Sa'd 2:64; Tabari 2:408; Ibn Sayyid al-Nās 1:224; Kahālah, *Mu'jam Qabā'il al-'Arab* 3:991

[27] Wāqidi 1:182, 403, 3:992; Ibn Hishām 3:50; Ibn Sa'd 2:2-5; Ibn Sayyid al-Nās 1:304

[28] Ibn Sa'd 2:2-5; Tabari 2:564, 3:36, 100

[29] Wāqidi 1:173, 184, 191; Ibn Sa'd 2:18-21, 66; Ibn Sayyid al-Nās 2:39

[30] Wāqidi 1:76; Ibn Hishām 3:50; Ibn Sa'd 2:19; Ibn Khayyāt 1:27; Tabari 2:479; Ibn Hazm: 154

[31] Zuhri: 71; Wāqidi 1:363; Bukhāri 5:88; Tabari 2:552

[32] Zuhri: 79; Wāqidi 2:496; Ibn Hishām 3:244; Ibn Sa'd 2:53; Tabari 2:71

[33] Zuhri: 84; Wāqidi 2:633; Ibn Sa'd 2:77; Ibn Sayyid al-Nās 2:130

[34] Wāqidi 1:76, 2:363, 496, 633

[35] Wāqidi 2:651; Ibn Hishām 3:344; Ibn Qayyim 2:292

36 Wāqidi 1:181; Ibn Hishām 3:47; Ibn Sa'd 2:20; Ibn Khayyāt 1:28; Tabari 2:483

37 Wāqidi 1:182, 193, 2:551, 555; Ibn Hishām 3:46; Ibn Sa'd 2:21, 24; Ibn Khayyāt 1:27; Ibn Hazm: 152; Ibn Sayyid al-Nās 1:292, 304

38 Wāqidi 1:193, 395, 550; Ibn Hishām 3:213; Ibn Sa'd 2:43, 58, 61, 85; Tabari 2:556; Ibn Sayyid al-Nās 2:52, 79, 146

39 Wāqidi 1:347, 355; Ibn Hishām 3:194; Ibn Sa'd 2:36; Tabari 2:583; Ibn Hazm: 178

40 Wāqidi 1:402, 2:560, 3:992; Ibn Hishām 4:15; Ibn Sa'd 2:44, 92, 118; Tabari 3:100; Ibn Hazm: 184; Ibn 'Asākir, *al-Tārikh al-Kabir* 1:107; Ibn Sayyid al-Nās 2:54

41 Zuhri: 106 onwards; Wāqidi 3:992; Ibn Hishām 3:159; Ibn Sa'd 2:118; Suhayli 4:195; Ibn Sayyid al-Nās 2:215

42 Wāqidi 1:182; Ibn Hishām 3:50; Tabari 3:63, 100; Suhayli 3:163; Ibn Sayyid al-Nās 2:153, 215

43 Wāqidi 2:568; Ibn Hishām 4:290; Muslim 3:1296; Kalā'i 1:162

44 Wāqidi 1:76, 363, 496, 633; Ibn Atheer 2:186

45 Zuhri: 52, 55; Wāqidi 1:347, 2:560, 573; Ibn Sa'd 2:36; Ibn Hazm: 208; Kalā'i 1:161

46 Ibn Hanbal 3:475; Khabbāri (al-Diyāt 22, al-Madhālim 605); Abu Dāwud (al-Malāhim 17); Tirmidhi (al-Fitan 8, al-Isti'dhān 30)

47 Ibn Sa'd 2:105, 3:11, 118; Ibn Sayyid al-Nās 2:184, 200, 207

48 Wāqidi 3:973, 980; Ibn Hishām 4:226; Ibn Sa'd 2:115; Ibn Sayyid al-Nās 2:202, 203; Ibn Qayyim 2:471

49 Wāqidi 1:1-8; Ibn Hishām 4:257; Ibn Sa'd 2:1; Tabari 3:155 onwards; Ibn Atheer 2:301; Kalā'i 1:57; Ibn Sayyid al-Nās 1:223

50 Wāqidi 1:11 onwards; Ibn Hishām 3:224, 4:15, 279; Ibn Sa'd 2:2-6, 19, 24, 61, 86; Ibn Hazm: 184, 220; Ibn Sayyid al-Nās 2:54, 108, 153

51 Wāqidi 1:403; Ibn Hishām 3:342; Ibn Sa'd 2:44; Suhayli 4:56; Kalā'i 1:130

52 Wāqidi 1:1-8; Ibn Hishām 4:257; Ibn Sa'd 2:1; Tabari 3:152 onwards; Ibn Atheer 2:303; Ibn Sayyid al-Nās 1:223

53 Wāqidi 1:76, 2:363, 496, 633; Ibn Sa'd 2:2, 19, 39, 96

54 Ibn Hishām 2:257, 3:46, 64, 213, 224; Ibn Hanbal 4:262; Bukhāri (al-Maghāzi 29)

55 Wāqidi 1:324, 2:440; Ibn Hishām 3:192, 224; Ibn Sa'd 2:35-47; Tabari 2:546, 565

[56] Bukhāri (al-'Itq 13); Muslim 2:1357; Abu Dāwud (al-Jihād 83); al-Nasā'i (al-Mawāqeet 26)

[57] Tabari 2:408, 604, 3:9-38; Ibn Atheer 1:137, 173, 185, 216

[58] *Ibid.*

[59] Wāqidi 1:177, 368; Ibn Hishām 3:46, 50, 231; Ibn Sa'd 2:109; Dhahabi, *Tārikh al-Islām* 1:267

[60] Wāqidi 2:722, 3:923; Ibn Sa'd 1:85, 113; Ibn Sayyid al-Nās 2:145, 200

[61] Wāqidi 1:403; Ibn Hishām 3:342

[62] Wāqidi 2:722; Ibn 'Abd al-Barr 3:1144; Ibn Atheer 2:226; Ibn Hajar al-Isābah 3:279

[63] For details about the tribe of 'Ajz Hawāzin see: al-Bakri, *Mu'jam Masta'jam* 1:308; Hamawi, *Mu'jab al-Buldān* 2:21

[64] Wāqidi 2:722; Ibn Qayyim 2:358

[65] Wāqidi 3:923; Ibn Sa'd 2:133; Ibn 'Abd al-Barr 2:757; Ibn Atheer 3:54; Ibn Sayyid al-Nās 2:200; Ibn Hajar 3:286

[66] Ibn Sa'd 2:113

[67] Wāqidi 2:923; Ibn Sa'd 2:113

[68] Wāqidi 2:822; Ibn Hishām 4:47, 49; Ibn Sa'd 2:98; Ibn Sayyid al-Nās 2:172, 174

[69] Wāqidi 2:534, 550; Ibn Hishām 3:249; Tabari 3:126; Ibn Katheer 3:246

[70] Zuhri: 71; Ibn Hanbal 1:49, 87, 207; Bukhāri (al-Jihād 122); Abu Dāwud (al-Jihād 22); Dārimi (al-Siyar 29)

[71] Zuhri: 52; Ibn Hishām 3:107; Tabari 2:326; Ibn Hazm: 175; Kalā'i

[72] Wāqidi 3:948; Ibn Sa'd 2:118; Ibn 'Abd al-Barr 3:1098; Ibn Atheer 4:16; Ibn Sayyid al-Nās 2:207; Ibn al-Qayyim 3:948

[73] Suhayli 1:107; Yāqut Himyari, *Majma' al-Buldān* 4:2273; Jawād 'Ali 6:278

[74] Yāqut Himyari 1:536; Ibn Mandhur, *Lisān al-'Arab* 2:278

[75] Wāqidi 3:1080

[76] Wāqidi 3:875; Ibn Hishām 4:70, 73; Ibn Sa'd 2:196; Tabari 3:66; Ibn Hazm: 235; Kalā'i 1:143; Ibn Sayyid al-Nās 2:185; Ibn Hajar 2:98

[77] Wāqidi 3:875; Ibn Sa'd 2:106

[78] This event only affirms the fact that Khālid bin Walid, who became a Muslim a little while before the Conquest of Makkah, still had a tendency to act as the Arabs of the Age of Jāhiliyya used to act. His killing of Mālik ibn Nuwayra and forcefully fornicating with his wife on the same night is recorded in history (see: Ibn Hajar 'Asqalāni, al-Isābah fi Tamyiz al-Sahāba 3:337 and Dhahabi, Tārikh al-Islām 1:353)

[79] Q4:84; Q8:65; Ibn Hishām 2:279; Ibn Hanbal 1:117; Tabari 2:448

[80] Ibn Hanbal 4:354; Bukhāri (al-Anbiyā' 54, al-Adab 10); Abu Dāwud (al-Jihād 24); Nasā'i (al-Zakāh 85, al-Buyu' 98)

[81] Bukhāri (al-Maghāzi 17); Muslim (al-Imārah 117)l Tirmidhi (al-Zuhd 48)

[82] Ibn Hanbal 5:324, 406; Muslim (al-Musāfirun 305); Abu Dāwud (al-Jihād 22)

[83] Ibn Hishām 2:179; Ibn Hanbal 3:137; Ibn Atheer, *Usd al-Ghābah* 2:143

[84] Ibn Hishām 2:208; Suhayli 3:48; Ibn Atheer 2:26; Ibn Sayyid al-Nās 1:257

[85] Wāqidi 1:21, 88; Ibn Hishām 3:70; Tabari 2:505; Ibn Sayyid al-Nās 2:6

[86] A large flag (Tr.)

[87] Wāqidi 1:12; Ibn Hishām 2:251, 3:342; Ibn Hazm: 102, 108; Ibn Sayyidah, *al-Mukhassis* 6:204; Ibn Sayyid al-Nās 1:246; Ibn Katheer 3:246, 260

[88] Wāqidi 1:388, 408; Ibn Hishām 3:342; Ibn Sa'd 2:45, 48; Ibn Hazm: 212

[89] Wāqidi 1:22, 2:822; Suhayli 4:96; Ibn Katheer 3:245-247

[90] Wāqidi 2:649, 824; Ibn Hishām 2:264; Ibn Mājah (al-Jihād 20); Abu Dāwud (al-Jihād 69); Nasā'i (al-Hajj 106)

[91] Ibn Hanbal 4:297; Abu Dāwud (al-Jihād 69); Tirmidhi (al-Jihād 10)

[92] A banner (Tr.)

[93] Wāqidi 2:800, 812, 819

[94] *Ibid.*

[95] Ibn Hishām 3:342; Ibn Hanbal 1:31; Bukhāri (al-Maghāzi 44, 48; al-Jihād 10); Abu Dāwud (al-Jihād 69); Suhayli 3:32

[96] Wāqidi 1:239; Ibn Hishām 4:19-21; Ibn Khayyāt, *Tārikh* 1:29; Tabari 3:37; Ibn al-Qayyim 2:375

[97] Wāqidi 1:220, 2:499; Kalā'i 1:101

[98] Wāqidi 1:225; Ibn Hishām 4:19 onwards; Tabari 3:237; Suhayli 4:81

[99] Wāqidi 1:203, 2:763; Ibn Hishām 4:21; Tabari 2:513, 3:40; Kalā'i 1:136

[100] Wāqidi 1:71, 72, 2:466; Ibn Hishām 3:237, 4:51

[101] Wāqidi 1:54, 2:460, 504; Ibn Sayyid al-Nās 1:246; Ibn Katheer 4:121

[102] 'Ammād Talās, *al-Rasul al-'Arabi*: 174; al-Lawā Khattāb, *al-Rasul al-Qā'id*: 123; Wāqidi 1:8

[103] Wāqidi 1:722, 3:1117; Ibn Hishām 4:291; Ibn Sa'd 2:85, 136; Tabari 3:184; Ibn Sayyid al-Nās 2:146, 281; Ibn al-Qayyim 2:358

[104] Zuhri: 79, 151; Wāqidi 2:496, 3:1117; Ibn Hishām 2:251, 3:224, 293, 4:291; Ibn Sa'd 2:1, 53, 58; Ibn Hazm: 103, 191, 201; Ibn Sayyid al-Nās 1:227, 2:68

[105] Wāqidi 2:539, 545, 3:1057; Ibn Sa'd 2:1; Ibn Sayyid al-Nās 1:227

[106] Wāqidi 1:512; Ibn Hishām 2:251; Ibn Sa'd 2:1; Ibn Sayyid al-Nās 1:227

[107] Zuhri: 79; Wāqidi 2:294; Ibn Hishām 3:244; Ibn Sa'd 2:53; Ibn Hazm: 191; Tabari 2:181; Suhayli 3:280; Ibn Sayyid al-Nās 2:68

[108] Wāqidi 2:489; Ibn Hishām 3:244; Muslim 3:1392

[109] Wāqidi 2:357; Ibn Hishām 2:293; Ibn Sa'd 2:58; Tabari 2:601; Ibn Hazm: 201; Kalā'i 1:123; Ibn Sayyid al-Nās 2:84

[110] Wāqidi 2:539; Ibn Sa' 2:58; Muslim 3:1433; Tabari 2:602; Kalā'i 1:123

[111] Zuhri: 151; Wāqidi 3:1117; Ibn Hishām 4:291; Ibn Sa'd 2:136; Tabari 3:184; Ibn Atheer 2:33; Ibn Sayyid al-Nās 2:281

[112] Wāqidi 3:1122

[113] Wāqidi 3:1117; Ibn Sa'd 1:136

[114] Majmu'ah min al-Mu'allifeen al-'Askariyyeen, *al-Mawsu'ah al-'Askariyya* 1:286

[115] Wāqidi 1:19, 159, 2:780, 3:992; Ibn Hishām 2:257, 3:50, 4:31, 159

[116] Zuhri: 86, 106; Wāqidi 2:780, 3:989; Ibn Hishām 4:31, 159; Ibn Sa'd 2:96; Tabari 3:42, 100; Ibn Hazm: 233, 249; Kalā'i 1:137, 151; Ibn Sayyid al-Nās 2:163, 215; Ibn Qayyim 2:385, 3:3

[117] Wāqidi 1:19, 181, 252; Ibn Hishām 2:257, 3:50; 213; Ibn Sa'd 2:9, 24; Ibn Khayyāt, *Tārikh* 1:16, 28; Tabari 2:267; Ibn Atheer 2:188; Kalā'i 1:85, 124; Ibn Sayyid al-Nās 1:241, 2:52

[118] Wāqidi 1:193, 195; Ibn Hishām 3:302, 4:39; Ibn Sa'd 2:24; Ibn Hazm: 182; Kalā'i 1:138

[119] Wāqidi 3:990

[120] Wāqidi 3:1057; Ibn Hishām 3:244; Muslim 3:1391; Ibn Atheer 2:185; Ibn Sayyid al-Nās 2:216

[121] Wāqidi 2:800, 812, 819, 823, 3:895, 916; Ibn Hishām 4:42, 46-49; Ibn Sa'd 2:108; Suhayli 4:96

[122] Wāqidi 3:927; Ibn Sa'd 2:119; Tabari 3:73; Suhayli 4:163

[123] Q8:74; Wāqidi 1:20; Ibn Hishām 2:279, 4:261; Bukhāri (al-Jihād 2, 31)

[124] Wāqidi 1:20; Ibn Hishām 2:279; Ibn Sa'd 2:26; Bukhāri (al-Anbiyā' 54, al-Jihād 110); Muslim (al-Imārah 117); Abu Dāwud (al-Jihād 20)

[125] Ibn Hanbal 1:117; Tabari 2:448

[126] Ibn Hanbal 3:354; Tirmidhi (al-Zuhd 48)

[127] Wāqidi 3:990; Ibn Sa'd 2:70; Ibn 'Abd al-Barr, *al-Isti'āb* 4:1473; Ibn al-Qayyim 2:303

[128] Wāqidi 1:335; Ibn Hishām 3:226; Ibn Hazm: 186, 251; Kalā'i 1:105; Ibn Qayyim 3:4, 7, 9, 16; Ibn Katheer 4:12

[129] Zuhri: 794; Wāqidi 2:496; Ibn Hishām 3:244; Ibn Sa'd 2:53, 58; Muslim 3:1433; Ibn Hazm: 191; Suhayli 3:280; Tabari 2:539, 602; Ibn Sayyid al-Nās 2:68

[130] Wāqidi 1:181, 2:1117; Ibn Hishām 2:251; Ibn Sa'd 2:1; Tabari 2:483; Ibn Hazm: 155; Ibn Sayyid al-Nās 1:296

[131] Wāqidi 3:991, 994; Ibn Hishām 4:161; Ibn Katheer 5:4

[132] Zuhri: 71, 79, 84; Wāqidi 1:176, 363; Ibn Hishām 3:50, 199, 244, 342; Ibn Sa'd 2:19, 40, 53, 77; Tabari 2:479, 552; Ibn Hazm: 154, 181, 191, 211; Kalā'i 1:111, 130; Ibn Sayyid al-Nās 1:294, 2:48, 68

[133] Wāqidi 2:457, 458; Ibn Hishām 3:244, 232; Ibn Atheer 2:186; Ibn al-Qayyim, *Zād al-Ma'ād* 2:292; Heiderābādi, *Majmu'ah al-Wathā'iq al-Siyāsiyya lil-'Ahd al-Nabawi wal-Khilāfah al-Rāshidah*: 25, 26

[134] Wāqidi 1:12, 2:357; Ibn Hishām 2:251, 3:293; Ibn Sa'd 2:1, 58; Tabari 2:601; Ibn Hazm: 103, 201; Kalā'i 1:123; Ibn Sayyid al-Nās 1:227

[135] Wāqidi 2:616, 640; Ibn Sa'd 2:7, 69; Ibn Hazm: 108 onwards; Hamawi, *Mu'jam al-Buldān* 1:480

[136] Wāqidi 1:220, 2:642; Ibn Hishām 2:257, 3:323 onwards; Hamawi 3:380

[137] Wāqidi 2:800, 802-804; Bakri 1:303; Hamawi 2:14

[138] Wāqidi 1:20, 3:1117, 1123; Ibn Hishām 2:57 onwards; Ibn Sa'd 2:25; Ibn Hazm: 156; Hamawi 2:128

[139] Wāqidi 2:993, 1006; Ibn Hishām 2:257 onwards; Hamawi 2:14; Kalā'i 1:85; Ibn Sayyid al-Nās 1:241 onwards

[140] Ibn Hishām 3:69; Ibn Sa'd 2:59; Tabari 3:9; Ibn Sayyid al-Nās 2:131

[141] Wāqidi 1:13, 2:632; Ibn Sa'd 2:96; Hamawi 1:214; Ibn Sayyid al-Nās 2:54; Ibn Katheer 3:261

[142] Ibn Hishām 2:268 onwards, 3:69, 90; Ibn Sa'd 2:96; Bakri 3:742

[143] Wāqidi 1:56, 2:535; Ibn Katheer 3:261

[144] Wāqidi 1:403, 2:534, 557; Ibn Hishām 3:279; Ibn Sa'd 2:44, 56; Kalā'i 1:58; Ibn Sayyid al-Nās 2:54, 79

[145] Wāqidi 1:13, 2:252, 800; Ibn Hishām 2:252; Ibn Hazm: 802

[146] Wāqidi 1:403, 2:536; Ibn Hishām 3:292; Ibn Sa'd 2:61, 117; Ibn Atheer 2:188; Ibn Sayyid al-Nās 2:103

[147] Wāqidi 1:217, 2,602

[148] Ibn Hishām 2:264; Ibn Sa'd 2:12; Ibn Hazm: 108; Qurtubi, *al-Jāmi' li Ahkām al-Qur'ān* 4:306; Ibn Katheer 3:260, 5:9

[149] Wāqidi 1:20, 335, 3:1117; Ibn Hishām 2:257; Ibn Sa'd 2:25, 136

[150] Wāqidi 2:800, 812, 820, 3:895, 995, 1034; Ibn Hishām 4:24, 49; Ibn Sa'd 2:108; Ibn Hazm: 231; Ibn 'Asākir, *Tārikh Dimishq* 1:111

[151] Wāqidi 1:20; Ibn Hishām 2:257; Ibn Sa'd 2:25, 92; Kalā'i 1:135; Ibn Katheer 4:240

[152] Wāqidi 1:20, 21; Ibn Hishām 3:70; Ibn Hazm: 159

[153] Wāqidi 3:927; Ibn Sa'd 2:119; Tabari 3:73; Suhayli 4:163

[154] Wāqidi 3:1117; Ibn Hishām 2:257; Ibn Sa'd 2:25

[155] Wāqidi 1:145, 198, 500; Ibn Hishām 2:320; Kalā'i 1:112; Ibn Katheer 4:282

[156] Ibn Hanbal 1:307; Bukhāri (al-Jihād 110); Abu Dāwud (al-Jihād 24)

[157] Wāqidi 1:13, 56, 217; Ibn Sa'd 2:96; Ibn Katheer 3:216

[158] Wāqidi 1:12 onwards,2:573, 3:995; Ibn Hishām 2:241, 251, 3:202, 321, 342; Ibn Sa'd 2:119; Ibn Khayyāt 1:71; Ibn 'Abd al-Barr 3:1023; Ibn Sayyid al-Nās 2:167

[159] Wāqidi 1:215, 388, 2:822, 3:995; Ibn Hishām 3:342, 4:42; Ibn Sa'd2:34, 45; Ibn Khayyāt 1:29; Ibn Hazm: 212; Ibn Atheer 4:16 onwards

[160] Wāqidi 1:10-13, 48, 2:800, 819, 820; Ibn Hishām 2:241, 251, 4:42; Ibn Sa'd 2:1, 4; Ibn Hazm: 100; Ibn Sayyid al-Nās 1:226

[161] Wāqidi 1:396; Ibn Hishām 2:264; Tabari 3:102; Muslim 3:1429

[162] Q8:42; Wāqidi 1:53; 2:445; Ibn Hishām 3:69, 231

[163] Mount Uhud is was used like a strong fort that was positioned behind the Muslim army (Tr.)

[164] Wāqidi 2:445; Ibn Hazm: 186, 187; Tabari 3:9; Kalā'i 1:130; Ibn Sayyid al-Nās 2:231

[165] Wāqidi 1:53, 2:643; Ibn Hishām 3:234; Ibn Hazm: 186

[166] Wāqidi 1:54; Ibn Hishām 3:344; Kalā'i 1:130; Ibn Sayyid al-Nās 1:251, 2:231

[167] Wāqidi 1:56, 220; Harawi, *al-Hiyal al-Harbiyya*: 97

[168] Wāqidi 1:199, 220; Ibn Hishām 1:53

[169] Wāqidi 1:56, 220; Harawi: 97

[170] Ibn Hishām 3:302; Muslim (al-Imārah 178); Ibn Hanbal 2:327; Tabari 507; Bakri 2:229, 1220; Hamawi 5:118

[171] Wāqidi 2:644, 646

[172] Wāqidi 1:54; Ibn Hishām 3:344; Kalā'i 1:130; Ibn Sayyid al-Nās 1:251, 2:131

[173] Wāqidi 1:176, 363, 496, 2:633 onward, 992; Ibn Hishām 3:50, 199, 244 onwards 4:121; Ibn Sa'd 2:19, 40, 53, 114; Ibn Hazm: 181, 191; Ibn Sayyid al-Nās 2:68, 130, 201

[174] Wāqidi 1:177, 368, 449; Ibn Hishām 3:199; Kalā'i 1:111

[175] Wāqidi 2:651, 652, 804; Ibn Hishām 3:344; Kalā'i 1:130; Ibn Sayyid al-Nās 2:131

[176] Wāqidi 1:53, 2:445; Ibn Hishām 3:69; Kalā'i 1:130; 'Imād Talās, *al-Rasul al-'Arabi*: 310-311

[177] Wāqidi 1:53, 54, 220; Tabari 3:9; Kalā'i 1:130

[178] Wāqidi 2:462, 464; Ibn Hishām 4:85; Tabari 2:568

[179] Wāqidi 1:55, 220, 2:644; Ibn Sayyid al-Nās 1:131; Ibn Katheer 4:199; Harawi: 87

[180] Wāqidi 1:56, 224, 2:649; Ibn Hishām 3:231; Ibn Sa'd 2:48; Ibn Sayyid al-Nās 2:48

[181] Wāqidi 1:19, 27, 225, 2:645, 3:1002; Ibn Hishām 2:264; Muslim 3:1430

[182] Wāqidi 1:56, 2:445; Ibn Hishām 3:69, 231; Ibn Sayyid al-Nās 2:131

[183] Wāqidi 1:56, 219, 2:819-823; Ibn Hishām 3:218, 4:46

[184] Zuhri: 86; Wāqidi 1:219 onwards, 405, 2:522, 801, 1122; Ibn Hishām 3:23

[185] Wāqidi 1:56, 219; Tabari 6:573; Ibn Hazm: 239

[186] Wāqidi 1:219, 224; Ibn Hishām 3:243, 4:49; Ibn Sa'd 2:2 onwards; Suhayli 4:96; Kalā'i 1:113

[187] Wāqidi 1:217, 2:504; Ibn Sa'd 2:48; Tabari 2:567

[188] Wāqidi 1:217, 2:504, 800, 820; Ibn Hishām 4:42, 46-49; Suhayli 4:60

[189] Ibn Hishām 2:279; Ibn Hanbal 1:117; Bukhāri (al-Anbiyā' 54, al-Jihād 110); Tabari 2:448

[190] Wāqidi 1:58 onwards; Ibn Hishām 4:161; Ibn Hanbal 3:137; Bukhāri (al-Maghāzi 17)

[191] Wāqidi 1:71, 2:466, 3:1117; Ibn Hishām 3:237, 4:291; Ibn Sa'd 3:85; Ibn Sayyid al-Nās 2:146

[192] Shaybāni 1:58; Wāqidi 1:220, 2:778; Tabari 2:507

[193] Wāqidi 1:68, 3:923; Ibn Hishām 4:49; Ibn Sa'd 2:113; Colonel Akram, *Sayfullah Khālid*: 114

[194] Shaybāni 1:58; Wāqidi 1:67, 68; Ibn Hishām 2:278; Muslim 3:1362; Ibn Qutayba *'Uyun al-Akhbār* 2:107

[195] Wāqidi 1:343, 3:1117; Ibn Hishām 2:281; Ibn Sa'd 2:35; Tabari 3:184; Ibn Sayyid al-Nās 2:39

[196] Wāqidi 1:13, 3:897; Ibn Sa'd 2:44, 281

[197] Wāqidi 1:177; Ibn Hishām 2:325-327; Ibn Sa'd 2:70; Ibn Hazm: 28; Kalā'i 1:134

[198] Wāqidi 1:13, 203, 2:535, 3:1123; Ibn Hishām 4:15, 39; Ibn Sa'd 2:56, 65; Kalā'i 1:138

[199] Wāqidi 1:13, 2:796; Ibn Hishām 2:252; Ibn Sa'd 2:5, 96; Ibn Hazm: 104; Ibn Sayyid al-Nās 2:161

[200] Wāqidi 1:13, 343; Ibn Sa'd 2:35; Ibn Hazm: 105; Ibn Sayyid al-Nās 2:39; Ibn al-Qayyim 2:358

[201] Wāqidi 1:13, 363; Ibn Sa'd 2:40; Suhayli 3:136; Kalā'i 1:121, 122; Ibn Sayyid al-Nās 2:109

[202] Wāqidi 1:13, 2:636; Ibn Sa'd 2:96; Ibn Atheer 2:188; Ibn Sayyid al-Nās 2:54

[203] Wāqidi 2:796, 802-805; Ibn Hishām 4:39; Ibn Hanbal 3:456; Bukhāri (al-Jihād 103, al-Maghāzi 79); Muslim (al-Tawba 254); Abu Dāwud (al-Jihād 92)

[204] Wāqidi 1:195; Ibn Hishām 3:50, 4:39; Ibn Sa'd 2:24, 92; Ibn Atheer 2:188

[205] Wāqidi 1:203, 204; Ibn Hishām 2:268, 4:39; Ibn Sa'd 1:207; Tabari 2:436; Kalā'i 1:113

[206] Wāqidi 1:404, 406; Ibn Hishām 2:268; Suhayli 3:43

[207] Wāqidi 1:11, 13, 196, 198, 2:815; Ibn Hishām 3:53; Ibn Sa'd 2:24; Tabari 2:494; Ibn Hazm: 102

[208] Wāqidi 2:815

[209] al-Mawsu'ah al-'Askariyya 1:261

[210] Wāqidi 1:19, 207, 218; Ibn Hishām 2:268, 4:37, 42; Kalā'i 1:87

[211] Shaybāni 1:118; Wāqidi 2:445-452, 449; Ibn Sa'd 2:70; Ibn Hazm: 208; Kalā'i 1:144; Ibn al-Qayyim 2:303

[212] Wāqidi 1:10, 197, 2:550, 755, 3:1011; Ibn Hishām 2:245, 3:53, 224, 268, 269; Ibn Sa'd 2:2-5, 61, 85, 89, 209; Ibn Hazm: 102, 226, 227; Ibn Atheer 2:209, 226, 303; Ibn Sayyid al-Nās 1:224, 2:39

[213] Wāqidi 1:207, 218, 445, 461; Ibn Hishām 3:243; Ibn Sa'd 2:25; Kalā'i 1:113; Ibn Katheer 4:103

[214] Wāqidi 1:207, 218, 3:996; Ibn Hishām 3:232; Ibn Sa'd 2:119

[215] Wāqidi 1:54, 220, 2:651, 922; Ibn Hishām 3:50, 69, 264; Ibn Sa'd 2:45; Ibn Sayyid al-Nās 2:68

[216] Ibn Hanbal 2:471, 3:487; Bukhāri (al-Jihād 184); ibn Mājah (al-Jihād 3); Tirmidhi (Fadhā'il al-Jihād 20)

[217] Wāqidi 3:991; Ibn Hishām 4:261; Bukhāri (al-Jihād 2, 31)

[218] Wāqidi 1:68 onwards; Ibn Hishām 4:49; Ibn Sa'd 2:113

[219] Wāqidi 2:445; Ibn Hishām 2:264; Ibn Sa'd 2:!2; Tabari 2:568

[220] Ibn Hishām 2:150; Ibn Sa'd 2:1; Suhayli 2:252

[221] Q49:10; Bukhāri (al-Adab 27); Muslim (al-Birr 66)

[222] Wāqidi 1:334, 384; Ibn Hishām 3:128, 220; Ibn Sa'd 2:34, 42; Ibn Hazm: 175, 184; Kalā'i 1:104; Ibn Sayyid al-Nās 2:37, 52; Ibn Katheer 4:84, 87

[223] Wāqidi 1:324, 384; Ibn Hishām 3:128, 321; Ibn Sa'd 2:34, 42; Ibn Hazm: 175

[224] Wāqidi 1:335, 3:990, 1091; Ibn Sa'd 2:119; Suhayli 4:196

[225] Wāqidi 1:334; Ibn Hishām 3:220; Ibn Sa'd 2:42, 45; Tabari 2:564

[226] Wāqidi 1:11, 13, 340, 550; Ibn Hishām 2:245, 251; Ibn Sa'd 2:56, 61, 65; Ibn Atheer 2:207; Kalā'i 1:58

[227] Wāqidi 1:334; Ibn Hishām 3:128; Ibn Sa'd 3:34; Ibn Khayyāt 1:38; Tabari 3:29; Ibn Hazm: 175; Kalā'i 1:104; Ibn Sayyid al-Nās 2:37; Ibn Katheer 4:48

[228] Wāqidi 1:402; Ibn Hishām 3:224; Ibn Sa'd 2:44; Ibn Hazm: 184; Ibn Sayyid al-Nās 2:54

[229] Wāqidi 1:385, 287

[230] Wāqidi 1:387

[231] Wāqidi 1:326

[232] Wāqidi 1:334, 384, 2:822; Ibn Hishām 4:64, 47; Ibn Sa'd 2:34, 42, 70, 92; Ibn Hazm: 209; Ibn Qayyim 2:306

[233] Zuhri: 5; Ibn Hanbal 1:229; Bukhāri (al-Hajj 80); Kalā'i 1:105; Ibn Sayyid al-Nās 2:116

[234] Zuhri: 58; Wāqidi 1:338, 3:990, 1124; Ibn Sa'd 2:119; Suhayl 4:196

[235] Wāqidi 1:338; Ibn Hishām 4:19, 21, 47; Ibn Sa'd 2:98; Ibn Atheer 2:236, 246; Kalā'i 1:105

[236] Zuhri: 79; Wāqidi 1:337, 338; Ibn Sayyid al-Nās 2:64, 170; Ibn al-Qayyim 2:390

[237] Wāqidi 3:928; Ibn Hishām 4:122; Suhayli 3:250; Kalā'i 1:111; Ibn Katheer 4:77, 346

[238] Ibn Hishām 4:44; Ibn Sa'd 2:97; Tabari 3:52; Ibn Atheer 2:144; Ibn Sayyid al-Nās 2:168

[239] Wāqidi 2:819, 820, 822; Ibn Hishām 4:46, 47

[240] Wāqidi 2:614; Abu Dāwud (al-Manāsik 12)

[241] Wāqidi 2:736; Ibn Hishām 4:13; Tabari 3:24; Ibn Sayyid al-Nās 2:148

[242] Wāqidi 2:734, 735; Tabari 3:24

243 Wāqidi 2:735; Abu Dāwud (al-Tawāf 3, al-Raml 1)

244 Wāqidi 2:735; Ibn Hishām 4:13; Tabari 3:24

245 Through this he (s) displayed the strength and might of his army to the enemy (Tr.)

246 Ibn Hishām 4:13; Ibn Hanbal 1:229; Tirmidhi (al-Hajj 39); Nasā'i (al-Manāsik 176)

247 Wāqidi 1:821, 195; Ibn Hishām 3:46,213, 292; Ibn Sa'd 2:21, 43; 56; Ibn Hazm: 152, 182, 200; Kalā'i 1:122; Ibn Sayyid al-Nās 1:294

248 Wāqidi 1:335, 371, 2:799; Ibn Hishām 3:224; Tabari 3:101; Ibn Hazm: 202; Ibn Katheer 4:12

249 Ibn Sa'd 2:4, 19,24, 43, 56, 108; Ibn Atheer 2:173, 188, 192

250 Wāqidi 1:182, 195; Ibn Hishām 3:46; Ibn Sa'd 2:21, 24, 35, 43-45, 62, 95; Ibn Hazm: 152; Ibn Sayyid al-Nās 1:294

251 Wāqidi 2:560, 3:1125; Ibn Hishām 4:169, 239; Ibn Sa'd 2:64, 119, 122; Ibn Atheer 2:209, 293; Ibn Sayyid al-Nās 2:108, 220; Ibn al-Qayyim 2:299, 3:11

252 Zuhri: 71, 84, 89; Wāqidi 1:176, 363, 2:496, 633; Ibn Hishām 3:50, 199, 244, 342; Ibn Sa'd 2:19, 40, 53, 77; Ibn Hazm: 154, 181, 191, 211; Ibn Sayyid al-Nās 1:294, 2:48, 64, 130

253 Wāqidi 1:182, 193, 195; Ibn Hishām 3:46; Ibn Sa'd 2:21, 24, 35, 43-45; Ibn Hazm: 152, 182; Ibn Atheer 2:207; Ibn Sayyid al-Nās 1:294, 304, 2:52, 54

254 Ibn Sa'd 2:122; Bukhāri (al-Jihād 143); Muslim (al-Jihād 2, Fadhā'il al-Sahābah 35); Ibn Mājah (al-Jihād 38); Abu Dāwud (al-Jihād 82)

255 Wāqidi 1:176, 363, 2:496; Zuhri: 71, 89; Ibn Hishām 3:50, 199; Ibn Sa'd 2:19, 40; Ibn Hazm: 154, 181; Ibn Sayyid al-Nās 1:294, 2:48

256 Wāqidi 1:176, Suhayli 3:137, Ibn Atheer 2:137; Ibn Sayyid al-Nās 2:294

257 Wāqidi 1:365; Ibn Sa'd 2:41; Tabari 2:552; Ibn Sayyid al-Nās 2:49

258 Ibn Sa'd 2:41; Tabari 2:552; Ibn Sayyid al-Nās 2:49; Ibn Katheer 4:75

259 *Ibid.*

260 Ibn Sa'd 2:41; Ibn Hazm: 182; Ibn Sayyid al-Nās 2:49; Ibn Katheer 4:75

261 Shaybāni 1:58; Wāqidi 1:67, 2:649; Bukhāri (al-Jihād 130); Tabari 2:502

262 Zuhri: 151; Wāqidi 2:778; Ibn Hishām 4:291; Ibn Sayyid al-Nās 2:161

[263] Wāqidi 2:778; Ibn Hanbal 6:11; Bukhāri (al-Jihād 130); Ibn Qutaybah, *'Uyun al-Akhbār* 1:108

[264] Wāqidi 2:778, 3:1117; Ibn Sayyid al-Nās 2:281

[265] Tabari 3:75; Ibn 'Abd al-Barr, *al-Isti'āb* 2:810; Kalā'i 1:144

[266] Ibn Mājah (al-Jihād 8); Abu Dāwud (al-Jihād 102); Dārimi (al-Siyar 6, al-Riqāq 5); Harawi: 98

[267] Wāqidi 1:62; Ibn Sa'd 2:10; Ibn Qutaybah 1:108

[268] Majmu'at Muhādharāt Alqaytu fi al-Akādimiyya al-'Askariyya al-'Ulyā al-Suriyyah

[269] There are many examples of this during the eight years of war between Iran and 'Iraq (Tr.)

[270] Wāqidi 1:68, 225; Ibn Hishām 2:277, 3:72; Ibn Sa'd 2:10, 27; Tabari 2:445; Ibn Sayyid al-Nās 1:254, 2:10

[271] Wāqidi 1: 68, 225, 2:472; Ibn Hishām 2:277, 3:235; Ibn Sa'd 2:10, 49; Tabari 2:445, 574; Ibn Sayyid al-Nās 1:254, 2:61

[272] *Ibid.*

[273] Wāqidi 1:68, 225; Ibn Hishām 2:277, 3:72; Ibn Sa'd 2:10, 27; Tabari 2:445

[274] Zuhri: 63 onwards; Wāqidi 1:68; Ibn Hishām 2:277; Ibn Sa'd 2:10; Tabari 2:445; Kalā'i 1:88; Ibn Sayyid al-Nās 1:254

[275] Wāqidi 1:225; Ibn Hishām 3:72; Ibn Sa'd 2:28; Tabari 2:513; Ibn Sayyid al-Nās 2:10

[276] Wāqidi 1:68, 225, 2:471; Ibn Hishām 2:277, 3:72, 335; Ibn Sa'd 2:10, 28, 49; Tabari 2:245, 574; Ibn Sayyid al-Nās 1:254

[277] *Majmu'ah al-Ta'leef fi Akādimiyya Ferunzi al-'Askariyya – Takteek*: 376 onwards; *Majmu'at Muhādharāt Alqaytu fi al-Akādimiyya al-'Askariyya al-'Ulyā al-Suriyyah*

[278] Ibn Sayyidah, *al-Mukhassis* 6:81; Ibn Khaldun, *al-Muqaddimah* 2:657

[279] Bukhāri (al-Maghāzi 31, 37); Muslim (al-Zakāh 136, al-Jihād 42); Abu Dāwud (al-Jihād 107)

[280] Muslim (al-Jihād 78); Tabari 2:445 onwards; Ibn Sayyid al-Nās 1:252

[281] Shaybāni 1:58; Ibn Hanbal 3:456, 498; Tabari 1:446

[282] Shaybāni 1:58; Wāqidi 1:67; Ibn Hishām 2:278; Ibn Hanbal 3:456, 498; Tabari 2:446

[283] Wāqidi 1:223; Ibn Hishām 2:264; Ibn Hanbal 5:420

[284] Wāqidi 1:219 onwards, 2:800, 812, 819; Muslim (al-Zakāh 136); Abu Dāwud (al-Jihād 107)

[285] Wāqidi 1:225, 230, 2:645; Ibn Atheer 2:185, 192, 239

[286] Wāqidi 2:653; Ibn Hishām 2:344, 4:49; Ibn Sa'd 2:98

[287] Wāqidi 1:55, 225, 2:457; Ibn Hishām 2:272, 3:69; Ibn Sa'd 2:9, 27; Tabari 1:426, 440, 507

[288] Wāqidi 1:177, 363, 2:496, 670; Ibn Hishām 3:245, 344, 347; Ibn Sa'd 2:40; Tabari 2:573; Ibn Sayyid al-Nās 1:295

[289] Wāqidi 2:653, 700, 2:927; Ibn Hishām 3:344, 357, 4:129; Tabari 3:9

[290] Wāqidi 2:658, 3:927; Ibn Sayyid al-Nās 2:201

[291] Wāqidi 1:177 onwards, 363, 371, 2:466, 499; Ibn Hishām 3:200 onwards; Ibn Sa'd 2:114; Ibn Qayyim 2:330; Harawi: 103

[292] Wāqidi 1:37, 2:496, 643; Ibn Katheer 4:199

[293] Wāqidi 2:499, 666, 3:928; Ibn Hishām 3:200, 344, 4:132; Tabari 2:554; Kalā'i 1:111

[294] Wāqidi 1:177; Ibn Sa'd 2:19; Ibn Khayyāt 1:27; Tabari 2:480; Ibn Sayyid al-Nās 1:295

[295] Wāqidi 1:363; Ibn Sa'd 2:40; Ibn Hazm: 182; Ibn Katheer 4:76; Dianna, *Muhammad Rasulullah*: 278

[296] Wāqidi 2:496, 501; Ibn Hishām 3:245; Tabari 2:583; Ibn Hazm: 193

[297] Wāqidi 2:666; Ibn Sa'd 2:77; Tabari 3:16; Suhayli 4:59; Ibn Sayyid al-Nās 2:143, 145; Ibn Katheer 4:198; Nāsif, *al-Tāj* 4:422

[298] Wāqidi 3:927; Ibn Sa'd 2:114; Ibn Sayyid al-Nās 2:201

[299] Wāqidi 2:647 onwards; Ibn Hishām 3:344; Tabari 3:9; Ibn Sayyid al-Nās 2:132

[300] Wāqidi 2:652, 658, 664; Tabari 3:9; Ibn Sayyid al-Nās 2:132, 134

[301] Wāqidi 2:677; Ibn Sayyid al-Nās 2:133; Ibn Katheer 4:198

[302] Wāqidi 2:667, 669; Ibn Atheer 2:217; Ibn Katheer 4:198

[303] Wāqidi 2:680; Tabari 3:10, 14; Ibn Atheer 2:218; Ibn Sayyid al-Nās 2:134

[304] Wāqidi 2:652 onwards; Ibn Atheer 2:217

[305] Wāqidi 2:652; Ibn Hishām 3:344; Tabari 13:9; Ibn Sayyid al-Nās 2:131

[306] Wāqidi 2:644; Ibn Hishām 3:347; Ibn Sa'd 2:77; Ibn Katheer 4:194

[307] Wāqidi 2:640; Tabari 3:17; Suhayli 4:65

[308] Wāqidi 2:644; Ibn Hishām 3:344; Tabari 3:9; Kalā'i 1:130; Ibn Sayyid al-Nās 2:131

[309] The Ghatfān were a large tribe that was made up of many clans and lived near Khaybar. Ibn Sa'd 2:77; Suhayli 2:181; Hamawi 2:409

[310] Wāqidi 2:652, 670; Ibn Hishām 3:344; Ibn Atheer 2:217

[311] Wāqidi 2:671; Tabari 2:16; Suhayli 4:60; Ibn Hazm: 212; Ibn Sayyid al-Nās 2:136, 145

[312] Ibn Hishām 3:344; Tabari 3:9; Ibn Atheer 2:216; Ibn Sayyid al-Nās 2:131

[313] Wāqidi 2:652 onwards and 667 onwards

[314] Wāqidi 2:652; Ibn Hishām 3:344; Tabari 3:9; Ibn Sayyid al-Nās 2:131

[315] Wāqidi 2:658-662, 668-670

[316] Ibn Katheer 4:95; al-'Umayd al-Shā'ir, *al-Malāji wal-Tahsilāt*: 22-37

[317] Wāqidi 2:445; Tabari 2:566; Ibn Khaldun, *Muqaddimah* 2:657 onwards

[318] Wāqidi 2:470, 492; Tabari 2:574; Ibn Sayyid al-Nās 2:61

[319] Wāqidi 2:445, 446; Tabari 2:570; Ibn Hazm: 186; Hamawi 1:256, 262; Ibn Sayyid al-Nās 2:58

[320] Wāqidi 2:446; Ibn Hishām 3:231; Ibn Sa'd 2:47; Tabari 2:566

[321] Wāqidi 2:445; Ibn Sa'd 2:48; Tabari 2:567, 568

[322] Wāqidi 2:448; Ibn Hishām 3:226, 227; Ibn Sa'd 2:47, 50; Tabari 2:566; Ibn Sayyid al-Nās 2:55

[323] Wāqidi 2:445; Ibn Sa'd 2:48

[324] Wāqidi 2:446

[325] *Ibid.*

[326] Wāqidi 2:452

[327] Wāqidi 2:450; Ibn Hishām 3:260; Tabari 2:569; Kalā'i 1:114; Ibn Sayyid al-Nās 2:57

[328] Wāqidi 2:445; Tabari 2:568; Ibn Mandhur, *Lisān al-'Arab* 8:93

[329] Wāqidi 2:445; Ibn Sa'd 2:48; Ibn Sayyid al-Nās 2:57

[330] Wāqidi 2:445; Ibn Hishām 3:231; Ibn Sa'd 2:47; Ibn Hazm: 186

[331] Wāqidi 2:464; Ibn Sa'd 2:48; Tabari 2:568

[332] Wāqidi 2:460; Ibn Sa'd 2:48; Suhayli 3:279; Ibn Sayyid al-Nās 2:58

333 Ibn Hishām 3:233; Ibn Sa'd 2:48; Tabari 2:572; Ibn Atheer 2:180; Ibn Sayyid al-Nās 2:60

334 Wāqidi 2:471; Ibn Hishām 3:235; Ibn Sa'd 2:49; Tabari 2:574; Ibn Sayyid al-Nās 2:62; 'Amr ibn 'Abd Wudd was one of the bravest soldiers among the Arabs and his strength was legendary. He was among the few who were successful in crossing over the trench. After crossing over, he began to recite poems of valor and boast that none from the Muslim army would be ready to meet him in one-on-one combat. Sure enough, none from the Muslim army showed any willingness to face him and when the Prophet (s) asked who would go, only the young 'Ali ibn Abi Tālib ('a) stood up. As 'Ali ('a) walked into battle to face the giant Ibn 'Abd Wudd, the Prophet (s) remarked: Today the whole of Eimān is going to fight against the whole of Kufr (Tr.)

335 Wāqidi 2:446

336 Wāqidi 2:796, 802-805; Ibn Sa'd 2:96; Ibn Hazm: 226, 230; Suhayli 3:28, 29; Kalā'i 1:138; Ibn Sayyid al-Nās 2:161, 167, 170; Ibn al-Qayyim 2:386; Ibn Katheer 4:280

337 Wāqidi 2:792, 803, 822, 823; Ibn Hishām 4:44; Ibn Sa'd 1:98; Ibn Hazm: 230; Tabari 3:52, 54; Ibn Atheer 2:241; Ibn Sayyid al-Nās 2:170; Ibn Qayyim 21:389

338 Wāqidi 2:825, 875; Ibn Hishām 4:49; Ibn Sa'd 2:98, 101; Tabari 3:56; ibn Atheer 2:226; Kalā'i 1:139; Ibn Sayyid al-Nās 2:172

339 Wāqidi 2:25, 728, 875; Ibn Atheer 2:246; Ibn Sayyid al-Nās 2:173

340 Wāqidi 2:818, 825; Ibn Hishām 4:49; Ibn Sa'd 2:98; Tabari 3:56; Ibn Atheer 2:246; Ibn Katheer 4:296

341 Wāqidi 2:825; Ibn Hishām 4:51, 75; Ibn Sa'd 2:98, 99

342 Ibn Hishām 4:46,47; Ibn Sa'd 2:98; Tabari 3:56; Ibn Sayyid al-Nās 2:169 onwards

343 Ibn Hishām 4:47; Ibn Sa'd 2:98; Tabari 3:56; Ibn Sayyid al-Nās 2:170

344 Wāqidi 2:822, 878; Ibn Hishām 4:53; Tabari 3:57

345 Wāqidi 2:823; Ibn Hishām 4:44; Tabari 3:54; Ibn Atheer 2:246; Ibn Sayyid al-Nās 2:170; Ibn al-Qayyim 2:390

346 The way that the Holy Prophet (s) planned the Conquest of Makkah was so perfect that the city was taken without any bloodshed or fighting. Once Makkah was taken, the Prophet (s) proceeded to the Ka'bah and broke all the idols in it. (Tr.)

347 Majmu'at Muhādharāt Alqaytu fi al-Akādimiyya al-'Askariyya al-'Ulyā al-Suriyyah

348 Wāqidi 1:13, 343, 2:723, 726; Ibn Hishām 2:245, 4:165; Ibn Sa'd 2:56, 61, 64; Suhayli 4:252; Ibn Atheer 2:207; Kalā'i 1:158, 162; Ibn Sayyid al-Nās 2:105; Ibn al-Qayyim 2:297; Ibn Katheer 4:220-223

349 Wāqidi 1:343, 2:723; Ibn Hishām 4:265; Ibn Sa'd 2:61, 65; Suhayli 4:252; Ibn Atheer 2:207

350 Wāqidi 1:13, 2:551; Ibn Hishām 2:252; Ibn Sa'd 2:61; Ibn Sayyid al-Nās 2:104, 105; Ibn Qayyim 2:197, 297

351 Zuhri: 150; Wāqidi 2:769; Ibn Hishām 4:272;Ibn Sa'd 2:94; Tabari 3:31; Ibn Sayyid al-Nās 2:157

352 Wāqidi 2:391; Ibn Hishām 3:278; Ibn Hazm: 200; Kalā'i 1:121; Ibn Katheer 4:139

353 Wāqidi 1:11; Ibn Hishām 2:245; Ibn Hazm: 103, 105; Tabari 2:295

354 Wāqidi 2:534, 550, 562; Ibn Sa'd 1:56, 61-65; Ibn Atheer 1:207, 209; Kalā'i 1:158; Ibn Sayyid al-Nās 2:79, 103, 105, 109

355 Wāqidi 2:726; Ibn Hishām 4:265; Ibn Sa'd 2:64; Ibn Atheer 2:207; Kalā'i 1:158

356 Wāqidi 2:535; Ibn Atheer 2:226; Ibn Sayyid al-Nās 2:105, 206; Ibn Katheer 4:220

357 Wāqidi 2:770; Ibn Sa'd 2:95; Ibn Sayyid al-Nās 2:157

358 Wāqidi 1:11, 13, 2:769; Ibn Hishām 2:245, 252; Ibn Sa'd 2:1, 95; Tabari 2:259; Ibn Hazm: 04; Ibn Sayyid al-Nās 1:225; Ibn Katheer 3:248

359 Wāqidi 1:19; Ibn Hishām 2:257; Ibn Sa'd 2:29; Ibn Khayyāt 1:16; Tabari 2:267; Ibn Hazm: 107; Kalā'i 1:58; Ibn Sayyid al-Nās 1:241; Ibn Katheer 2:261

360 Q8:42; Wāqidi 1:53; Ibn Hishām 2:266, 272

361 Wāqidi 1:56 onwards; Ibn Hishām 2:278; Ibn Hanbal 3:157; Muslim (al-Jihād 42); Abu Dāwud (al-Jihād 107)

362 Wāqidi 1:11 onwards; Ibn Hishām 2:254; Ibn Sa'd 2:10 onwards; Tabari 2:259; Ibn Hazm: 104

363 Wāqidi 1:20, 87, 91; Ibn Hazm: 108

364 Wāqidi 1:20; Suhayli 3:51

365 Wāqidi 1:48 onwards; Ibn Hishām 2:262; Ibn Katheer 3:262, 267

[366] Shaybāni 1:118; Wāqidi 1:67; Ibn Hishām 3:69; Ibn Sa'd 2:8; Tabari 2:426; Ibn Sayyid al-Nās 2:188

[367] Q4:84; Ibn Hishām 2:279; Ibn Hanbal 1:307; Bukhāri (al-Jihād 110)

[368] Wāqidi 1:23, 27, 39; Ibn Hishām 2:269; Ibn Sa'd 2:7; Tabari 2:423, 431 onwards; Ibn Atheer 2:118; Ibn Sayyid al-Nās 1:244

[369] Wāqidi 1:181; Ibn Khayyāt 1:28; Tabari 2:483; Ibn Hazm: 155; Ibn Sayyid al-Nās 1:296

[370] Ibn Is'hāq: 310; Wāqidi 1:181; Tabari 2:483; Ibn Sayyid al-Nās 1:296

[371] Wāqidi 1:197m 198; Tabari 2:492

[372] Wāqidi 1:197; Ibn Hishām 3:53; Ibn Sa'd2:24; Tabari 2:492; Ibn Sayyid al-Nās 1:305

[373] Zuhri: 76; ; Wāqidi 1:199; Ibn Hishām 3:64; Ibn Sa'd 2:25; Khayyāt 1:29; Tabari 3:9; Ibn Hazm: 956; Kalā'i 1:104; Dhahabi, *Tārikh al-Islām* 1:183

[374] Wāqidi 1:221-229; Ibn Hishām 3:82; Ibn Sa'd 2:28; Tabari 2:517 onwards; Ibn Sayyid al-Nās 2:11

[375] Wāqidi 1:229 onwards; Ibn Hishām 3:82; Ibn Sa'd 2:29; Tabari 2:515 onwards; Ibn Sayyid al-Nās 2:11

[376] Wāqidi 1:249; Ibn Sa'd 2:29; Tabari 2:510; Ibn Atheer 2:54; Ibn Sayyid al-Nās 2:11

[377] Wāqidi 1:241; Ibn Hishām 3:89; Tabari 2:518; Ibn Atheer 2:157; Ibn Sayyid al-Nās 2:14 onwards

[378] *Ibid.*

[379] Wāqidi 1:241 onwards; Ibn Hishām 3:82, 91; Tabari 2:521; Ibn Sayyid al-Nās 2:15

[380] Wāqidi 1:334; Ibn Hishām 3:128; Ibn Sa'd 3:34; Ibn Khayyāt 1:38; Tabari 3:29; Ibn Hazm: 175; Kalā'i 1:104; Ibn Sayyid al-Nās 2:37; Ibn Katheer 4:48

[381] Wāqidi 1:335; Ibn Hishām 3:107; Ibn Sa'd 2:34; Tabari 2:534; Kalā'i 1:105

[382] Wāqidi 1:335 onwards; Ibn Hishām 3:107; Ibn Sa'd 2:34; Tabari 2:534; Ibn Sayyid al-Nās 2:37

[383] Wāqidi 1:338; Ibn Hishām 3:108; Ibn Sa'd 2:35; Tabari 2:535; Ibn Sayyid al-Nās 2:37

[384] Wāqidi 1:340, 362, 391, 404; Ibn Hishām 3:199; Ibn Sa'd 2:75

[385] Ibn Hishām 3:226; Ibn Sa'd 2:47; Ibn Hazm: 186

386 Zuhri: 79; Wāqidi 2:440; Ibn Hishām 2:244; Ibn Sa'd 2:47; Tabari 2:565; Ibn Hazm: 185; Suhayli 3:276; Kalā'i 1:114; Ibn Sayyid al-Nās 2:55; Ibn Qayyim 2:288

387 Wāqidi 2:457; Ibn Hishām 3:231; Ibn Sa'd 2:47

388 Wāqidi 2:492; Ibn Hishām 2:230; Ibn Hazm: 186, 187

389 Wāqidi 2:445, 449, 453; Ibn Hishām 3:262

390 Wāqidi 2:462, 464, 471; Ibn Hishām 2:235; Ibn Sa'd 2:48; Tabari 2:586; Suhayli 3:279; Ibn Atheer 2:180; Ibn Sayyid al-Nās 2:61

391 Wāqidi 1:492; Ibn Hishām 3:243; Ibn Sayyid al-Nās 2:65

392 Wāqidi 2:445; Ibn Hishām 2:231; Tabari 2:570; Ibn Hazm: 186; Ibn Sayyid al-Nās 2:58

393 Wāqidi 2:443; Ibn Sa'd 2:48, 48; Ibn Qayyim 2:289; Watt, *Muhammad fi al-Madina*: 58

394 Wāqidi 2:443; Ibn Hishām 3:260; Muslim 3:1362; Kalā'i 1:114; Ibn Sayyid al-Nās 2:65

395 Zuhri: 79; Wāqidi 2:479; Muslim 3:1361; Ibn Sayyid al-Nās 2:64; Ibn Qayyim 2:192

396 Zuhri: 79; Ibn Hishām 2:232, 262; Ibn Sa'd 2:47; Bukhāri (al-Maghāzi 29)

397 Ibn Hishām 3:241; Ibn Sa'd 2:50; Tabari 2:578; Ibn Sayyid al-Nās 2:65

398 Ibn Hishām 3:243; Ibn Sa'd 2:51; Ibn Atheer 2:184; Ibn Sayyid al-Nās 2:65

399 Ibn Hishām 3:243; Ibn Atheer 2:184; Ibn Sayyid al-Nās 2:65

400 Wāqidi 2:492; Ibn Katheer 4:113

401 Zuhri: 79; Wāqidi 2:479; Ibn Hishām 3:234, 262; Qurtubi, *al-Jāmi li Ahkām al-Qur'ān* 14:133

402 Ibn Sa'd 2:53; Tabari 2:579; Ibn Atheer 2:184

403 Ibn Sa'd 2:54; Ibn Hazm: 188; Ibn Katheer 4:103

404 Wāqidi 2:496; Ibn Hishām 3:145; Ibn Sa'd 2:53; Tabari 2:583; Ibn Hazm: 193

405 Ibn Hishām 3:266; Ibn Hanbal 4:262; Bukhāri (al-Maghāzi 29)

406 Ibn 'Abd al-Barr 2:542; Ibn Atheer 2:224; Ibn Hajar, *al-Isābah* 3:24

407 Wāqidi 2:553; Ibn Sa'd 2:63; Ibn Atheer 2:207; Ibn Sayyid al-Nās 2:106; Ibn Qayyim 2:297

408 Ibn Hishām 3:325, 327; Ibn Sa'd 2:70; Ibn Hazm: 208; Ibn Katheer 4:170

[409] Ibn Hishām 3:232; Tabari 2:635; Ibn Atheer 2:204; Kalā'i 1:130, 137

[410] Zuhri: 86, 87; Wāqidi 2:780; Ibn Hishām 4:31; Ibn Sa'd 2:96; Ibn Khayyāt 1:56

[411] Wāqidi 2:796, 799, 892; Ibn Hishām 4:39; Ibn Sa'd 2:96; Ibn Hazm: 226, 228, 230; Suhayli 4:97; Kalā'i 1:38; Ibn Sayyid al-Nās 2:161, 167; Ibn Qayyim 2:309

[412] Wāqidi 2:800, 818, 825; Ibn Sa'd 2:98; Kalā'i 1:137; Ibn Sayyid al-Nās 2:172, 174; Ibn Katheer 4:288

[413] Wāqidi 2:822, 823; Ibn Hishām 4:47; Ibn Sa'd 2:98; Ibn Atheer 2:246

[414] Wāqidi 2:825; Ibn Hishām 4:49; Ibn Sa'd 2:98; Tabari 3:61; Ibn Atheer 2:246; Kalā'i 1:139

[415] Wāqidi 3:873; Ibn Hishām 4:56; Ibn Sa'd 2:105; Ibn Hazm: 235; Ibn Qayyim 2:398

[416] Wāqidi 1:1-8; Ibn Hishām 4:256; Ibn Sa'd 2:1; Tabari 3:152; Ibn Sayyid al-Nās 3:223

[417] Wāqidi 1:1-8; Ibn Hishām 4:257; Ibn Sa'd 2:51; Tabari 3:155; Kalā'i 1:57; Ibn Sayyid al-Nās 1:223

[418] Wāqidi 1:173, 184; Ibn Hishām 3:54, 287; Ibn Sa'd 2:21; Ibn Hazm: 184, 198

[419] For more details about this tribe see: Kahālah, *Mu'jam Qabā'il al-'Arab* 2:543

[420] Ibn Sa'd 2:21

[421] Bahrān was a place between Makkah and Madina; Ibn Sa'd 2:24

[422] Ibn Sa'd 2:62; Bakri 2:394

[423] Suhayli 3:136; Kahālah 1:144, 3:888

[424] Wāqidi 1:193; Hamawi 1:252

[425] Ibn Sa'd 2:44, Hamawi 2:398

[426] Wāqidi 1:404; Ibn Hishām 3:302; Ibn Sa'd 2:45; Ibn Sayyid al-Nās 2:91

[427] Ibn Sa'd 2:45; Bakri 4:1240

[428] Kahālah 3:190

[429] Ibn Hishām 3:292

[430] Bakri 1:77; Kahālah 1:147

[431] Ibn Sa'd 2:108; Suhayli 4:138; Bakri 2:471

[432] Kahālah 1:21, 22

[433] Wāqidi 1:342; Ibn Sa'd 2:35

[434] Ibn Sa'd 1:61; Bakri 3:1002

[435] Ibn Sa'd 2:56; Zarqāni, *Sharh al-Mawāhib* 2:166; Kahālah 1:92

[436] Ibn Sa'd 2:56; Bakri 1:269, 3:859; Hamawi 3:457

[437] Zarqāni 2:178

[438] Ibn Sa'd 2:161; Hamawi 4:366

[439] Ibn Sa'd 2:36

[440] Ibn Sa'd 2:63; Kahālah 1:174

[441] Ibn Sa'd 2:63; Bakri 2:446; Hamawi 2:258

[442] Hamawi4:338; Kahālah 3:918

[443] Hamawi 4:338

[444] Kahālah 2:513

[445] Ibn Sa'd 2:65; Bakri 3:1015

[446] Bakri 1:308, Hamawi 2:21

[447] Ibn Sa'd 2:85; Bakri 1:308; Hamawi 2:21; Ibn Katheer 4:221

[448] Kahālah 3:918, 990

[449] *Majma' al-Buldān* 5:261; Kahālah 3:1231

[450] Ibn Sa'd 2:117; Hamawi 3:133, 457

[451] Kahālah 3:1072

[452] Hamawi 4:238

[453] Kahālah 1:143

[454] Ibn Sa'd 2:186; Bakri 4:1284

[455] Kahālah 3:888

[456] Ibn Sa'd 2:87; Bakri 2:395, 4:1400; Hamawi 2:98, 164, 5:449

[457] Ibn Sa'd 2:95; Hamawi 2:388

[458] Kahālah 3:1173

[459] Bakri 3:925, 4:1119; Hamawi 4:442

[460] Ibn 'Abd al-Barr 3:1323; Bakri 1:17

[461] Ibn Sa'd 2:92; Hamawi 1:218

[462] Kahālah 2:1231, 2:708

[463] Ibn Sa'd 2:92; Bakri 3:772

[464] Wāqidi 1:7; Ibn Sa'd 2:116; Kahālah1:126

465 Suqyā is the name of a well and Masjid near Madina from which the Holy Prophet (s) drank water or performed ablution when he passed by it in some of the battles. (Tr.)

466 Wāqidi 2:754; Ibn Sa'd 2:117; Bakri 1:301

467 Wāqidi 3:981; Hamawi 5:125

468 Wāqidi 1:182, 193; Ibn Hishām 3:46, 50; Ibn Sa'd 2:21; 43; Ibn Hazm: 152, 182

469 Wāqidi 1:182, 193, 404; Ibn Hishām 3:213, 4:272; Ibn Sa'd 2:21, 43; Ibn Hazm: 152

470 Wāqidi 1:183, 535; Ibn Sa'd 2:61; Ibn Atheer 2:226; Ibn Sayyid al-Nās 2:93, 105

471 Wāqidi 1:23, 27; Ibn Sa'd 2:21; Ibn Sayyid al-Nās 1:226

472 Wāqidi 1:23, 27, 39; Ibn Sa'd 2:21; Ibn Sayyid al-Nās 1:226

473 Wāqidi 2:534, 552, 3:1022; Ibn Sa'd 2:56

474 Ibn Sa'd 2:12, 35, 45, 56, 63, 108; Bakri 1:17, 301, 308, 3:446, 3:1015, 4:1274, 1400; Hamawi 1:308, 2:21, 3:133, 4:238

475 Wāqidi 1:193, Ibn Hishām 3:302; Ibn Sa'd 2:44, 45, 56, 61; Suhayli 3:136

476 Wāqidi 1:12, 2:537; hi 2:251, 3:293; Ibn Sa'd 2:1, 58; Tabari 2:601; Ibn Hazm: 201; Ibn Atheer 2:188; Ibn Sayyid al-Nās 1:227, 2:84

477 Wāqidi 1:342; Ibn Hishām 3:203; Ibn Sa'd 2:21, 35, 43-45, 62, 95; Ibn Hazm: 203; Ibn Sayyid al-Nās 2:39

478 Wāqidi 1:193; Ibn Sa'd 2:21, 23; Suhayli 3:136, 142; Ibn Atheer 2:142

479 Wāqidi 1:342, 403; Ibn Sa'd 2:35, 44; Ibn Sayyid al-Nās 2:39; Ibn Katheer 4:61; Nāsif, *al-Tāj* 4:347

480 Wāqidi 1:69, 5:563; Ibn Sa'd 2:24; Tabari 3:75; Ibn Sayyid al-Nās 1:304; Ibn Qayyim 2:299

481 Wāqidi 1:182, 194, 395, 406; Ibn Sa'd 2:61, 63-65, 85, 89; Tabari 3:29; Suhayli 4:252; Ibn Sayyid al-Nās 2:39

482 Wāqidi 1:182; Ibn Hishām 3:46; Ibn Sa'd 2:21; Ibn Khayyāt 1:27; Ibn Hazm: 152

483 Wāqidi 1:10, 12; Ibn Hishām 2:241; Ibn Sa'd 2:1-4; Tabari 2:259; Ibn Hazm: 100; Suhayli 3:17; Hamawi 1:92, 3:350, 4:136

484 Wāqidi 1:182; Ibn Hishām 3:46, 50; Ibn Sa'd 2:21, 24; Ibn Hazm: 152; Hamawi 1:193, 341; Ibn Sayyid al-Nās 1:264, 304

485 Wāqidi 1:404, 2:535, 752; Ibn Hishām 3:302; Ibn Sa'd 2:45, 56, 95; Tabari 3:29; Ibn Hazm: 200; Kalā'i 1:124; Ibn Sayyid al-Nās 2:83, 91, 152; Ibn Qayyim 2:278, 293

486 Wāqidi 1:12, 2:560, 3:1079; Ibn Hishām 3:3:249; Ibn Sa'd 2:64, 122; Tabari 3:131; Bakri 2:564; Hamawi 1:503, 536; Ibn Sayyid al-Nās 1:224, 271; Ibn Mandhur 1:278

487 Wāqidi 1:182, 195, 2:560, 3:1025; Ibn Hishām 3:46, 50; Ibn Sa'd 2:21, 24, 62, 86; Ibn Sayyid al-Nās 1:294, 304; Ibn Sa'd 2:83, 95; Suhayli 3:136

488 Ibn Hishām 2:241; Suhayli 2:252; Haiderābādi: 15-21; this pact had forty conditions that were to be abided by both the Arab Muslims and Jews residents of Madina. (Tr.)

489 Wāqidi 1:176; Ibn Hishām 3:50; Ibn Sa'd 2:19; Ibn Sayyid al-Nās 1:294

490 Wāqidi 1:176; Suhayli 3:137; Ibn Atheer 2:137; Ibn Sayyid al-Nās 2:294

491 Wāqidi 1:177; Ibn Hishām 3:45; Ibn Hazm: 193; Ibn Sayyid al-Nās 2:295

492 Wāqidi 1:184, 391; Ibn Hishām 3:54, 286; Ibn Hazm: 154, 198

493 Wāqidi 1:391; Ibn Hishām 3:55; Ibn Sa'd 2:21; Ibn Hazm: 154, 198

494 Wāqidi 1:391; Ibn Hishām 3:52, 286; Ibn Sa'd 2:21; Ibn 'Abd al-Barr 3:946, 1377; Ibn Atheer 3:304, 4:330

495 Zuhri: 71; Wāqidi 1:363; Ibn Hishām 3:199; Bukhāri 5:88

496 Wāqidi 1:365; Ibn Hishām 3:199; Ibn Sayyid al-Nās 2:48

497 Wāqidi 1:363 onwards; Ibn Hishām 3:199; Ibn Sa'd 2:40; Ibn Sayyid al-Nās 2:48

498 Zuhri: 71; Wāqidi 1:363; Ibn Hishām 3:200; Ibn Sa'd 2:40; Ibn Hazm: 181, 182

499 Wāqidi 2:443, 445, 457; Ibn Hishām 3:225, 232; Suhayli 3:278; Ibn Qayyim 2:289, 292

500 Wāqidi 2:497; Ibn Sa'd 2:54; Ibn Hazm: 188; Ibn Katheer 4:103

501 Zuhri: 79; Wāqidi 2:496; Ibn Hishām 3:244; Ibn Sa'd 2:53; Tabari 2:181; Ibn Hazm: 191; Ibn Sayyid al-Nās 2:68; Ibn Qayyim 2:292

502 Wāqidi 2:497, 498, 510; Ibn Hishām 3:244; Ibn Sa'd 2:53; Muslim 2:1391

503 Wāqidi 2:496, 501; Ibn Hishām 3:245; Ibn Qutaybah, *'Uyun al-Akhbār* 2:114; Tabari 2:583; Ibn Sayyid al-Nās 2:72; It mentioned that the Prophet (s) gave authority to Sa'd ibn Mu'ādh who was in allegiance with them to make the decision about their punishment. He (s) also ensured that their punishment was in accordance to the Jewish holy scriptures and the command of God. It is then that he ordered that they be put to

death and their families be taken as prisoners. However, there are many doubts that can be raised about this account: (1) the number of killed is put at 900 but there could not have been that many fighters of the Bani Quraydha at the time (2) these reports have been narrated by persons who had just accepted Islām and it is possible that they wanted to express a feeling of oppression against the Jews [as even today, while it is clear that it is they who are the oppressors, they still portray themselves as the oppressed] (3) it is said that two people were given the task of killing these men yet the short span of time mentioned makes it impossible for two men to kill 900; and many other questions that make this narration suspicious and not easy to accept outright. (Tr.)

[504] Zuhri: 84; Wāqidi 2:633; Ibn Hishām 3:342; Ibn Sa'd 2:77; Ibn Khayyāt 1:50; Tabari 3:9; Ibn Hazm: 211; Ibn Atheer: 216; Kalā'i 1:130; Ibn Sayyid al-Nās 2:130; Ibn Qayyim 2:324

[505] Wāqidi 2:666, 685, 700; Ibn Hishām 3:357; Ibn Katheer 4:198, 199

[506] Wāqidi 2:706, 709; Tabari 3:106; Hamawi 2:37, 42, 238, 338; Ibn Sayyid al-Nās 2:143, 145

[507] Wāqidi 1:176, 2:633; Ibn Hishām 3:50, 342; Ibn Sa'd 2:19, 53, 77; Tabari 2:479, 552; Ibn Hazm: 154, 181, 211; Ibn Sayyid al-Nās 2:48, 68, 130

[508] Wāqidi 1:368, 2:496, 647, 671 onwards; Ibn Hazm: 192; Suhayli 6:65; Ibn Katheer 4:185, 198

[509] Wāqidi 1:368, 2:637, 640, 643

[510] Wāqidi 1:368, 2:637, 664, 670; Ibn Sayyid al-Nās 1:134; Ibn Qayyim 2:330, 331

[511] Wāqidi 1:177, 377, 2:510, 667; Ibn Sa'd 2:41; Suhayli 4:65; Ibn Sayyid al-Nās 4:72

[512] Wāqidi 1:176, 2:640

[513] Wāqidi 1:177, 2:454, 510, 574, 642, 650

[514] Wāqidi 1:179, 374, 634, Kalā'i 1:130

[515] Wāqidi 1:179, 2:634, 637; Ibn Atheer 1:656

[516] Wāqidi 1:370; Ibn Hishām 3:50, 199, 244, 342; Ibn Sa'd 2:19, 40, 53, 77; Tabari 2:479, 552, 3:9

[517] Wāqidi 1:177, 363, 2:499, 503; Ibn Hishām 2:245; Ibn Sa'd 2:40; Tabari 357

[518] Wāqidi 1:177 onwards, 363, 2:499, 666; Ibn Hishām 3:200, 344; Ibn Sa'd 2:114; Ibn 'Abd al-Barr: 181; Ibn Qayyim 2:330

[519] Wāqidi 1:371, 2:496; Ibn Katheer 4:199

[520] Wāqidi 2:671, 683; Ibn Hishām 3:344; Tabari 3:9; Ibn Atheer 2:217

[521] Wāqidi 1:378, 2:496, 670; Tabari 2:552; Ibn Hazm: 182

[522] Wāqidi 2:496 onwards; Ibn Hishām 3:200, 344; Ibn Atheer 2:217; Ibn Sayyid al-Nās 1:295

[523] Wāqidi 1:371, 2:501; Tabari 3:9; Kalā'i 1:130; Ibn Sayyid al-Nās 2:131

[524] Wāqidi 1:176, 2:496, 652 onwards; Ibn Hishām 3:50, 244; Ibn Sa'd 2:19, 40, 77; Ibn Hazm: 154, 181, 191, 211

[525] Wāqidi 1:176; Ibn Hishām 3:50; Ibn Sa'd 2:19; Ibn Hazm: 59; Ibn Sayyid al-Nās 1:294

[526] Wāqidi 1:363; Ibn Hishām 3:199; Ibn Sa'd 2:40; Tabari 2:479; Ibn Sayyid al-Nās 2:48

[527] Wāqidi 2:496; Ibn Hishām 3:244; Ibn Sa'd 2:53; Tabari 2:552; Ibn Hazm: 191

[528] Wāqidi 2:633; Ibn Hishām 3:342; Ibn Sa'd 2:77; Tabari 3:9; Ibn Sayyid al-Nās 2:130

[529] Wāqidi 1:177, 2:497, 670; Ibn Hishām 3:200; Tabari 1:116, 117; Ibn Qayyim 4:330

[530] Wāqidi 1:420; Ibn Hishām 3:224; Ibn Sa'd 2:44; Ibn Hazm: 184; Suhayli 3:276; Ibn Sayyid al-Nās 2:54; Ibn Katheer 4:92

[531] Tabari 3:378; Hamawi 2:487; Jawād 'Ali 1:590, 611, 624, 3:106

[532] Ibn Hishām 3:224; Ibn Atheer 2:395 onwards; Ibn Sayyid al-Nās 2:220

[533] Wāqidi 2:560, 3:1025; Ibn Hishām 3:169; Ibn Sa'd 2:119; Kahālah 3:991; Watt, *Muhammad fi al-Madina*: 157

[534] Ibn Sa'd 2:64, 119; Bakri 2:564; Hamawi 2:15, 487

[535] Wāqidi 2:560; Ibn Sa'd 2:64; Ibn Atheer 2:209; Ibn Sayyid al-Nās 2:108; Ibn Qayyim 299

[536] Wāqidi 2:560; Ibn Sa'd 2:64; Ibn Qayyim 2:300

[537] Wāqidi 2:560, 561; Ibn Sa'd 2:64; Hamawi 2:487; Jawād 'Ali 1:590, 592, 624

[538] Wāqidi 2:755; Ibn Hishām 4:15; Ibn Sa'd 2:92; Ibn Khayyāt 1:56; Tabari 2:36; Ibn 'Asākir 1:92; Ibn Hazm: 220; Ibn Sayyid al-Nās 2:153

539 Ibn Hishām 4:30; Ibn Sa'd 2:92; Ibn Hazm: 220, 221; Kalā'i 1:176; Ibn Sayyid al-Nās 2:154

540 Wāqidi 2:755; Kalā'i 1:136; Ibn Sayyid al-Nās 2:215

541 Wāqidi 2:760, 761; Suhayli 4:81; Ibn Hazm: 220; Ibn Sayyid al-Nās 2:154

542 Zuhri: 106; Ibn Hishām 4:159; Ibn Sa'd 2:118; Ibn Khayyāt 1:64; Tabari 3:100; Ibn Hazm: 249; Ibn 'Asākir 1:107; Kalā'i 1:151; Ibn Sayyid al-Nās 2:215

543 Wāqidi 2:765; Ibn Hishām 4:19-21; Ibn Sa'd 2:119; Ibn Atheer 2:36; Ibn Qayyim 2:375

544 Wāqidi 2:990; Ibn Sa'd 2:119

545 Zuhri: 151; Wāqidi 3:117; Ibn Hishām 4:291; Ibn Sa'd 2:136; Tabari 3:184; Ibn 'Abd al-Barr 1:75; Ibn Sayyid al-Nās 2:281; Ibn Hajar 1:29

546 Zuhri: 58; Wāqidi 3:1091, 1124; Ibn Khayyāt 1:103; Ibn Katheer 6:316; Watt, Muhammad fi al-Madina: 158, 177; Initially this mission was delayed because of the objections raised by some companions about the young age of the appointed commander Usāma bin Zayd. (Tr.)

547 Wāqidi 3:990; Ibn Sayyid al-Nās 2:44, 119

548 Wāqidi 1:2, 4, 2:560, 3:989, 1117; Ibn Sa'd 2:44, 64, 119, 136

549 Zuhri: 58; Wāqidi 3:1035; Ibn Hishām 3:244, 4:291; Tabari 3:100; Ibn Hazm: 253; Bakri 2:538; Ibn 'Asākir 1:111, 112; Hamawi 1:489

550 Wāqidi 3:1018, 1039; Ibn Sa'd 2:44; Bakri 2:564; Hamawi 2:14; Ibn Katheer 5:9

551 Wāqidi 1:403; Ibn Hishām 4:169; Ibn Sa'd 2:64, 119; Kahālah 2:991

552 Wāqidi 2:560; Ibn Hishām 4:169; Ibn Sa'd 2:64; Ibn Atheer 2:280; Ibn Qayyim 3:210

553 Wāqidi 2:769; Ibn Hishām 4:30; Ibn Sa'd 2:293; Ibn Hazm: 222; Kalā'i 1:136; Watt: 158, 159. 177

554 Wāqidi 2:760, 3:990; Ibn Sa'd 2:119; Hindi, *al-Jaysh al-'Arabi fi 'Asr al-Futuhāt*: 26

555 Wāqidi 2:755, 756, 760; Ibn Hishām 4:16, 19; Ibn Hazm: 22; Suhayli 4:81; Ibn Sayyid al-Nās 2:153

556 Wāqidi 3:1117, 1123; Ibn Hazm: 220 onwards; Kalā'i 136; Ibn Sayyid al-Nās 2:281

557 Wāqidi 3:117, 1122, 1123; Ibn Hishām 4:291; Ibn Sa'd 2:281; Kalā'i 1:136; Ibn Sayyid al-Nās 2:153

558 Wāqidi 2:760; Ibn Hishām 4:16, 17; Tabari 3:37; Ibn Atheer 2:235; Ibn Sayyid al-Nās 2:153

559 Wāqidi 2:120, 3:1019, 1124; Ibn Sayyid al-Nās 3:220, 383

560 Wāqidi 2:560, 755, 3:990; Ibn Sa'd 2:64, 110; Hamawi 2:487; Kalā'i 1:136; Jawād 'Ali 1:529, 611, 2:38

561 Wāqidi 1:404, 3:990, 1091; Ibn Hishām 4:279; Ibn Sa'd 2:44, 199; Suhayli 4:196; Kalā'i 1:136

562 Wāqidi 1:403, 2:560; Ibn Hishām 4:169; Ibn Sa'd 2:64, 119; Ibn Atheer 2:280

563 Wāqidi 1:402; Ibn Hishām 4:15, 191; Kalā'i 1:152; Tabari 3:100; Ibn Hazm: 184; Ibn 'Asākir 1:107; Ibn Sayyid al-Nās 2:108

564 Ibn Sa'd 2:92; Ibn Hazm: 220, 221; Suhayli 4:81; Kalā'i 1:136; Ibn Sayyid al-Nās 2:154

565 Wāqidi 3:763; Ibn Hishām 4:19; Ibn Sa'd 2:94; Ibn Hazm: 221; Ibn 'Abd al-Barr 2:427; Ibn Atheer 2:101; Kalā'i 1:136; Ibn Katheer 4:249

566 Wāqidi 2:764; Ibn Hishām 4:21; Dianna, *Muhammad Rasulullah*: 296

567 Wāqidi 2:763, 1025; Ibn Sa'd 2:94

568 Wāqidi 2:760; Ibn Hishām 4:17; Suhayli 4:80

569 Wāqidi 1:403, 2:535; Ibn Hishām 2:230; Qurtubi 4:306; *al-Mawsu'ah al-'Askariyya* 1:264

570 Wāqidi 1:174; Ibn Sa'd 2:61; Ibn 'Abd al-Barr 3:1218; Ibn Atheer 2:248

571 Wāqidi 2:534; Ibn Hishām 4:265; Ibn Sa'd 2:61; Ibn Atheer 2:207; Ibn Sayyid al-Nās 2:104; Ibn Qayyim 2:297

572 Wāqidi 2:755; Ibn Sa'd 2:632; Kalā'i 1:158; Ibn Sayyid al-Nās 2:106

573 Wāqidi 2:755; Ibn Sa'd 2:92, 98; Ibn Hishām 4:15, 49

574 Zuhri: 76; Wāqidi 1:199; Ibn Hishām 2:257; Ibn Sa'd 2:47; Tabari 2:267; Ibn Hazm: 223; Ibn Atheer 2:276

575 Zuhri: 92; Wāqidi 1:207, 2:457; Ibn Hishām 2:245; Ibn Sa'd 2:45; Ibn Sayyid al-Nās 1:224

576 Ibn Is'hāq: 307; Shaybāni 2:58; Wāqidi 1:10, 67; Ibn Hishām 2:278

577 Wāqidi 1:68, 225; Ibn Hishām 2:277; Ibn Sa'd 2:10, 28; Tabari 2:445; Ibn Atheer 2:152; Ibn Sayyid al-Nās 2:10; Ibn Katheer 4:15

578 Wāqidi 1:67; Muslim 3:1362; Abu Dāwud (al-Jihād 102); Ibn Qutayba, *'Uyun al-Akhbār*

579 Ibn Sa'd 2:61; Muslim 3:1433; Kalā'i 1:123

580 Wāqidi 2:496, 633; Ibn Hishām 3:213, 244, 342; Ibn Hazm: 18, 191, 211; Tabari 2:181, 556

581 Wāqidi 3:1117; Ibn Sa'd 2:56, 61, 85; Ibn Katheer 4:61

582 Wāqidi 1:13, 2:636; Ibn Hishām 4:265; Ibn Sa'd 2:96; Ibn Sayyid al-Nās 2:54; Ibn Katheer3:261

583 Wāqidi 1:19; Ibn Hishām 4:265; Ibn Sa'd 2:63; Ibn Sayyid al-Nās 2:106, 110; Ibn Katheer 4:222

584 Wāqidi 1:403, 2:534; Bukhāri (al-Maghāzi 28); Abu Dāwud (al-Jihād 57)

585 Wāqidi 1:13, 2:774; Ibn Hishām 2:264; Ibn Sa'd 2:12, 108; Ibn Sayyid al-Nās 2:206; Ibn Katheer 5:9

586 Wāqidi 1:53, 2:445; Ibn Hishām 3:69, 231, 344; Tabari 3:9; Ibn Hazm: 186; Kalā'i 1:130

587 Wāqidi 3:991; Ibn Hishām 4:161; Bukhāri (al-Jihād 38, 184); Ibn 'Asākir 1:104

588 Wāqidi 1:182, 194; Ibn Hishām 3:46; Ibn Sa'd 2:21, 35, 43, 62, 95; Ibn Hazm: 203; Ibn Atheer 2:142

589 Wāqidi 1:396; Ibn Sa'd 2:21; Tabari 2:268; Suhayli 3:28; Ibn Sayyid al-Nās 1:304

590 Wāqidi 1:20, 88; Muslim (al-Eimān 8); Tabari 2:513

591 Wāqidi 2:562, 729; Tabari 2:554

592 Wāqidi 1:58; Bukhāri (al-Maghāzi 17); Muslim (al-Imārah 117); Abu Dāwud (al-Jihād 120, 149)

593 Wāqidi 1:81, 240, 3:897; Ibn Hishām 2:279; Ibn Sa'd 2:15, 39, 109; Tabari 3:75, 181; Kalā'i 1:144; Ibn Qayyim 2:440

594 Wāqidi 2:634, 3:1039; Ibn Sa'd 2:120; Suhayli 4:805; Kalā'i 1:131; Ibn Sayyid al-Nās 2:218

595 Wāqidi 1:177, 363, 2:496, 670; Ibn Hishām 3:200, 344; Ibn Sa'd 2:40; Tabari 583; Ibn Hazm: 154

596 Wāqidi 2:446; Ibn Hishām 3:231; Ibn Sa'd 2:47; Tabari 2:583

597 Wāqidi 2:796, 825, 875; Ibn Hishām 3:39, 44, 49; Ibn Sa'd 2:96, 101; Ibn Hazm: 226, 230; Ibn Sayyid al-Nās 2:161, 169, 173; Ibn Qayyim 2:386, 390; Ibn Katheer 4:282, 289

598 Bukhāri (al-Salāh 41, al-Jihād 56-58, al-I'tisām 16); Muslim (al-Imārah 6); Ibn Mājah (al-Jihād 44); Nasā'i (al-Khayl 2)

599 Wāqidi 1:2-7, 3:1039; Bukhāri (al-Jihād 80, al-Manāqib 4, al-Maghāzi 10); Tirmidhi (Fadhā'il al-Jihād 11)

600 Wāqidi 1:10, 193, 2:551; Ibn Sa'd 2:4, 62

601 *Ibid.*

602 Wāqidi 1:11, 13, 2:769; Ibn Hishām 2:245, 252, 4:272; Ibn Sa'd 2:1, 94; Tabari 2:259; Ibn Hazm: 103; Ibn Sayyid al-Nās 2:157, 161

603 Zuhri: 71, 79, 84; Wāqidi 1:76, 363, 2:496, 553, 564, 633; Ibn Sa'd 2:19, 40, 53, 77; Tabari 2:479, 553; Suhayli 4:252; Kalā'i 1:158; Ibn Sayyid al-Nās 1:105, 110

604 W8:7; Wāqidi 1:21, 49; Ibn Hishām 3:68; Tabari 2:503; Ibn Qayyim 2:231

605 Wāqidi 1:12 onwards, 200 onwards; Ibn Hishām 2:257 onwards, 3:10 onwards; Kalā'i 1:85, 104; Ibn Sayyid al-Nās 1:241, 2:2

606 Q33:22; Wāqidi 2:444, 3:890; Ibn Katheer 4:104

607 Wāqidi 1:28; Ibn Hishām 3:213; Ibn Sa'd 2:43; Ibn Atheer 2:185; Kalā'i 1:116; Ibn Sayyid al-Nās 1:296

608 Q3:152, Q9:26; Ibn Hishām 4:85; Ibn Sa'd 2:109; Kalā'i 1:143; Dhahabi, *Tārikh al-Islām* 1:267

609 Shaybāni 1:58; Wāqidi 1:378, 2:510; Ibn Hishām 2:278; *al-Mawsu'ah al-'Askariyya* 1:207

610 Bukhāri (al-Jihād 22, 56); Muslim (al-Jihād 20, al-Sulh 7, al-Maghāzi 44)

611 Ibn Sa'd 2:171; Tabari 3:176; Ibn Sayyid al-Nās 2:318

612 Ibn Hanbal 2:50; Bukhāri (al-Jihād 88); Ibn Sayyidah, *al-Mukhassis* 6:26 onwards

613 Ibn 'Abd Rabbih, al-'Iqd al-Farid 1:186 onwards; Ibn Sayyidah 6:37 onwards

[614] Ibn Hanbal 4:144 onwards; Dārimi (al-Jihād 14); Ibn Mājah (al-Jihād 18); Abu Dāwud (Fadhā'il al-Jihād 11)

[615] Abu Dāwud (al-Jihād 18); Tirmidhi (al-Jihād 17); Tabari 3:177

[616] Ibn Sa'd 2:172; Ibn Hanbal 1:80; Bukhāri (al-Istiqrādh 1); Abu Dāwud (al-Nikāh 35); Nasā'i (al-Nikāh 76)

[617] Ibn Sa'd 2:174; Tabari 2:177; Ibn Atheer 2:316

[618] Bukhāri (al-Jihād 75); Ibn Sayyidah 6:73

[619] Bukhāri (al-Libās 17); Tirmidhi (al-Jihād 18); Ibn Mandhur 5:26

[620] Bukhāri (al-Jihād 169, al-Maghāzi 48, al-Libās 17); Muslim (al-Hajj 450); Ibn Mājah (al-Jihād 18); Abu Dāwud (al-Jihād 117); Tirmidhi (al-Jihād 18); Nasā'i (al-Manāsik 107)

[621] It is reported that the Arabs learnt how to create the catapult from the Persians and would use it to throw large boulders (and later fireballs) at the enemy (Tr.)

[622] Wāqidi 3:927; Ibn Hishām 3:121; Ibn Sa'd 2:14; Kala'i 1:146; Ibn Sayyidah 6:14; The *Dabbābah* was a primitive version of today's tanks. It was a means used to break walls and barriers set up by the enemy. (Tr.)

[623] Bukhāri (al-Jihād 56, 58; al-Maghāzi 38; al-Adab 80); Muslim (al-Imārah 65, al-Jihād 132); Ibn Mājah (al-Jihād 9, 44); Abu Dāwud (al-Jihād 6, al-Khayl 12)

[624] Wāqidi 1:27; Ibn Hishām 2:321; Ibn Sa'd 2:7; Tabari 2:478

[625] Ibn Sa'd 2:78; Ibn Atheer 2:216; Ibn Sayyid al-Nās 2:129

[626] Wāqidi 2:812, 819

[627] Bukhāri (al-Buyu' 37, Tafseer of Surah 19); Tirmidhi (al-Jihād 12); Nasā'i (al-Jihād 26); Tabari, *Tafseer al-Tabari* 14:119

[628] Ibn Mājah (al-Jihād 18); Abu Dāwud (al-Jihād 23); Tirmidhi (Fadhā'il al-Jihād 11); Nasā'i (al-Jihād 26, al-Khayl 80)

[629] Wāqidi 3:927; Ibn Hishām 4:121; Ibn Sa'd 2:114; Kala'i 1:146

[630] Bukhāri (al-Buyu' 108, al-Maghāzi 2); Abu Dāwud (al-Jihād 24, al-Buyu' 26); Tirmidhi (al-Jihād 20); Nasā'i (al-Khayl 3)

[631] Bukhāri (al-Jihād 80); Muslim (al-Musāfirun 139, al-Jihād 49); Abu Dāwud (al-Imārah 19); Tirmidhi (al-Jihād 39); Nasā'i (al-Fay' 1)

[632] Wāqidi 1:96, 373, 2:510, 544, 658, 3:987; Ibn Sa'd 2:20, 41, 120

[633] Wāqidi 1:178; Ibn Hishām 3:201; Ibn Sa'd 2:80; Ibn Sayyid al-Nās 2:50

[634] Ibn Hanbal 3:1; Dārimi (al-Buyu' 56); Abu Dāwud (al-Buyu' 88)

[635] Bukhāri (al-Jihād 24, 56) Ibn Mājah (al-Jihād 29, al-Nikāh 50); Tirmidhi (al-Fitan 39); Nasā'i (al-Khayl 13, 16)

[636] Bukhāri (al-Jihād 12, 22, 88,156); Muslim (al-Jihād 92); Ibn Mājah (al-Fitan 10, al-Hudud 34); Abu Dāwud (al-Jihād 64, 108)

[637] Bukhāri (al-Riqāq 17, al-Maghāzi 56, al-Manāqib 4, al-Jihād 38); Muslim (al-Zuhd 12, Fadā'il al-Sahābah 41); Ibn Mājah (al-Muqaddimah 11); Abu Dāwud (al-Jihād 23); Tirmidhi (Fadhā'il al-Jihād 11, al-Sayd 1); Nasā'i (al-Jihād 26, al-Khayl 8)

[638] Wāqidi 2:648; Ibn Hishām 4:126; Ibn Sa'd 2:114; Ibn Sayyid al-Nās 2:201

[639] Bukhāri (al-Maghāzi 56, al-Jihād 80); Muslim (Fadhā'il al-Sahābah 41); Ibn 'Abd al-Barr 2:606, 764

[640] Bukhāri (al-Manāqib 28, al-Jihād 192); Muslim (al-Imārah 96, 99); Ibn Mājah (al-Jihād 14); Abu Dāwud (al-Jihād 41, 45, 60); Nasā'i (al-Khayl 8, 12)

[641] Ibn Mājah (al-Jihād 19); Abu Dāwud (al-Jihād 23); Tirmidhi (Fadhā'il al-Jihād 11); Nasā'i (al-Jihād 8, 26)

[642] Wāqidi 3:927

[643] Bukhāri (al-Jihād 12, 88, al-Shurut 15); Muslim (al-Jihād 20, al-Imārah 146); Abu Dāwud (al-Fitan 1, al-Buyu' 13, al-jihād 64, 108)

[644] Ibn Hanbal 1:88; Ibn Mājah (al-Jihād 18)

[645] Bukhāri (al-Jihād 88); Ibn Mājah (al-Jihād 18); Ibn Sayyid al-Nās 2:318

[646] Bukhāri (al-Maghāzi 44)

[647] Bukhāri (al-Jihād 88); Ibn Sa'd 2:171; Tabari 3:176

[648] Ibn Hanbal 1:193; Ibn Hishām 3:106; Ibn Sayyid al-Nās 2:24

[649] Wāqidi 2:743; Ibn Sa'd 2:87; Bakri 4:1385; Hamawi 5:424

[650] Ibn Hanbal 5:86; Muslim (al-Imārah 172, 175, 176); Abu Dāwud (al-Jihād 33)

[651] Abu Dāwud (al-Jihād 233); Wāqidi 3:1057; Ibn Sa'd 2:120

CHAPTER SIX
DEPARTMENT OF SUPPLIES AND REINFORCEMENTS

This department was responsible for matters pertaining to reinforcements, supplies, means of transport, food for the soldiers, the type of clothes and shelter of the forces, dividing the spoils of war, medical issues and all related concerns.

(A) Department of Supplies and Reinforcements

The responsibility of this department was to secure the material resources and assistance to the armed forces in general. This included personal accessories and other necessities like water, tents, clothes and moving the residents away from areas where military operations were taking place.[1]

The Rear

This comprised of groups whose work was to prepare and supply material provisions, military equipment and other needed supplies to the troops.[2] The most important groups that were present in the rear were the guards, those responsible for munitions and supplies, the camp of the commander, and the non-combatants (i.e. womenfolk). They carried some amount of supplies and munitions[3] with them and each one of these groups would be supervised by a commander who would oversee their work.[4] The Prophet (s) would emphasize on keeping the supplies and military equipment well hidden. He (s) would only specify where the rear of the army began[5] and would not give importance to where it ended.

The limits of the rear of the army during encampment was defined as the last lines of the army,[6] and while marching also, it was the last group.[7] The main missions of this department was to secure the facilities and material resources needed by the army, carry out medical treatment, assist the injured and handicapped and carry them away from the battlefield, burying the martyrs and gathering the spoils of war.[8]

1) Types of supplies and support:

Madina was known as the main center for supplies and munitions, and reinforcement and support during battle would rarely take place from there;[9] because the backing and rear of the army would usually take the necessary supplies with them, and from the very beginning whatever wa needed by the army would be put at their disposal. They would go to the battle and whenever their mission was complete, they would return to their own lands.[10] Despite this, in some of the battles, the army had to face severe hunger,[11] like what happened in the battles of Khaybar and Tabuk, but they would bear this pressure and difficulty.[12] This is precisely what they did in the Sariya of al-

Khabt. Sometimes they would also benefit from the abundant local resources.[13]

The sources of food and supplies for the army in the areas where the battles were fought included: In the Battle of Badr from the hunting of deer; in the Battle of Dhāt al-Ruqā' from cucumbers and ostrich eggs; in the Battle of Hudaybiyya from cucumbers, the meat of deer, wild donkeys and other animals whose meat is permissible to eat, and yoghurt; and in the Battle of Khaybar from a variety of different sources. Full reinforcements from Madina only came when Sa'd ibn 'Ubādah had the responsibility of bringing the reinforcements[14] in the Battle of Hamrā al-Asad. At this time he would slaughter two to three animals (whose meat was permissible to eat) every day. In the battles of Dhi Qurā and Waddān, he brought reinforcements with dates and meat from slaughtered animals.[15] At times, like in the Sariya of 'Amr ibn 'Aās, the supplies were sent by soldiers on foot.[16]

As for the food for horses and camels, it was provided for from the abundant grazing grounds especially in the areas where the army was camped.[17] In the Battle of Uhud, the Quraysh used the grazing grounds and fields that belonged to the Ansār. In the battles of Badr and Bani al-Mustalaq, the Muslim army took benefit from the wells of Badr and Murisiyya'. Muslim soldiers would sometimes use crushed date seeds to feed their horses and camels[18] while in the Battle of Khandaq, the Quraysh carried corn as fodder for their horses.[19]

Relief in its true and complete sense during battle was not done except through giving drinking water.[20] This was done by means of water bags which were carried by soldiers,[21] or through injured and handicapped soldiers.[22] The women would also at times participate in this exercise and would carry the water bags for long distances and exchange them for empty water bags. These relief operations continued even in the time when the heat of battle had subsided[23] and some of the helpers would take water to the supreme commander and the troops during this time.[24]

2)   The main points of relief support

These points were the very same routes that were used by the troops, and the rear wound usually not move in one position behind the main ranks of the army;[25] like in the battles of Badr and Tabuk. The movement from these points by the rear of the army would not take place more than once, because this would cause a split and a cessation of the relief support operations. For the soldiers, there was more than one central point for supplies but despite this, they would always use the closest point like Madina in the Battle of Hudaybiyya and from there (the route) to Fadak would be used.[26] Of course

218

the original and primary points of relief supply were Makkah and Madina which had links with the outside and were considered the main centers of relief support.[27] Between Makkah and outside it there were two roads to the west (coastal) and east (desert), and between Madina and outside it there was an important road that led towards the land of Shām (Syria) and there was continuous relief support conducted using different means between these two routes. Whenever these central points were cut off for any reason, the army forces would face hardships in terms of lack of sufficient relief supplies and provisions.

Similarly, in the beginning the Muslim army tried to cut off the supply routes of the Quraysh and they would be so harsh on them that at times they would be pushed to the brink of destruction.[28] When the point of supply from Madina was partially cut off, the supreme commander would reopen them by gaining victory of the tribes that were responsible for closing the route.[29]

3) Places of rest for the army

After marching a specified distance, the Muslim army would stop for a brief period in a suitable location.[30] At this time, the troops would carry out repairs and maintenance on their battle equipment, and would eat and drink. Then they would refill their vessels with water and continue their march.[31] The army would usually stop at a place where there was a well and plentiful grass for grazing.[32] The places of rest for the army would be selected according to the length of their journey, the army's size and the suitability of the area for remaining hidden and concealed.[33]

The time of these rest-stops would be in accordance to the mission given to the forces, the weather or time of day (and night).[34] In the Battle of Dumat al-Jundal, the rest was taken at night and during the Conquest of Makkah, because of the speed required, it was only for a brief period of time. Aside from this, the period of rest would be determined by the state of the troops and the distance they had covered and would be short or long accordingly.[35] And if there was a serious need to reach the enemy (as quick as possible), the rest-stops would be shortened. If this was not done, like in the Sariya of Muhammad ibn Maslamah against the Bani Bakr, the duration would be prolonged. In some of the Sariya missions, the army would rest the whole day and would march at night in order to carry out a surprise attack.

4) Modes of transport

The modes of transport were mainly camels and then followed by donkeys. Camels would be used to traverse long distances of up to eight hundred kilometers, like in the Battle of Dumat al-Jundal[36] which was located at a distance of 'ten stations of Madina' and 'seven stations of the Damascus', or the Battle of Muta[37] near the province of Dir'ā from the land of Balqā' in Shām,[38] or the Battle of Tabuk[39] which was at a distance of twelve stations from Madina and was close to Shām. The same was the case of the Battle of Abnā[40] in the land of al-Sarrāh near Balqā' which was a village in Muta between Palestine and Shām.

The camel is known for its ability to bear thirst and hunger and carry heavy loads in the dry and hard desert.[41] However, donkeys were mostly used for non-military purposes[42] to cover short distances in and around Madina. A number of troops would bring camels to the battlefield.[43] They would carry their battle gear and rations and also the special fodder for camels on the camels' backs.

Women would also sit in howdahs on these animals at the rear of the army and would be taken along.[44] The army would be divided into sections depending on the number of soldiers and camels that were used for transport. Each section had two to four soldiers[45] who would put the equipment that could be carried on the backs of camels like one big caravan.[46] The length of these sections when marching depended on the number of camels and soldiers in it.[47]

5) Foods and rations

The most important foodstuffs that were used by the Muslim forces in battle included: dates,[48] locusts,[49] meat[50] (mostly from animals that were halāl[51]), wheat,[52] raisins, bread,[53] barley flour[54] and some of the foods that were prepared from wheat,[55] flour,[56] cucumbers[57] and milk.[58] Among these, dates were the staple food that the soldiers would be provided with when attacking or defending, travelling or remaining back, and they would always have with them a little under three kilos (one Sā')[59] of dates and if something (from the dates produced) would remain, they would store it in their house and would use it throughout the year.

6) Sources for procuring the food

From the troops,[60] locals and residents of the area,[61] and some of the wealthy soldiers – who were sometimes responsible for providing the food – and also through other means[62] of securing it.[63] Rations in the Muslim army were such that each person would eat one portion per day before marching or prior to the start of battle or when he felt hungry.[64] Most of the times, these rations i.e. a few dates[65] or a slaughtered animal whose meat was shared among a hundred men, would not be sufficient[66] and it was common for the forces to remain hungry due to lack of sufficient food; that is why in some of the battles it was necessary for them to economize and forbear.[67] So much so that in some situations the troops were left with no option but to eat some of the grass, leaves,[68] the remainder of the food eaten by others[69] and at times they would slaughter the animals that were used for transport[70] and use the meat; meaning they would eat the meat of horses, wild and tame donkeys, deer etc.[71]

At times a day or two would pass before they ate anything[72] and the Holy Prophet (s) was forced to take a loan from the rich[73] and divide it among the soldiers in order for them to buy food, until things improved and the financial situation became better, then he would repay the loan.

7) Water

The most important of all things that were considered in the battles were: drinking water,[74] washing the injured[75] and treating some of the sick.[76] War between the two opposing sides would take place in a place that had plenty of water.[77] Each of the two sides would try to take advantage of the well and gain the upper hand over the other, preventing him from coming near it.[78] For this reason, gaining access to water was considered an important factor in victory or surrender and defeat.[79]

In all the battles, the Holy Prophet (s) would choose a land that had abundance of life-giving water and would take control over it while keeping the enemy at bay;[80] just as he had eventually blocked it from the fortresses of Khaybar etc.[81] in order to speed up the surrender of the inhabitants of those fortresses.[82] He (s) would forbid the drinking of unhygienic water.[83] In the end, there were many hardships faced in securing water while marching through the dry, harsh, scorching deserts[84] especially in the long routes.

8) Sources of nourishment

The most important sources of nourishment were foods the animals, edible plants and the drinking water that were found in the fields in the area where the military operations were conducted. The most important animals included: fawns,[85] wild donkeys,[86] rabbits,[87] deer,[88] cows and camels,[89] sheep,[90] birds (that were permissible to eat),[91] cucumbers,[92] fruits of the Miswāk tree[93] and other types of edibles.[94]

The above-mentioned foods made up a large portion of the supplies that were required during battle and through this the Muslim army was saved from starvation and severe thirst and gave them the ability to carry out their mission effectively. In the Battle of Khaybar, the Muslim soldiers suffered a lot of hunger[95] and in the Battle of Tabuk, the soldiers were about to collapse out of severe hunger.[96]

9) Shelter, tents and clothes

In Madina there were many tents but in the battles, tents would rarely be used.[97] Mattresses and beddings as we see today never existed.[98] In those days, tents were made of skin or fur,[99] or both together.[100] As for the clothing, it remained the same as it was before the advent of Islām.[101]

10) Storing foodstuffs

The portion of food that was extra would be stored inside storehouses and homes to such as extent that it would suffice for the soldiers for some time.[102] The storing of food by the Muslim army was done differently to the way the Jewish army or other armies did it, as it was done based on the material resources, military mission, type of enemy and other factors.[103] The Muslim army did not have many resources. When the army would prepare for war, they would come under pressure out of the insufficiency and lack of resources; that is why this army was an offensive army and did not have much need for storing foodstuffs. Aside from this, donation and generosity and not hoarding and storing are matters that were emphasized by the new religion (Islām), and this was also considered one of the factors.

The supreme commander and his soldiers took to storing the excess foodstuffs in times when the supplies were abundantly available. This took place especially after the Battle of Bani Nadhir and after gaining access to a lot of necessary resources.[104] However, in the earlier period and during the start of the first wars there was no thought given to this type of action.[105] The Holy Prophet (s) would keep some barley and dates - to the extent that would suffice for a number of days - in his house.[106] We have no other report that suggests that storing foodstuffs was considered a priority for the Muslim army. Even in the Battle of Khandaq, when they dug the trench by which Madina was saved, they did not make any efforts with regards to storing supplies.[107] The enemy, however, went to great lengths to store foodstuffs, especially the Jews who store provisions and water inside their fortresses – to the extent that would suffice them for the duration of a long war.[108] The Muslim army had no choice but to completely cut off the enemy's relief supplies,[109] besiege them from all sides,[110] attack their front-line,[111] conduct psychological warfare,[112] and all those actions that would force the Jews to surrender quickly, before their stores were empty.[113]

11) Clearing the field of operations

Another one of the responsibilities of the 'department of supplies (and relief support)' was clearing the following from the battlefield:

- All the people who would cause the military operations to be delayed, like the womenfolk, the children, the old and those who were unable to fight[114]
- Those considered enemies and those who were not from their side[115]
- The equipment and weapons that were broken or needed repair for use in the next battle

The first group was transferred to a suitable place where the 'living conditions' were better.[116] The second group was also taken to far off places that were outside the domain and control of the Muslim army.[117] As for the equipment, it was carried to the appropriate place where it could undergo repair and maintenance after which it would be distributed to the soldiers, and sometime a group would carry out repairs on the weapons right there on the battlefield.

12) Trade and agriculture

After the military missions were completed, the Holy Prophet (s) would give permission to the soldiers to embark on trade. He (s) had tolerated their exchange of goods in Badr al-Aākhar,[118] and the forces returned back to Madina after having made a handsome profit.[119] In this way, aside from battle operations, the army would engage in trade also. The Ansār would also pursue their own agricultural work.[120]

13) Welcoming the soldiers

After achieving victory in battle, the army would send the glad tidings and news of their return to Madina.[121] All the people of Madina, men, women and children, would come out to welcome the victorious soldiers.[122] The supreme commander had also come out with a group of tribesmen to welcome the army that was returning from Muta.[123] In his caliphate, Abu Bakr also came out to welcome the army of Usāma.[124]

14) The minimum age for being accepted into the army

Joining the army was something done voluntarily[125] and was not done as it is today i.e. joining the armed forces (for training) becomes mandatory at a certain age. The Holy Prophet (s) had laid down some conditions for those wishing to join the army. The volunteers had to be at least fifteen or sixteen years old,[126] strong and of sound body, and capable of fighting in battle.[127] For this reason, the young boys who had stepped forward for the Battle of Uhud, like 'Abdullah ibn 'Umar,[128] Barrā' ibn 'Aāzib and others, were not accepted while 'Umayr ibn Abi Waqqās got permission to join the army in the Battle of Badr when he was sixteen years old.[129] Ibn 'Umar himself said: The Holy Prophet (s) turned me back on the day of Uhud when I was fourteen years old and later accepted me in the Battle of Khandaq when I was fifteen.[130]

Today, the minimum age for recruitment differs from country to country and most countries have kept the minimum age at eighteen years and have stipulated that the person should be healthy.

15) Teaching and education

The Holy Prophet (s) gave importance to teaching and education[131] and emphasized on its promotion. Due to this emphasis, he instructed Mundhir ibn 'Amr al-Sā'idi to go with seventy teachers and educate the Bani 'Aāmir.[132] He (s) also sent Ibn Abi Murthid[133] with ten 'reciters' in order to teach the tribes of Adhal and al-Qārrah.[134] The Prophet (s) would also employ those prisoners who were not able to pay the ransom to secure their freedom to teach others.[135]

16) Securing relief support in pre-emptive battle

For securing relief support in this type of battle which was conducted against the enemy, the Holy Prophet (s) was not in need of a strong 'rear'[136] in the army as this would act as a burden and would hold back the army preventing them from swift movement and battle maneuvers; rather he would only take the rear when a large army was required.[137] Single units and small contingents did not usually have a rear[138] and would carry the necessary provisions like dates, some foodstuffs and water, along with them[139] or would depend on the locally available resources.[140] This type of securing of supplies needed quick transport, but because this was not fully and abundantly available (in the Muslim army), a clever soldier could make up for this deficiency[141] by carrying whatever supplies he needed himself.

17) Securing reinforcements when capturing fortresses

The enemy forces would usually take refuge in forts and would store provisions that would last for a long time.[142] In the same way, supply centers were divided along the line of defense.[143] In these situations, more than three supply centers were set up with the needed supplies.[144] The Muslim army would not fight between the fortresses, rather they would attack the forts from the front and from different sides[145] and besiege it for long periods of time.[146] During this time, they would take advantage of the resources available in the area[147] or that which was possessed by the enemy.[148]

18) Difficulties in securing supplies

The Muslim army faced numerous difficulties when trying to secure supplies. These included: Lack of adequate means of transport,[149] even camels that were used by a number of soldiers[150] to carry provisions and water. Food rations were also not enough.[151] Many of the soldiers faced severe hunger especially during the final days of the battles[152] and had to eat hunted prey[153] and some of the plants and herbs.[154] Similarly, the lack of wells[155] and sufficient water especially in the hot months, would cause the soldiers to be overcome[156] by thirst.[157] Lack of weapons and battle equipment,[158] which was difficult to buy or procure due to poor resources and also the suitable clothes for fighting against the enemy in the desert were not easy to come by.[159] Many of the soldiers came to face the enemy without any armor[160] while some did not even have anything to cover themselves.[161]

These harsh weather conditions in the heart of the dry, scorching desert with frequent strong sandstorms[162] effected the strength and ability of the forces to fight in battle. The rays of the midday sun would be like arrows attacking the soldiers and the sand would cover their possessions in dust.[163] This army, especially in the battles against the Jews when the duration of the siege was prolonged, faced difficulties with supplies.[164] During this time the food supplies that were consumed by the soldiers depleted very quickly and put the army under threat of starvation. In the Battle of Khaybar, the field of operations had become polluted with disease and cholera,[165] to such an extent that it was not possible to remain in that place for a long period of time and it would cause the forces to be afflicted by other sicknesses.[166]

In the same way, the Muslim army was always faced with great economic pressures that had been put against the Muslims by the Jews;[167] because they had numerous economic centers and interests in the Arabian peninsula. Another of the hardships related to supplies that the army faced was the distance between the battlefields and the city of Madina (which was a center for procurement of supplies)[168] especially in the battles of Dumat al-Jundal, Abnā and Tabuk which were towards the north of the Arabian peninsula and also those that took place in Yemen.[169]

19) The division for training and exercise

Military training would be conducted in the actual battles and wars. The army would travel long distances[170] in the desert until they would reach the enemy, and along the way, the army would undergo training in the following: bearing hunger[171] and thirst[172] on the way,[173] the harsh conditions of the desert, including its heat, winds and dryness,[174] staying in prolonged military expeditions,[175] sleeping in open spaces,[176] economizing on food rations[177] and being satisfied with small portions of it, being generous with provisions despite the hard times,[178] helping other soldiers,[179] how to take advantage of locally available resources,[180] digging trenches and pits,[181] hunting animals,[182] how to deal with prisoners,[183] arrangements that needed to be made when the army stopped at any place,[184] gathering the war booty and accepting the system of its distribution,[185] finding clean water,[186] and in the end, how to bury those who had been killed.[187]

These matters gave the Muslim army a special zeal for battle and made them capable, strong and ready for fighting the enemy.

(B) Department of War Booty

This was the department that was answerable for collecting the booty, arranging it and distributing it. All the wealth of the enemy forces that was taken by overpowering them or winning the battle was considered as war booty.[188] The first war booty that was obtained by the Muslims was in the second year after Hijra which was the year when the fighting was first ordained. During this time, the Holy Prophet (s) sent 'Abdullah ibn Jahash, accompanied by seventy men, for a mission. He gave a letter to the commander of the Sariya and ordered him to open it after he had travelled for two days and then follow the path directed therein. This was done in order to protect military secrets. The commander of the Sariya did as he was instructed and when he opened the letter he found the order to raid the caravan of the Quraysh at Nakhlah. He did just that and took the wealth of the caravan as booty.[189]

1) Ways of using the booty on the battlefield

Once the appropriation of the war booty was completed, there would be no delay in taking advantage of it especially with regards to the foodstuffs, drinks, fodder for animals, firewood and all the other requirements; whether those who used it were rich or poor, because even the rich would have to bear the difficulty of carrying foodstuffs and fodder from Madina to the battlefield.[190]

2) The rules of distribution of war booty

The Noble Prophet (s) organized the booty and ordered that it be gathered up in a suitable place.[191] He appointed certain people to count and distribute it and would specify the people who would use it,[192] forbidding anyone to take anything (from it) before its distribution[193] while being very strict with those people who infringed on these instructions.[194]

The booty would be divided into five parts and was distributed as follows:[195]
The first part would be given to the following: orphans, needy, those who were travelers but had no more money (Ibn al-Sabil), and for basic

requirements like buying battle equipment and things that were needed by the army including foodstuffs, weapons, battle gear, clothes etc.

The four remaining parts would be distributed to the soldiers and every Muslim who participated in the battle, meaning one who was part of the army and entered the battlefield with the intention of fighting, whether he fought or not, would get a share; because frightening the enemy is akin to participating in the battle.

As for the gauge of merit by which it each person got what they deserved, it was relative. For example, for the soldiers who were on horseback three portions were allotted (two portions for the horse and one for the soldier) while the one who was on foot got one portion. The reason for this was that a horse had to be specially treated and readied for battle and this incurred an extra expense. It is obvious that the expense incurred by a soldier on horseback was more than one who was on foot. As for the women and young children who were present in the battle, they would not get a full share, because they were not considered part of the forces. Rather, they got a small share i.e. smaller than one full portion, depending on what the supreme commander decided based on their contribution and participation during the battle.

3)   The place where the booty was divided

Division of the booty took place in a secure location or after it had been carried back to the Muslim lands. The supreme commander could transfer the army along with the booty to another area if the current location was not deemed to be safe.[196] The division would either be done personally by the commander or by someone who was appointed by him to carry out this task.[197]

4)   Sources of booty

One of the important sources for acquiring booty were the Jews[198] and the Muslim army had taken possession of a lot of weapons, wealth and farming lands from them as war booty.[199] As for the (enemy) Arab tribes, they took sheep, camels and some horses from them. This booty was used to cater for the material needs of the army.

5)   Prisoners

Prisoners were enemy combatants and those who were considered part of the enemy's army that were captured alive.[200] Generally, prisoners would either be killed,[201] or secure their release through the payment of ransom or by being exchanged for Muslim prisoners,[202] or they would be forgiven and freed;[203] and this was decided according to what was in the best interests (of the Muslims). The Holy Prophet (s) had ordered the killing of 'Aqabah ibn Abi Mu'eet and Nadhr bin Hārith in the Battle of Badr,[204] 'Amr ibn al-Jamhā, the poet of the Age of Ignorance, in the Battle of Uhud[205] and also the Bani Quraydha after the siege.[206] A number of prisoners of Badr were freed by ransom.[207] Some of them who did not have wealth had to teach ten youths of Madian (in order to secure their freedom)[208] and two prisoners from the Sariya of Abdullah ibn Jahash were also freed by ransom.[209]

The exchange of prisoners with the Quraysh began after the Treaty of Hudaybiyya.[210] A woman from the Bani Kilāb was given as a ransom to secure the freedom of a prisoner from the Muslims who had been captured by the Quraysh.[211] This woman had been taken prisoner in the Sariya of Abu Bakr against the Bani Kilāb. Abi 'Uzza al-Jamhā was freed as an act of kindness because of his poverty.[212] The same was done with Abi al-'Aās ibn Rabee'[213] and other prisoners of Badr,[214] prisoners of Bani al-Mustalaq,[215] Tamāmah ibn Athāl al-Hanafi after his imprisonment in the Sariya of Muhammad ibn Maslamah against the Bani Bakr,[216] and also a man from Bani Tha'labah who had become a Muslim[217] after his imprisonment in the Sariya of Abi 'Ubaydah ibn Jarrāh for the revenge against the Bani Tha'labah.

Similarly, a woman who had divulged sensitive information to the enemy in the Sariya of Zayd ibn Hāritha against the Bani Saleem and was taken prisoner, was forgiven and set free.[218]

The Holy Prophet (s) would deal mercifully and humanely with the prisoners[219] and would urge that they be treated well[220] and forgiven when victory had been gained over them.[221] Whenever he (s) would hear the cries of any of them he would open their tied hands.[222] The result of this kind treatment to the prisoners was that they would become believers in Islām[223] and out of their own free will, accept this new religion. Usually the prisoners would be tied up and not left free, and they would be kept in a place where hygiene[224] was good. They would be imprisoned in the Masjid[225] or in the house of the soldiers to whom they had been given[226] or were imprisoned all together in the house of one of the soldiers.[227] This would be done to prevent any of them from fleeing. These houses were not built as prisons and if they were not tied, the prisoners could escape at any time.

The Glorious Qur'ān has encouraged the feeding of prisoners[228] and the Holy Prophet (s) would also recommend it.[229] The troops would also give precedence to the prisoners when it came to food and would sacrifice their own food for them.[230] Like 'Aziz ibn 'Umayr who used to eat bread and good foods. The food of the prisoners was dates.[231] When the supreme commander was requested for some food by a prisoner, he replied with kindness and generosity[232] and asked the companions to prepare some food for him.[233] They immediately gave him milk and delicious food.

At the same time, the prisoners were covered with proper clothes. For instance, the supreme commander gave a shirt to 'Abbās ibn 'Abd al-Muttalib[234] and while giving some clothes as a gift to Safānah bint Hātim Tā'i, the Prophet (s) favored her by setting her free.[235]
He (s) would never force any prisoner to divulge secret military information,[236] however, if he tried to deceive the Muslim army by giving them false information, he would be pressurized and would even be beaten.[237] If a prisoner did not give up secret information about the enemy, he would never be beaten or abused. However, if he did give up any vital information, he would be set free.[238]

(C) Department of Medical Services

1) Designation and goals of the department of medical services

The goal of this department was the preservation of the health of soldiers. To this end, offering medical assistance to the injured and taking them from the battlefield to the medical camps for treatment were the functions that this department was responsible for. Other functions included taking preventative measures to stop the spread of different diseases and epidemics and taking care of the hygiene in the places where the troops and commanders camped and ensuring the cleanliness and soundness of these places.[239]

The supreme commander would also participate in giving medical assistance,[240] for instance when Qatāda ibn Nu'mān was injured in the Battle of Uhud and the news reached him, he (s) wrapped Qatāda in his cloak and gave him treatment, such that he regained his health and returned to his previous state.[241] In the same way, he (s) treated the injury of Sa'd ibn Ma'ādh, who was injured in the Sariya of Muhammad ibn Maslamah (that was undertaken) to assassinate Ka'b ibn Ashraf.[242] The Prophet (s) put his own saliva on the eyes of 'Ali ('a), who was suffering from an ailment in his eyes, and he was cured and could continue fighting the battle.[243]

The support forces would always provide the required medicines to those who were sick or injured.[244] General medical services in the Muslim army were based on the individual,[245] collective[246] and the women.[247] When the supreme commander was attacked and became injured, Abi 'Ubaydah ibn Jarrāh would pull out the chains of his helmet from his cheeks[248] and Fātima ('a) also would put a heated mat with palm leaves on his wounds.[249] The injured would come as outpatients and would get their wounds dressed and this would happen after they had returned to Madina.[250] Some of the wounds would be given basic treatment and dressing during the battle.

Another responsibility of this department was evacuating the injured to a specific location for treatment in Madina. When Sa'd ibn Mu'ādh was injured in the Battle of Khandaq, he was transferred to a tent in Masjid al-Nabi (s).[251] In the same way, when Muhammad ibn Maslamah[252] was injured in battle against the Bani Tha'labah and 'Awāl, he was taken to Madina (for treatment). The medications and medical equipment that were used to treat and cure the injured were very basic and the most important among these included: water, (heated) mats, fabrics[253] that were used by men in their trousers or the turbans[254] that they wore on their heads – and this would be used to dress the wounds and cuts. Honey,[255] oil,[256] a special type of dates,[257] milk, camel urine,[258] salt with water[259] and other remedies (were used).[260] The Holy Prophet (s) would take it upon himself to find out about the situation of hygiene in the army. He (s) would send some troops to check this and give him news about the situation[261] and to select (hygienic and) sound locations.[262] He would choose such (clean and hygienic) locations for the army to set up camp. He would select clean and suitable water for drinking[263] and would only permit the using of water that had not changed in smell or color for washing hands and cleaning wounds.[264]

2) Losses

Losses in the battlefield would be suffered because of a number of reasons, the most important among which were:

- Their resources and conditions of warfare and those of the enemy
- The type of battle (offensive, defensive, siege etc.)
- The types of weapons used
- Preparation for war and the type of terrain
- The time of day (whether day or night)
- The zeal and morale of the soldiers
- Ability and precaution[265]

In the battle of Badr, the resources were equally accessible to both the sides. The type of war was defensive in Khandaq and offensive in the Conquest of Makkah. Entering the fortresses, the conditions of terrain and time of the battle (during the last hours of the night) in Khaybar, the type of weapons used in the Battle of Tā'if, the preparation in the Battle of Bani Quraydha and the great care and precaution taken in the Battle of Dhāt al-Ruqā' were all important factors. The losses faced by the Muslim army in the first defensive battles were greater. In the Battle of Badr fourteen people,[266] in Uhud eighty[267] and in Khandaq six people[268] were martyred. But in the offensive battles, the numbers were relatively less. In the Battle of Muta nine people,[269] in the Conquest of Makkah two people,[270] in Hunayn fourteen people,[271] in conquering the fortresses of Khaybar fifteen people[272] and in Ṭā'if twelve people[273] were martyred. When conquering the fortresses of Bani Qaynuqā', Bani Nadhir and Bani Quraydha, the Muslim army suffered no losses at all.[274]

As for the losses faced in the Sariya missions, they included: ten people[275] were martyred in the Sariya of Muhammad ibn Maslamah against the Bani Tha'labah, three people[276] in the Sariya of Bashir ibn Sa'd al-Ansāri against the Bani Murrah, five people[277] in the Sariya of Abi al-'Awjā al-Sulami against the Bani Saleem and fifteen people[278] in the Sariya of Kalā'i'b ibn 'Umayr al-Ghaffāri against the Bani Qudhā'ah. In missions where the enemy ambushed the Muslims, many losses were suffered. Like the event of Bi'r Ma'unah where seventy people[279] and Rajee' where ten people were martyred.[280]

By studying these numbers one can see that the losses in defensive war were greater than those in offensive war, and this was because after the Battle of Khandaq, the Muslim army had gained experience and were better trained.[281] The losses in some of the Sariya missions[282] were higher due to the commanders not having taken all the necessary precautions, a stronger enemy army, the element of surprise was not there in their attack, the secretive nature of the military operation and the inability to assist the injured because of which they would die.

3) The number of martyrs in the battles

The percentage of those who were martyred were as follows: Badr[283] – 5% of the forces, Uhud[284] – 10%, Khandaq[285] – 0.002%, Khaybar[286] – 1%, Muta[287] – 2.5%; Conquest of Makkah[288] – 0.002%, Hunayn[289] – 0.003%, Ṭā'if[290] – 0.02% and in the Sariya and other missions put together[291] - 10%. The highest number of martyrs was in the Battle of Uhud (70) and the lowest was in the Conquest of Makkah (2).

4) Burying the Martyrs

The Holy Prophet (s) gave the order that the martyrs should be buried in the battlefield,[292] just as is done in some of the battles of our time. He (s) would not give permission to take their bodies back to Madina and it has been said that some of the heirs had taken the corpses of their dead back to Madina, but the Prophet (s) ordered that they be taken back. The announcer of the supreme commander would call out: 'Return those who have been killed to their place of rest (i.e. the place where they fell in battle).[293] The reason for this was that transferring the dead to another place would put their families under financial strain and other difficulties and it was possible that the change in weather conditions could affect the corpses and cause them to be cut into pieces. Aside from this, the means of transport were not abundant and could not even cater for all the soldiers. Most important of all, burying the fallen soldiers in the battlefield was a secret for keeping their memory alive, heightening emotions about them and expressing the meaning of courage by their example.

The Holy Prophet (s) would honor the martyrs,[294] put them on the pedestal of respect and glory in this world and the hereafter[295] and would give the glad tidings about this to the family and relatives of the martyred;[296] so their hearts would be filled with happiness. The Prophet (s) would bury one, two or three martyrs in a single grave[297] depending on their closeness with each other or their relationship (to each other) or the amount of Qur'ān they had memorized in their lifetimes.

The Prophet (s) forbade the disfigurement and cutting off of parts of the enemy corpses[298] and gave the order that once they were identified, they were to be buried without taking any revenge on their dead bodies by burning, drowning or decapitating them.[299] The supreme commander would also instruct the commanders and leaders of Sariya missions not to disfigure the corpses of the enemy[300] and preserve the respect of their dead.[301] This was despite the fact that the Quraysh had disfigured the body of Hamza and others in the Battle of Uhud, and Hind bint 'Aqabah, the wife of the commander of the enemy's army i.e. Abu Sufyān, had chewed the liver of this martyr (Hamza).[302] Despite all this, if the enemies were keen to take their corpses, the Prophet (s) would allow them to do so.[303]

5) The role of women in securing supplies and relief support

Women had an important role in (securing) supplies and relief support of the Muslim army. They would prepare food for the soldiers,[304] give water to the thirsty,[305] carry water-bags on their shoulders and take them to the troops in the battlefield,[306] treat the injured by burning medicinal herbs and teas[307] and putting them on heated mats which would be placed on the injuries,[308] and assist in evacuating the injured to specific areas such as Masjids. There role in lifting the morale and encouraging the soldiers before battle was important.[309] They would force those fleeing from battle to return,[310] repair clothes and coverings and stitch water-bags[311] and assist in medical evacuations.[312] The women would share their advice with the supreme commander[313] and would, in times of desperation, fight[314] and would guard and protect the weapons and military equipment.[315]

By allowing the women to participate in battle, the Prophet (s) raised their status. In the Battle of Hudaybiyya, he took their advice when leaving for 'Umrah[316] and they had told him to go ahead and do whatever he saw fit as the Muslims would all follow him. In the Conquest of Makkah, the women pledged allegiance to him just as the men did[317] and when making the Treaty of Hudaybiyya with the Quraysh, even though the men did not agree to the conditions[318] and protested them, the women did not do so.[319] It was at this point that the verses of the Qur'ān[320] were revealed that elevated their status. The place of the women in the battles[321] while marching or camping, was in the rear of the army and in Madina and the fortresses[322] during defense,[323] it was behind the men and they would give the necessary assistance and support to the soldiers.[324] Whenever they participated in the battle, they would be behind the male soldiers.[325]

An Analysis of the Military Management

A study of all the battles that were fought by the Muslim army in all the front-lines establishes the fact that possessing greater forces and resources was not sufficient for achieving victory. Rather, the organization of resources and proper utilization of the same at the right place and right time,[326] even if these resources were few[327] or even lacking,[328] was considered the most evident cause of victory. It is because of this that the Muslim army was able to attain victory over the Jews who were stronger in terms of resources,[329] the Romans who had a variety of different types of resources[330] and even the enemy tribes who possessed thousands of sheep, mules and horses.[331]

After gaining victory over the enemy, the Muslims added the acquired resources to what little they had and began organizing it.[332] The Prophet (s) would never face the enemy altogether, rather he would face them separately attacking one after the other.[333] This was the strategy that made the forces develop gradually in different fields, to such a degree that in time, they were able to overcome larger enemy forces.[334] In the beginning the army fought against the Bani Qaynuqā' and took over the few material resources that they had.[335] The Prophet (s) fought against the Bani Qaynuqā' at a time when the resources of the Muslim army were incomparable[336] to those that were used in the Battle of Khaybar that took place a few years later, in which they overcame the enemy, and in this way each battle would increase the resources and capability of the Muslim army.

In his battles, the Holy Prophet (s) would use methods that required fewer material resources, like the pre-emptive battles,[337] surprise attacks,[338] full scale and revolutionary attacks,[339] because these methods created a high morale,[340] swiftness in attack,[341] strong faith and steadfastness,[342] complete general readiness[343] and fear in the enemy.[344]

NOTES AND REFERENCES

[1] Zuhri: 93; Ibn Hishām 2:372, 3:264; Faryābi, *Dalā'il al-Nubuwwah*:12

[2] Wāqidi 3:996; Ibn Hishām 2:264

[3] Wāqidi 1:217, 23, 3:996; Ibn Hishām 4:24, 49; Ibn Sa'd 2:48; Tabari 2:568

[4] Ibn Hishām 2:264; Ibn 'Abd al-Barr 3:1924; Kalā'i 1:130

[5] Wāqidi 3:996; Ibn Hishām 2:264

[6] Dārimi (al-Muqaddimah 2); Muslim (3:895); Abu Dāwud (al-Jihād 107)

[7] Wāqidi 3:996

[8] Wāqidi 1:25, 230, 2:645; Ibn Hishām 4:170; Tabari 2:568; Ibn Sayyid al-Nās 2:131

[9] Ibn Sa'd 2:1, 136; Tabari 2:408, 657, 3:9, 159; Ibn Sayyid al-Nās 1:222, 2:220

[10] Wāqidi 1:193, 391; Ibn Khayyāt 1:7; Ibn Hazm: 100

[11] Wāqidi 2:444, 658, 664, 3:1038; Ibn Hishām 3:260; Tabari 3:10; Kalā'i 1:114

[12] Wāqidi 2:774 onwards; Ibn Hishām 4:281; Tabari 3:32; Ibn Sayyid al-Nās 2:158

[13] Wāqidi 1:26, 398 onwards, 2:575, 658, 668; Ibn Hishām 2:346

[14] Wāqidi 1:338

[15] Wāqidi 2:546

[16] Bukhāri (al-Maghāzi 65); Muslim (al-Sayd 17, 19); Abu Dāwud (al-At'imah 46); Nasā'i (al-Sayd 35)

[17] Wāqidi 1:53; Ibn Hishām 2:271, 3:302; Ibn Sa'd 2:45; Bakri 4:1220

[18] Muslim (al-Salām 34)

[19] Wāqidi 2:444

[20] Wāqidi 1:53, 2:643; Ibn Hishām 2:276, 3:233

[21] Ibn Hishām 3:90; Tabari 2:519; Ibn Sayyid al-Nās 2:15

[22] Bukhāri (al-Jihād 67, al-Maghāzi 37); Muslim (al-Jihād 135); Tirmidhi (al-Qiyāmah 18)

[23] Bukhāri (al-Jihād 65, 67); Muslim (al-Jihād 137, 141); Abu Dāwud (al-Jihād 32); Tirmidhi (al-Siyar 22)

[24] Bukhāri (al-Maghāzi 37); Muslim (al-Jihād 135)

[25] Wāqidi 3:966; Ibn Hishām 2:263, 4:170; Tabari 2:433

[26] Wāqidi 1:13, 2:562, 571, 636; Ibn Sa'd 2:65; Ibn Sayyid al-Nās 2:54

[27] al-Fākihi, *Akhbāru Makkah* 2:3; Tabari 2:427; Hamawi 57, 87, 188

[28] Ibn Sa'd 2:2-6, 24; Ibn Atheer 2:113, 116

[29] Wāqidi 1:402; Ibn Hishām 3:224; Ibn Hazm: 184; Ibn Sayyid al-Nās 2:54

[30] Wāqidi 1:403 2:756; Ibn Hishām 2:257; Ibn Sa'd 2:92; Bakri 4:1172; Hamawi 5:219; Mawri, *Ghāyat al-Aāmāl fi Fann al-Harb wal-Qitāl* 2:14

[31] Ibn Hishām 2:68 onwards; 3:69, 90; Ibn Sa'd 2:96; Bakri 3:473

[32] Bukhāri (al-Anbiyā' 9); Muslim (al-Imārah 178); Abu Dāwud (al-Jihād 55)

[33] Wāqidi 1:253, 643; Ibn Hishām 4:234; Bajri 2:1190

[34] Zuhri: 86; Ibn Hanbal 3:305; Abu Dāwud (al-Jihād 57)

[35] Wāqidi 2:534; Ibn Hishām 3:244; Muslim 3:1391

[36] Ibn Sa'd 2:44; Bakri 2:564; Hamawi 2:487

[37] Ibn Sa'd 2:92; Bakri 4:1172; Hamawi 5:219

[38] Dir'ā is presently located in the south of Syria while Muta is in the north of Jordan. (Tr.)

[39] Bakri 1:303; Hamawi 2:14

[40] Ibn Sa'd 2:92, 136; Bakri 1:101

[41] Ibn Hanbal 2:267; Muslim (al-Imārah 178); Abu Dāwud (al-Tibb 24); al-Nuwayri, *Nihāyat al-Adab* 10:103

[42] Wāqidi 2:511; Abu Dāwud (al-Manāsik 65); Tirmidhi (al-Janā'iz 32); Ibn Sayyidah 6:25

[43] Wāqidi 1:17, 338; Ibn Hishām 2:264; Ibn Sa'd 2:12

[44] Ibn Hishām 3:311; Tabari 2:611; Ibn Sayyid al-Nās 2:96

[45] Bukhāri (al-Maghāzi 31); Muslim (al-Jihād 149); Abu Dāwud (al-Jihād 34)

[46] Wāqidi 1:274; Ibn Hishām 2:264; Ibn Sayyid al-Nās 2:206

[47] Ibn Sa'd 2:7, 13; Mawri, *Ghāyat al-Aāmāl fi Fann al-Harb wal-Qitāl* 2:25

[48] Bukhāri (al-Maghāzi 17); Muslim (al-Imārah 143)

[49] Bukhāri (al-Dhabā'ih 13); Muslim (al-Sayd 52); Tirmidhi (al-Asa'mah 22); Nasā'i (al-Sayd 37)

[50] Bukhāri (al-Riqāq 17, al-At'imah 23); Muslim (al-Zuhd 21); Abu Dāwud (al-Imārah 20)

[51] Ibn Hanbal 1:224; Muslim (al-Ashribah 83; Fadhā'il al-Sahābah 132)

[52] Bukhāri (al-Hibah 7, al-At'imah 8, 16, al-Maghāzi 38); Muslim (al-Sayd 46); Abu Dāwud (al-At'imah 28); Nasā'i (al-Sayd 26)

[53] Ibn Hanbal 6:456; Bukhāri (al-Maghāzi 29)

[54] Ibn Hanbal 3:488; Bukhāri (al-Maghāzi 35, 38, al-Jihād 123)

[55] Wāqidi 2:796

[56] Wāqidi 2:452, 476; Ibn Hishām 3:260

[57] Wāqidi 1:398, 2:500,577

[58] Wāqidi 2:577

[59] Wāqidi 2:24, 338; Kalā'i 2:112

[60] Wāqidi 1:24; Muslim (al-Jihād 49)

[61] Wāqidi 1:391

[62] Wāqidi 1:26, 2:576, 3:1035

[63] Wāqidi 1:338; Kalā'i 1:112

[64] Bukhāri (al-Maghāzi 38); Abu Dāwud (al-Jihād 145)

[65] Wāqidi 2:775; Ibn Hishām 4:281

[66] Wāqidi 1:238; Ibn Sayyid al-Nās 2:159

[67] Wāqidi 1:26; Ibn Hishām 3:346; Tabari 3:10

[68] Bukhāri (al-Maghāzi 65); Muslim (al-Sayd 17); Abu Dāwud (al-At'imah 46); Nasā'i (al-Sayd 35)

[69] Wāqidi 2:575 onwards, 3:1037; Ibn Sayyid al-Nās 2:123

[70] Wāqidi 2:661; Suhayli 4:58; Ibn Sayyid al-Nās 2:123

[71] Ibn Hanbal 6:346; Bukhāri (al-Dhabā'ih 28, al-Maghāzi 35); Tirmidhi (al-At'imah 6)

[72] Bukhāri (al-Maghāzi 29, al-Riqāq 17); Muslim (al-Zuhd 12); Tirmidhi (al-Zuhd 39)

[73] Wāqidi 2:863, 882

[74] Zuhri: 52; Ibn Sa'd 2:45; Bukhāri (al-Ashribah 16)

75 Bukhāri (al-Jihād 85); Muslim (al-Jihād 101)

76 Bukhāri (al-Tibb 28); Muslim (al-Islām 78); Tirmidhi (al-Tibb 25, 33)

77 Wāqidi 1:53; Ibn Sa'd 2:9; Mālik, *al-Muwatta'* (al-At'imah 83)

78 Ibn Hishām 2:272; Ibn Atheer 2:122; Ibn Qayyim 3:230

79 Ibn Sa'd 2:9; Ibn Qutayba 2:113; Harthami, *Mukhtasar Siyāsat al-Hurub*: 65

80 Q8:42; Wāqidi 1:53; Ibn Hishām 3:234; Ibn Sa'd 2:35, 45; of course this was not always done. For example, even though the Prophet (s) had gained control over the wells of Badr, he allowed the enemy to take some water from it. (Tr.)

81 Wāqidi 1:177, 368, 2:499, 680, 787; Ibn Qayyim, *Zād al-Ma'ād* 2:330

82 Wāqidi 2:685; Ibn Sa'd 2:114; Tabari 2:582

83 Bukhāri (al-Jihād 85); Muslim (al-Jihād 101)

84 Zuhri: 52; Wāqidi 2:587, 661, 3:1039; Ibn Hazm: 251; Kalā'i 1:152

85 Wāqidi 3:1018, 1035

86 Bukhāri (al-Sayd 3); Muslim (al-Sayd 37); Ibn Mājah (al-Dhabā'ih 10); Nasā'i (al-Sayd 32)

87 Bukhāri (al-Hibah 5, al-Dhabā'ih 10); Muslim (al-Sayd 53); Tirmidhi (al-At'imah 2)

88 Bukhāri (al-At'imah 14); Muslim (al-Sayd 42, 47); Nasā'i (al-Sayd 26)

89 Ibn Hanbal 1:100, 104

90 Ibn Hanbal 1:366; Muslim (al-Zakāh 170); Abu Dāwud (al-Buyu' 3)

91 Wāqidi 1:338, 2:775; Ibn Hanbal 1:260

92 Bukhāri (al-At'imah 39, 45); Ibn Mājah (al-At'imah 37); Tirmidhi (al-At'imah 37)

93 Bukhāri (al-At'imah 50, al-Anbiyā' 29); Muslim (al-Ashriba 165)

94 Wāqidi 2:577, 658, 664-670, 3:1035; Ibn Sa'd 2:95; Tabari 3:10

95 Wāqidi 2:658, 661, 670; Ibn Hishām 3:346; Kalā'i 1:132; Ibn Sayyid al-Nās 2:134

96 Wāqidi 3:1039; Ibn Hishām 4:164, 171; Kalā'i 1:152

97 Q27:80; Wāqidi 1:371, 2:822, 827; Tabari 2:568

98 Majmu'āt Muhādharāt Alqaytu fi al-Akādimiyya al-Askariyya al-'Ulyā al-Suriyya

99 Wāqidi 1:371; Ibn Hanbal 6:27; Ibn Mandhur 1:659

100 Bukhāri (al-Salāh 17, al-Libās 42, al-Maghāzi 56); Muslim (al-Salāh 250); Abu Dāwud (al-Salāh 36)

[101] Ibn al-Sikkeet, *Mukhtsar Tahdheeb al-Alfādh*: 407, 408; Ibn 'Abd Rabbih 2:225

[102] Bukhāri (al-Nafaqāt 3, al-Jihād 80); Muslim (al-Jihād 49); Nasā'i (al-Fay' 1)

[103] Q9:41; Wāqidi 3:991, 1019; Ibn Hishām 4:161, 3:226; Tabari 3:100

[104] Zuhri: 73; Wāqidi 1:377; Ibn Hishām 3:201; Ibn Sa'd 2:41; Ibn Sayyid al-Nās 2:50

[105] Ibn Sa'd 2:1, 39; Tabari 2:408, 493; Ibn Sayyid al-Nās 1:224, 2:2, 48

[106] Bukhāri (al-Nafaqāt 3, al-Jihād 80, al-Maghāzi 14); Muslim (al-Jihād 49); Abu Dāwud (al-Imārah 19); Nasā'i (al-Fay' 1)

[107] Wāqidi 2:444; Ibn Hishām 3:260; Kalā'i 1:114

[108] Wāqidi 1L368, 496, 2:637; Suhayli 4:65; Ibn Sayyid al-Nās 2:134

[109] Wāqidi 1:177, 363, 2:499, 644; Ibn Hishām 2:200, 344; Ibn Sa'd 2:114

[110] Ibn Sa'd 2:40; Tabari 2:583

[111] Wāqidi 2:671, 673; Ibn Hishām 3:344; Tabari 3:9

[112] Wāqidi 1:378, 2:496, 662; Tabari 2:554; Ibn Hazm: 182

[113] Ibn Hishām 3:245; Ibn Sa'd 2:19, 40, 77; Ibn Khayyāt 1:27; Ibn Hazm: 154, 182

[114] Wāqidi 1:179, 374, 2:453, 462; Ibn Sa'd 2:20, 41, 83; Tabari 2:481

[115] Wāqidi 1:179, 2:671; Ibn Sa'd 2:20, 41, 83; Ibn Sayyid al-Nās 2:50

[116] Wāqidi 2:453, 462; Ibn Hishām 3:264; Tabari 2:570

[117] Wāqidi 1:179, 374, 2:671; Ibn Atheer 2:138, 173, 221; Ibn Sayyid al-Nās 1:295, 2:50

[118] Q3:174; ibn Sa'd 2:42; Ibn Mājah (al-Jihād 23)

[119] Wāqidi 1:387

[120] Bukhāri (al-Harth 18, 20); Abu Dāwud (al-Buyu' 30, 54); Nasā'i (al-Eimān 45)

[121] Ibn Hanbal 5:45; Bukhāri (al-Jihād 192)

[122] Wāqidi 1:116 onwards; Ibn Hishām 2:197; Bayhaqi, *al-Sunan al-Kubrā* 9:175

[123] Wāqidi 2:765; Ibn Hishām 4:24; Tabari 3:42

[124] Wāqidi 3:1124; Ibn Sa'd 2:137; Ibn Sayyid al-Nās 2:282

[125] Wāqidi 1:20, 181, 194, 2:445; Ibn Mandhur 1:754

[126] Ibn Hanbal 2:17; Abu Dāwud (al-Hudud 18); Bayhaqi 9:21

[127] Wāqidi 1:21, 2:453; Bayhaqi 9:21

[128] Wāqidi 1:216; Ibn Hishām 3:70; Tabari 2:505

[129] Wāqidi 1:21

[130] Ibn Hanbal 2:17; Abu Dāwud (al-Hudud 18); Bayhaqi 9:21

[131] Bukhāri (al-'Ilm 1, 23, 26, 34); Ibn Mājah (al-Iqāmah 23); Tirmidhi (al-'Ilm 19)

[132] Bukhāri (al-Jizyah 8); Kalā'i 1:111; Details about this can be found in Wāqidi 1:347

[133] Murthid ibn Abi Murthid was one of the companions of the Prophet (s) who went with ten reciters in order to teach the tribes of Adhal and al-Qārrah but when they arrived at the well of Rajee', the tribes broke their pact with them and killed them (Tr.)

[134] Wāqidi 1:354; Ibn Sa'd 2:39; Ibn Hishām 3:178; Ibn Khayyāt 1:42

[135] Ibn Sa'd 2:14; Bayhaqi 6:322; Ibn Sayyid al-Nās 2:287

[136] Wāqidi 1:82; Ibn Hishām 3:49; Ibn Sa'd 2:21; Mishelah, *al-Harb al-Khātifah*: 77

[137] Wāqidi 3:996; Ibn Hishām 2:264

[138] Wāqidi 2:534, 550; Ibn Sa'd 2:56, 61; Ibn Sayyid al-Nās 2:79, 103

[139] Ibn Hanbal 4:456; Bukhāri (al-Dhabā'ih 13)

[140] Bukhāri (al-Sayd 3); Muslim (al-Sayd 53); Ibn Mājah (al-At'imah 27); Tirmidhi (al-At'imah 2)

[141] Muslim 3:1433; Abu Dāwud (al-Jihād 61)

[142] Wāqidi 1:177, 2:644, 685; Ibn Hishām 3:200; Ibn Sa'd 2:141

[143] Wāqidi 2:647, 644, 670; Ibn Hishām 3:344

[144] Wāqidi 2:647, 644, 670

[145] Wāqidi 2:671, 680; Ibn Hishām 3:344; Tabari 3:9

[146] Wāqidi 1:177, 363, 2:496; Ibn Hishām 3:245; Ibn Sa'd 2:40

[147] Bukhāri (al-Jihād 130); Muslim (al-Sayd 26)

[148] Wāqidi 2:639, 662

[149] Wāqidi 1:17; Ibn Hishām 2:264; Ibn Sa'd 2:5; Tabari 2:431

[150] Bukhāri (al-Maghāzi 31); Muslim (al-Jihād 149); Abu Dāwud (al-Jihād 34)

[151] Wāqidi 2:755; Ibn Hishām 4:281; Kalā'i 1:112

[152] Bukhāri (al-Maghāzi 65); Abu Dāwud (al-At'imah 46)

[153] Bukhāri (al-Sayd 3, al-Dhabā'ih 10, al-At'imah 14); Muslim (al-Sayd 37, 53); Abu Dāwud (al-At'imah 27)

[154] Bukhāri (al-At'imah 39, 45, 50, al-Anbiyā' 29, al-Maghāzi 65); Muslim (al-Ashribah 165); Abu Dāwud (al-At'imah 26)

155 Zuhri: 52; Bukhāri (al-Jihād 85)

156 Bukhāri (al-Maghāzi 35, 137); Muslim (al-Jihād 131)

157 Bukhāri (al-Maghāzi 79); Muslim (al-Tawba 53)

158 Dārimi (al-Buyu' 54); Abu Dāwud (al-Buyu' 88)

159 Ibn 'Abd Rabbih, *al-'Iqd al-Fareed* 2:225; Mas'udi, *Muruj al-Dhahab* 2:233; Lord Monister, *Risālah fi Harb 'ind al-'Arab*: 52; Farrukh, *Tārikh al-Jāhiliyya*: 30

160 Bukhāri (al-Jihād 97); Muslim (al-Jihād 78)

161 Q9:92; Ibn Hishām 4:161; Tabari 3:102; Qāsimi, *Mahāsin al-Ta'wil* 8:3233

162 Mas'udi 2:233; Watt: 16,17

163 Ibn Hanbal 4:372; Muslim (al-Sayd 100); Nasā'i (al-Mawāqeet 55)

164 Wāqidi 1:177; Ibn Hishām 3:245; Tabari 2:583; Dianna, *Muhammad Rasulullah*: 278

165 Wāqidi 2:644, 667; Ibn Hazm: 212; Ibn Katheer 4:!99

166 Bukhāri (al-Tibb 28); Muslim (al-Islām 78, 81); Tirmidhi (al-Tibb 25, 33)

167 Wāqidi 2:634; Kalā'i 1:130

168 Ibn Sa'd 2:44, 92, 136; Bakri 1:101, 303, 2:564; Hamawi 1:79, 2:14, 487

169 Wāqidi 3:1079; Ibn Hishām 4:239; Ibn Sa'd 2:122; Tabari 3:126

170 Ibn Sa'd 2:44, 56; Bukhāri (al-Maghāzi 28)

171 Dārimi (al-Jihād 22); Bukhāri (al-Maghāzi 20, al-Riqāq 117)

172 Zuhri: 52; Ibn Hazm: 251; Hamawi 2:350; Kalā'i 1:152

173 Wāqidi 3:1079; Ibn Hishām 3:203; Ibn Sa'd 2:45; Tabari 3:126;, 131; Bakri 1:101, 2:564, 4:1220

174 Kalā'i 1:151; Ibn Sayyid al-Nās 2:218; Watt: 16, 17

175 Wāqidi 3:1015; Ibn Khayyāt 1:17; Ibn Hazm: 253

176 Wāqidi 2:800-806; Ibn Hishām 3:264; Ibn Sa'd 2:45

177 Wāqidi 1:26; Ibn Hishām 3:346; Ibn Sa'd 2:95; Tabari 3:10

178 Wāqidi 3:991, 994; Ibn Hishām 4:161; Ibn Sa'd 2:120

179 Bukhāri (al-Maghāzi 16)

180 Bukhāri (al-Sayd 3, al-At'imah 39, 45, 50); Muslim (al-Sayd 37, 53)

181 Wāqidi 2:445, 448; Ibn Hishām 3:260; Tabari 2:568; Ibn Sayyid al-Nās 2:57

182 Bukhāri (al-Dhabā'ih 10); Abu Dāwud (al-At'imah 27); Nasā'i (al-Sayd 32)

183 Shaybāni 2:409; Ibn Hanbal 6:276; Muslim (al-Jihād 58); Bayhaqi 9:89

184 Wāqidi 1:53; Ibn Hishām 2:257; Ibn Sa'd 2:96

185 Q8:41; Bukhāri (al-Eimān 40); Muslim (al-Eimān 23); Abu Dāwud (al-Jihād 134); Tirmidhi (Aseer 14)

186 Bukhāri (al-Maghāzi 8); Muslim (al-Jihād 2); Abu Dāwud (al-Jihād 25)

187 Dārimi (al-Muqaddimah 7); Abu Dāwud (al-Janā'iz 32); Tirmidhi (al-Janā'iz 31)

188 Zuhayli, *al-Fiqh al-Islāmiyya wa Adillatih* 6:455

189 Suhayli 3:22 onwards

190 Zuhayli 6:458

191 Wāqidi 3:295; Dārimi (al-Siyar 35); Bukhāri (al-'Umrah 3)

192 Wāqidi 2:544; Ibn Sa'd 2:61

193 Bukhāri (al-Madhālim 20); Muslim (al-Adh'hā 20); Ibn Mājah (al-Fitan 3); Abu Dāwud (al-Hudud 14)

194 Bukhāri (al-Eimān 3); Muslim (al-Jihād 32)

195 Shāfi'i, *al-Umm* 4:64 onwards

196 *Ibid.*

197 Ibn Sa'd 2:46; Suhayli 4:65

198 Wāqidi 1:178, 377, 2:510, 524; Ibn Sa'd 2:41

199 Wāqidi 1:96, 2:535, 944, 3:943; Ibn Sa'd 2:61, 95

200 Ibn Qudāmah, *al-Mughni* 8:372 onwards; Ibn Sayyid al-Nās 2:287; Zuhayli, *Athār al-Harb fi Fiqh al-Islāmi*: 429

201 Shaybāni 2:409; Ibn Mājah (al-Diyāt 3); Tirmidhi (al-Siyar 18)

202 Dārimi (al-Siyar 27); Ibn Mājah (al-Jihād 32); Abu Dāwud (al-Jihād 124); Tirmidhi (al-Siyar 18)

203 Bukhāri (al-Khums 16); Abu Dāwud (al- Jihād 120); Tirmidhi (al-Siyar 18); Ibn Qudāmah 8:372

204 Wāqidi 1:138, 148; Ibn Hishām 2:298; Ibn Sa'd 2:11; Tabari 2:459

205 Wāqidi 1:142, 309; Ibn Hishām 3:110; Bayhaqi 6:320

206 Wāqidi 2:513; Ibn Hishām 3:249; Ibn Sa'd 2:56; Tabari3:593

207 Wāqidi 1:138 onwards; Ibn Sa'd 2:14; Ibn Hanbal 1:353

[208] Ibn Hanbal 1:247; Bayhaqi 6:322

[209] Wāqidi 1:16; Ibn Hishām 2:255; Ibn Sa'd 2:5; Tabari 2:413

[210] Wāqidi 2:602

[211] Dārimi (al-Siyar 27); Muslim 3:376; Ibn Mājah (al-Jihād 32)

[212] Wāqidi 1:142; Ibn Hishām 3:110; Ibn Atheer 2:165

[213] Ibn Hanbal 6:276; Abu Dāwud (al-Jihād 121); This was the husband of the Prophet's daughter Zainab (Tr.)

[214] Wāqidi 1:138 onwards; Abu Dāwud (al-Jihād 12)

[215] Wāqidi 1:407, 410; Ibn Hishām 3:307 onwards; Ibn Sa'd 2:46

[216] Ibn Sa'd 2:56; Muslim 3:1386; Bayhaqi 6:319

[217] Wāqidi 2:552; Ibn Sa'd 2:62; Ibn Sayyid al-Nās 2:105

[218] Ibn Sa'd 2:62; Ibn Atheer 2:207; Ibn Sayyid al-Nās 2:105; Ibn Qayyim 2:297

[219] Bukhāri (al-Ahkām 35); Muslim (al-Jihād 58); Tirmidhi (al-Siyar 18); Nasā'i (al-Qudhāt 17)

[220] Ibn Hishām 2:199; Tabari 2:46; Ibn Atheer 2:131

[221] Wāqidi 1:407, 410; Ibn Salām, *al-Amwāl* 1:106; Muslim 3:1386

[222] Tabari 2:463; Bayhaqi 9:89

[223] Wāqidi 2:252; Muslim 3:1368; Ibn Sayyid al-Nās 1:287

[224] Ibn Hanbal 3:377; Bukhāri (al-Jihād 144); Abu Dāwud (al-Eimān 31); Tirmidhi (al-Jihād 34)

[225] Dārimi (al-Farā'idh 43); Bukhāri (al-Salāh 75); Abu Dāwud (al-Jihād 97, 14); Nasā'i (al-Masājid 20)

[226] Ibn Hishām 2:199; Tabari 2:46; Ibn Sayyid al-Nās 1:265

[227] Ibn Sa'd 3:116; Bayhaqi 9:89; Ibn Sayyid al-Nās 2:203

[228] Q76:8

[229] Ibn Hanbal 5:294; Abu Dāwud (al-Buyu' 3)

[230] Ibn Hishām 1:300; Tabari 2:461; Ibn Atheer 2:131

[231] *Ibid.*

[232] Bayhaqi 6:230; Zuhayli, Athār al-Harb fi Fiqh al-Islāmi: 412

[233] Ibn 'Abd al-Barr 1:213; Ibn Atheer 1:246; Zuhayli: 412

242

[234] Bukhāri (al-Jihād 146); Qurtubi 4:3059

[235] Wāqidi 3:989; Bukhāri (al-Jihād 142)

[236] Abu Dāwud (al-Jihād 97, 116)

[237] Wāqidi 1:53, 2:563, 3:986; Ibn Hishām 2:268; Tabari 2:436

[238] Wāqidi 2:552; Abu Dāwud (al-Jihād 84)

[239] Zuhri: 93; Ibn Hanbal 5:309; Bukhāri (al-Madina 12); Nasā'i (al-Ashribah 40)

[240] Refer to the books on Tibb including Tibb al-Nabawi and the chapters on al-Tibb in Bukhāri and Muslim

[241] Ibn Is'hāq: 308; Wāqidi 1:241; Ibn Sayyid al-Nās 2:14

[242] Wāqidi 1:190; Ibn Hishām 3:60; Ibn Sayyid al-Nās 1:301

[243] Bukhāri (al-Maghāzi 38, 121); Muslim (Fadhā'il al-Sahābah 32, 35); The Prophet (s) had initially given the opportunity to his other companions like Abu Bakr, 'Umar and Sa'd ibn Abi Waqqās but they were unable to take down the fort of Khaybar. It is then that the Prophet (s) gave the command to 'Ali ibn Abi Tālib ('a) who finally gained victory over the Jews and brought down Khaybar (Ibn Hajar 2:503) (Tr.)

[244] Wāqidi 1:350, 2:644

[245] Wāqidi 1:87, 250, 334 onwards; Ibn Sa'd 2:34; Bukhāri (al-Maghāzi 16)

[246] Wāqidi 1:393, 2:551; Ibn Hishām 3:85; Ibn Sa'd 2:117

[247] Bukhāri (al-Jihād 67, Tibb 2); Muslim (al-Jihād 137, 141); Abu Dāwud (al-Jihād 32, 141); Tirmidhi (al-Siyar 22)

[248] Wāqidi 1:247; Ibn Hishām 3:85; Ibn Atheer 3:78; Ibn Sayyid al-Nās 2:12

[249] Ibn Hanbal 3:334; Bukhāri (al-Jihād 80, al-Tibb 27); Tirmidhi (al-Tibb 34)

[250] Wāqidi 1:334; Ibn Hishām 3:107; Ibn Sa'd 2:34; Tabari 2:534 onwards; Ibn Sayyid al-Nās 2:13

[251] Bukhāri (al-Maghāzi 30); Muslim (al-Jihād 66); Abu Dāwud (al-Janā'iz 4); Nasā'i (al-Masājid 18)

[252] Wāqidi 2:551; Ibn Sa'd 2:62; Ibn Sayyid al-Nās 2:104

[253] Shaybāni 1:127; Ibn Sa'd 2:34

[254] Bukhāri (al-Maghāzi 16)

[255] Bukhāri (al-Tibb 3, 5, al-Hajj 18); Muslim (al-Islām 18)

[256] Bukhāri (al-Tibb 52, 56); Muslim (al-Ashribah 155); Abu Dāwud (al-Tibb 12)

[257] Ibn Hanbal 6:77; Bukhāri (al-At'imah 43, al-Tibb 52); Ibn Mājah (al-Tibb 3)

[258] Wāqidi 2:569; Ibn Hanbal 6:380; Bukhāri (al-Tibb 6, 57); Ibn Mājah (al-Tibb 30)

[259] Ibn Hanbal 6:380; Abu Dāwud (al-Tahārah 120)

[260] Ibn Qayyim 3:134, 415; Ibn Katheer 4:195

[261] Wāqidi 1:53, 2:644; Ibn Hishām 3:69, 231; Kalā'i 1:130

[262] Wāqidi 2:644; Bukhāri (al-Madina 12); Tirmidhi (al-Ru'yā 10)

[263] Bukhāri (al-Jihād 85, al-Ashribah 16)

[264] Bukhāri (al-Anbiyā' 17); Muslim (al-Jihād 101); Abu Dāwud (al-Tahārah 33); Nasā'i (al-Tahārah 43)

[265] Zuhri: 79; Wāqidi 1:145, 152, 2:700, 825; Ibn Sa'd 2:43, 109; Ibn Hanbal 2:552; Nasā'i (al-Khawf 16); Kalā'i 1:112, 130; Ibn Sayyid al-Nās 2:52m 131

[266] Ibn Is'hāq: 289; Wāqidi 1:145; Ibn Sa'd 2:11; Tabari 2:477; Ibn Sayyid al-Nās 1:285

[267] Wāqidi 1:300 onwards; Ibn Sa'd 2:29; Ibn Hanbal 5:135

[268] Wāqidi 2:295; Ibn Hishām 3:263; Ibn Sayyid al-Nās 2:67

[269] Wāqidi 2:769; Ibn Hishām 4:30; Ibn Sayyid al-Nās 2:156

[270] Ibn Hishām 4:50; Ibn Sa'd 2:98; Ibn 'Abd al-Barr, *al-Durar fi Ikhtisār al-Maghāzi wal-Siyar*: 232; Ibn Sayyid al-Nās 2:173

[271] Wāqidi 3:922; Ibn Hishām 4:101; Ibn Sa'd 2:109; Ibn Sayyid al-Nās 2:192, 193

[272] Wāqidi 2:750; Ibn Hishām 3:357; Ibn Sayyid al-Nās 2:142

[273] Wāqidi 3:938; Ibn Hishām 4:129; Tabari 3:58; Ibn Sayyid al-Nās 2:202

[274] Zuhri: 71; Wāqidi 1:176; Ibn Sa'd 2:19, 40; Ibn Khayyāt 1:27; Kalā'i 1:111

[275] Wāqidi 2:551; Ibn Sa'd 2:61; Ibn Sayyid al-Nās 2:104; Ibn Qayyim 2:279

[276] Wāqidi 2:723; Ibn Sa'd 2:86; Ibn Sayyid al-Nās 2:146; Ibn Qayyim2:358

[277] Wāqidi 2:741; Ibn Sa'd 2:89; Ibn Atheer 5:266; Ibn Sayyid al-Nās 5:149

[278] Wāqidi 2:752; Ibn Sa'd 2:92; Tabari 3:29; Ibn Sayyid al-Nās 2:152

[279] Wāqidi 1:1:347; Ibn Sa'd 2:36; Bukhāri 5:41; Kalā'i 1:111

[280] Ibn Sa'd 2:39; Wāqidi 1:355; Ibn Hishām 3:178; Ibn Khayyāt 1:30 (some of whom mention different numbers)

[281] Bukhāri (al-Maghāzi 29); Abu Dāwud (al-Jihād 156); Ibn Hishām 4:49; Ibn Sa'd 2:98

[282] Wāqidi 2:551, 723, 741; Ibn Sa'd 2:61, 86, 89; Ibn Sayyid al-Nās 2:104, 146, 152

[283] Wāqidi 1:45, 152; Ibn Sa'd 2:6, 11; Tabari 2:431, 477; Ibn Sayyid al-Nās 1:245, 285

[284] Wāqidi 1:300; Ibn Hishām 3:68, 129; Ibn Sa'd 2:27, 29; Ibn Sayyid al-Nās 2:5, 27

[285] Ibn Hishām 3:231, 264; Ibn Sa'd 2:47; Tabari 2:570; Ibn 'Abd al-Barr: 194

[286] Wāqidi 2:574, 750; Ibn Hishām 3:231, 264; Ibn Sa'd 2:78; Ibn Sayyid al-Nās 2:153

[287] Wāqidi 2:756, 769; Ibn Hishām 4:15, 30; Ibn Sa'd 2:97; Tabari 3:36; Ibn Sayyid al-Nās 2:153

[288] Wāqidi 2:800, 812; Ibn Hishām 2:42, 50; Ibn Sa'd 2:97; Tabari 3:73, 81; Ibn 'Abd al-Barr: 232

[289] Wāqidi 3:889, 992; Ibn Hishām 4:83; Ibn Sa'd 2:108-110; Tabari 3:73, 81; Ibn 'Abd al-Barr: 242

[290] Wāqidi 2:889, 923, 938; Ibn Sa'd 2:114

[291] Wāqidi 2:551, 723, 741, 752; Ibn Sa'd 2:36, 39, 61, 86, 92; Bukhāri 5:41; Kalā'i 1:111; Ibn Sayyid al-Nās 2:104, 146, 149, 152

[292] Dārimi (al-Muqaddimah 7); Ibn Mājah (al-Janā'iz 28); Abu Dāwud (al-Janā'iz 23); Tirmidhi (al-Janā'iz 31)

[293] Abu Dāwud (al-Janā'iz 38); Tirmidhi (al-Janā'iz 31)

[294] Ibn Hanbal 4:185; Dārimi (al-Jihād 19); Ibn Mājah (al-Muqaddimah 110, al-Libās 2); Abu Dāwud (al-Jihād 25); Tirmidhi (Fadhā'il al-Jihād 13); Nasā'i (al-Qisāmah 18)

[295] Ibn Hanbal 1:288, 463; Dārimi (al-Jihād 16); Bukhāri (al-Jihād 2); Abu Dāwud (al-Jihād 26); Tirmidhi (Fadhā'il al-Jihād 25); Nasā'i (Fadhā'il al-Jihād 83)

[296] Ibn Hanbal 1:386; Dārimi (al-Jihād 18); Muslim (al-Aqdhiya 16); Abu Dāwud (al-Aqdhiya 13); Tirmidhi (Fadhā'il al-Jihād 13)

[297] Bukhāri (al-Janā'iz 73, 79); Abu Dāwud (al-Janā'iz 27); Tirmidhi (al-Janā'iz 46); Nasā'i (al-Janā'iz 62)

[298] Bukhāri (al-Salāh 109, Manāqib al-Ansār 45, al-Maghāzi 8); Muslim (al-Janā'iz 26); Abu Dāwud (al-Jihād 115); Nasā'i (al-Janā'iz 117)

[299] Bukhāri (al-Maghāzi 36); Muslim (al-Jihād 2, al-Birr 117, 119); Abu Dāwud (al-Jihād 113); Tirmidhi (al-Jihād 14)

[300] Bukhāri (al-Maghāzi 36, al-Dhabā'ih 25); Muslim (al-Jihād 2); Abu Dāwud (al-Jihād 82); Tirmidhi (al-Siyar 48, al-Jihād 14)

[301] Bukhāri (al-Janā'iz 75); Abu Dāwud (al-Adh'hā 11); Tirmidhi (al-Diyāt 14); Nasā'i (al-Dhahāyā 22, 26)

[302] Bukhāri (al-Janā'iz 34; al-Jihād 20); Muslim (Fadhā'il al-Sahābah 129); Tirmidhi (al-Janā'iz 31); Nasā'i (al-Janā'iz 12)

[303] Ibn Hanbal 1:248, 271; Abu Dāwud 2:279

[304] Ibn Hanbal 5:84; Dārimi (al-Jihād 30); Muslim (al-Jihād 141); Ibn Mājah (al-Jihād 37, al-Ahkām 14); Abu Dāwud (al-Buyu' 89, al-Salāh 70)

[305] Bukhāri (al-Jihād 67, al-Tibb 2); Abu Dāwud (al-Ashriba 44, al-Imārah 20, al-Adab 100)

[306] Bukhāri (al-Jihād 65, Manāqib al-Ansār 18, al-Maghāzi 18); Muslim (al-Jihād 136)

[307] Ibn Hanbal 5:84; Dārimi (al-Jihād 30); Muslim (al-Jihād 141); Ibn Mājah (al-Jihād 37); Bayhaqi 9:22, 30

[308] Bukhāri (al-Maghāzi 30); Muslim (al-Jihād 66, 141); Abu Dāwud (al-Janā'iz 4); Nasā'i (al-Masājid 18)

[309] Wāqidi 1:208; Ibn Hishām 3:72; Ibn Sayyid al-Nās 2:9 onwards

[310] Wāqidi 2:278, 3:903; Ibn Hishām 4:89; Tabari 3:77; Kalā'i 1:145

[311] Bukhāri (al-Jihād 66, al-Maghāzi 22); Tirmidhi (al-Libās 38)

[312] Ibn Hanbal 6:385; Bukhāri (al-Tibb 2, al-Jihād 67)

[313] Bukhāri (al-Hajj 316)

[314] Wāqidi 1:269, 3:904; Ibn Hishām 3:87, 88; Tabari 3:77; Kalā'i 1:145; Ibn Sayyid al-Nās 2:11, 13

[315] Ibn Hishām 3:106; Ibn Sayyid al-Nās 2:24

[316] Wāqidi 2:613; Ibn 'Abd al-Barr 4:1939; Ibn Atheer 2:205; Ibn Qayyim 2:308

[317] Bukhāri (al-Jihād 66, al-Maghāzi 22); Muslim (al-Imārah 89, al-Salām 89); Ibn Mājah (al-Jihād 43); Abu Dāwud (al-Zakāh 33)

[318] Wāqidi 3:629; Ibn Hishām 3:340; Tabari 2:640; Ibn Sayyid al-Nās 2:122

[319] For en example of the important role played by women in these battles see: Ibn Hishām 3:86

[320] Q60:10; Suhayli 1:26; Qāsimi, *Mahāsin al-Ta'wil* 16:5770

[321] Wāqidi 1:223, 3:897; Muslim 3:895; Abu Dāwud (al-Jihād 107)

[322] Wāqidi 2:996; Muslim 3:895; Abu Dāwud (al-Jihād 107)

[323] Wāqidi 2:262, 269; Ibn Hishām 3:262; Ibn Hanbal 1:164; Tabari 2:570

[324] Wāqidi 2:460; Ibn Hishām 3:239

[325] Wāqidi 1:269, 3:904; Ibn Hishām 3:87, 4:88; Kalā'i 1:145; Ibn Sayyid al-Nās 2:11, 13

[326] Wāqidi 2:661, 3:991; Ibn Hishām 4:159; Ibn Sa'd 2:120; Tabari 3:102

[327] Wāqidi 2:775; Ibn Hishām 4:281; Tabari 3:10; Kalā'i 1:112

[328] Bukhāri (al-Maghāzi 65); Muslim (al-Sayd 17); Abu Dāwud (al-At'imah 46); Nasā'i (al-Sayd 35)

[329] Wāqidi 3:368, 2:637; Ibn Sa'd 2:19; Kalā'i 1:130; Ibn Sayyid al-Nās 2:74; Wāqidi 2:644, 670, 680

[330] Wāqidi 1:755, 3:990; Ibn Hishām 4:16, 19; Ibn Sa'd 2:119

[331] Zuhri: 93; Wāqidi 1:183, 2:535, 3:943; Ibn Sa'd 2:61

[332] Ibn Sa'd 2:20, 41, 120; Bukhāri (al-Jihād 80); Muslim (al-Jihād 49)

[333] Wāqidi 1:176, 363, 2:496, 633, 267; Ibn Sa'd 2:1, 19, 40; Tabari 2:479, 581, 3:9; Ibn Hazm: 239

[334] Zuhri: 86; Ibn Shihāb 3:50 onwards; Ibn Sa'd 2:21, 44; Tabari 2:9; Kalā'i 1:130

[335] Wāqidi 1:187; Ibn Sa'd 2:20; Tabari 2:481; Ibn Sayyid al-Nās 1:296

[336] Wāqidi 2:658, 664, 470; Ibn Hishām 3:253; Ibn Sa'd 2:78

[337] Wāqidi 1:182, 194; Ibn Hishām 3:46; Ibn Sa'd 2:21, 35, 43, 62

[338] Wāqidi 1:396; Ibn Sa'd 2:21; Suhayli 3:28; Ibn Sayyid al-Nās 1:304

[339] Wāqidi 1:20, 88; Ibn Hishām 3:181; Tabari 2:513

[340] Zuhri: 87; Wāqidi 1:182, 2:749, 3:1123; Ibn Hishām 3:46; Ibn Sa'd 2:21, 28, 49, 97; Ibn Sayyid al-Nās 2:281

[341] Wāqidi 1:396; Kalā'i 1:123; Ibn Sayyid al-Nās 2:106

[342] Bukhāri (al-Jihād 122); Muslim (al-Masājid 3, 5); Tirmidhi (al-Siyar 5); Nasā'i (al-Jihād 1)

[343] Q8:65, Q9:19, 20, 41, 89; Bukhāri (al-Maghāzi 53, al-Jihād 110)

[344] Wāqidi 3:990 onwards, Tabari 3:101; Kalā'i 1:151

SECTION III

CONCLUSION

The organization and Islāmic government developed gradually after the migration of the Holy Prophet (s) to Madina. At this time the Prophet (s) made this city the capital of the Islāmic government, managed and supervised the affairs of the Muslims, planned and created a program for spreading the call of Islām and took steps which put him, in the short term, in situations of grave hardship. These steps were always taken with complete wisdom and awareness, and became a stepping stone and a basis for the expansion of the management and the great foundation of human reform.

The measures he (s) took made Madina a homeland for its residents and not a place of continuous disputes between its tribes. It became a peaceful home for those who upheld its sanctity. Madina welcomed the Muhājirs, from whatever tribe and group they may have been. Actually, this was the first time that a homeland in which the people lived as equals got its true meaning, and in which the people would take up responsibilities without looking at lineage of status.
The Holy Prophet (s) was successful in making leadership dignified and honored so that all the people could benefit from his guidance and leadership and would be ready to submit to and obey him after having been freed from the yoke of other tyrant rulers.[1] With the ingenuity and intelligence that he had been granted, the Prophet (s) understood that the head and guide who would be responsible for organizing affairs initially in Madina and later throughout the world cannot succeed without the strength of the divine call and guardianship of the Islāmic system, and this strength was found in the arms of the believers who decided to migrate with him to Madina and were the first group to form a Muslim army, which the Ansār also joined later.

The role of the Holy Prophet (s) in nurturing the military forces started when Jihād was made obligatory. During this time, he embarked on organizing, recruiting and training the army following the battles and Sariya missions that were aimed at attaining political and military goals; because in order to establish the government and expand the call to Islām, there was no other choice. He would give hope to the fighters and mobilize them to come together under the leadership of the unit commanders and would strive to increase the awe and eminence of the Muslims among the enemy. The supreme commander would always try to prepare the army and train them in the different arts of warfare, until they were fully prepared and well trained so that they could show the superiority of their skills when they came face to face with the enemy in battle.
His goal in these battles was self-defense,[2] safeguarding the call to Islām and defending it against those people who would act as hindrances in its way. As we study the progress of the battles that were commanded by the Holy Prophet (s) –

that we have mentioned in detail, we find the most evident factors that led to victory included:

First: the usage of certain methods of warfare by the Prophet (s) that the enemy did not have any knowledge of, such as 'siege', 'acquiring intelligence', 'specifying the goals and objectives', 'mobilizing the forces for the primary objective', 'surprise attacks', 'secret (Sariya) missions', 'swiftness', 'maneuvers' and 'spiritual force and securing all the military resources' which are all principles of present-day warfare.[3]

The types of warfare that were employed by the Holy Prophet (s) in his battles had a huge impact in victory over the enemy. For instance, psychological warfare[4] was an important means of reducing and weakening the morale of the enemy and in most of the battles, just by the enemy hearing the thunderous sounds of the Muslim army, it was enough to gain them victory. The same was the case of revolutionary and collective war where all the military and non-military groups were involved where he (s) used special methods to mobilize all of them together in a spirit of revolution. The result of this type of leadership was that the forces, having seen his just attitude and superior goal, accepted all that he gave them and believed in it. Similarly, the innovations in warfare that the Prophet (s) had brought led to the perplexity and reduced grandeur of the enemy and in the end led to their downfall.

More than anything else, the ingenuity of the supreme commander and the qualities that distinguished him as a leader, and also his uniqueness and superiority in politics, military management and a complete awareness of the principles and etiquettes of war both at the tactical and strategic levels, deserves praise.

Second: Islāmic training and nurturing – the Holy Prophet (s) gave full attention and importance to this. He (s) created a new force among the Muslim army which had never been witnessed by the Arabs before, and that was the force of spirituality that Islām put in their hearts and made them willing to sacrifice their lives and wealth in the way of spreading the true religion and made them volunteer for death. This was something that guaranteed their felicity and reward in this world and the hereafter.

The Muslim army was distinguished for its united leadership, sincerity and total obedience to them. The fact that Miqdād ibn 'Amr turned to the Holy Prophet (s) in the Battle of Badr and said: "If you march towards Bark al-'Imād (a remote place in Yemen), we will follow you with strength until we reach there!" and

Sa'd ibn Mu'ādh said: "If you give us the order to enter this sea, we will enter it with you and none of us will disobey you in this matter!" proves this point.

The invitation of the Holy Prophet (s) to Islām was a call based on reformation and peace, and war was not considered except when the hardheartedness and harsh treatment of the enemy upon the Muslims increased. In reality it was a defensive response of force against force. In this way, his battles were based on steadfastness from the very beginning and the Muslim army was never negligent of this. They would invite the people to the new religion, enact peace treaties with them, take Jizya tax or conquer their lands and fight against those who expressed enmity towards him.

The most important feature of the time of the Prophet (s) was his many battle and Sariya missions. Despite the fact the Jihād was ordained after migration to Madina, but in the span of seven years, the number of battles had reached 27, starting from the Battle of Waddān and ending with the Battle of Tabuk. The Holy Prophet (s) was present in nine of the battles. During this time, he (s) organized 47 Sariya missions where some of them were just to invite others to Islām or come face to face with those who posed a threat to the security of the Muslims.

A point worth noting here is that this military training and the battles that have been mentioned gave the Islāmic government eminence and put it in the category of the largest empires in human history, without this being the real goal. Accepting the notion that the primary goal of the Holy Prophet (s) was to establish an Islāmic empire would be contrary to the 'historical truth' because actually this matter was only part of the overall means of attaining the primary objective which was to destroy polytheism and spread Islām through peaceful and friendly means.

The way in which this government dealt with its enemies and other governments opened up a new door, because its principle of encounter and relationship were based on the rules and principles of justice and humanity, both in times of peace and war. The fact that after the supreme commander passed away the Muslim army continued its conquests and were able to capture the lands of Syria, Egypt and 'Iraq, and were able to bring the two largest empires of the time, i.e. the Romans and Persians, to submission, this was only because they gave importance and special significance to the fact that the Holy Prophet (s) was the first conqueror of these lands. Because during his time, he (s) laid the groundwork for them through his battles and wars and had given the army glad tidings about the expansion of their domain, and this was the reason for the increase in their morale and guarantee of gaining victory.

In reality, the Islāmic conquests during the reign of the Caliphs were the fruits of the seeds that were sowed by the Holy Prophet (s) in the battles that he led. There were always two factors that enabled the Muslim army to close the scrolls of the kings and overthrow them and overcome all the hardships and these were:

1) The love for Islāmic government and obedience to its leader.
2) Considering death to be insignificant.

It was because of these reasons that the domain of Islām reached China in the east and Andalusia in the west.

The Islāmic government will never achieve its past glory again unless the organization of its armies are once again based on the principles that the Holy Prophet (s) laid down, the most important of which were: Love for the (Islāmic) government, unity, sacrificing of lives and souls in the quest of achieving security and peace throughout the lands.

NOTES AND REFERENCES

[1] Hasan, Tārikh al-Islām al-Siyāsi wal-Dini wal-Ijtimā'i 1:85, 150

[2] Q2:190, 193

[3] Howard, Nadhariyat al-Harb Wāqidi Mumārasatiha: 16, 158

[4] Bukhāri (al-Salāh 438)

BIBLIOGRAPHY

Primary Sources

1.   Ibn Atheer, 'Ali ibn Muhammad ibn 'Abd al-Kareem al-Jarazi (630 AH): *al-Nihāyah fi Ghareeb al-Hadith wal-Athar*; Egypt, Dār al-Ihyā al-Kutub al-'Arabiyyah

2.   ____: *al-Kāmil fi al-Tārikh*; Beirut, Dār Beirut lil-Tibā'ah wal-Nashr (1965)

3.   ____: *Usd al-Ghābah fi Ma'rifat al-Sahābah*; Damascus, al-Maktabah al-Dhāhiriyyah

4.   Ibn Is'hāq, Muhammad ibn Is'hāq ibn Yasār al-Matlabi (151 AH): *al-Siyar wal-Maghāzi*; Beirut, Dār al-Fikr (1978)

5.   ____: *Bakr Wāqidi Taghlub*; Damascus, al-Maktabah al-Dhāhiriyyah

6.   ____: *Seerah Ibn Is'hāq* (also known as *al-Mubtada wal-Khabar*); Ma'had al-Dirāsāt wal-Abhāth, Marakesh (1978)

7.   Ibn Ayyās, Abu al-Barakāt Muhammad bin Ahmad (930 AH); *Tārikh ibn Ayyās*; Damascus, al-Maktabah al-Dhāhiriyyah

8.   Ibn Bakkār, Abu Abdillah al-Zubayr bin Bakkār (256 AH): *Jamharah Nasabu Quraysh Wāqidi Akhbārihā*; Cairo, al-Matba'ah al-Madani

9.   Ibn Thābit, Hassān ibn Thābit al-Ansāri (54 AH): *Diwān*; Egypt, al-Maktabah al-Tijāriyya al-Kubrā

10.   Ibn Jazari, Abu al-Khayr Muhammad ibn Muhammad al-Jazari (833 AH): *Ghāyah al-Nihāyah fi Tabaqāt al-Qurrā'*; Egypt, al-Maktabah al-Khānji (1933)

11.   Ibn Habeeb, Muhammad ibn Habeeb ibn Umayyah ibn 'Amr al-Hāshimi al-Baghdādi (245 AH): *al-Muhbar*; Beirut, al-Matba'ah al-Jadeedah

12.   Ibn Hazm, 'Ali ibn Ahmad al-Andalusi (456 AH): *Jawāmi' al-Seerah*; Egypt, Dār al-Ma'ārif

13.   ____: *Jamharah Ansāb al-'Arab*; Egypt, Dār al-Ma'ārif

14.   Ibn Hanbal, Ahmad ibn Muhammad (41 AH): *al-Musnad*

15.   Ibn Hajar 'Asqalāni, Abul-Fadhl Ahmad ibn 'Ali ibn Hajar (852 AH): *Tahdheeb al-Tahdheeb*; India, Matba'ah Dā'irat al-Ma'ārif al-Hindiyya

16.   Ibn Khaldun, 'Abd al-Rahmān ibn Muhammad (808 AH): *al-Muqaddimah*; Lajnat al-Bayān al-'Arabi (1985)

17.   Ibn Khallikān, Ahmad ibn Muhammad ibn Abi Bakr (681 AH): *Wafayāt al-A'yān Wāqidi Anbā'I Abnā' al-Zamān*; Beirut, Dār Sādir

18.   Ibn Khayyāt, Khalifa ibn Khayyāt (240 AH): *Tārikh Khalifa ibn Khayyāt*; Syria, Wizārat al-Thaqāfah wal-Irshād (1967)

19.   Ibn Sa'd, Muhammad ibn Munee' al-Zuhri (230 AH): *al-Tabaqāt al-Kubrā*; Leiden, Brill Press

20.   Ibn Salām, Qāsim (224 AH): *al-Amwāl*; Syria, al-Maktabah al-Dhāhiriyyah

21. Ibn Sayyid, Abu al-Hasan 'Ali ibn Ismā'il al-Andalusi (458 AH): *al-Mukhassas*; Egypt, al-Matba'ah al-Ameeriyya al-Kubrā

22. Ibn Sayyid al-Nās, Abu Fath al-Deen Muhammad ibn Muhammad Andalusi al-Ashbili (733 AH): *'Uyun al-Athar fi Funun al-Maghāzi wal-Shamā'il was-Siyar*

23. Ibn Shajari, Hibatullah ibn 'Ali (542 AH): *al-Hamāsah*

24. Ibn Shu'ayb, Muhammad ibn Hārun ibn Shu'ayb Ansāri (353 AH): *Sifat al-Nabi*; Damascus, al-Maktabah al-Dhāhiriyyah

25. Ibn Tufayl, 'Aāmir (11 AH): *Diwān* (Riwāyat Abi Bakr Muhammad ibn al-Qāsim al-Anbāri); Beirut, Dār Sādir

26. Ibn 'Abd Rabbih, Ahmad ibn Muhammad ibn 'Abd Rabbih al-Andalusi (327 AH): *al-'Iqd al-Fareed*; Lajnat al-Ta'leef wal-Tarjuma wan-Nashr (1948)

27. Ibn 'Abd al-Barr, Abu 'Umar Yusuf ibn 'Abd al-Barr al-Namari (463 AH): *al-Durar fi Ikhtisār al-Maghāzi wal-Siyar*; Cairo, al-Majlis al-A'lā li al-Shu'un al-Islāmiyya

28. ____: *al-Isti'āb fi Ma'rifat al-As'hāb*; Egypt, al-Matba'ah al-Nahdhah

29. Ibn 'Asākir, Abu al-Qāsim 'Ali ibn 'Abdillah (571 AH): *al-Tārikh al-Kabir*; Damascus, al-Matba'ah al-Rawdhah al-Shām (1911)

30. Ibn 'Ayyādh, 'Ayyādh ibn Musā ibn 'Ayyadh al-Yahsabi (544 AH): *al-Shifā bi Ta'reef Huquq al-Mustafā*; Egypt, al-Matba'ah al-'Uthmāniyya

31. Ibn 'Imād, Abu al-Fallāh 'Abd al-Hayy ibn al-'Imād al-Hanbali (1089 AH): *Shadharāt al-Dhahab fi Akhbār man Dhahab*; Egypt, al-Maktabat al-Qudsi

32. Ibn Qutaybah, 'Abdullah ibn Muslim ibn Qutayba al-Daynuri (276 AH): *al-Imāmah wal-Siyāsah*; Egypt, al-Matba'ah al-Futuh al-Adabiyyah

33. ____: *'Uyun al-Akhbār*; Cairo, al-Matba'ah Dār al-Kutub al-Misriyya (1925)

34. ____: *al-Ma'ārif*; Cairo, al-Matba'ah Dār al-Kutub (1960)

35. Ibn Qayyim Jawzi, Muhammad ibn Abi Bakr (752 AH): *Zād al-Ma'ād fi Huda Khayril-'Ibād*; Egypt, Dār al-Kutub al-Misriyya

36. ____: *al-Furusiyya al-Muhammadiyya*; Scanned copy from Mu'assasah al-Risālah

37. Ibn Katheer, Ismā'il ibn Katheer al-Qarashi al-Damishqi (744 AH): *Tafseer al-Qur'ān al-'Adheem*; Beirut, Dār Ihyā al-Turāth al-'Arabi (1969)

38. ____: al-Seerah al-Nabawiyya; Cairo, al-Matba'ah 'Isā al-Bābi al-Halabi (1964)

39. ____: *al-Bidāya wal-Nihāya*; Egypt, al-Maktaba al-Ma'ār (1966)

40. Ibn Mājah, Muhammad ibn Yazid al-Qazwini (275 AH): *Sunan*; Cairo, Dār Ihyā al-Kutub al-'Arabiyya

41. Ibn Mandhur, Abul-Fadhl Muhammad ibn Mukrim ibn Mandhur al-Afriqi (711 AH): *Lisān al-'Arab*; Beirut, Dār Beirut li al-Tabā'ah wal-Nashr (1955)

42. Ibn Nadim, Abul-Faraj Muhammad ibn Is'hāq (385 AH): *al-Fihrist*; Egypt, al-Maktabah al-Tijāriyya al-Kubrā

43. Ibn Hishām, 'Abdul Malik ibn Hishām ibn Ayyub al-Himyari (218 AH): al-Seerah al-Nabawiyya; Egypt, al-Matba'ah Mustafa al-Bābi al-Halabi (1936)

44. Abu Dāwud, Sulaymān ibn al-Ash'ath al-Sijistāni al-Azadi (275 AH): *Sunan*; Egypt, al-Maktabah al-Tijāriyya

45. Abul Faraj Isfahāni, 'Ali ibn al-Husayn (356 AH): *al-Aghāni*; Cairo, Wizārat al-Thaqāfah wal-Irshād al-Qawmi

46. Abu Na'im Isfahāni, Ahmad ibn 'Abdillah (430 AH): *Hilyat al-Awliyā' Wāqidi Tabaqāt al-Asfiyā'*; Egypt, al-Maktabah al-Khānji

47. Azraqi, Muhammad ibn 'Abdillah ibn Ahmad (244 AH): *Akhbāru Makkah*; Damascus, al-Maktabah al-Dhāhiriyyah

48. Azhari, Abu Mansur Muhammad ibn Ahmad (370 AH): *Tahdheeb al-Lughah*; Dār al-Kitāb al-'Arabi (1967)

49. Asma'i, 'Abd al-Malik ibn Qareeb ibn 'Abd al-Malik (216 AH): *al-Asma'iyyāt*; Egypt, Dār al-Ma'ārif (1964)

50. Bukhāri, Muhammad ibn Ismā'il ibn Ibrāhim Bukhāri al-Ju'fi (256 AH): *Sahih al-Bukhāri*; Egypt, al-Matba'ah Dār al-Kutub al-Misriyyah (1964)

51. Bakhtari, Abu 'Ibādah al-Walid ibn Ubayd (284 AH): *al-Hamāsah*; Beirut, Dār al-Kutub al-'Arabi (1967)

52. Bakri, 'Abdullah ibn 'Abd al-'Aziz al-Bakri al-Andalusi (487 AH): *Mu'jam Masta'jam*; Cairo, Dār al-Nashr (1969)

53. Balādhuri, Abu al-'Abbās Ahmad ibn Yahyā ibn Jābir (279 AH): *Futuh al-Buldān*

54. Baydhāwi, 'Abd al-Rahmān ibn 'Umar al-Shirāzi (719 AH): *Anwār al-Tanzil wa Asrār al-Ta'wil*; Egypt, Dār al-Kutub al-'Arabi

55. Bayhaqi, Muhammad ibn al-Husayn ibn 'Ali (458 AH): *al-Sunan al-Kubrā*; Heidarābād, al-Dukun al-Hindiyya

56. Tirmidhi, Muhammad ibn 'Isā ibn Sawrah (279 AH): *Jāmi' al-Tirmidhi*

57. Tim Quraysh, Mu'ammar ibn Muthanna al-Timi (209 AH): *Kitāb al-Khayl*; India, Dā'irat al-Ma'ārif al-'Uthmāniyya

58. Tha'ālibi, Abu Mansur 'Abd al-Malik ibn Muhammad Ismā'il: *Fiqh al-Lugha wa Sirr al-'Arabiyya*; Egypt, al-Matba'ah al-Bābi al-Halabi (1938)

59. Jāhidh, Abu 'Uthmān 'Amr ibn Bahr (255 AH): *al-Bayān wa al-Tibyān*; Cairo, al-Matba'ah li al-Ta'leef wal-Tarjumah wal-Nashr (1948)

60. Jamhi, Muhammad ibn Salām (231 AH): *Tabaqāt Fuhul al-Shu'arā'*; al-Matba'ah al-Madani

61. Halabi, Abul-Faraj 'Ali ibn Burhān ibn Ibrāhim ibn Ahmad (1044 AH): *Unsān al-'Uyun fi Seerat al-Amin wal-Ma'mun* (also known as *al-Seerah al-Halabiyya*); Egypt, al-Maktabah al-Tijāriyya (1962)

62. Hamawi, Abu 'Abdillah Yāqut ibn 'Abdillah al-Rumi al-Hamawi al-Baghdādi (who was known as Shihāb al-Deen): *Mu'jam al-Udabā'*; Egypt, Maktabah 'Isā al-Bābi al-Halabi

63. ____: *Mu'jam al-Buldān*; Egypt, al-Matba'ah al-Sa'ādah (1906)

64. Hamidi, 'Abdullah ibn Zubayr (219 AH): *al-Musnad*; Manshurāt al-Majlis al-'Ilmi

65. Khashni, Abu Dharr Muhammad ibn Mas'ud (604 AH): *Sharh al-Seerah al-Nabawiyya*; Egypt, al-Matba'ah al-Hindiyya

66. Khufāji, Ahmad ibn Muhammad al-Shihāb (1069 AH): *Naseem al-Riyādh fi Sharh Shifā al-Qādhi 'Ayyādh*; Damascus, al-Maktabah al-Dhāhiriyyah

67. Khateeb Baghdādi, Abu Bakr Muhammad ibn 'Ali al-Khateeb (463 AH): *Tārikh Baghdād*; Cairo, al-Maktaba al-Khānji

68. Khateeb Tabrizi, Yahya ibn 'Ali ibn Muhammad al-Shaybāni al-Tabrizi (502 AH): *Sharh al-Qasā'id al-'Ashar*; Halab, al-Maktabah al-'Arabiyya

69. Dārimi, 'Abdullah ibn 'Abd al-Rahmān (255 AH): *Sunan*

70. Dhahabi, Muhammad ibn Ahmad ibn 'Uthmān (748 AH): *Tārikh al-Islām wa Tabaqāt al-Mashāheer wal-A'lām*; Cairo, al-Maktabah al-Quds

71. ____: *Tadhkirat al-Huffādh*; Damascus, al-Maktabah al-Dhāhiriyya

72. Rāzi, Abu Bakr (311 AH): Jumal *Ahkām al-Firāsah*; Halab, al-Matba'ah al-'Ilmiyya (1929)

73. Rajabiyāni, Mustafa (1165 AH); *Matālib Awla al-Nahy fi Sharh Ghāyat al-Muntahā*; Damascus, Manshurat al-Maktab al-Islāmi

74. Zubaydi, Muhammad Murtadhā al-Husayni al-Wasati (205 AH): *Tāj al-'Arus*; Egypt, al-Matba'ah al-Khayriyya

75. Zarqāni, Muhammad ibn 'Abd al-Bāqi (1122 AH): *Sharh al-Mawāhib al-Daniyyah li al-Qastalāni*; Beirut, Dār al-Ma'ārif lil-Tibā'ah wal-Nashr

76. Zarākali, Khayr al-Deen: *al-A'lām* (A dictionary of the biographies of the most famous men and women among the Arabs and the Orientals); Damascus, al-Maktabah al-Dhāhiriyyah

77. Zuhri, Muhammad ibn Muslim ibn 'Abdillah ibn Shihāb (124 AH): *al-Maghāzi al-Nabawiyya*; Dār al-Fikr (1980)

78. Sikkeet, Abu Yusuf Ya'qub ibn Is'hāq (244 AH): *Mukhtasar Tahdheeb al-Alfādh*; Beirut, al-Matba'ah al-Kātukiyya (1897)

79. Sam'āni, Abu Sa'eed ibn 'Abd al-Kareem ibn Muhammad ibn Mansur al-Tamimi (562 AH): *al-Ansāb*; Beirut (1981)

80. Suhayli, 'Abd al-Rahmān ibn 'Abdillah ibn Ahmad (581 AH): *al-Rawdh al-Anf fi Tafseer al-Seerah al-Nabawiyya li Ibn Hishām*; Beirut (1987)

81. Suyuti, Jalāl al-Deen (911 AH): *al-Itqān fi 'Ulum al-Qurān*

82. ____: *Kifāyat al-Tālib al-Labeeb fi Khasāis al-Habeeb* (al-Khasāis al-Kubrā); Heidarābād, al-Dukan

83. Shāfi'i, Muhammad ibn Idrees (204 AH): *al-Umm*; Egypt, Dār al-Sha'b

84. Shaybāni, Muhammad ibn al-Hasan (179 AH): *Sharh Kitāb al-Siyar al-Kabeer*; Ma'had al-Makhtutāt bi Jāmi'ah al-Duwal al-'Arabiyya

85. Tabari, Muhammad ibn Jareer (310 AH): *Jāmi' al-Bayān fi Tafseer al-Qur'ān*; Egypt, al-Matba'ah al-Kubrā al-Ameeriyya

86. ____: *Tārikh al-Tabari* (Tārikh al-Rusul wal-Muluk); Egypt, Dār al-Ma'ārif

87. Tabarāni, Sulaymān ibn Ahmad (360 AH): *al-Mu'jam al-Kabeer*; Irāq, Dār al-'Arabiyya lil-Tibā'ah al-A'dheemah

88. Tarsusi, Mardhi ibn 'Ali Mardhi (589 AH): *Tabsirat Arbāb al-Albāb fi Kayfiyat al-Najāt fi al-Hurub*

89. Sābi, Hilāl ibn al-Muhsin: *Rusum Dār al-Khilāfa*; Baghdād, al-Matba'ah al-Bāni

90. Faryābi, Ja'far ibn Muhammad ibn al-Hasan al-Mustafādh (301 AH): *Dalā'il al-Nubuwwah*; al-Maktabah al-Dhāhiriyya

91. Feiruzābādi, Abu Tāhir Muhammad ibn Ya'qub ibn Muhammad ibn Ibrāhim (816 AH): *al-Qāmus al-Muheet*; Beirut, Dār al-Kutub al-'Arabi

92. Qāsimi, Muhammad Jamāl al-Deen (1332 AH): *Tafseer al-Qāsimi* (also known as Mahāsin al-Ta'weel); Egypt, Dār Ihyā al-Kutub al-'Arabiyya

93. Qurtubi, Muhammad ibn Ahmad al-Ansāri (681 AH): *Tafseer al-Qurtubi – al-Jāmi' li Ahkām al-Qur'ān*; Cairo, Dār al-Sha'b

94. Qastalāni, Ahmad ibn Muhammad ibn Abi Bakr (923 AH): *al-Mawāhib al-Daniyya*; Damascus, al-Maktabah al-Dhāhiriyya

95. Qalqashandi, Ahmad ibn 'Ali (812 AH): *Subh al-A'shā*; Cairo, al-Matba'ah al-Ameeriyya

96. Katbi, Muhammad ibn Shākir ibn Ahmad (764 AH): *Fawāt al-Fawayāt – Tahqeeq al-Wafayāt*; Egypt, al-Matba'ah al-Sa'ādah

97. Kalā'i, Sulaymān ibn Musa ibn Sālim al-Himyari al-Kalā'i al-Balansi (634 AH): *al-Iktifā' min Maghāzi Sayyidinā Rasulillah (s) wa Maghāzi al-Sādah al-Thalātha al-Khulafā – Abu Bakr al-Siddiq wa 'Umar al-Fāruq wa 'Uthmān Dhi al-Nurayn*; Damascus, al-Maktabah al-Dhāhiriyya

98. Kalbi, Hishām ibn Sā'ib (204 AH): *al-Asnām*; Cairo, Dār al-Qawmiyya li al-Tibā'ah wal-Nashr

99. Mālik, Mālik ibn Anas (179 AH): *al-Muwatta'*; Egypt, al-Maktabah al-Tijāriyya al-Kubrā (1939)

100. Marzbāni, Abu 'Abdillah Muhammad ibn 'Imrān ibn Musa (384 AH): *Mu'jam al-Shu'arā'*; Egypt, Dār Ihyā al-Kutub al-'Arabiyya

101. Mas'udi, 'Ali ibn al-Husayn ibn 'Ali (346 AH): *Muruj al-Dhahab wa Ma'ādin al-Jawhar*; Cairo, al-Maktabah al-Tijāriyya

102. Muslim, Muslim ibn Hajjāj ibn Muslim al-Qushayri al-Naishāburi (261 AH): *Sahih al-Naishāburi*

103. Nabāhi, Abu al-Hasan 'Ali ibn 'Abdillah ibn al-Hasan al-Nabāhi al-Māliqi (776 AH): *Tārikh Qudhāt al-Andalus – al-Martabah al-'Ulyā fi man Yastahiq al-Qadhā al-Futyā*; Beirut, al-Maktab al-Tijāri lil-Sabā'ah wa al-Nashr wa al-Tawzi'

104. Al-Nabhāni, Yusuf ibn Ismā'il (1350 AH): *al-Anwār al-Muhammadiyya min al-Mawāhib al-Daniyya*; Beirut, al-Matba'ah al-Adabiyya

105. Nasā'i, Ahmad ibn Shu'ayb ibn 'Ali ibn Bahr (303 AH): Sunan

106. Al-Nasafi, 'Abdullah ibn Ahmad ibn Mahmud (701 AH): *Tafseer al-Qur'ān al-Jaleel* (also known as *Madārik al-Tanzeel wa Haqā'iq al-Ta'weel*); Beirut, Dār al-Ma'rifah

107. Nuwairi, Ahmad ibn 'Abd al-Wahhāb (733 AH); *Nihāyat al-Urb fi Funun al-Adab*; Egypt, Wizārah al-Thaqāfah

108. Harthami (Sāhib Ma'mun): *Mukhtasar Siyāsat al-Hurub*; Egypt, al-Mu'assasah al-Misriyya al-'Aāmmah

109. Harawi, 'Ali ibn Abi Bakr (611 AH): *al-Tadhkirah al-Harawiyya fi al-Hiyal al-Harbiyya*; Syria, Wizārat al-Thaqāfah wal-Irshād

110. Wāqidi, Muhammad ibn 'Umar (207 AH): *al-Maghāzi*; Oxford University Press

Secondary Sources

111. Arnold, Thomas: *al-Da'wah ilal Islām*, translated into Arabic by Hasan Ibrāhim Hasan, 'Abd al-Majeed 'Aābideen and Ismā'il al-Nahrāwi; Cairo (1947)

112. Akādimiyya al-'Askariyya al-'Ulyā fi al-Jumhuriyya al-'Arabiyya al-Suriyya: *Hujum Firqat Mashāh 'alā Difā'i 'Aduw Muhadhar* (1976)

113. ____: *Difā' Firqat Mashāh fi al-Madina* (1979)

114. ____: *Hujum Firqat Mashāh (al-Dabābāt) fi al-Madina* (1979)

115. Akram, A. (Colonel); *Khālid ibn Walid Sayfullah*; Damascus (1976)

116. Ansāri, Muhammad ibn Abi Tālib: *al-Siyāsa fi 'Ilm al-Firāsah*; al-Matba'ah al-Watab (1882)

117. Boudley, R. F.: *al-Rasul – Hayātu Muhammad (s)*, translated into Arabic by Muhammad Faraj; Egypt, Dār al-Kitāb al-'Arabi

118. Buolatif, al-'Aqeed: *al-Mufāja'at al-Taktikiyya*, translated into Arabic by 'Abd al-Hameed al-Jummal, Syria (1971)

119. Jād al-Mawla, Muhammad Ahmad: *Ayyām al-'Arab fil-Jāhiliyya*; Egypt: al-Matba'ah 'Isā al-Bābi al-Halabi (1942)

120. Hasan, Hasan Ibrāhim: *Tārikh al-Islām al-Siyāsi wal-Ijtimā'i wal-Deeni*; Egypt, al-Maktabah al-Nahdha al-Misriyya (1948)

121. Hakim, Philemon: *al-Firāsah*; Halab, al-Matba'ah al-'Ilmiyya (1929)

122. Hakeem As'ad: *Masā'il Manhajiyya 'Ilmiyya fī Nadhariyyat al-Harb wa Tatbiqātihā min Wijhat al-Nadhar al-Sufitiyya*; Syria, Markaz al-Dirāsāt wal-Abhāth al-'Askariyya (1981)

123. Hamdi, Ahmad Pasha: *Matālib al-Harb al-Hadithah*; Egypt, al-Maktabah al-Nahdha al-Misriyya (1945)

124. Hanafi, Sayyid: *al-Furusiyya al-'Arabiyya fī al-'Asr al-Jāhili*; Egypt, Dār al-Ma'ārif (1960)

125. Haiderābādi, Muhammad Hamidullah: *Majmu'at al-Wathā'iq al-Siyāsiyya lil-'Ahd al-Nabawi wal-Khilāfa al-Rāshidah*; Cairo, al-Matba'ah Lajnat al-Ta'leef wal-Tarjuma wal-Nashr (1956)

126. Khattāb, Mahmud Sheit: *al-Rasul al-Qā'id*; Beirut, Dār al-Fikr (1974)

127. Dianna, Atin: *Muhammad Rasulullah*, translated into Arabic by 'Abdul-Haleem Mahmud; Egypt, Maktabah al-Nahdhah

128. Zuhayli, D. Wahbah: *Athār al-Harb fī Fiqh al-Islāmi*; Damascus, Dār al-Fikr

129. ____: *al-Fiqh al-Islāmi wa Adillatih*; Damascus, Dār al-Fikr

130. Sirāj al-Deen, 'Abdullah: *Sayyidina Muhammad Rasulullah* (also known as *Shamā'ilat al-Hameedah wa Khasālt al-Majeedah*); Halab, Jamee'at al-Ta'leem al-Shar'i

131. Sa'eed, Muhammad 'Aātif: *al-Shakhsiyya al-'Askariyya*; Egypt, Dār al-Ma'ārif (1962)

132. ____: *Fusul fī 'Ilm al-Nafs al-'Askari*; Egypt, al-Shirkah al-'Arabiyya li al-Tibā'ah wal-Nashr (1949)

133. Shā'ir, Muhammad Ibrāhim: al-*Malājee' wal-Tahseenāt*; Damascus (1974)

134. Talās, al-'Imād Mustafā: *al-Rasul al-'Arabi wa Fann al-Harb*; Beirut (1977)

135. 'Adawi, Ibrāhim Ahmad: *al-Dawlah al-Islāmiyya wa Imperātoriyyat al-Rum*; Egypt, al-Maktabah al-Anjalo al-Misriyya (1968)

136. 'Azmi, Muhammad: *Dirāsāt fī Harb al-Khātifah*; Beirut (1972)

137. 'Askari, Majmu'ah min al-'Askariyyeen: *al-Mawsu'ah al-'Askariyya*; Beirut (1977)

138. 'Aqqād, Abbās Muhammad: *al-'Abqariyyat al-Islāmiyya*; Cairo, Dār al-Futuh lil-Tibā'ah (1957)

139. 'Ali, Jawād: *al-Mufassal fī Tārikh al-'Arab Qabl al-Islām*; Beirut, Dār al-'Ilm lil-Malāyeen (1974)

140. Faraj, Muhammad: *al-'Abqariyya al-'Askariyya fī Ghazawāt al-Rasul*; Dār al-Fikr al-'Arabi (1958)

141. Furukh, 'Umar: *Tārikh al-Jāhiliyya*; Beirut, Dār al-'Ilm lil-Malāyeen (1964)

142. Ferunzi, Majmu'at al-Ta'leef fi Akādimiyya Ferunzi al-'Askariyya: *al-Takteek*, translated into Arabic by 'Abd al-Razzāq al-Duri; Syria, Wiārat al-Difā' (1967)

143. Fuller, J.F.C. (Colonel): *Idārat al-Harb*, translated into Arabic by Akram Dayri; Dār al-Nahdha al-'Arabiyya lil-Ta'leef wal-Nashr (1971)

144. Carlayl, Thomas: *Muhammad Rasul al-Hudā wal-Rahmah wal-Shari'at al-Khālidah*, translated into Arabic by Muhammad al-Sabā'i; Beirut, al-Maktabah al-Ahliyya

145. Katāni, Sharif Muhammad ibn Ja'far (1345 AH): *al-Risālah al-Mustatrafah*; Damascus, al-Matba'ah Dār al-Fikr

146. Kahālah, 'Umar Ridhā: *Mu'jam Qabā'il al-'Arab al-Qadimah wal-Hadithah*; Damascus, al-Matba'ah al-Hāshimiyya

147. Cobold, Evelyn: *al-Bahth 'an Allāh*, translated into Arabic by 'Umar Abu Nasr; Beirut, al-Maktabah al-Ahliyya (1934)

148. Lumbard, Morris: *al-Geographiya al-Tārikhiyya lil-'Aālam al-Islāmi Khilāl al-Qurun al-'Arba'ah al-Ula*, translated into Arabic by 'Abd al-Rahmān 'Ameedah; Damascus, Dār al-Fikr

149. Mārgoliyuth: *Dirāsāt 'an al-Muwarrikheen al-'Arab*, translated into Arabic by Husain Nassār; Beirut, Dār al-Thaqāfah

150. Mawri, Asst. Syrian Defense Minister: *Ghāyat al-Amāl fi Fann al-Harb wal-Qitāl*; al-Matba'ah 'Umum Arkān Harb al-Jihādiyya

151. Monister, Lord: *Risālah fi Fann al-Harb 'indal-'Arab*; al-Majallah al-'Askariyya (1964)

152. Meishān, Benoit: *Tārikh al-Jaysh al-Almāni*, translated into Arabic by Muhammad Samee' al-Sayyid; Damascus (1976)

153. Mikshah, F. W.: *al-Harb al-Khātifah*, translated into Arabic by Kamāl 'Ismat al-Sharif; Beirut, Dār al-Talee'ah (1970)

154. Nāsif, Mansur 'Ali: *al-Tāj al-Jāmi' li Usul fi Ahādith al-Rasul*; Dār Ihyā al-Kutub al-'Arabiyya (1961)

155. Hard, Michael: *al-Mi'at al-Awā'il*, translated into Arabic by Khālid As'ad 'Isā; Damascus, Dār Qutaybah

156. Hindi, Ihsān: *al-Jaysh al-'Arabi fi 'Asr al-Futuhāt*

157. Howard, Michael: *Nadhariyat al-Harb wa Mumārasatuhā*, translated into Arabic by Markaz al-Dirāsāt wal-Ab'hāth al-'Askariyya (1980)

158. Watt, Montgomery: *Muhammad fi Makkah*, translated into Arabic by Sha'bān Barakāt; Beirut, al-Maktabah al-'Asriyya

159. _____: Muhammad fi al-Madina, translated into Arabic by Sha'bān Barakāt; Beirut, al-Maktabah al-'Asriyya

160. Watr, Muhammad Dhāhir: *Makān al-Mar'ah fi Shu'un al-Idāriyya wal-Butulāt al-Qitāliyya*; Beirut, Mu'assasah al-Risālah (1979)

161. _____: *al-Istratigiyya al-Idāriyya*; Beirut, Mu'assasah al-Risālah (1980)

162. Yazbek, Yusuf Ibrāhim: *al-Jawād al-'Arabi* (al-Tuhfat al-Kanz); Paris, al-Nāshirun al-'Arab (1981)

www.ingramcontent.com/pod-product-compliance
Lightning Source LLC
Chambersburg PA
CBHW071556030726

47593CB00001BA/194